Employee Stock
Ownership
and
Related Plans

New Titles from
QUORUM BOOKS

The Uses of Psychiatry in the Law: A Clinical View of Forensic Psychiatry
WALTER BROMBERG

Abuse on Wall Street: Conflicts of Interest in the Securities Markets
THE TWENTIETH CENTURY FUND

The Politics of Taxation
THOMAS J. REESE

Modern Products Liability Law
RICHARD A. EPSTEIN

U.S. Multinationals and Worker Participation in Management: The American
Experience in the European Community
TON DEVOS

Our Stagflation Malaise: Ending Inflation and Unemployment
SIDNEY WEINTRAUB

Employee Stock Ownership and Related Plans

ANALYSIS AND PRACTICE

Timothy C. Jochim

QUORUM BOOKS

WESTPORT, CONNECTICUT • LONDON, ENGLAND

Library of Congress Cataloging in Publication Data

Jochim, Timothy C.
   Employee stock ownership and related plans.

   Bibliography: p.
   Includes index.
   1. Employee ownership—United States.
I. Title.
HD5660.U5J63   658.3'225   81-5888
ISBN 0-89930-007-3 (lib. bdg.)   AACR2

Copyright © 1982 by Timothy C. Jochim

Library of Congress Catalog Card Number: 81-5888
ISBN: 0-89930-007-3

First published in 1982 by Quorum Books

Greenwood Press
A division of Congressional Information Service, Inc.
88 Post Road West, Westport, Connecticut 06881

Printed in the United States of America

10 9 8 7 6 5 4 3 2 1

Contents

Figures

Tables

Introduction and Acknowledgments

The subject matter of this book concerns an old but timeless topic: the means whereby the great majority of employees and citizens can accumulate a significant amount of capital wealth while acquiring a significant degree of control over their economic destiny. It also concerns a more cyclical but no less timely secondary topic: the means whereby the United States economy can increase its rate of savings, capital formation, and productivity. There is a tertiary topic of more specific interest to managers, accountants, lawyers, and stockholders: the means whereby a company can improve its cash flow, labor relations, and productivity.

The means can be designated as stock ownership plans (SOPs) and, in particular, employee stock ownership plans (ESOPs). They could be the nascent forms of the American response to the efficient economic institutions of Japan and West Germany. In essence, ESOPs and SOPs constitute "democratic capitalism" requiring distinct but cooperative roles for management, labor, and government. Management and labor will need to develop new standards of communication and performance as employees become owners while government will provide the appropriate tax incentives and controls to assure the effective and equitable utilization of the plans.

The Chrysler Corporation could provide a symbolic, though unusual, illustration of the operation of the ESOP technique and philosophy. As part of the $1.5-billion federal loan guarantee, Chrysler has set up a companywide

ESOP that is to accumulate over $165 million in company stock over four years and so assure that the company will be 25-30 percent employee owned. At the same time, the president of the United Auto Workers, Douglas Fraser, is to serve as a member of the Chrysler Corporation board of directors.

ESOPs are intended to operate through trusts as deferred compensation plans qualified under the Internal Revenue Code. As such, conforming contributions of cash or employer stock to the trust are tax deductible by the employer company. The trust is not taxed on income earned by plan assets, and participants or their beneficiaries are granted tax preferences when distributions are made to them from the plan. Further, the ESOP trust, or the company on its behalf, may borrow to finance the purchase of company stock. This provides financing for the company, which subsequently amortizes the loan such that both principal and interest are tax deductible.

The common features of all ESOPs and variations thereof are that the employees accumulate company stock and that the companies obtain tax preferences and/or financing. Some plans are addressed specifically to the investment tax credit (TCESOPs), and some plans can be established by the various states for all the citizens of the state (GSOPs). Plans can also be developed to give consumers an equity interest in the public utilities or government enterprises that serve them (CSOPs).

The format and content of this book have been influenced by several earlier works in the ESOP area. The first is *The Capitalist Manifesto* by Louis Kelso and Mortimer Adler; the second is *A Guide to Employee Stock Ownership Plans* by Charles A. Scharf; and the third is *How to Analyze, Design and Install an Employee Stock Ownership Plan* by John D. Menke. An acknowledgment must also go to the office staff of Congressman John F. Seiberling of Ohio and to several staff members of the Senate Committees on Finance and Small Business for assisting me in gathering documents and material. Several companies also provided me with access to their plan documents. These include Harco Corporation; Parr, Inc.; and Dalton, Dalton, Newport and Little, all located in Ohio.

Norman Kurland, an ESOP consultant who heads Kurland and Associates of Washington, D.C., was a factor in stimulating my interest in ESOPs and encouraging me to do some consulting and publishing in the area. Kurland was formerly associated with an ESOP consulting firm headed by Louis Kelso. A special thanks to Julien Suso, an Ohio development planner, and to James L. Green and R. Bruce Jones, both of the University of Georgia, for reviewing portions of the manuscript. Also, to Frank Musick of the Research Department, United Auto Workers, an acknowledgment for the valuable UAW research data and policy documents on ESOPs provided to me on a timely and consistent basis.

Like the books by Scharf and Menke, this book is an ESOP practice guide. It includes Internal Revenue Service and Department of Labor codes, all essential forms, and a sample plan for a basic ESOP. It also develops a hypothetical financial and managerial analysis of ESOP companies. Like the book by Kelso and Adler, this book develops a theoretical treatment of ESOPs. It includes an economic analysis and a comparison of ESOPs with Western European plans. This book also presents major labor union positions, numerous case studies, congressional testimony, and a government performance and policy evaluation.

The reader is assumed to have some knowledge of economics, finance, and the Internal Revenue Code (IRC). Text and footnote citations and a bibliography provide source materials for the more curious. However, this book is intended for a diverse group of readers: managers, lawyers, union officials, accountants, economists, employees, stockholders, industrial psychologists, and government officials.

*Employee Stock
Ownership
and
Related Plans*

CHAPTER

1

Definitions and Development

DEFINITIONS

The topic of employee ownership in general and employee stock ownership plans (ESOPs) in particular involves numerous dimensions and disciplines. There are implications for management theory and practice when the traditional status and role of the employee change to include ownership. Legal rights and responsibilities may be altered with respect to employee compensation and benefits, labor-management relations, and control of the employee stock trust and the company. Implications for economic theory and policy are inherent in allowing the acquisition of equity by credit and/or by tax preference, in broadening the base of capital ownership, and in altering the balance of employee income from labor to capital. Significant financial considerations are involved where a company can increase its working capital and profits and reduce taxes. Finally, all of the above may affect the social relationships of the work place and the larger community.

Employee ownership can be analogized to the fable of the elephant and the five blind men, each of whom perceived the animal in a different manner. So too, different interests and perceptions concerning the subject matter of this book are common and prevalent. Employees of a plant or subsidiary may view it as a better alternative to a shutdown or divestiture by a parent company. A retiring majority shareholder of a close-held company may wish to use it as a means of "cashing out" while assuring the continued existence of the company. Management may use it to "go private" to prevent a takeover or to make an expansion or acquisition with pretax income. Labor union officials may perceive it as a threat to their authority, as an undesirable risk for workers, as a means of saving jobs, or as a new frontier for union influence.

Employee ownership is a general concept covering different employee classifications, different degrees of ownership, different degrees of participation or control, different business and tax entities, and different plan classifications. For the purposes of this book, the following categories and conventions will be followed:

Employee Classifications: Management; salaried personnel (neither management nor production personnel); workers (production personnel whether on wage or salary and whether union or nonunion).

Employee Owned: Actual or beneficial ownership of at least 50 percent of the company lies with the employees in substantial proportionate representation by employee classification (e.g., if workers constitute 60 percent of company employees, they must own a substantial percentage of all the employee-owned stock, which must be at least 50 percent of all company stock issued and outstanding).

Employee Controlled: Actual or beneficial influence on the relevant company decision-making bodies in substantial proportionate representation by employee classification (e.g., if workers constitute 60 percent of company employees, they must have substantial decision-making authority over production matters and significant influence or representation on the board of directors).

Business/Tax Entities: One or more of the business and tax entities that could be involved in employee ownership includes the partnership or joint venture, the co-op or cooperative, the conventional stock corporation, and the trust [in most cases an IRC Section 401(a) qualified trust].

Direct Employee-Owned Companies (DEOCs): Employees participate directly in the ownership and control of the business as owners of partnership interests, co-op shares, or shares of a conventional stock corporation. The trust instrument is not used to hold, allocate, vote, or distribute employee interests. The results may be more direct employee influence, more simplicity, and lower administrative costs, but the tax advantages of utilizing a qualified trust are lost. DEOCs may or may not involve stock bonus or money purchase provisions.

Employee Stock Ownership Plan (ESOP): Section 4975(e) (7) of the Internal Revenue Code states that "employee stock ownership plan" means a defined contribution plan that is a stock bonus plan or a stock bonus and money purchase plan, both of which are qualified under Section 401(a), that is designed to invest primarily in employer securities, and that meets additional requirements of Section 409A and issued regulations. Section 407(d) (6) of the Employee Retirement Security Act (ERISA) of 1974 states that the term "employee stock ownership plan" means an individual account plan that is a qualified stock bonus plan or a stock bonus plan and money purchase plan, both of which are qualified under Section 401(a), that is designed to invest primarily in qualifying employer securities, and that meets other requirements as may be prescribed by regulation.

Variations of the ESOP concept include the LESOP (leveraged employee stock ownership plan), the TCESOP (tax credit employee stock ownership plan), the GSOP (general stock ownership plan), the CSOP (consumer stock ownership plan), and the ISOP (individual stock ownership plan). The GSOP is intended for general equity participation under state authorization, while the TCESOP permits an additional 1 percent investment tax credit for utilizing companies. The LESOP may borrow money to purchase company stock.

An ESOP may be considered a form of a stock bonus plan because stock is contributed to the trust for the account of the participating employees as a supplement to money compensation. In addition, or in the alternative, the employer company may contribute the money that is then used by the trust to purchase the stock, thus constituting a form of money purchase plan. The plan and trust must be for the exclusive and general benefit of the participating employees and their beneficiaries under IRC Section 401(a). The company may be only an incidental beneficiary even though the ESOP may help finance the company.

General Stock Ownership Plan (GSOP): Variation of an ESOP that is not a deferred compensation plan. It is open to eligible residents of each state that authorizes the plan under charter as a special corporation. A GSOP corporation, or GSOC, may not be affiliated with any other corporation and may not acquire more than 20 percent of the stock of any corporation. Stock purchases are funded by private loans guaranteed by the state, and net dividends are paid out as ordinary income when earned. The GSOP authorization was provided by Section 601 of the Revenue Act of 1978 and added Sections 1391-97 to the Internal Revenue Code.

Tax Credit Employee Stock Ownership Plan (TCESOP): Variation of an ESOP under IRC Section 409A, as added by the Revenue Act of 1978, amending Section 48 and replacing Section 301 of the Tax Reduction Act of 1975 as amended by the Tax Reform Act of 1976. A TCESOP is a qualified plan allowing an additional 1 percent investment tax credit for the employer company in return for a contribution of equal value in employer stock or purchase money for the stock with other requirements. An additional 0.5 percent is available for employee-matched contributions.

Defined Benefit Plan: As per Section 3(35) of ERISA, a pension plan in which the retirement pension is fixed or definitely determinable by the plan formula. That is, the annual contribution is determined by actuarial methods in order to accumulate a fund sufficient to provide each employee's pension when he/she retires.

Defined Contribution Plan: As per Section 3(34) of ERISA, a plan that provides for an individual account for each participant and for benefits based solely upon the amount contributed to the participant's account and upon income, expenses, gains and losses, and any forfeitures of accounts of any other participants that may be allocated to such participant's account. The term "defined contribution plan" thus includes profit-sharing plans, employee stock ownership plans, and money purchase pension plans.

Individual Account Plan: As per Section 3(34) of ERISA, a defined contribution plan. An individual account plan is also defined by Section 407(d) of ERISA to mean an individual account plan that is a profit-sharing, stock bonus, thrift, or savings plan or an employee stock ownership plan.

Profit-Sharing Plan: A plan in which the annual contributions are made out of current or accumulated profits, usually in the form of cash. The amount of each employee's retirement or other benefit will depend upon the sum that has accumulated in his/her account during his/her years of participation in the plan.

Stock Bonus Plan: As defined in Internal Revenue Service Regulation Section 1.401-1(b), a stock bonus plan is an employee benefit plan similar to a profit-sharing plan except that employer contributions are not necessarily dependent upon profit and benefits are distributable in the form of stock. Like the profit-sharing plan, it is also a defined contribution and individual account plan.

Money Purchase Plan: A defined contribution plan and a form of pension plan with fixed or determinable annual contributions not necessarily based on profits. This is generally not an individual account plan, and generally any reduction in the money contribution will impair or partially terminate the plan.

Consumer Stock Ownership Plan (CSOP): Variation of an ESOP. A CSOP is similar in operation to a cooperative in that the equity or ownership interest of the consumer or customer would be tied to the monthly or annual billing accounts between the business and the consumer. A trust or escrow account is utilized to allocate and hold individual consumer or customer stock accounts. A CSOP may be nonleveraged, leveraged, or contributory and is most appropriate for a capital-intensive company with a broad and secure customer base. Examples would include utility companies, public transit companies, and energy companies.

Individual Stock Ownership Plan (ISOP): A trust account having a relationship to other types of ESOPs analogous to the relationship of an individual retirement account to other IRC Section 401(a) qualified deferred compensation or retirement plans. After vesting and other requirements of other ESOPs are met, the securities could be rolled over or transferred to the ISOP without any adverse tax consequences. The roll-over could be delayed until scheduled distributions are made from the other ESOPs. The ISOP, like the GSOP, would have a diversified securities portfolio obtained through low-cost credit, which in turn would be repaid through portfolio earnings.

Stock Ownership Plans (SOPs): Generic term applied to ESOPs, TCESOPs, GSOPs, ISOPs, CSOPs, and variations thereof.

DEVELOPMENT

The concept of employee ownership of the DEOC variety is not a recent development. The cooperative, the joint venture or partnership, and the conventional stock corporation have a long history in the United States and Western Europe. The development of technology, mass production markets, public capital markets, large bureaucratic corporations, and professional management during the twentieth century altered the traditional American concept of individual initiative and private enterprise. *The Modern Corporation and Private Property* by A. A. Berle, Jr., and Gardner C. Means was one of the first major treatments of the evolution of American capitalism.[1] Twenty-four years later, *American Capitalism: The Concept of Countervailing Power*, by John Kenneth Galbraith, further developed the political economy of institutionalized wealth and power.[2]

The path of individual initiative and private enterprise was not being successfully pursued by the average American employee. Then, however, *The Capitalist Manifesto*, a book of portentous title, was published in 1958, two years after the publication of *American Capitalism*. Authored by academic and philosopher Mortimer J. Adler and by lawyer and investment banker Louis O. Kelso, the book advanced the notion that the benefits of capitalism should be and could be made significantly more available to the average American worker. A second book, *Two Factor Theory: The Economics of Reality*, by Kelso and Patricia Hetter, expanded the premise and the underlying analysis rather than developing the plan in detail.

The premise is that two-factor economic theory is the one true and realistic theory and that the classical, socialist, and Keynesian schools of theory are in error.[3] The promise is "universal capitalism," to be attained through a set of general policies and specific proposals derived from the premise. These may be summarized as follows:

General Policies

1. To broaden the ownership of existing enterprises.
2. To encourage the formation of new enterprises and new capitalists.
3. To discourage the excessive concentration of the ownership of capital.

Specific Proposals

1. Increase the use of equity-sharing plans in industry.
2. Modify estate and gift tax laws to encourage the creation and survival of capital estates.
3. Gradually eliminate the corporate income tax.
4. Eliminate government programs that promote the concentration of capital ownership.
5. Develop effective government regulation to assure that free and workable competition is maintained in all markets.
6. Assure all households of a reasonable opportunity to participate in the production of wealth.
7. Require mature corporations to pay out 100 percent of their net earnings.
8. Selective use of tax and credit devices to encourage viable capital holdings by all households and to discourage concentrated or monopolistic capital holdings.
9. Primary use of the credit system to promote new capital formation and ownership rather than consumption.[4]

The principal equity-sharing vehicles would be stock-bonus/profit-sharing plans, financed in part by deductions against current income taxes and made more attractive by the phase-in of the 100 percent net income pay-out for mature corporations.[5] New enterprises for new capitalists would be financed by the equivalent of a modern day Homestead Act for pioneer capitalists, and insurance policies could be written on capital holdings to reduce the risk of major financial losses from investments.[6] Debt financing would be made available at "pure credit" interest rates (i.e., interest rates covering only loan administrative costs and no-risk lender profit).

Kelso's application of investment banking and corporate finance to the major deficiencies of contemporary American capitalism gave birth to the leveraged ESOP. His first application involved Peninsula Newspapers, Inc., of Palo Alto, California, which utilized an ESOP to purchase the company from its retiring founder in 1956 and thus to prevent a takeover by the Ridder chain. Many proposals enumerated above, however, are neither novel nor original, such as the elimination of the corporate income tax and the 100 percent corporate net earnings pay-out.[7]

In its generic form an ESOP is a stock bonus plan that has roots in the Revenue Act of 1921. IRS Revenue Ruling 46 in 1953 permitted the use of a qualified employee trust to borrow for the purpose of investing in the securities of the sponsoring employer corporation. Over the years numerous functions and variations have evolved. These both stimulated and developed from federal legislation, including the Regional Rail Reorganization Act (RRRA) of 1973, ERISA of 1974, the Foreign Trade Act of 1974, the Tax Reduction Act of 1975, the Tax Reform Act of 1976, the Revenue Act of 1978 (which supersedes the two previous acts as to ESOPs), the Chrysler Corporation Loan Guarantee Act of 1979, and the Small Business Employee Ownership Act (SBEOA) of 1980.[8]

The legal requirements for a qualified ESOP and its variations are detailed, numerous, and ever changing. ERISA added Section 4975 to Title 26 of the U.S. Code (Taxes) and Sections 407 and 408 (relating to ESOPs) and various other sections to Title 29 of the U.S. Code (Labor). The Revenue Act of 1978 added Sections 409A, 1391-97, and 6699 to the IRC and amended or replaced other sections as amended by the Technical Corrections Act of 1979. The Economic Recovery Tax Act of 1981 amended various sections of the IRC and provided an alternative tax credit based on payroll rather than capital investment.

NOTES

1. A. A. Berle, Jr., and Gardner C. Means, *The Modern Corporation and Private Property* (New York: Commerce Clearing House, 1932).

2. John Kenneth Galbraith, *American Capitalism: The Concept of Countervailing Power* (Boston: Houghton Mifflin, 1956).

3. Louis O. Kelso and Patricia Hetter, *Two Factor Theory: The Economics of Reality* (New York: Vintage Books, 1967), pp. 31, 36.

4. Louis O. Kelso and Mortimer J. Adler, *The Capitalist Manifesto* (New York: Random House, 1958), pp. 169, 170.

5. Ibid., pp. 190, 191.

6. Ibid., pp. 229, 243.

7. Nobel economist Milton Friedman and consumer advocate Ralph Nader are among the proponents of such measures. See Friedman, *An Economist's Protest* (Glen Ridge, N.J.: Thomas Horton and Co., 1972).

8. Among other provisions, the act authorizes the Small Business Administration (SBA) to make loans and loan guarantees to ESOPs.

2

An Economic Analysis

PRODUCTION AND DISTRIBUTION THEORY

The basic thrust of the Kelso plan, of which the leveraged ESOP is a part, is a combination of supply-side and welfare economics: production theory, growth theory, and distribution theory. Kelso begins with Karl Marx's critique of capitalism and private productive property—the system and the tool, respectively, of greed, exploitation, inequality, and instability.[1] Marxian distribution theory was based primarily on the labor theory of value. All productive value came from labor, whether direct, imputed, or historical, and thus all returns accrued to labor.

Kelso rejects the Marxian critique of capitalism and offers instead "two factor theory" and "universal capitalism." The latter is the goal, and the former is both the means and the premise. By comparison, Kelso asserts that the goal of classical, socialist, and Keynesian theory is full employment, and the premise of all three is symbolic logic: monetary theory.[2] The "invisible hand" and government spending, respectively, are the means of classical theory and Keynesian theory.

Further, the latter two, like socialist (Marxian) theory, end up being "one factor" (of production) theories. Classical theory does because monetary theory and the invisible hand are inadequate to deal with the productive power of real capital and the consequences (as per Marx) of its concentration.[3] Keynesian theory does because its essence is aggregate demand and full employment at the expense of productivity and capital ownership.[4]

The nexus between production theory and distribution theory is critical. While recognizing the difficulty of measuring aggregate factor productivity, Kelso, nevertheless, asserts that "physical labor" accounts for 10 percent and "capital instruments" account for 90 percent of wealth production.[5] The distribution principle of "private property" is consistent with production, whereas the principle of "needism," advocated by both Keynesianism and socialism, is based on need.[6] Thus Keynesian capitalism, while boosting aggregate demand and employment in the short run, must inevitably succumb to inflation, capital deficiency, and reduced productivity in the long run.

In Kelso's analysis, technology and capital deepening have meant that capital ownership in the United States has become too highly concentrated; the result is excessive and needless economic inequality and instability that the government ameliorates with welfare and employment programs at the expense of productivity (new and dispersed capital formation). Thus, the factor distribution of national income would be artificially shifted from capital to labor despite the tremendous growth of capital. Another result would be inflation if the Federal Reserve finances the government deficits that could be expected to result from such program expenditures. Nobel laureate in economics Paul A. Samuelson has commented as follows:

Kelsoism is not accepted by modern scientific economics as a valid and fruitful analysis of the distribution of income, but rather it is regarded as an amateurish and cranky fad . . . the principal learned journals of economic science—e.g., the American Economic Review, the Royal Economic Journal, the Harvard Quarterly Journal of Economics, the Chicago Journal of Political Economy—have steadfastly withheld recognition and approval from the doctrines of Kelsoism. Its central tenet is contradicted by the findings of economic empirical science: according to statistical study of macroeconomic trends by such distinguished scholars as Professor Simon Kuznets of Harvard (Nobel laureate in economics for 1971), Senator and Professor Paul H. Douglas (award winner for his Cobb-Douglas statistical measurement of the aggregate production function), MIT Professor Robert M. Solow, . . . the contribution of labor to the totality of GNP is in the neighborhood of 75 percent, with only 25 per cent attributable to land, machinery and other property.

Moreover, an increasing proportion of labor productivity is attributable in modern economics . . . to investment of "human capital" in the form of education and skill enrichment. This 75-25 per cent breakdown is diametrically opposite to the Kelso presuppositions, which are purely speculative and not based upon econometric analysis of the observed statistics of nations at different stages of development.[7]

The production function is $Q = b \sqrt{0.75L \times 0.25K}$, where Q is real output and b is a technical coefficient times the geometric mean of the product of labor

(L) and capital or property (K) inputs. As Samuelson indicates above, the 0.75 and 0.25 represent the empirical determination of the relative contribution of labor and capital to output and, consequentially, the income distribution of that output. The production function is the technical relationship indicating the maximum output for specified quantities of specified inputs with a given state of technology and subject to diminishing returns.[8]

This does not mean that the prices attached to those inputs are free-market competitive prices, nor does it mean that the resultant factor income can be altered with impunity through government programs, taxing, and spending. The actual combination of inputs that a company selects will be determined by the relative marginal productivity and prices of the inputs ($MP_L/P_L = MP_K/P_K = 1$). If the competitive market optimum is distorted by government or by private economic power, the result will be resource waste and higher prices at both the micro (plant) level and the macro (aggregate) level. The aggregate technical coefficients may or may not be $0.75L$ and $0.25K$ either before or after the distortion, but it is assumed that factor payments (national income) are consistent with the coefficients.

The essence of the preceding paragraph is illustrated by figure 1 and figure 2. Both are aggregate supply and demand graphs illustrating the functional distribution of national income using the 75 percent labor and 25 percent capital split. In the first graph, labor is the primary factor and capital is the residual. For the second, the reverse is true.

On figure 1, S_L and D_L (marginal product of labor, or MP_L) represent the optimal competitive market aggregate supply and demand for labor. The wage rate (price) is at A, and the quantity of labor demanded is at F. Labor's share (L) of national product and income is $OAEF$, and the residual, ACE, is attributed to capital.

Subsequent transfer and subsidy programs, anticompetitive regulations and institutions, compulsory wage and benefit laws, and labor-management practices restrict the supply (increase the cost) to S_L'. Labor supply also becomes less price elastic (less responsive to price changes). Sub-pay, unemployment compensation, occupation and trade barriers, tax rates, and "make work" jobs all have an effect. The marginal product of labor may fall to D_L' from D_L—as may the marginal product of capital on figure 2 (D_K to D_K')—since the ratio of capital to labor has increased. Thus, labor productivity has decreased despite the increased ratio of capital to labor.

At the same time, anticompetitive regulations, government debt financing, inflation, regulatory costs, subsidies, economic concentration, archaic management, and easy credit for consumption are retarding innovation, small business growth, and new capital formation. The supply of capital becomes more

FIGURE 1 **Labor Income**

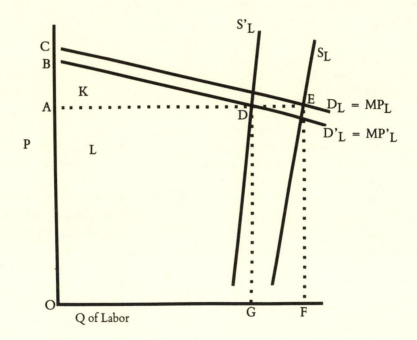

FIGURE 2 **Capital Income**

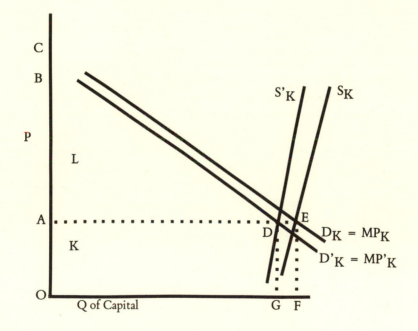

restricted and concentrated and less price elastic, and thus it moves to S'_K from S_K on figure 2. The effect is to reduce further the marginal product of labor on figure 1 to D'_L from D_L and of capital on figure 2 to D'_K from D_K.

Labor's real output and earned income continue to be 75 percent of the total and at the same real price (wage), but total real output and income have declined. Nominal (inflated) personal income may remain the same since government transfers and debt financing have compensated for the decline. Figure 1 now shows *OADG* for labor and *ABD* for capital. Figure 2 shows the same loss of real output, disregarding graphing disproportions.

Thus, the economy depicted here has the same production function and factor distribution of income before and after. It is merely less productive than it could be because of the inefficient use of government regulatory and fiscal tools. Monetary expansion, whether 4 percent or 16 percent per annum, is in error only when it cannot be used for real corresponding increases in capital and output.

However, the issue of the scientifically optimal factor distribution of income has been a source of continuing historical debate within the economics profession and will not be resolved here. It may be more productive to determine what mode of distribution most efficiently furthers important economic objectives and social goals. Several respected economists, notably Joan Robinson and Nicholas Kaldor, reject the notion of accurate technical determination of the aggregate production function of capital and labor and are even more skeptical that any such determination can be used to explain wages and profits and relative factor income shares.[9]

In addition, as far back as the late nineteenth century, other respected economists have proposed a broad-based second income from broad-based capital ownership. Such proposals should not be considered original to Kelso. The German economist Johann H. Von Thunen, a contemporary of Marx, developed a natural wage theory that required that interest from investment must be added to the wage rate to provide a subsistence-level income for workers.[10] Von Thunen set up a profit-sharing plan on his own estates such that employee allocations were reinvested in the estate. Employees were paid interest as earned and received their respective equity allocations upon retirement.

John Maynard Keynes proposed a mandatory wage earners' investment fund in 1940 to curb inflation and escalating wage increases such that workers would be given "a share in the claims on the future which would otherwise belong to the entrepreneurs."[11] In 1964, J. E. Meade, an English economist, advocated "employee share schemes whereby workers can gain a property interest in business firms."[12] This constituted an important element in his proposal for a property-owning democracy.

COMPARATIVE ANALYSIS: PLANS, PROGRAMS, AND PERFORMANCE

On December 11 and 12, 1975, the Joint Economic Committee of the U.S. Congress, chaired by the late Senator Hubert Humphrey, conducted intensive and comprehensive hearings on ESOPs. Among those submitting prepared statements and presenting testimony was Hans Brems, professor of economics at the University of Illinois and a specialist in U.S. and Western European employee equity plans or wage earners' investment funds. Brems cited the several purposes of such plans as follows (his citations omitted):

[It]... would be one step in the direction of equalizing wealth distribution. Directly it would serve the dual purpose of giving labor a share of, first, the capital gains accruing to stockholders in an inflationary economy and, second, the co-determination rights inherent in stock ownership.

...Perhaps the fund would raise the propensity to save national output and thus relieve a possible capital shortage. Perhaps a tax-exempt fund would enable the parent firm to borrow on more favorable terms and thus raise the inducement to invest. Perhaps the fund would reduce alienation and raise labor productivity—or at least raise labor tolerance of profit-making and of income policies involving money-wage restraint.[13]

John Maynard Keynes, in 1940, was perhaps the first economist to develop and propose an employee investment wage and fund.[14] His was a compulsory plan to limit demand for consumer goods, to increase savings and investment, and to promote the "accumulation of working class wealth under working class control." It was adopted in limited form as a temporary wartime measure. The Federal Republic of Germany established a voluntary investment-wage program for all companies in 1961, and France followed with a compulsory profit-sharing plan for major corporations in 1967.

The stated purpose of Brems' monograph was the comparative analysis of ESOPs and the Western European plans (WEPs) and their comparative effects upon corporate control, savings, investment, productivity, and resource allocation. Reasons for differential effects can be inferred from table 2.1, which compares the characteristics of ESOPs and the West German plans. No comparison was made for GSOPs since these did not exist at the time.

Normally ESOP contributions are not intended to be a wage deduction, as in the case of WEPs, but companies with ESOPs may tend to limit wage or employee benefit increases. Employee voting rights in ESOPs are required for public companies, but may be restricted for close-held ones to supramajority

TABLE 2.1
Comparison of ESOPs and the West German Plan (WGP)

	ESOPs	WGP
VOTING RIGHTS	Yes, limited[a]	Yes
CONTRIBUTION	Common or convertible preferred or cash	Stocks, bonds, or cash
GOVERNMENT AID	Tax deductions and preferences	Subsidy
DIVERSIFIED	No	Yes
PLAN LEVEL	Company	Industry or region
PARTICIPATION	Voluntary 2%[b]	Voluntary 60%
UNION ROLE	Little	Major
REDEMPTION	Termination or retirement	7 Years

SOURCE: [a]WGP data from Brems as cited in Joint Economics Committee, U.S. Congress, *Employee Stock Ownership Plans* (Washington, D.C.: U.S. Government Printing Office, 1976), pt. 1.

[a]IRC Sections 401 (a), 4975, and 409A have extended limited voting rights.

[b]Calculated from recent Treasury Department estimate of 3,000 companies or 2,000,000 employees.

issues (e.g., mergers). Employers can deduct up to 25 percent of payroll for ESOP contributions, and employees/beneficiaries may obtain tax preferences (e.g., capital gains) upon redemption. ESOP equity is company tied, but not so for the WEPs. The major difference is the extent and degree of participation—union and employee. An additional difference is that current dividends may be taken from ESOPs, but not WEPs.

Brems indicates probable effects as follows:

1. Over the long run (at least eight years), investment of 5 percent of the total corporate wage bill would yield control of 10-17 percent of corporate stock.

2. As per the above, for WEPs and WGPs, disposable income (DI) as a percentage of gross national product (GNP) should drop by about 2 percent. Thus, aggregate national savings should correspondingly increase. The capital fund enlarges at the expense of disposable income, but not at the expense of the disposable income of the wage earner-participants.

3. Even without tax deductions or credits, ESOPs will also lower the DI/GNP ratio and increase savings. The degree and amount are directly related to leverage (amount and frequency of borrowing) and to the holding period (contribution to redemption). It is assumed that contributions will not decline over time.

4. If all nonfarm nonfinancial corporations had had tax credit ESOPs in 1972, the federal tax loss could have been $21 billion ($429 billion payroll times 10 percent contribution deduction is $43 billion; $74 billion corporate profits minus the $43 billion leaves $31 billion and reduces the tax from $35 billion to $15 billion; then deduct tax credit of 1 percent of $101 billion for $14 billion tax).

5. WEPs, by forcing companies to issue more stock, may lower stock prices and earnings and induce less risky investment projects. A tax incentive may be necessary to maintain or accelerate capital formation.

6. ESOPs may accelerate capital formation not because of any inherent quality, but because liberal federal fiscal policy (tax deductions and credits) reduces the cost of capital. The Federal Reserve may also "monetize" this capital formation by rediscounting ESOP notes given to the lender.

7. There are several types of productivity increases: A. short-run increases at local, plant, or company level with existing types of technology, capital, and labor; B. long-run increases at aggregate or industry level with new technology, new capital, and new labor. Type A is largely influenced by employee attitudes and involvement. Type B is largely influenced by technology development and mobility of resources. ESOPs may do well by type A, but poorly by type B unless portfolio diversification is permitted. "Suprafirm funds" (i.e., WGPs) may do less well by type A, but better by type B, especially if diversified.

8. ESOPs, because they are more decentralized and less diversified than WGPs or WEPs, involve a greater risk of loss for participating employees.[15]

Brems' analysis and conclusions may be generally accurate and correct. Empirical tests still remain to be performed. As to effects (5), (6), and (7), if (2) and (3) above are correct, it will be the business savings component (S_B) of national savings (S) that is increased. Government and consumer access to the increased S is foreclosed. Thus, the price of monetary capital should fall and the capital formation rate should increase even in the absence of fiscal and monetary incentives. If technological change, innovation, or other productivity increases fail to occur, the marginal efficiency of capital of companies using ESOPs and WEPs should eventually decline. This decline may be offset by both product and portfolio diversification.

As to effect (6), an employee-owned and -controlled ESOP may experience both A- and B-type productivity increase. Type A would be a direct and readily apparent result (see chapter 7 on case studies), and type B may occur because the employee owners/controllers may actually promote capital investment and technical change for several reasons. First, such investment and change may directly increase the value of their stock and/or its earning power; and second, the price of capital is lower for them than for an ordinary corporation. At the minimum, such employees should not be expected to resist such developments, as is frequently the case in conventional corporations.

Point (8) seems to be valid at the present time. Insurance could minimize the employee participant's risk if diversification is not possible, and regulations could permit gradual diversification after a minimum holding period (e.g., seven years). The corporate control effect cited in (1) may be of concern to many managers and stockholders, but its economic effect is uncertain. Elsewhere, by means of microeconomic analysis, it has been postulated that ESOPs will increase plant/company productivity, but that the long-run labor supply curve will shift to the left as employees become wealthier.[16]

Two critical economic questions remain. First, are fiscal and monetary expansion alone an efficient alternative to ESOPs in increasing savings, investment, and output and in equalizing wealth distribution? Second, are existing programs (e.g., capital gains, tax credits, block grants) more efficient alternatives to ESOPs with respect to the four stated objectives?

These questions require empirical time series as well as theoretical analysis. The preceding analysis by Brems and the subsequent discussion favor WEPs, if not ESOPs, in theory. Tables 2.2, 2.3, and 2.4 support this analysis by revealing the meager absolute and comparative results from consistent monetary and fiscal expansion and alternative capital/business incentive programs since 1960.

Table 2.2 shows the real changes (1972 constant dollars) in selected GNP accounts, debt, prices, and productivity for selected years from 1955 to 1980.

TABLE 2.2
Changes in U.S. GNP Accounts, Debt, Prices, and Productivity, 1955-80
(in billions of constant 1972 dollars)

	1955	1960	1965	1970	1975	1979	1980
GNP	658	737	929	1,086	1,234	1,484	1,481
% Change	-	+ 13	+ 26	+ 17	+ 14	+ 20	0
Consumption	394	452	558	672	780	931	933
C/GNP	.60	.61	.60	.62	.65	.63	.63
Savings[a]	102	110	155	167	205	217	238
S/GNP	.16	.15	.17	.16	.17	.15	.16
Investment[a]	104	105	152	159	155	233	204
I/GNP	.16	.14	.16	.15	.13	.16	.14
Government[b]	152	173	210	251	267	282	290
G/GNP	.23	.23	.23	.23	.22	.19	.20
Transfer Payments	30	42	55	88	140	157	186
TP/GNP	.05	.06	.06	.08	.11	.11	.13
Federal Debt	409	422	436	421	432	512	516
FD/GNP	.62	.57	.47	.39	.35	.35	.35
Private Credit[c]	920	1,084	1,416	1,624	1,861	2,086	-
PC/GNP	1.40	1.47	1.53	1.50	1.51	1.41	-
IPD[d]	61	69	74	91	126	163	177
Productivity[e]	68	73	87	93	102	107	106

SOURCES: *U.S. Statistical Abstract, 1970* and *1979*; and *Economic Report of the President, 1970, 1980, and 1981* (Washington, D.C.: U.S. Government Printing Office).

[a]Gross private domestic.

[b]Federal, state, and local expenditures.

[c]Nonfinancial institution private debt.

[d]GNP implicit price deflator: 1972 = 100.

[e]Nonfarm private sector, output per work hour: 1972 = 100.

The percentage changes in GNP are from one selected year to the next, not annual averages. The most significant trends over the twenty-five years are the following:

1. The rising ratio of GNP going to consumption from 0.60 to 0.65.
2. The rising ratio of GNP going to transfer payments (social security, federal employee retirement, unemployment compensation, public assistance, economic impact relief, etc.) from 0.05 to 0.13.
3. The accelerating rate of general price increases since 1970 as measured by the implicit price of deflator (IPD).
4. The steady decline in productivity increases from over 3 percent to less than 1 percent per annum.

The remaining GNP accounts, including federal debt and private credit outstanding, have been stable as a ratio of GNP. It can be inferred that the key to lagging capital formation and productivity lies in the increasing rate of consumption fueled by the increasing rate of transfer payments. Paying a worker a high percentage of his/her former wage because of displacement by foreign competition does nothing to increase the productivity of the worker or the capital of the employer company. By contrast, ESOPs can transfer private credit and federal debt into accelerated investment and capital formation even with a restrictive monetary policy. The result should be higher productivity and less inflation without any detrimental effect upon employment.

Economist James L. Green of the University of Georgia included the following in a statement submitted to the Joint Economic Committee hearing on ESOPs in 1975:

As recently as 1955, federal transfer payments to persons (income received for which no current economic services are rendered) amounted to 5.8 per cent of total wage and salary income earned. In 1974, transfer payments to persons amounted to $128 billion. The proportion had grown to 17 per cent of total earned wage and salary income. In 1975, the proportion is estimated to be 22 per cent or more. The "taking by command" of this sizeable proportion of earned income from those who are working is deadening to the work ethic. The motivations to excel, to strive for quality, to work more efficiently and productively lose their potency as workers turn pragmatically toward bargaining for more pay for less work and in some cases to no work at all as they become wards of government.[17]

Tables 2.3 and 2.4 reveal that in recent history the United States has ranked *last* among the seven major industrialized nations of the world (the Soviet Union excluded) in the percentage of GNP going to investment. Further,

TABLE 2.3

Comparative Growth Rates and Economic Ratios, I

	AVERAGE ANNUAL % CHANGE IN REAL GNP		% OF GNP IN 1977			INFLATION AND UNEMPLOYMENT RATES IN 1979	
	1960-70	*1970-80*	C	I	G	CPI[a]	UR[b]
United States	3.9	3.0	65	17	18	217	6.3%
Canada	5.2	3.9	57	23	20	221	8.0%
West Germany	4.7	2.8	56	21	20	170	3.3%
Japan	11.1	5.3	58	31	10	262	2.1%
United Kingdom	2.8	1.6	59	18	21	359	6.0%
France	5.6	3.7	62	23	15	259	5.5%
Italy	5.5	3.1	64	20	14	338	3.7%

SOURCES: *U.S. Statistical Abstract, 1979, 1980*, and *Economic Report of the President, 1979, 1981*.

KEY:
C   Consumption
I   Investment
G   Government spending
CPI Consumer price index
UR   Unemployment rate
[a]1967 = 100.
[b]Average of 1977, 1978 and 1979.

TABLE 2.4

Comparative Growth Rates and Economic Ratios, II

	INVESTMENT AS % OF GNP[a]	CONSUMPTION AS % OF GNP	GOVERNMENT EXPENDITURES AS % OF GNP
United States	14.96	62.85	22.15
Canada	22.70	58.05	19.59
United Kingdom	18.63	62.96	18.58
Japan[b]	38.21	51.48	8.18
West Germany	26.21	53.78	17.66
France[b]	27.56	59.46	12.29
Italy	21.71	64.45	14.12

SOURCE: James L. Green as cited in Joint Economic Committee, U.S. Congress, *Employee Stock Ownership Plans (ESOPs), Hearings* (Washington, D.C.: U.S. Government Printing Office, 1976), pt. 2, p. 835.

[a]Data from the early 1970s with residential construction excluded.

[b]1973.

among those same nations the United States ranks next to last in percentage growth in GNP since 1960. Conversely, the United States ranks second in the percentage of GNP going to current consumption. Nor does the United States compare favorably on inflation and unemployment if recent data are considered. Government spending as a percentage of GNP is near the top. But what is critical in this account is not revealed: the output and productivity return on government expenditures—including tax expenditures (revenue losses). Government expenditures are not neutral with respect to returns in the form of technology, capital formation, and productivity.

Table 2.5 indicates selected federal program expenditures and percents for the 1979 fiscal year. Transfer payments constitute almost half of the total: $197.7 billion of the $434.4 billion. There may be many transfer payment "double dippers." There may also be many "triple dippers." Consistent with table 2.2 is the fact that transfer payments have shown remarkable growth as a percentage of total federal expenditures over the past twenty years, reaching 40 percent in 1979.

Grants in aid at $79.3 billion are the next largest item. Urban development action grants (UDAG), block grants, and economic development grants are included under community and regional development. Many of the direct loans and loan guarantees also go toward economic development efforts (e.g., SBA and Farmers Home Administration). Loan guarantees at $26.1 billion represent the government participation amount (i.e., its "at-risk" position), not direct expenditures. Of the tax expenditure (estimated revenue loss) items, capital gains—individual and business—rank first at $17.7 billion, followed by the investment tax credit at $16.5 billion. If the special 1 percent ESOP extra credit is added, the total becomes $17.2 billion.

The items cited in the preceding paragraph and others are specifically intended to increase capital formation, output, and employment (i.e., urban development and economic development grants, block grants, SBA and FHA loans and guarantees, capital gains and investment tax credits, jobs credit, depletion allowances, domestic international sales corporations, etc.). What is the return on these expenditures? The federal government owns nothing, it has made no purchase of goods or capital. It may own some of both if the loans go bad. Assuming a 1979 GNP (ΔQ) of $1,483 billion and a national capital stock (K) of $4,449 billion, a possible increase in output (ΔQ) can be calculated. Should the economy experience, for example, $92.9 billion in additional investment (ΔI) from the above items and new output (ΔQ) of $31.0 billion ($\Delta Q = \Delta I \times Q/K$) over several years? At least the return on these items should be greater than for transfer payments.

TABLE 2.5

Selected Federal Program Expenditures and Returns, 1979
(direct, indirect, or tax expenditures, fiscal year, in billions of dollars)

PROGRAM	EXPENDITURE	BUDGET %
1. Transfer Payments	$197.7	40.0%
Social Security	$99.4	
Retired Civil Service	12.3	
Unemployment	9.6	
Medicare	28.1	
Veterans	14.0	
Retired Military	10.1	
Other	24.2	
2. Grants in Aid	79.3	16.1
Community and Regional Development	6.4	
Revenue Sharing	6.8	
Transportation	9.6	
Income Security	11.3	
Medicaid	12.4	
Other	32.8	
3. Loan Guarantees	26.1[a]	5.3
4. Direct Loans	19.6	4.0
5. State and Local Taxes	18.9	3.8
6. Capital Gains	17.7	3.8
7. Investment Tax Credit	16.5	3.3
8. Medical Plans	14.2	2.9
9. Retirement Plans	13.1[b]	2.7
10. Mortgage Interest Deduction	10.7	2.2
11. Residential Property Tax Deduction	6.8	1.4
12. Municipal Bonds	4.1	0.8
13. Resource Depletion and Development Deduction	3.6	0.7
14. Consumer Interest Deduction	3.1	0.6
15. Domestic International Sales Corporation	1.2	0.2
16. Jobs Credit	1.1	0.2
17. ESOP Tax Credit	0.7	0.1
Total	434.4	TOTAL BUDGET 493.6

SOURCE: Office of Management and Budget, *Special Analysis Budget of the United States Government, 1981* (Washington, D.C.: U.S. Government Printing Office).

[a]Amount of government participation.

[b]Includes tax loss from contributions to qualified ESOP trusts, but not tax credit.

Returns could best be measured by controlled experimentation, but this being improbable, the results of tables 2.2, 2.3, and 2.4 may be utilized. By such a test, it would seem reasonable to infer that present capital formation and economic development programs are ineffective and inefficient—perhaps they nearly achieve an offset to the deleterious effects of transfer payments. A recent study made this comment:

The General Accounting Office has concluded that the $19 billion in investment tax credits in 1978 produced very little noticeable increase in new investment or productivity. Before we rush to give more giant tax breaks to industry, the virtually free option of giving people a stake in what they're doing ought to be considered.[18]

ESOPs may not be "virtually free," but they may never reach the universal use cost cited by Brems in point (4) of his analysis wherein corporate tax liability was reduced 60 percent (from $35 billion to $14 billion with 1972 data). For 1979 this would reduce federal corporate tax liability from $78.4 billion to $31.4 billion, a cost of $47.0 billion.[19] The actual tax credit ESOP (TCESOP) tax cost was $0.7 billion, as indicated in table 2.5. The basic ESOP tax cost, or contribution deductions from pretax income, is included in item 9 of table 2.5: deductible contributions to qualified retirement and other deferred compensation plans. This amount is estimated to be from $1.2 to $1.8 billion [prior to 1979 a pure tax credit ESOP did not also have to be an IRC Section 401(a) qualified plan], for a total of $1.9 to $2.5 billion.

What is the return on the ESOP expenditure? This has not been directly determined. Table 2 6 compares the recent three-year performance (1976-78) of seventy-five ESOPs with that of all nonfarm corporations. Data on seventy-five ESOP firms were collected by the U.S. Senate Finance Committee (SFC) in 1979. The average ESOP was three years old and 21 percent employee owned. The profit and tax payment growth record for the ESOPs was more than double that for all corporations. For employment it was triple; and for productivity increases, quadruple. Conventional corporations had a higher overall tax rate, 51 percent to 38 percent, but the rate for ESOPs was only one percentage point less than it was before they became ESOPs.

Assuming the ESOP sample would have had performance data similar to all corporations had they not adopted ESOPs, the employment, profit, and tax changes would have been 3,990 (plus 12 percent), $40.0 million (plus 75 percent), and $16.4 million (plus 70 percent), respectively. Thus, for a 1 percent lower tax rate on $99,550,000, or a tax loss of $995,500 over the three years, the economy gained 8,310 in new jobs, $53.4 million in additional profits, and

TABLE 2.6
Performance Comparisons of All Corporations vs. ESOP Sample, 1976-78
(current dollar totals for the years 1976, 1977, and 1978)

	ALL CORPORATIONS	ESOP SAMPLE[a]
Sales Change	$529 billion[b]	$1 billion
% Change	+39%	+72%
Employment Change	9,501,000[b]	12,300
% Change	+12%	+37%
Profit Change	$71.8 billion	$93.4 million
% Change	+75%	+157%
Tax Change	$34.7 billion	$35.1 million
% Change	+70%	+150%
Tax Rate	51%	38%[c]
Productivity	+6%[b]	+25%[d]
%Profit/Sales	5.4%[e]	6.0%[f]

SOURCES: *Economic Report of the President, 1980*; ESOP Sample from Committee on Finance, U.S. Senate, 1979.

NOTE: 1976-1978 are estimated dates of latest three-year data reported in SFC sample.

[a] $N = 75$. Average ESOP in sample was three years old and 21 percent employee owned.

[b] Nonfarm.

[c] Pre-ESOP rate = 39%.

[d] Based on sales per employee.

[e] All manufacturing.

[f] Pre-ESOP rate = 4.1%.

$18.7 million in additional taxes. To the public this represents a return on investment of 1,879 percent ($18.7/0.995), or 626 percent per annum.

The Senate Finance Committee sample was based upon voluntary questionnaire returns, a technique that does not assure a representative ESOP sample. However, from 1971 to 1979 about sixty new ESOPs were formed as an alternative to shutdown or divestiture moves initiated because of poor profitability.[20] This indicates that real economic gains are likely to result from these ESOP adoptions.

The average firm in the Senate Finance Committee survey was of moderate size: an average of 602 employees and $33,780,000 in sales at the time of the survey. With 21 percent employee stock ownership, the average firm was neither employee owned nor employee controlled. They were also ESOPs rather than DEOCs.

The Senate Finance Committee findings tend to support a previous report prepared in 1978 by the Survey Research Center of the University of Michigan as a technical assistance project for the Economic Development Administration of the Department of Commerce.[21] Over 472 ESOPs and DEOCs were located, but detailed information was collected on only 98 firms in which all employees owned at least 50 percent of the equity (i.e., employee owned). Again, the firms were of moderate size. The 68 ESOPs averaged about $40 million in sales and 400 employees, while the 30 DEOCs averaged about $17 million in sales and 200 employees.

While selections may not have been made on the basis of profitability *a priori*, profit data was published on only 30 firms. These did have profit levels 50 percent higher than similar conventional firms in their industries, and the single most important correlate of profitability among the numerous characteristics of ownership measured was "worker" ownership.[22] The greater the percentage of worker ownership, the greater the profitability. Profitability seemed to be unrelated to percentage of employee participation, worker representation on the boards of directors, employee stockholder voting rights, and the firm's status as an ESOP or DEOC.

Profitability was calculated using the ratios of pretax profits to sales of the sample divided by the same ratio for the relevant industry in 1976 (i.e., Comparative Profit = Profit S/Sales S ÷ Profit I/Sales I). This ratio, adjusted to union wage scale in five companies where profit was part of the wage, was 1.5 in favor of the sample—1.7 unadjusted. The finding, while of analytical significance, was not of statistical significance due to the small sample size ($N = 30$) and the large variance in profitability.

As of this writing, no serious economic analysis has discredited the ESOP concept. Both the theoretical and empirical work, while generally supportive, have been exploratory and sporadic. No similar analysis has been made of GSOPs (general stock ownership plans) authorized by the Revenue Act of 1978. These plans are state chartered, multicompany, multi-industry, and they are intended to stem the rising tide of transfer payments as a source of personal income.

NOTES

1. Refer to Karl Marx, *Capital and the Capitalist Manifesto* (New York: The Modern Library, 1959).

2. Louis O. Kelso and Patricia Hetter, *Two Factor Theory: The Economics of Reality* (New York: Vintage Books, 1967), pp. 31, 36.

3. Ibid., p. 34.

4. Ibid., p. 35.

5. Louis O. Kelso and Mortimer J. Adler, *The Capitalist Manifesto* (New York: Random House, 1958), p. 41.

6. Kelso and Hetter, *Two Factor Theory*, p. 13.

7. From a statement by Paul A. Samuelson on House Bill 1708, concerning the Proprietary Fund of Puerto Rico (a provincewide ESOP loan fund and guarantee), as printed in the *Congressional Record*, 92d Cong., 2d sess., vol. 118, no. 93, June 8, 1972.

8. Paul A. Samuelson, *Economics*, 10th ed. (New York: McGraw-Hill, 1976), p. 537.

9. Joan Robinson, *Accumulation of Capital* (London: Macmillan & Co., 1956); and Nicholas Kaldor, *Essays on Value and Distribution* (London: Duckworth Publishing Co., 1960).

10. J. J. Jehring, *The Significance of Von Thunen's Theory of Wages for Profit Sharing and a Free Economy* (Evanston, Ill.: Profit Sharing Research Foundation, 1960).

11. John Maynard Keynes, *How to Pay for the War* (London: Macmillan & Co., 1940).

12. J. E. Meade, *Efficiency, Equality and the Ownership of Property* (London: Allen & Unwin, 1964).

13. Joint Economic Committee, U.S. Congress, *Employee Stock Ownership Plans (ESOPs) Hearings* (Washington, D.C.: U.S. Government Printing Office, 1976), pt. 1, p. 525.

14. Keynes, *How to Pay for the War*.

15. Joint Economic Committee, *ESOPs*, pt. 1, pp. 528-37.

16. Timothy P. Roth, "Employee Stock Ownership Trusts, Myopia and Intertemporal Profit Maximization," *Quarterly Review of Economics and Business*, vol. 18, Summer 1978. It is not probable that the supply curve would move to the left due to the decreased marginal disutility of labor with an ESOP.

17. Joint Economic Committee, *ESOPs*, pt. 2, p. 836.

18. Karl Frieden, *Workplace Democracy and Productivity* (Washington, D.C.: National Center for Economic Alternatives, 1980).

19. Corporate tax total taken from the Office of Management and Budget, *Special Analysis: Budget of the United States Government, 1981* (Washington, D.C.: U.S. Government Printing Office), p. 72.

20. Select Committee on Small Business, U.S. Senate, *The Role of the Federal Government and Employee Ownership of Business* (Washington, D.C.: U.S. Government Printing Office, 1979), p. iv.

21. A summary of this report appears in Michael Conte and Arnold S. Tannenbaum, "Employee-Owned Companies: Is the Difference Measurable?" *Monthly Labor Review*, vol. 10 (July 1978): 23-28.

22. Ibid., p. 25. The research was conducted primarily through telephone interviews with company financial officers. Several regression tables are presented.

CHAPTER

3

Financial and Tax Analysis

FINANCIAL SCENARIOS

Under present legislation, as discussed previously, deferred compensation plans have very limited utility as vehicles of corporate finance. ESOPs are the exception since they are intended to invest primarily in employer securities and are permitted to extend credit to the employer company. The principal methods of corporate finance include retained surplus revenues (internal), equity securities, debt securities, and borrowing. An ESOP may be used as a substitute for or a supplement with one or more of these. In most cases the use of an ESOP will involve the issuance to the trust of additional equity securities. This may eventually involve the payment of additional dividends or additional cash contributions for cash distributions or for the repurchase of stock distributions.

To compare and contrast the financial characteristics of ESOPs and conventional corporations efficiently and effectively, nine hypothetical companies will be analyzed using both tables and graphs to present significant financial data.[1] The tables contain, for each company, a simplified balance sheet, a simplified income statement, and a simplified financial position (working capital) statement. Three companies are conventional, and six are ESOPs. Four ESOPs are leveraged: in two the trust obtains a bank loan and in the others the company obtains a bank loan. Two ESOPs are internally financed. One conventional company uses internal financing, another obtains a bank loan, and the third uses equity financing.

It will be assumed, contrary to prior analysis, that the level of productivity and profitability of the ESOPs is the same as that of the conventional companies. In all significant respects the companies are assumed to be identical: productivity, income to assets (20 percent), product and geographic market, management, tax rate (50 percent), stock price ($10 per share), capital requirements, and stock outstanding (10,000 shares, common only). All bank loans will be for a five-year term at 8 percent per annum interest, due in end-of-the-year annual installments. All earnings are retained and added to the asset base, which in turn determines earnings for the following year.

Several of the assumptions may not be realistic, among them the no-dividend provision and the interest rate. Another is that small companies (starting assets of $100,000) could issue and sell securities quickly with only nominal cost. Another is the constant stock price of $10 per share. However, the analysis is intended to be comparatively accurate and not empirically accurate. The focus is upon comparative internal financial conditions under similar circumstances and constraints over a ten-year period.

Summary of assumptions and conditions

1. Beginning assets and equity equal $100,000.
2. Gross income is 20 percent of the assets of the prior year.
3. Basic income tax rate is 50 percent.
4. All earnings are retained (no dividends) and added to assets.
5. Beginning stock outstanding is 10,000 shares common at constant price of $10 per share.
6. All bank loans are for a five-year term at 8 percent interest per annum.
7. All loan payments, principal and interest, are made in five equal annual installments.
8. Contributions to the ESOP do not exceed 15 percent of payroll.
9. All accounts and payments are calculated once per year at year end.
10. All funds are allocated to assets or debt reduction.
11. New stock issues are common stock sold immediately and at no expense.
12. Earnings per share are based on net income, not dividends.

A summary of company scenarios is reported in tables 3.1-3.9.

Table 3.1. Internally financed company. Assets and equity grow from $100,000 to $259,374 over ten years. No new debt or securities are required. Income per share grows to $2.36 from $1.00. Increases in working capital grow to $23,579 from $10,000 and net income from $10,000 to $23,579.

Table 3.2. Debt-financed company that borrows $50,000 at the start of the ten-year period. Debt service consumes $10,000 per year of working capital increases for the first five years, but interest expense is deductible from taxable income. Assets increase from $150,000 to $278,192; equity from $100,000 to $278,192; net income per share from $1.30 to $2.53; working capital additions from $3,000 to $25,290; and net income from $13,000 to $25,290.

Table 3.3. Equity-financed company that sells new issue of stock at start of ten-year period: 5,000 shares at $10 per share. Thus, no deduction from income or working capital for debt service is necessary. Assets and equity grow from $150,000 to $389,061; net income from $15,000 to $35,369; net income per share from $1.00 to $2.36; and additions to working capital from $15,000 to $35,369. The increase in shares outstanding from 10,000 to 15,000 affects per share net income.

Table 3.4. Internally financed company as in table 3.1 except that the company adopts a nonleveraged ESOP to which it transfers 1,000 shares of treasury stock for each of the first five years. This permits a deduction of $10,000 from taxable income for each of the five years (1,000 shares at $10 per share). The ESOP holds 5,000 shares or one-third of the total shares outstanding. Assets and equity grow from $100,000 to $308,579; net income from $15,000 to $28,052 (includes value of ESOP contribution); net income per share from $1.36 to $1.87; and working capital additions from $15,000 to $28,052. Net income and net income per share experience a temporary drop in the sixth year when the ESOP contribution deduction is lost.

Table 3.5. An ESOP company in which the trust obtains the bank loan of $50,000, which is secured by company stock held by the trust or guaranteed by the company, and is transferred to the company in exchange for 5,000 shares of its stock. The company amortizes the loan in five annual payments to the trust and thence to the bank. Both principal and interest are excluded from taxable income. Assets and total equity grow from $150,000 to $327,354; net income from $8,000 to $29,760; net income per share from $0.53 to $1.98 (total outstanding shares); and working capital additions from $8,000 to $29,760. Since the loan amortization payments are qualified plan contributions, no debt reductions show on the financial statement. However, all 5,000 shares transferred to the trust are included to determine per share net income, resulting in very low values at the start of the period. The trust holds 5,000 of the 15,000 outstanding shares.

Table 3.6. An ESOP company in which the company obtains a $50,000 bank loan directly and offsets the loan principal payments with stock contributions to the trust. Thus both principal and interest payments are made from pretax income, even though debt servicing payments of $10,000 reduce working capital. Assets increase to $327,354 from $150,000; equity to $327,354 from $100,000; net income to $29,760 from $18,000; net income per share to $1.98

from $1.64; and working capital additions from $8,000 to $29,760. Stock contributions are 1,000 shares per annum for the first five years, leaving the trust with 5,000 of 15,000 outstanding shares.

Table 3.7. An ESOP company in which the employees purchase the company directly and through the trust from the parent company or from founding stockholders. This is a buy-out in which the ESOP trust acquires 50 percent of the company (5,000 shares). Fifty thousand dollars of the purchase money is contributed by key employees from various sources, and $50,000 is obtained through a bank loan. The company then amortizes the loan with cash contributions. The result is reduced net income and net income per share. Assets grow from $100,000 to $197,668; equity from $50,000 to $197,668; and net income additions from $3,000 to $17,970 per year.

Table 3.8. A buy-out similar to the example in table 3.7 except that the ESOP company obtains a $50,000 loan directly and holds 5,000 shares as treasury stock. Key employees put up $50,000 for the other 5,000 shares. As the loan is amortized by the company, the principal payments are matched by deductible stock contributions to the ESOP trust. Both equity and income per share dilution are less than with a trust-financed acquisition, although working capital increases are the same. Equity per share increases from $10.00 to $19.77, and net income per share decreases from $2.16 to $1.80. The higher net income is offset by debt reduction payments, but outstanding shares remain lower over the term compared to trust financing.

Table 3.9. A third type of employer stock acquisition by the ESOP trust, but in this instance no loan is obtained by either the company or the trust to purchase the stock. Rather, the purchase is made on an installment basis of 1,000 shares per year for five years, using tax-deductible cash contributions made to the trust. This could also represent a partial buy-out of a controlling stockholder or a repurchase of stock distributed by the trust. Shares outstanding are constant at 10,000, and since there is no debt burden, the financial performance exceeds that of the leveraged-acquisition ESOPs. Assets and equity grow from $100,000 to $210,388; net income from $5,000 to $19,126; and per share income from $0.50 to $1.91.

As the tables indicate, the tax and working capital advantages are significant for ESOPs, but come at the expense of equity dilution and reduced per share income. While the nominal market price per share remains $10, the ESOPs have per share book values about 20 percent lower than the conventional companies after ten years. However, total assets and equity are comparable.

The equity ESOP reduces its first year taxes by half ($10,000 to $5,000), and the savings goes directly to working capital. This effect is less pronounced with leveraged ESOPs, which have the double burden of loan amortization and earnings/stock dilution. To a lesser degree, the effect of the equity ESOP or the company-financed ESOP—but not a trust-financed ESOP—could be achieved with a qualified stock bonus plan. Contributions to the trust by any of the ESOP companies are made at half the actual cost of the money or the stock contributed because of the 50 percent tax rate. The remaining half of the contribution cost is either compensation or a bonus to plan participants. An ESOP company with no tax liability would have no benefit from the tax deduction and would thus pay the entire cost of any contributions.

As to the leveraged ESOPs, the company-financed version appears to offer numerous advantages over the trust-financed version. These include the following:

1. Company-financed ESOP income and equity per share suffer less dilution when based on total shares outstanding. The treasury stock method could be used partially to remedy this, such that the balance of the unearned employee deferred compensation could be used to purchase the excess outstanding stock. The effect, if practiced, would be a reduction of working capital.

2. The trust-financed ESOP company incurs an obligation to the trust to amortize the loan requiring the reduction in equity and equity per share as indicated in tables 3.5 and 3.7.[2]

3. If the value of the contribution is overstated, the loss for the company-financed ESOP probably is the loss of part of the deduction, while for the trust-financed ESOP a penalty tax could be imposed under IRC 4975(a) or even possible plan disqualification.

4. Company financing permits more flexibility in contributions during loss years and in loan renegotiation.

The principal advantage of trust financing over company financing with an ESOP is that an alternate form of financing is available to acquire the company or assure its continuance as a viable business entity when the company is unable to act. The most common examples, ones giving birth to many ESOPs, are impending shutdowns or divestitures of companies by parent firms or retiring owners of close-held companies. These scenarios are illustrated by the acquisition ESOPs of tables 3.7, 3.8, and 3.9.

Figures 3, 4, 5, and 6 summarize and compare in graphic form the data from the preceding tables on total assets, net income, net income per share, and working capital changes. Figure 3 reveals the strong asset growth of the equity-financed company, followed by the three ESOPs closely grouped together. The lower initial starting point of the equity ESOP results from its reliance on incremental tax leveraging rather than on a lump-sum capital increase. The debt-financed company shows the burden of five years of debt service.

TABLE 3.1
Internal Financing—Conventional Company

| | BEGINNING | \multicolumn{10}{c}{END OF YEAR} | | | | | | | | | |
		1	2	3	4	5	6	7	8	9	10
BALANCE SHEET											
Assets	$100,000	$110,000	$121,000	$133,100	$146,410	$161,051	$177,156	$194,872	$214,359	$235,795	$259,374
Liabilities	-	-	-	-	-	-	-	-	-	-	-
Equity	100,000	110,000	121,000	133,100	146,410	161,051	177,156	194,872	214,359	235,795	259,374
Equity per Share	10.00	11.00	12.10	13.31	14.64	16.11	17.72	19.49	21.44	23.58	25.94
INCOME STATEMENT											
Gross Income		$20,000	$22,000	$24,200	$26,620	$29,282	$32,210	$35,431	$38,974	$42,872	$47,159
Other Expenses		-	-	-	-	-	-	-	-	-	-
Taxable Income		$20,000	$22,000	$24,200	$26,620	$29,282	$32,210	$35,431	$38,974	$42,872	$47,159
Taxes		10,000	11,000	12,100	13,310	14,641	16,105	17,715	19,487	21,436	23,580
Net Income		$10,000	$11,000	$12,100	$13,310	$14,641	$16,105	$17,716	$19,487	$21,436	$23,579
Outstanding Shares		10,000	10,000	10,000	10,000	10,000	10,000	10,000	10,000	10,000	10,000
Income per Share		$1.00	$1.10	$1.21	$1.33	$1.46	$1.61	$1.77	$1.95	$2.14	$2.36

36

CHANGES IN
FINANCIAL POSITION

Sources:										
Net Income	$10,000	$11,000	$12,000	$13,310	$14,641	$16,105	$17,716	$19,487	$21,436	$23,579
Applications:										
Reduction of Debt	-	-	-	-	-	-	-	-	-	-
Increase (Decrease) in Working Capital	$10,000	$11,000	$12,100	$13,310	$14,641	$16,105	$17,716	$19,487	$21,436	$23,579

SOURCE: Hewitt Associates, "ESOPs: An Analytical Report" [1976] in Select Committee on Small Business, U.S. Senate, *The Small Business Employee Ownership Act, Hearings* (Washington, D.C.: U.S. Government Printing Office, 1979), pp. 399-455.

37

TABLE 3.2
Debt Financing—Conventional Company

	Beginning	\multicolumn{10}{c}{End of Year}									
		1	2	3	4	5	6	7	8	9	10
Balance Sheet											
Assets	$150,000	$153,000	$156,700	$161,170	$166,487	$172,736	$190,009	$209,010	$229,911	$252,902	$278,192
Liabilities	50,000	40,000	30,000	20,000	10,000	-	-	-	-	-	-
Equity	100,000	113,000	126,700	141,170	156,487	172,736	190,009	209,010	229,911	252,902	278,192
Equity per Share	10.00	11.30	12.67	14.12	15.65	17.27	19.00	20.90	22.99	25.29	27.82
Income Statement											
Gross Income		$30,000	$30,600	$31,340	$32,234	$33,297	$34,547	$38,002	$41,802	$45,982	$50,580
Interest		4,000	3,200	2,400	1,600	800	-	-	-	-	-
Taxable Income		26,000	27,400	28,940	30,634	32,497	34,547	38,002	41,802	45,982	50,580
Taxes		13,000	13,700	14,470	15,317	16,248	17,274	19,001	20,901	22,991	25,290
Net Income		$13,000	$13,700	$14,470	$15,317	$16,249	$17,273	$19,001	$20,901	$22,991	$25,290
Outstanding Shares		10,000	10,000	10,000	10,000	10,000	10,000	10,000	10,000	10,000	10,000
Income per Share		$1.30	$1.37	$1.45	$1.53	$1.62	$1.73	$1.90	$2.09	$2.30	$2.53

CHANGES IN
FINANCIAL POSITION

Sources:										
Net Income	$13,000	$13,700	$14,470	$15,317	$16,349	$17,373	$19,001	$20,901	$22,991	$25,290
Applications:										
Reduction of Debt	10,000	10,000	10,000	10,000	10,000	-	-	-	-	-
Increase (Decrease) in Working Capital	$3,000	$3,700	$4,470	$5,317	$6,249	$17,273	$19,001	$20,901	$22,991	$25,290

SOURCE: Hewitt Associates, "ESOPs."

TABLE 3.3

Equity Financing—Conventional Company

	Beginning	End of Year 1	2	3	4	5	6	7	8	9	10
BALANCE SHEET											
Assets	$150,000	$165,000	$181,500	$199,650	$219,615	$241,576	$265,734	$292,308	$321,538	$353,692	$389,061
Liabilities	-	-	-	-	-	-	-	-	-	-	-
Equity	150,000	165,000	181,500	199,650	219,615	241,576	265,734	292,308	321,538	353,692	389,061
Equity per Share	10.00	11.00	12.10	13.31	14.64	16.11	17.72	19.49	21.44	23.58	25.94
INCOME STATEMENT											
Gross Income		$30,000	$33,000	$36,300	$39,930	$43,923	$48,315	$53,147	$58,462	$64,308	$70,738
Other Expenses		-	-	-	-	-	-	-	-	-	-
Taxable Income		30,000	33,000	36,300	39,930	43,923	48,315	53,147	58,462	64,308	70,738
Taxes		15,000	16,500	18,150	19,965	21,962	24,157	26,573	29,231	32,154	35,369
Net Income		$15,000	$16,5000	$18,150	$19,965	$21,961	$24,158	$26,574	$29,231	$32,154	$35,369
Outstanding Shares		15,000	15,000	15,000	15,000	15,000	15,000	15,000	15,000	15,000	15,000
Income per Share		$1.00	$1.10	$1.21	$1.33	$1.46	$1.61	$1.77	$1.95	$2.14	$2.36

CHANGES IN
FINANCIAL POSITION
Sources:
Net Income $15,000 $16,500 $18,150 $19,965 $21,961 $24,158 $26,574 $29,231 $32,154 $35,369
Applications:
Reduction of Debt   -   -   -   -   -   -   -   -   -   -

Increase (Decrease)
in Working Capital $15,000 $16,500 $18,150 $19,965 $21,961 $24,158 $26,574 $29,231 $32,154 $35,369

SOURCE: Hewitt Associates, "ESOPs."

41

TABLE 3.4
Equity ESOP—Internal Financing
(stock contributions to ESOP)

	Beginning	\multicolumn{10}{c}{End of Year}									
		1	2	3	4	5	6	7	8	9	10
Balance Sheet											
Assets	$100,000	$115,000	$131,500	$149,650	$169,615	$191,577	$210,734	$231,838	$255,022	$280,527	$308,579
Liabilities	-	-	-	-	-	-	-	-	-	-	-
Equity	100,000	115,000	131,500	149,650	169,615	191,577	210,734	231,838	255,022	280,527	308,579
Equity per Share	10.00	10.45	10.96	11.51	12.12	12.77	14.05	15.46	17.00	18.70	20.57
Income Statement											
Gross Income		$20,000	$23,000	$26,300	$29,930	$33,923	$38,315	$42,147	$46,368	$51,004	$56,105
Contribution (Stock)		10,000	10,000	10,000	10,000	10,000	-	-	-	-	-
Taxable Income		10,000	13,000	16,300	19,930	23,923	38,315	42,147	46,368	51,004	56,105
Taxes		5,000	6,500	8,150	9,965	11,962	19,158	21,073	23,184	25,502	28,053
Net Income		$15,000	$16,500	$18,150	$19,965	$21,961	$19,157	$21,074	$23,184	$25,502	$28,052
Outstanding Shares		11,000	12,000	13,000	14,000	15,000	15,000	15,000	15,000	15,000	15,000
Income per Share		$1.36	$1.38	$1.40	$1.43	$1.46	$1.28	$1.40	$1.55	$1.70	$1.87

CHANGES IN FINANCIAL POSITION

Sources:										
Net Income	$15,000	$16,500	$18,150	$19,965	$21,961	$19,157	$21,074	$23,184	$25,502	$28,052
Applications:										
Reduction of Debt	-	-	-	-	-	-	-	-	-	-
Increase (Decrease) in Working Capital	$15,000	$16,500	$18,150	$19,965	$21,961	$19,157	$21,074	$23,184	$25,502	$28,052

43

TABLE 3.5
ESOP Financing by Trust

	BEGINNING	END OF YEAR 1	2	3	4	5	6	7	8	9	10
BALANCE SHEET											
Assets	$150,000	$158,000	$167,200	$177,720	$189,692	$203,261	$223,587	$245,946	$270,540	$297,594	$327,354
Liabilities:											
Obligation to ESOT		40,000	30,000	20,000	10,000	-	-	-	-	-	-
Equity	100,000	118,000	137,200	157,720	179,692	203,261	223,587	245,946	270,540	297,594	327,354
Equity per Share	6.67	7.67	9.15	10.51	11.99	13.55	14.91	16.40	18.04	19.84	21.82
INCOME STATEMENT											
Gross Income		$30,000	$31,600	$33,440	$35,544	$37,938	$40,652	$44,718	$49,189	$54,108	$59,520
Contribution (Cash) and Interest		14,000	13,200	12,400	11,600	10,800					
Taxable Income		16,000	18,400	21,040	23,944	27,138	40,652	44,178	49,189	54,108	59,520
Taxes		8,000	9,200	10,520	11,972	13,569	20,326	22,359	24,595	27,054	29,760
Net Income		$8,000	$9,200	$10,520	$11,972	$13,569	$20,326	$22,359	$24,594	$27,054	$29,760
Outstanding Shares "Fully Outstanding"		15,000	15,000	15,000	15,000	15,000	15,000	15,000	15,000	15,000	15,000
Income per Share "Fully Outstanding"		$0.53	$0.61	$0.70	$0.80	$0.90	$1.36	$1.49	$1.64	$1.80	$1.98

CHANGES IN
FINANCIAL POSITION

Sources:										
Net Income	$8,000	$9,200	$10,520	$11,972	$13,569	$20,326	$22,359	$24,594	$27,054	$29,760
Applications:										
Reduction of Debt	-	-	-	-	-	-	-	-	-	-
Increase (Decrease)										
in Working Capital	$8,000	$9,200	$10,520	$11,972	$13,569	$20,326	$22,359	$24,594	$27,054	$29,760

SOURCE: Hewitt Associates, "ESOPs."

45

TABLE 3.6
ESOP Financing by Company

	Beginning					End of Year					
		1	2	3	4	5	6	7	8	9	10
BALANCE SHEET											
Assets	$150,000	$158,000	$167,200	$177,720	$189,692	$203,261	$223,587	$245,946	$270,540	$297,594	$327,354
Liabilities	50,000	40,000	30,000	20,000	10,000	-	-	-	-	-	-
Equity	100,000	118,000	137,200	157,720	179,692	203,261	223,587	245,946	270,540	297,594	327,354
Equity per Share	10.00	10.73	11.43	12.13	12.84	13.55	14.91	16.40	18.04	19.84	21.82
INCOME STATEMENT											
Gross Income		$30,000	$31,600	$33,440	$35,544	$37,938	$40,652	$44,718	$49,189	$54,108	$59,520
Contribution (Stock) and Interest		14,000	13,200	12,400	11,600	10,000	-	-	-	-	-
Taxable Income		$16,000	$18,400	$21,040	$23,944	$27,138	$40,652	$44,718	$49,189	$54,108	$59,520
Taxes		8,000	9,200	10,520	11,972	13,569	20,326	22,359	24,595	27,054	29,760
Net Income		$18,000	$19,200	$20,520	$21,972	$23,569	$20,326	$22,359	$24,594	$27,054	$29,760
Outstanding Shares		11,000	12,000	13,000	14,000	15,000	15,000	15,000	15,000	15,000	15,000
Income per Share		$1.64	$1.60	$1.58	$1.57	$1.57	$1.36	$1.49	$1.64	$1.80	$1.98

Changes in Financial Position

Sources:										
Net Income	$18,000	$19,200	$20,520	$21,972	$23,569	$20,326	$22,359	$24,594	$27,054	$29,760
Applications:										
Reduction of Debt	10,000	10,000	10,000	10,000	10,000	-	-	-	-	-
Increase (Decrease) in Working Capital	$8,000	$9,200	$10,520	$11,972	$13,569	$20,326	$22,359	$24,594	$27,054	$29,760

TABLE 3.7
Acquisition ESOP—Trust Financed

	Beginning	End of Year									
		1	2	3	4	5	6	7	8	9	10
BALANCE SHEET											
Assets	$100,000	$103,000	$106,700	$111,170	$116,487	$122,736	$135,009	$148,511	$163,362	$179,698	$197,668
Liabilities	50,000	40,000	30,000	20,000	10,000	-	-	-	-	-	-
Equity	50,000	63,000	76,700	91,170	106,487	122,736	135,009	148,511	163,362	179,698	197,668
Equity per Share	5.00	6.30	7.67	9.12	10.65	12.27	13.50	14.85	16.34	17.97	19.77
INCOME STATEMENT											
Gross Income		$20,000	$20,600	$21,340	$22,234	$23,297	$24,547	$27,002	$29,702	$32,672	$35,940
Contribution (Cash) and Interest		14,000	13,200	12,400	11,600	10,800	-	-	-	-	-
Taxable Income		$6,000	$7,400	$8,940	$10,634	$12,497	$24,547	$27,002	$29,702	$32,672	$35,940
Taxes		3,000	3,700	4,470	5,317	6,249	12,274	13,501	14,851	16,336	17,970
Net Income		$3,000	$3,700	$4,470	$5,317	$6,248	$12,273	$13,501	$14,851	$16,336	$17,970
Outstanding Shares		10,000	10,000	10,000	10,000	10,000	10,000	10,000	10,000	10,000	10,000
Income per Share		$0.30	$0.37	$0.45	$0.53	$0.62	$1.23	$1.35	$1.49	$1.63	$1.80

CHANGES IN FINANCIAL POSITION

Sources:										
Net Income	$3,000	$3,700	$4,470	$5,317	$6,248	$12,273	$13,501	$14,851	$16,336	$17,970
Applications:										
Reduction of Debt	-	-	-	-	-	-	-	-	-	-
Increase (Decrease) in Working Capital	$3,000	$3,700	$4,470	$5,317	$6,248	$12,273	$13,501	$14,851	$16,336	$17,970

TABLE 3.8
Acquisition ESOP—Company Financed

	Beginning	End of Year 1	2	3	4	5	6	7	8	9	10
BALANCE SHEET											
Assets	$100,000	$103,000	$106,700	$111,170	$116,487	$122,736	$135,009	$148,511	$163,362	$179,698	$197,668
Liabilities	50,000	40,000	30,000	20,000	10,000	-	-	-	-	-	-
Equity	50,000	63,000	76,700	91,170	106,487	122,736	135,009	148,511	163,362	179,698	197,668
Equity per Share	10.00	10.50	10.96	11.40	11.83	12.27	13.50	14.85	16.34	17.97	19.77
INCOME STATEMENT											
Gross Income		$20,000	$20,600	$21,340	$22,234	$23,297	$24,547	$27,002	$29,702	$32,672	$35,940
Contribution (Stock) and Interest		14,000	13,200	12,400	11,600	10,800	-	-	-	-	-
Taxable Income		6,000	7,400	8,940	10,234	12,497	24,547	27,002	29,702	32,672	35,940
Taxes		3,000	3,700	4,470	5,317	6,249	12,274	13,501	14,851	16,336	17,970
Net Income		$3,000	$3,700	$4,470	$5,317	$6,248	$12,273	$13,501	$14,851	$16,336	$17,970
Outstanding Shares		6,000	7,000	8,000	9,000	10,000	10,000	10,000	10,000	10,000	10,000
Income per Share		$2.16	$1.96	$1.81	$1.72	$1.62	$1.23	$1.35	$1.49	$1.63	$1.80

CHANGES IN
FINANCIAL POSITION

Sources:										
Net Income	$13,000	$13,700	$14,470	$15,317	$16,248	$12,273	$13,501	$14,851	$16,336	$17,970
Applications:										
Reduction of Debt	10,000	10,000	10,000	10,000	10,000	-	-	-	-	-
Increase (Decrease) in Working Capital	$3,000	$3,700	$4,470	$5,317	$6,248	$12,273	$13,501	$14,851	$16,336	$17,970

TABLE 3.9
Acquisition ESOP—Internally Financed

| | Beginning | End of Year ||||||||||
		1	2	3	4	5	6	7	8	9	10
Balance Sheet											
Assets	$100,000	$105,000	$110,500	$116,550	$123,305	$130,635	$143,698	$158,068	$173,875	$191,262	$210,388
Liabilities	-	-	-	-	-	-	-	-	-	-	-
Equity	100,000	105,000	110,500	116,550	123,305	130,635	143,698	158,068	173,875	191,262	210,388
Equity per Share	10.00	10.50	11.05	11.66	12.33	13.06	14.37	15.81	17.39	19.13	21.04
Income Statement											
Gross Income		$20,000	$21,000	$22,100	$23,310	$24,661	$26,127	$28,740	$31,614	$34,775	$38,252
Contribution (Cash)		10,000	10,000	10,000	10,000	10,000	-	-	-	-	-
Taxable Income		10,000	11,000	12,100	13,310	14,661	26,127	28,740	31,614	34,775	38,252
Taxes		5,000	5,500	6,050	6,655	7,331	13,064	14,370	15,807	17,388	19,126
Net Income		$5,000	$5,500	$6,050	$6,655	$7,330	$13,063	$14,370	$15,807	$17,387	$19,126
Outstanding Shares		10,000	10,000	10,000	10,000	10,000	10,000	10,000	10,000	10,000	10,000
Income per Share		$0.50	$0.55	$0.61	$0.67	$0.73	$1.31	$1.44	$1.58	$1.74	$1.91

CHANGES IN
FINANCIAL POSITION
Sources:
Net Income $5,000 $5,500 $6,050 $6,655 $7,330 $13,063 $14,370 $15,807 $17,387 $19,126
Applications:
Reduction of Debt   -   -   -   -   -   -   -   -   -   -
                          _____ _____ _____ _____ _____ _____ _____ _____ _____ _____
Increase(Decrease)
In Working Capital $5,000 $5,500 $6,050 $6,655 $7,330 $13,063 $14,370 $15,807 $17,387 $19,126

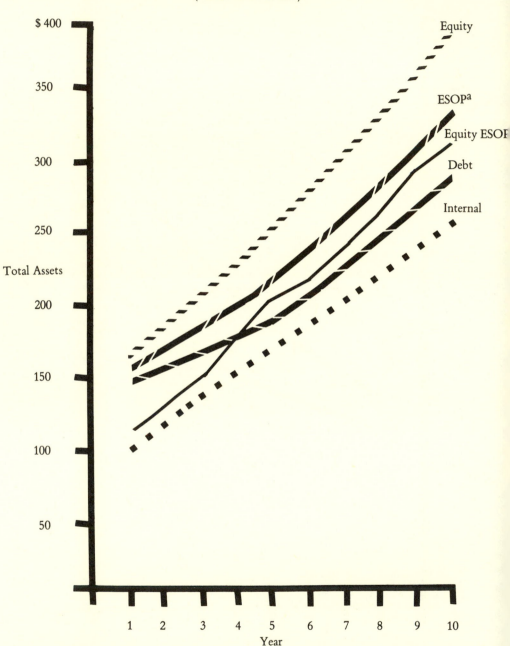

FIGURE 3
Total Assets by Type of Financing
(thousands of dollars)

SOURCE: Hewitt Associates, "ESOPs: An Analytical Report" [1976] in Select Committee on Small Business, U.S. Senate, *The Small Business Employee Ownership Act, Hearings* (Washington, D.C.: U.S. Government Printing Office, 1979), pp. 399-455.

[a]Trust financed.
[b]Company financed.

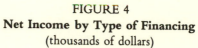

FIGURE 4
Net Income by Type of Financing
(thousands of dollars)

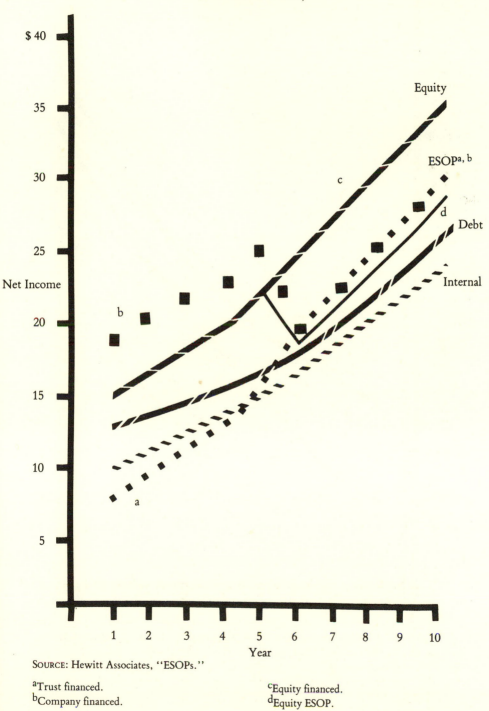

SOURCE: Hewitt Associates, "ESOPs."

[a]Trust financed.   [c]Equity financed.
[b]Company financed.   [d]Equity ESOP.

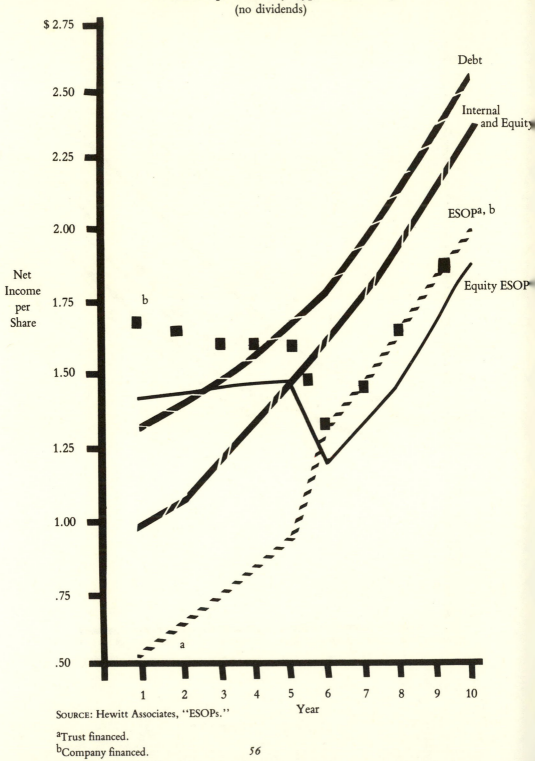

FIGURE 5
Net Income per Share by Type of Financing
(no dividends)

SOURCE: Hewitt Associates, "ESOPs."

Year

[a]Trust financed.
[b]Company financed.

56

FIGURE 6
Working Capital by Type of Financing
(increases in thousands of dollars)

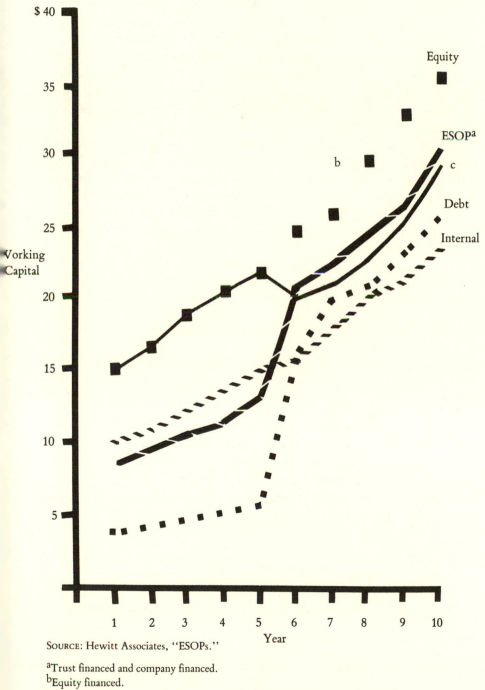

[a]Trust financed and company financed.
[b]Equity financed.
[c]Equity ESOP.

Figure 4 also shows superior performance by the conventional equity-financed company. Again the ESOPs end up close together after dissimilar starts. Earnings dropped for the equity ESOP when it lost its tax preference deduction in the sixth year, the same year in which earnings jumped for both debt-financed ESOPs due to complete loan repayment. As in figure 3, the conventional internally financed company lags behind by a significant margin.

Figure 5 reveals the advantage of leverage for the conventional debt-financed company on per share net income and dramatic early-year dilution for the leveraged ESOPs since the leverage was accompanied by additional stock contributions. This effect is not significant for the equity ESOP until it loses its tax deductions in the sixth year.

Figure 6 is almost identical to figure 4 since net income is either transformed into working capital or used for debt service. The latter is the reason for the low increases in working capital during the early years for the debt-financed company. The graph and table indicate only changes in working capital—not its total. All companies, except the internally financed equity ESOP and conventional company, received large initial working capital additions from outside financing.

In summation, the ESOP companies as a whole have financial characteristics slightly superior to conventional companies, under the assumptions made herein, with two exceptions:

1. Net income per share may be significantly lower even in the long run than with conventional companies.

2. A conventional equity-financed company shows generally superior financial characteristics to any ESOP.

A quick and ready market for the stock of the equity-financed company is a necessity for this conclusion, and the stock may have to be issued to "outsiders" or "raiders." Further, dividend payments will most adversely affect the equity company and the ESOPs. The ESOPs may be assisted in this matter and in capital acquisition in general because the trust provides an internal market that is financed up to 50 percent by tax reductions. This factor can be increased up to an additional 1 percent of the tax if a TCESOP is used plus up to an additional 0.5 percent for qualified employee contributions.

REPURCHASE BURDEN

The ESOPs used as examples in this section, with one exception, are neither employee owned nor controlled since the trust in each instance holds only one third of the outstanding stock. With continued contributions of stock (not cash) to the trust, the equity ESOP may have continued its high growth rate in assets and net income while permitting net income per share to rise at a slow but steady rate. The reason is that the resulting tax reductions may more than compensate for the dilution factor as more stock is issued each year. However, the more stock that is issued to the trust, the more likely it is that the company will have to make significant cash contributions to the trust, also tax deductible, as employees seek to cash out upon separation or retirement. This could be particularly detrimental to the net income and working capital of a company having no public market for its securities.

An IRC 409A-type plan may provide for a cash distribution, and any ESOP may provide a "put" option upon separation or retirement. Table 3.10 illustrates the effect upon the equity ESOP of table 3.4 of trust stock repurchases following distribution. In years 11, 12, 13, 14, and 15, such distributions and repurchases are 500 shares per year financed by company cash contributions at $10 per share. Since the contribution is deductible from taxable income (50 percent tax rate), the reduction in net income and working capital is only $2,500 per year or $12,500 in total.

Compared with the conventional internally financed company in table 3.1, for the first ten years the equity ESOP has a cumulative net income advantage of $49,172. This continues to increase over the years as per the original assumptions on company scenarios. At the end of fifteen years this amount would be $79,213. To obtain the net cumulative advantage, the actual out-of-pocket cost for the repurchases, or $2,500, must be subtracted for years 11, 12, 13, 14, and 15, leaving $66,713.

The amount of the net annual advantage will depend upon the repurchase burden required of the ESOP company. Assuming 500 shares per annum, this would represent a 10 percent annual turnover rate through retirement and separation with all such employees requesting repurchase of all stock vested in their accounts. Despite this repurchase burden, the ESOP's financial advantage persists. Additional stock contributions could be made to the trust to increase existing employee allocations or to cover additional employees. This again would result in a sharp increase in assets and net earnings and, eventually, in a higher repurchase burden.

The IRS may require the employer company to repurchase stock distributions where such securities are not readily tradable on an established market. A repurchase burden should not be likely for companies listed on a national securities exchange. This decreased repurchase burden will probably be transformed to a dividend burden for public companies. Private companies and over-

TABLE 3.10
Equity ESOP Stock Repurchase
(from table 3.4)

	END OF YEAR					
	10	11	12	13	14	15
Trust Shares	5,000	5,000	5,000	5,000	5,000	5,000
Distributed and Repurchased	0	500	500	500	500	500
Cash Contribution Required	0	$5,000	$5,000	$5,000	$5,000	$5,000
Change in Net Income and Working Capital	0	$(2,500)	$(2,500)	$(2,500)	$(2,500)	$(2,500)
Tax Saving	0	$2,500	$2,500	$2,500	$2,500	$2,500
Cumulative Income Gain[a]	$49,172	$54,093	$59,506	$65,460	$72,009	$79,213
Cumulative Net Income Gain[b]	$49,172	$51,593	$54,506	$57,960	$62,009	$66,713

[a]Cumulative difference between table 3.4 and table 3.1 type of companies before repurchase contribution.

[b]Cumulative difference between table 3.4 and table 3.1 type of companies after repurchase contribution.

the-counter companies will have a lighter dividend burden and a heavier repurchase burden. No ESOP company should face both a heavy dividend burden and a heavy repurchase burden.

In conclusion, the financial advantages of an ESOP are directly related to the sponsoring company's tax rate, growth rate, immediate cash needs, and degree of foreclosure from conventional financing. ESOP disadvantages are directly related to company sensitivity to equity and income per share dilution, dividend rate, tax losses and deductions, long-term debt, equity market access, and the repurchase rate. Stagnant public companies with adequate dividends and share prices are poor ESOP risks. The best candidates would be small to medium private companies or corporate subsidiaries with growth potential and restricted access to capital.

However, the repurchase burden is potentially more devastating to private than to public companies. The repurchase scenario of table 3.10 represents a favorable situation of steady growth in company assets and earnings and carefully planned stock contributions and repurchases. The stock holdings of the ESOP trust are limited to one-third of total shares outstanding, and annual contributions never exceed 10 percent of total shares outstanding. Distributions and repurchases never exceed 5 percent of total shares outstanding or 20 percent of the shares held by the trust. A company permitting an excessive repurchase burden must either go public to provide a market for plan beneficiaries or end up insolvent or in breach of its repurchase obligation.[3]

NOTES

1. Much of the data and most of the assumptions are based on a 1976 report prepared for the Profit Sharing Council of America by Hewitt Associates, Lincolnshire, Illinois. The report is titled "ESOPs: An Analytical Report" and is reproduced in Select Committee on Small Business, U.S. Senate, *The Small Business Employee Ownership Act, Hearings* (Washington, D.C.: U.S. Government Printing Office, 1979), pp. 399-455.

2. This reflects "Accounting for Stock Issued to Employees," in *Opinion No. 25* of the Accounting Principles Board, American Institute of Certified Public Accountants, in *APB Accounting Principles* (Chicago: Commerce Clearing House, Inc., 1973), p. 6735. Not shown on tables 3.5 and 3.7 is an offsetting entry for unearned employee compensation.

3. Refer to "Employee Stock Plans: An Economic Cure-All or a Dubious Benefit?" *Wall Street Journal*, December 8, 1980, p. 1.

4

Comparative Characteristics

DEFERRED COMPENSATION PLANS

A pension plan, profit-sharing plan, stock bonus plan, money purchase plan, and ESOP are all forms of deferred compensation plans that may qualify for preferential tax treatment under IRC Sections 401(a), 402(a)(e), 404(a), and 501(a). Other code sections that generally must be met include 410, 411, 412, 413, 414, 415, and 4975. In addition, all must meet most provisions of ERISA Sections 3(14), 3(18), 102, 104, 402, 403(a), 404(a), 406(a), 407, and 408. The major differences between other plans and ESOPs may be cited without most of the statutory and regulatory detail.

Pension Plans: Contributions must be made annually in cash only and must be actuarially determined on the basis of defined benefits to be distributed under the plan. Contributions and distributions are based upon actuarial solvency and not upon profit. The amount contributed need not be the same each year unless it is a money purchase pension plan.

The employer may deduct contributions from pretax income to the extent necessary to fund actuarially the pensions due to participants without significant restrictions by profit or payroll. In general, pension benefits must be determined by years of employment and compensation. Benefit payments must be made in cash periodic payments or annuity payments. Being a defined benefit plan, a pension is not an individual account plan.

The lending of money or extending of credit by a pension trust to certain parties—including the sponsoring company, a fiduciary, or certain controlling stockholders—is prohibited by both IRC Section 4975 and ERISA Section 406(a). Further, under Sections 404(a) and 407(a) of ERISA the trust must diversify its asset holdings such that no more than 10 percent thereof are in the form of qualified sponsoring company property and securities.

Profit-Sharing Plans: Contributions, generally in the form of cash, may be made only out of current or accumulated earnings. Benefits may be distributed in the form of employer stock, cash, or an annuity.

A profit-sharing plan may borrow funds, but not from the sponsoring company nor with its guarantee. In addition, it may not engage in a credit transaction with the sponsoring company as per IRC Section 4975 and ERISA Section 406(a), including any installment purchase.

It may also purchase qualifying securities of the sponsoring company, but is not required to do so, as in an ESOP, and under certain circumstances such purchases may exceed 10 percent of the value of its plan assets. A profit-sharing plan is an individual account plan under ERISA Section 407(d) and, if authorized by the plan, it is permitted to exceed the usual diversity requirement of Sections 404(a) and 407(a) within the constraints of prudence. Major elements of the prudence test include the rate of return and appreciation.

Stock Bonus Plans: According to IRS Regulation 1.401-1(b), a stock bonus plan is a plan established and maintained by an employer to provide benefits similar to those of a profit-sharing plan, except that the contributions by the employer are not necessarily dependent upon the profits and the benefits are distributable in stock of the employer company. For the purpose of allocating and distributing the stock of the employer that is to be shared among the employees or their beneficiaries, such a plan is subject to the same requirements as a profit-sharing plan. As in a profit-sharing plan, the amount of each employee's retirement benefits will depend upon the amount accumulated in the account over the years of participation.

A stock bonus plan is both an individual account plan and a defined contribution plan. An ESOP is a form of stock bonus plan as defined in IRC Section 4975(e)(7) and in ERISA Section 407(d)(6). A stock bonus plan may borrow and invest in qualifying employer securities beyond 10 percent, but with the same restraints as apply to profit-sharing plans.

Section 406(a)(1)(B) of ERISA and Section 4975(c)(1)(B) of the IRC prohibit any direct or indirect lending of money or any other extension of credit between any type of plan and a "party in interest" (e.g., sponsoring company or controlling stockholder). ERISA Section 408(b)(3) and IRC Section 4975(d)(3) exempt from such prohibitions any loan to an ESOP if such loan is primarily for the benefit of participants and beneficiaries, if it is granted at reasonable interest, and if any collateral given consists only of qualifying employer securities. Unlike an ESOP or LESOP, a stock bonus plan may not and is not intended both to engage in financing for the sponsoring company and to invest primarily in its securities.

Money Purchase Plans: In this form of pension plan and defined contribution plan the annual contribution to a member's account is fixed or definitely determinable. Like a stock bonus plan or an employee stock ownership plan, contributions are not necessarily dependent upon profits. Unlike a profit-sharing plan, stock bonus plan, or employee stock ownership plan, the contribution rate, once established, cannot be decreased without resulting in a curtailment or partial termination of the plan. A money purchase pension plan differs from a defined benefit pension plan in that, under a money purchase plan, the amount of each employee's retirement or other benefit will depend upon the sum accumulated in the account.

Combined with a stock bonus plan, it forms part of the definition of an ESOP under ERISA Section 407(d)(6) and IRC Section 4975(e)(7). Standing alone, it cannot invest more than 10 percent of the value of its assets in employer securities nor can it engage in financing.

Employee Stock Ownership Plans: Section 4975(e)(7) states that an employee stock ownership plan means a defined contribution plan that is a stock bonus plan or a stock bonus and money purchase plan, both of which are qualified under Section 401(a), that is designed to invest primarily in employer securities, and that meets additional requirements of Section 409A. ERISA Section 407(d)(6) states that the term "employee stock ownership plan" means an individual account plan that is a qualified stock bonus plan or a stock bonus plan and money purchase plan, both of which are qualified under Section 401(a), that is designed to invest primarily in qualifying employer securities, and that meets other requirements as may be prescribed by regulation. IRC Section 409A states that a tax credit employee stock ownership plan (TCESOP) means a defined contribution plan that meets the requirements of Section 401(a), is designed to invest primarily in employer securities, and meets additional requirements subsequently enumerated.

An ESOP is a stock bonus plan that is designed to invest primarily in employer securities and that may engage in financing for the employer company by borrowing and extending credit as a leveraged ESOP or LESOP. It may also qualify the employer company for an additional 1 percent investment tax credit (TCESOP) under Section 409A plus another 0.5 percent for employee matching. As a qualified Section 401(a) plan, employer cash or stock contributions of up to 15 percent (25 percent for a LESOP) of payroll before carryforward are deductible from pretax income under Section 404(a). Earnings of the plan and trust are not taxed as per Section 501(a), and capital gain and income averaging are available for distributions to employees or their beneficiaries under Sections 402(a) and 691(c). For a stock bonus and money purchase ESOP, being a combined plan, the deduction from pretax income is also 25 percent of payroll.

In contrast to other plans, Section 409A(e) requires that plan participants be allowed to vote the securities allocated to their accounts if the securities are registered on a national exchange. If not so registered, the voting rights need be given only where state law or the corporate charter requires a supramajority. Employer securities contributed to a LESOP or TCESOP must be voting common stock or, in certain cases, readily convertible preferred under Section 409A(l). A participant may elect to require the employer to repurchase securities upon distribution (put option) if no established market exists.

MANAGEMENT AND LABOR RELATIONS

Bureaucratic structure, organizational hierarchy, and a labor-management dichotomy are common in contemporary commercial and industrial companies.[1] If an ESOP or DEOC results in an employee-owned and -controlled company, there may be significant consequences in how the company is organized, in how decisions are made and who makes them, and in how managers and workers interact both professionally and socially.

Figure 7 illustrates the typical corporate hierarchy. It will vary in size, complexity, and centralization depending upon the size of the company and the nature of its product(s) or service(s).[2] A heavy line separates the worker from supervisory and management personnel to emphasize the legal, functional, and organizational division that tends to exist between the two groups. This may be apparent and pronounced in large, unionized manufacturing companies.

Figure 8 reflects the same phenomenon as it might appear in a labor union. The rank-and-file member may enjoy a situation parallel to that of the worker in figure 7. Again, the tendency may be more apparent and pronounced if the union is large and is associated with large manufacturing companies. Government could be expected to have a similar hierarchy, but separate treatment is not warranted here.

A general rule of hierarchies is that income, influence, and privilege tend to increase in moving from the bottom to the top. The literature in management and organization indicates the difficulty in generating a consistent and reliable body of knowledge covering the optimum allocation of these scarce economic goods for the profit-dependent company in a heterogenous economy.[3]

FIGURE 7   **Corporate Hierarchy**

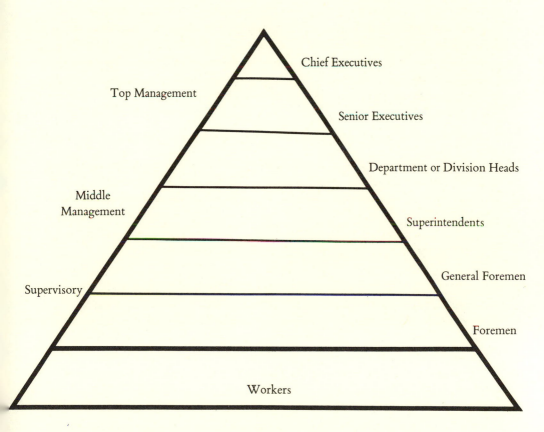

SOURCE: Dalton E. McFarland, *Management: Foundations and Practices*, 5th ed. (New York: Macmillan Co., 1979).

FIGURE 8 **Union Hierarchy**

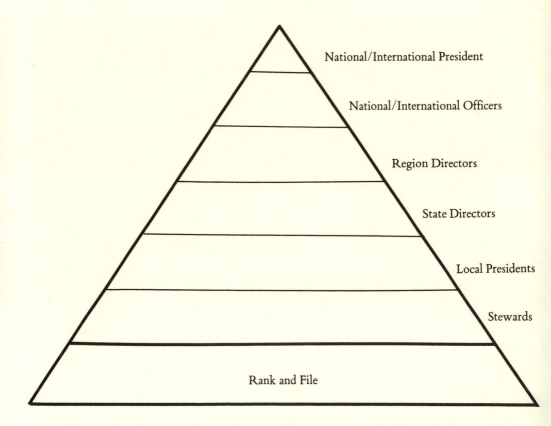

Figure 9 illustrates the departmental/functional organization for a typical small- to medium-sized corporation engaged in manufacturing photocopying machines and related products. The company could have $20 million in annual sales from 600 employees with a pretax profit of $1 million for a 16 percent return on equity and 10 percent on total assets. The company has a relatively tall hierarchy and a conventional line and staff organization. One vice-president has primary staff responsibility, and the other has primary operations responsibility. It will also be assumed that the production workers are unionized and that management has good relations with the company local, but resents and resists regional and national union influence within the company.

It is further assumed that the company is publicly traded over the counter with 50 percent of all outstanding shares held by two members of the founding family. These members are the chairman of the board and the president of the company. Both are traditional in management and labor relations philosophy, and both are ready to sell out their interests and retire. What would be the probable organizational and labor-management relations implications if an ESOP were established to buy out their holdings?

If such an event occurred, it is possible that very little would change. The perceptions, attitudes, and aspirations of the employees and management are critical if anything more than a formal structural change in the employee benefit plan is to happen. The initial decision point lies with management. In most cases it is management that initiates, implements, and administers an ESOP. If the intent is to buy out the founders but to maintain the status quo, there will be minimal management effort to develop the full potential of an ESOP. Motivation for the latter is usually provided by an imminent sale or shutdown.

The present ERISA and IRC requirements, however, do assure a certain level of management involvement and employee participation. Of particular significance are requirements for common voting stock (or convertible preferred), voting rights, minimum employee participation and vesting standards, the employee meeting of explanation, the summary plan description (employee handbook), and the copies of the summary annual report and annual registration to be distributed to employees. Both employees and unions may initiate a plan, and ESOPs are appropriate subjects in collective bargaining.

It is probable, therefore, that some significant organizational changes will result. In the lexicon of organizational development, an ESOP could be considered an adaptive, if not a dynamic, system.[4] Figure 10 represents the structural transformation of the company from figure 9 after implementation of an ESOP. In the new concept of the company the stockholders are at the top of the chart with the trust as the dominant stockholder, controlling 50 percent of

FIGURE 9 **Organization of Conventional Corporation**
(manufacturing, small- to medium-sized)

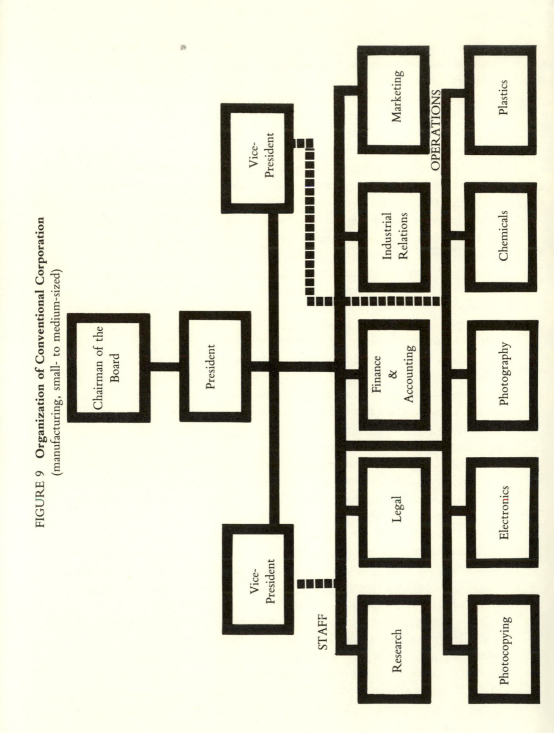

all outstanding shares. "ESOT" is used rather than "ESOP" since it is the trust that actually holds the stock. The trust (ESOT) is part of the plan (ESOP).

It will be assumed that 80 percent of all company employees participate in the plan in each classification: management, salaried, and worker personnel. The company is thus employee owned, but not necessarily employee controlled. It will be further assumed that the seven directors are the president of the company, the president of the union local, the chief financial officer, the director of marketing, one of the two plant managers, the senior plant foreman, and the president of the company's primary bank (which serves as ESOT trustee and which made the loan to the ESOP to buy out the founders). The company president serves as chairman of the board and of the executive committee. The president of the union local serves as chairman of the personnel/compensation committee, the plant manager as chairman of the productivity committee, and the chief financial officer (CFO) as head of the finance committee.

The personnel/compensation committee has partially displaced one of the former vice-presidents, who now serves on all four committees and acts as the new vice-president and ESOP administrator. The other former vice-president is now president. The finance function is now located in the finance committee, the head of which is also a director and member of the executive committee. The personnel/compensation committee has also replaced the industrial relations department, the former director of which now serves on all four committees and is assistant to the president. Both personnel and compensation decisions are decentralized to department levels, and the committee serves review, advisory, and coordinating roles.

The effective power in the company lies with the directors and the executive and finance committees, in that order. The title of president is more formal than substantive. The president is chief executive officer and decision maker by virtue of his positions on the board and executive committee, while the vice-president is chief administrative officer. The executive committee also includes the two plant managers and the directors of marketing, legal, and research. The finance committee also includes the president and the directors of accounting, legal, and marketing. The CFO is the company treasurer, and the legal director is secretary. According to the ESOP, the trustee of the ESOT must be appointed by the board for two-year periods and can be neither an officer nor a director of the company.

Significant reorganization and decentralization of authority have occurred in the company. One employee from each department serves on the personnel/compensation committee, and each employee participating in the ESOP may direct the trustee as to the voting of shares allocated to that particular em-

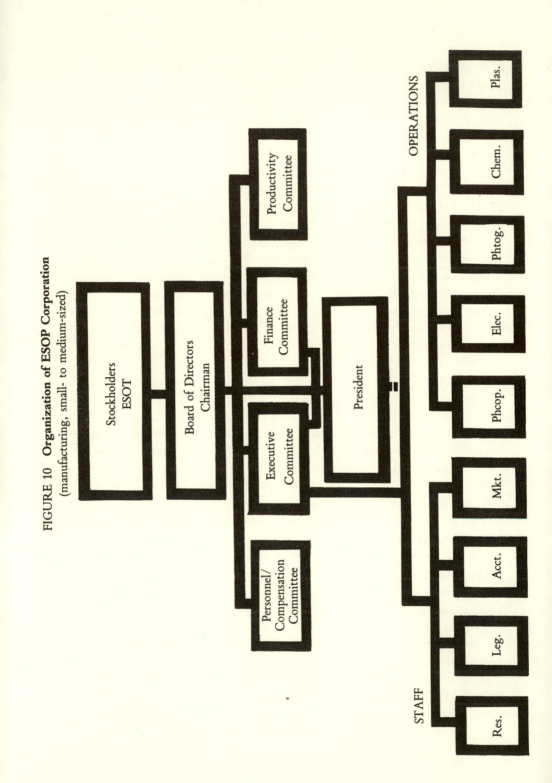

FIGURE 10 **Organization of ESOP Corporation**
(manufacturing, small- to medium-sized)

ployee. Each department, whether line or staff, also has a productivity council that has the authority to modify short-run operating procedures within existing resource constraints. Membership on the council is determined by the department employees. From among the council members the president selects the coordinator, who is also the department representative to the productivity committee. The coordinators also replace supervisors or foremen.

Figure 11 represents the new form of the hierarchy as changed from the hierarchy of figure 7. The two most obvious and significant changes are the increased flatness of the hierarchy and the vertical, rather than horizontal, lines of division up to the executive-committee level. These changes reflect the broadened base of management and supervision and the increased vertical access to the same.

The company is substantially both employee owned and controlled. Both of these terms are used as defined previously and in a relative rather than an absolute context. Employees own 50 percent of the company, and this ownership is general throughout the company. That is, all major classifications and levels of employees are represented in ownership, not merely managerial employees or the highly compensated. The same test applies to control in that control is general among all major classifications of employees: workers, salaried, and managerial. Significant worker representation exists from the department level to the board of directors. Such representation is lacking only on the executive and finance committees, whose functions tend to involve a high level of professional expertise.

The role of the union local at the company has been redefined and enlarged. The president of the local is a member of the board of directors and of the personnel/compensation committee. Union members serve on the productivity councils, and several have been chosen as coordinators for their departments by the president. The union is thus in a better position than before to serve the interests of the workers. This realization is gradually neutralizing the earlier national union opposition to union participation in the ESOP. The result is the recognition of the ESOP as a bona fide worker benefit within the collective bargaining context.

The brief scenario presented here is not intended to be the representative or ideal result of an ESOP implementation. No significant increase in profits or economic position or reallocation of compensation was assumed in this example. It merely presents a selected composite of actual changes that have resulted in ESOP companies, some of which will be cited and analyzed in subsequent chapters. This does indicate how it is possible for an ESOP to address many of

FIGURE 11 ESOP Corporate Hierarchy

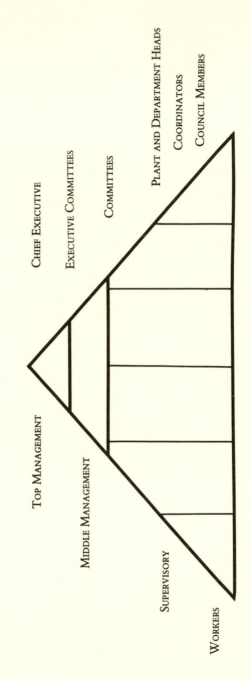

TOP MANAGEMENT

CHIEF EXECUTIVE

EXECUTIVE COMMITTEES

COMMITTEES

MIDDLE MANAGEMENT

PLANT AND DEPARTMENT HEADS

COORDINATORS

COUNCIL MEMBERS

SUPERVISORY

WORKERS

the problems, concepts, and practices central to management, industrial relations, and organizational development. The critical factors include the attitude and involvement of managers and employees.

NOTES

1. See generally James C. March and Herbert A. Simon, *Organizations* (New York: John Wiley & Sons, 1958); Peter F. Drucker, *The Practice of Management* (New York: Harper & Row, 1954); Rensis Likert, *The Human Organization* (New York: McGraw-Hill, 1967); Peter M. Blau, *On the Nature of Organizations* (New York: John Wiley & Sons, 1974); Victor A. Thompson, *Modern Organization* (New York: Alfred A. Knopf, 1961); Studs Terkel, *Working* (New York: Pantheon, 1974); and Paul Bernstein, *Workplace Democratization: Its Internal Dynamics* (Kent, Ohio: Kent State University Press, 1976).

2. Dalton E. McFarland, *Management: Foundations and Practices*, 5th ed. (New York: Macmillan Co., 1979), p. 301.

3. The literature warrants closer study, but such study is not essential here. Refer to notes 1 and 4.

4. Refer to Warren G. Bennis, *Organization Development: Its Nature, Origins and Prospects* (Reading, Mass.: Addison-Wesley Co., 1969); David G. Bowers, *Systems of Organization: Management of the Human Resource* (Ann Arbor: University of Michigan Press, 1977); Ervin Williams, ed., *Participative Management: Concepts, Theory and Implementation* (Atlanta: Georgia State University, 1976); William Foote Whyte, *Organizational Behavior: Theory and Application* (Homewood, Ill.: Richard D. Irwin Co., 1969); and Bernstein, *Workplace Democratization*.

CHAPTER

5

Special Legislated ESOPs

Thus far, employee stock ownership plans and direct employee owned companies have been discussed in fundamental terms. The principal variations of the basic ESOP included the leveraged ESOP, or LESOP, and the tax credit ESOP, or TCESOP. This chapter will focus upon federal legislation authorizing or requiring special-purpose ESOPs, usually as part of a specific industry or company assistance and regulatory scheme. This legislation includes the Regional Rail Reorganization Act of 1973, the Foreign Trade Act of 1974, the Revenue Act of 1978 (only as to general stock ownership plans, or GSOPs), and the Chrysler Corporation Loan Guarantee Act of 1979.

Excluded will be the Employee Retirement Income Security Act of 1974, the Tax Reduction Act of 1975, the Tax Reform Act of 1976, the Revenue Act of 1978 (excepting GSOP provisions), and the Economic Recovery Tax Act of 1981. ERISA and the 1978 act treat ESOPs in general. Section 301 of the 1975 act first provided for the TCESOP an additional 1 percent investment tax credit for 1975 and 1976 only. This was extended through 1980 by the 1976 act and through 1983 by the 1978 act. The 1981 act replaced the property-based tax credit with a lower, payroll-based credit starting in 1983 and expiring after 1987. Both the LESOP and TCESOP are treated herein as variations of the basic ESOP and not as special-purpose ESOPs. Variation plans retain the general purpose and general qualification criteria, while special-purpose plans have specific purposes and specific qualification criteria.

THE REGIONAL RAIL REORGANIZATION ACT OF 1973

This act provided authorization for the Conrail system and also endorsed a special type of ESOP as a "technique" of corporate finance and as a means of spreading capital ownership among railroad employees. Section 102(5) of the act defines an ESOP as follows:

"employee stock ownership plan" means a technique of corporate finance that uses a stock bonus trust or a company stock money purchase pension trust which qualifies under Section 401(a) of the Internal Revenue Code of 1954 (26 U.S.C. 401(a)) in connection with the financing of corporate improvements, transfers in the ownership of corporate assets, and other capital requirements of a corporation and which is designed to build beneficial equity ownership of shares in the employer corporation into its employees substantially in proportion to their relative incomes, without requiring any cash outlay, any reduction in pay or other employee benefits, or the surrender of any other rights on the part of such employees.

The probable perception of Congress was that an ESOP could be used both as an instrument of corporate finance in the new rail system and as a means of building equity ownership for participating employees. The basic purpose of the act was to consolidate and rehabilitate the railroad system of the central and northeastern United States. To do this a new corporation was established, the Consolidated Rail Corporation (Conrail), which was authorized, but not required, to utilize ESOPs in its plan. The following considerations were to be included in the decision-making process thereon as stated in the act:

the manner in which employee stock ownership plans may, to the extent practicable, be utilized for meeting the capitalization requirements of the Corporation, taking into account (A) the relative cost savings compared to conventional methods of corporate finance; (B) the labor cost savings; (C) the potential for minimizing strikes and producing more harmonious relations between labor organizations and railway management; (D) the projected employee dividend incomes; (E) the impact on the quality of service and the prices to railway users; and (F) the promotion of the objectives of this Act of creating a financially self-sustaining railway system in the region which also meets the service needs of the region and the nation.

Subsequently, the United States Railway Association (USRA), created as the administrative agency under the act, commissioned several studies concerning the use of an ESOP by Conrail. Ultimately, the use of an ESOP for Conrail was rejected by the USRA. The following were cited in committee as among the major reasons thereof:

1. Conrail's need for funds far exceeds the current value of the securities it could issue to the trust at fair market value. Conrail needs the government to supply nearly $700 million in the first year alone.

2. An ESOP would increase Conrail's requirement for government financing, if the trust is to purchase Conrail stock at fair market value, under the assumptions of the studies.

3. For the foreseeable future, an ESOP would not provide Conrail with any tax benefits since Conrail is in a position to eliminate or defer income taxes for at least ten years (1975-85).

4. Since Conrail has a very large number of employees, since a large number of these are older employees, and since an individual employee's trust accumulation is not expected to reach a high enough value, there is little evidence that an ESOP would improve employee motivation.

5. Under the act, the exchange of rail properties owned by the bankrupt entities and estates must be "fair and equitable" and must include the securities of Conrail. A proposal to require the common stock of Conrail to be issued to an ESOP could subject the United States to suit for deficiencies under the Tucker Act.[1]

THE FOREIGN TRADE ACT OF 1974

One of the purposes of this act was to provide procedures to protect U.S. industry and labor from unfair or injurious import competition and to assist industry, labor, companies, and communities to adjust to changes in international trade. Among other provisions directed thereto, the secretary of commerce is authorized to guarantee loans for working capital made to private borrowers by private lenders in trade-impacted areas. Section 273(f)(1) of the act provides that the secretary shall give preference to a corporation that agrees to have 25 percent of the loan principal supplied by the lender paid to an ESOP trust established by the company as per the act and, by contract with the lender and the ESOP, agrees to pay off the loan with contributions to the trust.

The trade act ESOP, like the rail act ESOP, is viewed as a technique of corporate finance, one that utilizes a qualified stock bonus plan and is designed to invest primarily in qualifying employer securities. These are to be allocated at the close of each plan year to the employee accounts based upon the relative compensation paid each employee. Section 273(f)(5)(c) defines "qualified employer securities" as

common stock issued by the recipient corporation or by a parent or subsidiary of such corporation with voting power and dividend rights no less favorable than the voting power and dividend rights on other common stock issued by the issuing corporation and with voting power being exercised by the participants in the employer stock ownership plan after it is allocated to their plan accounts.

These provisions are more restrictive than comparable ERISA requirements and are similar to the IRC Section 409A provisions added by the Revenue Act of 1978. The trade act ESOP is further developed in the committee report as follows:

As defined in this bill, an "employee stock ownership plan" is a technique of corporate finance which utilizes a stock bonus plan which is qualified, or a stock bonus and a money purchase pension plan both of which are qualified, under Section 401 of the Internal Revenue Code of 1954, and which is designed to invest primarily in qualifying employer securities. The employee stock ownership plan and the qualified trust forming a part of the plan must also be designed: (i) to meet general financing requirements of the corporation, including capital growth and transfers in the ownership of corporate stock; (ii) to build into employees beneficial ownership of stock of their employer or its affiliated corporations, substantially in proportion to their relative incomes, without requiring any cash outlay, any reduction in pay or other employee benefits, or the surrender of any other rights on the part of such employees; and (iii) to receive loans or other forms of credit to acquire stock of the employer corporation or its affiliated corporations, with such loans and credit secured primarily by a legally binding commitment by the employer to make future payments to the trust in amount sufficient to enable such loans to be repaid.

THE REVENUE ACT OF 1978

Section 601 of the Revenue Act of 1978 authorized the legislatures of the several states, or the residents thereof through a statewide referendum, to charter a special-purpose corporation between January 1, 1979, and December 31, 1983. It would be known under the act as a general stock ownership corporation (GSOC). GSOC is further defined as a private corporation, not a member of an affiliated group of corporations, that may issue one class of stock to residents of a state. At least one share, but no more than 10 percent of all shares, may be issued to any qualified resident. A GSOC may invest in properties, but not through eminent domain, and not more than 20 percent of the stock of any single company may be acquired.

A GSOC may elect for federal tax-exempt status such that income and tax liability pass through to shareholders and that at least 90 percent of such income is paid out by January 31 following the close of such taxable year. Any amount not so distributed as to meet the minimum distribution shall be taxed at 20 percent. The GSOC would keep individual shareholder accounts to which income would be allocated pro rata and included as part of the shareholder's gross income. Any investment tax credit and recapture would also be allocated pro rata to individual accounts.

Allocations to an account are ordinary income and are not eligible for the partial dividend exclusion or the maximum tax on earned income. Distributions from the account allocation are subject to 25 percent withholding, though refund credits and exemptions are available. Distributions, which may exceed the account allocation (i.e., previously taxed income), are taxed in the same manner as distributions from a regular corporation under IRC Section 301(c). Distributions from previously taxed income would reduce the tax basis of the GSOC shares, while allocations prior to distribution would increase the tax basis.

The corporation (GSOC) is the central instrument of the plan to create a means by which general equity ownership could become more broadly based among the residents of a state and could aid in reducing the percentage of passive or unearned income of those residents derived from transfer payments. The initial GSOC funds for investment would be borrowed from private lenders with a guarantee by the state granting the charter. The loan would be amortized from the earnings of the portfolio before income allocations would be made to shareholders. If earnings should prove to be insufficient to meet the debt service, state intervention would be necessary.

The hearings on GSOPs by the Senate Finance Committee and the committee report provide additional insight concerning the basis and purpose of the plans.[2] While the GSOP is a version of an ESOP, the former is not a deferred compensation plan and has a regional scope that significantly expands the category of eligible individuals and company securities. Except for its leveraged feature, it has similarities to the Western European plans discussed in chapter 2. It also has an origin in legislation pending in Alaska that would permit the state to purchase nearly a 16 percent interest in the Alaska oil pipeline. It has some characteristics of an IRC Subchapter S corporation and a real estate investment trust in that earnings are taxed to the shareholders rather than to the corporation.

The Senate Finance Committee included the following in its report on Section 201 of the committee bill filed October 1, 1978:

The committee believes that many citizens should have a greater ownership stake in the private enterprise system, and that this would lead to better understanding of the system and would encourage individuals to invest in other business enterprises. Also, in the case of individuals now receiving various forms of transfer payments from Federal,

State, or local governments, the receipt of dividend income from a General Stock Ownership Corporation (GSOC) would, to some extent, reduce the need for such payments. The committee believes that an experimental program permitting States to form such private corporations for the benefit of their citizens may enable the Congress to study a method of replacing transfer payments with dividend income.

...Under the committee bill, a State would be authorized to establish a GSOC for the benefit of its citizens. It is anticipated that the GSOC would be authorized to borrow money to acquire business enterprises. The cash flow from the operation of the business would be used to pay the loan, and the corporate revenues would be distributed to the GSOC shareholders (i.e., the citizens of the State).

...The bill provides that a corporation must meet certain statutory tests in order to be treated as a GSOC. First, the corporation must be chartered by an official act of the State legislature or by a State-wide referendum. Second, the GSOC's corporate charter must provide for the issuance of all authorized shares to eligible individuals provided that at least one share is issued to each eligible individual, and such eligible individual does not elect within one year after the date of issuance not to receive such share, and provides for certain restrictions on the transferability of the share. The transfer restriction must provide that the share cannot be transferred until the earliest to occur of (1) the expiration of 5 years from issuance, (2) death or (3) failure to meet the State's residency requirements. In no event may shares of stock of a GSOC be transferred to nonresidents. Also, an individual may not acquire more than 9 shares by purchase. Third, the charter must provide that the GSOC is empowered to invest in properties (not including properties acquired by it or for its benefit through the right of eminent domain). Fourth, the GSOC may not be affiliated with any other corporation. Fifth, the GSOC must be organized after December 31, 1978, and before January 1, 1984. An eligible individual is any individual who is a resident of the chartering State as of the date specified in the corporate charter. A State may define a resident for purposes of its GSOC so long as such definition is consistent with constitutional principles.

THE CHRYSLER CORPORATION LOAN GUARANTEE ACT OF 1979

Perhaps the most publicized special-purpose ESOP to date involved its incorporation in the Chrysler Corporation Loan Guarantee Act of 1979. Section 7 of the act makes the establishment of an ESOP, as approved by the loan guarantee board, a condition precedent to the guarantee or commitment to guarantee any loan under the act after 180 days of the enactment.

The fatal defect of the Regional Rail Reorganization Act was avoided. The rail act made ESOP implementation discretionary with the governing agency. Significant and successful efforts were made by long-time ESOP advocates in

Congress, such as Senator Russell Long of Louisiana, and more recent additions to Congress, such as Senator Donald Stewart of Alabama, to make the ESOP a mandatory and major provision of the act. Chrysler contributions to the ESOP must total less than $162,500,000 before the close of the fourth year of operation of the plan. At $6 to $7 per share this would constitute about 25 million shares or 28 percent of the total then issued and outstanding.

The administration of the act is under the authority of the loan guarantee board as established by Section 3 of the act. Membership consists of the secretary of the treasury as chairperson, the chairman of the Board of Governors of the Federal Reserve System, and the comptroller general. The secretaries of labor and transportation shall be ex officio nonvoting members. The authority of the board to extend loan guarantees shall not at any time exceed $1.5 billion in the aggregate principal amount outstanding, and all such loan guarantees shall be made no later than December 31, 1983, and repaid in full not later than December 31, 1990.

In addition, Chrysler must obtain $1.43 billion in nonfederally guaranteed assistance to include loans from U.S. and foreign banks, proceeds from the sale of corporate assets, state and local government assistance, and concessions from suppliers and dealers. Section 6 requires employee wage and benefit reductions of $462,500,000, to be proportioned between union and nonunion members, over a three-year period, September 1979 to September 1982.

The Chrysler act ESOP provision reads as follows:

Section 7.

(a) No guarantee or commitment to guarantee any loan may be made under this Act until the Chrysler Corporation, in a written agreement with the Board which is satisfactory to the Board, agrees—

(1) to establish a trust which forms part of an employee stock ownership plan meeting the requirements of subsection (c);

(2) to make employer contributions to such trust in accordance with such plan; and

(3) to issue additional shares of qualified common stock at such times as such shares are required to be contributed to such trust.

(b) No guarantee or commitment to guarantee any loan may be made under this Act after the close of the one hundred and eighty-day period beginning on the date of the enactment of this Act unless the Chrysler Corporation has established a trust which forms part of an employee stock ownership plan meeting the requirements of subsection (c).

(c) An employee stock ownership plan meets the requirements of this subsection only if—

(1) such plan is maintained by the Chrysler Corporation;

(2) such plan satisfies the requirements of section 4975(e)(7) of the Internal Revenue Code of 1954 (determined without regard to subparagraph (A) of section 410(b)(2) of such Code);

(3) Such plan provides that—

(A) employer contributions to the trust may be made only in accordance with requirements of subsection (d);

(B) each participant in the plan has a nonforfeitable right to the participant's accrued benefit under the plan;

(C) each employer contribution to the trust shall be allocated in equal amounts (to the extent not inconsistent with the requirements of section 415(c) of such Code) to the accounts of all participants in the plan; and

(D) distributions from the trust under the plan will be made in accordance with the requirements of section 401(k)(2)(B) of the Internal Revenue Code of 1954; and

(4) such plan benefits 90 percent or more of all employees of the Corporation, excluding the employees who have not satisfied the minimum wage and service requirements, if any, prescribed by the plan as a condition of participation.

(d)(1) Employer contributions meet the requirements of this subsection only if such contributions—

(A) will total not less than $162,500,000 before the close of the four-year period beginning not later than the one hundred and eightieth day after the date of the enactment of this Act;

(B) are made in such amounts and at such times that no time during such four-year period will the amount of employer contributions to the trust be less than the amount such contributions would have been if made in installments of $40,625,000 made at the end of each year in such period; and

(C) are made in the additional qualified common stock which the Chrysler Corporation issues by reason of subsection (a)(3).

(2)(A) In the case of a qualified loan to the trust for the purchase of qualified common stock the amount of such stock purchased with the proceeds of such loan shall be treated for purposes of paragraph (1) as an employer contribution to the trust made on the date such stock is so purchased.

(B) For purposes of subparagraph (A), the term "qualified loan" means any loan—

(i) which may be repaid only in substantially equal installments;

(ii) which has a term of not more than ten years; and

(iii) the proceeds of which are used only to purchase an amount of the additional qualified common stock which the Chrysler Corporation issues by reason of subsection (a)(3).

(e) For purposes of this section, the term "qualified common stock" means stock of the class of common stock of the Chrysler Corporation which is outstanding on October 17, 1979, and which is readily tradeable on an established securities market.

(f) An amount equal to $162,500,000 of the additional qualified common stock issued by the Corporation by reason of subsection (a)(3) shall not be treated for purposes of this Act as assistance received by the Chrysler Corporation from other than the Federal Government pursuant to section 4(c).[3]

The ESOP precondition to loan guarantee is a two-part test. First, prior to any guarantee or commitment to guarantee, Chrysler must submit its ESOP agreement to the board for approval. Second, after 180 days from the date of enactment of the act, no guarantee or commitment to guarantee may be made unless Chrysler has established a trust that forms part of an IRC Section 4975(e)(7) ESOP. At the same time, the president of the United Auto Workers, presently Douglas Fraser, is to serve as a director of the corporation.

The ESOP must meet the voting rights and distribution provisions of IRC Section 409A(e) and (h) and the general IRC Section 401(a) qualified plan provisions. The minimum participation test of 90 percent of all employees is higher than the IRC Section 410(b) and 401(a) test of 70 percent or 80 percent of 70 percent. The minimum contribution schedules must be no less than the equivalents of $40,625,000 in annual year-end installments made in the form of additional qualified common stock. The ESOP trust will obtain private loans guaranteed by the board to purchase the stock, and Chrysler will amortize the loans by the end of 1990.

Certain of the testimony before the Senate Committee on Banking, Housing, and Urban Affairs concerning the use of an ESOP to assist Chrysler in its financial difficulty and to require the same in any federal aid package is reproduced here. Senator Russell Long submitted the following letter to the committee:

U.S. SENATE,
Committee on Finance
Washington, D.C., November 19, 1979

Hon. William Proxmire,
Chairman, Committee on Banking, Housing and Urban Affairs,
Washington, D.C.

Dear Mr. Chairman: As you know, I am Floor Manager for H.R. 3919, "The Crude Oil Windfall Profit Tax Act of 1979." Floor debate on this bill will continue throughout the day, and accordingly I will be unable to testify before your Committee on the question of an employee stock ownership plan for Chrysler Corporation. However, I believe so strongly about this issue that I would appreciate having my views made known to the Members of the Committee.

I believe that it would be a serious mistake for this Congress to enact legislation to provide financial assistance for Chrysler Corporation unless we combine with that assistance a requirement that Chrysler Corporation provide a significant amount of stock ownership for its employees through an employee stock ownership plan. To pass this legislation without the requirement which I and other Senators feel is so essential to the financial recovery of Chrysler Corporation would amount to nothing more than a $1.5 billion "windfall" for that company's shareholders and creditors. I do not believe we can justify the use of taxpayers' money in such a manner.

These shareholders and creditors cannot contribute anything to Chrysler Corporation's financial recovery and revitalization; in fact, an argument can be made that the shareholders have helped put this company in the serious financial condition it is in today by voting their stock in support of past management decisions.

However, it is absolutely clear that the employees of Chrysler Corporation can have a significant impact on its financial future. Studies which have been conducted in the past few years indicate that companies which have provided a significant amount of stock ownership for their employees are much more profitable and successful than nonemployee-owned companies. This fact should mandate that employee stock ownership be included in any Chrysler relief legislation.

A study conducted by Mr. Paul Bernstein, entitled "Worker-Owned Plywood Firms Steadily Outperform Industry," World of Work Report, June 24, 1977, reflected that employee-owned firms had a 30 percent higher productivity and 25 percent higher wages than conventional firms.

In the Survey Research Center study of 100 employee-owned firms, profits were 1.5 times higher in employee-owned firms than in nonemployee-owned firms and conversations with managers of these employee-owned firms indicated much higher levels of employee satisfaction through employee ownership and greater productivity and improved work atmosphere.

In addition, the Senate Finance Committee has been conducting a survey among American companies which have established stock ownership plans. To date, 75 companies have responded to our request for information, and they have advised us as follows:

At the time of the ESOP installation, which took place an average of three years ago, the typical company had been in business for 24 years and had attained annual sales of $19,596,000. This company employed 438 people and averaged $44,700 sales per employee. This generated an annual profit in the three years prior to the ESOP installation of $794,000 per year and the company paid taxes which averaged $312,000 per year.

Over the past three years, an average of 7 percent of the ownership of the company has been transferred each year; today, the Employee Stock Ownership Plan now has an average of 20.6 percent of the company stock. The incentive provided by this ownership has resulted in sales increasing to $33,780,000—up 72 percent. This created the need to increase the number of employees to 602 employees, an increase of 37 percent. The average sales per employee increased to $56,000 (+ 25 percent). The combination of this increased productivity and higher level of sales increased the profits of the company in the three years following ESOP installation to an average of $2,039,000—up 157 percent—and the typical company paid an average of $780,000 per year in taxes—up 150 percent.

Finally, I would like to have introduced into the Hearing Record a copy of an article which appeared in last Sunday's Washington Post. This article explains the financial recovery of South Bend Lathe, a company in South Bend, Indiana. In 1975, this company set up an employee stock ownership plan; prior to that time, the company had been extremely unprofitable and the parent corporation was planning on liquidating it. Since establishing the ESOP, the company has increased its earnings per share from $20 per share to $69 per share, realized in 1977 and 1978 the highest sales in the company's 70-year history, and increased each employee's stock ownership under the ESOP from $2,500 to $9,000. I take personal pleasure in the success of this company because I helped them get $5 million from the Federal Government in an ESOP very much like what we are proposing for Chrysler, and I would commend this article to every Member of this Committee.

There is no question but that Chrysler Corporation is in serious financial shape. If we are going to attempt to help this company, we should do everything possible to assure that our efforts are successful. I and other Senators believe that the inclusion of an employee stock ownership plan requirement for Chrysler is an important step in this direction. In fact, I do not believe I can support this legislation unless employee stock ownership is included in it.

Mr. Chairman, I thank you for your courtesy and consideration.

With every good wish, I am,

Sincerely,

Russell B. Long, Chairman[4]

Also giving testimony before the Committee was Neil A. Wassner, CPA and partner of the New York CPA firm of Main Hurdman & Cranstoun. His statement included the following:

As a CPA practicing in the ESOP field, I have had a good deal of practical experience working with our clients in determining the feasibility of ESOPs for them. I hope that my contribution will be helpful to the committee....

Contributions made to an ESOP, in cash or stock are tax deductible to the employer. Shares purchased by the trust are distributed to the employees when they retire, die or terminate their employment.

It is my understanding that one proposal for Chrysler aid would call for the establishment of a leveraged ESOP. The Government would guarantee a loan of, for example, $150 million to a newly established Chrysler ESOP. The ESOP would then purchase stock of the corporation say 25 million common shares at $6 per share. This would represent approximately 28 percent of the common shares that would be outstanding after this issuance.

Each year Chrysler would make a tax-deductible contribution in cash to the ESOP and the ESOP would use the contribution to repay the loan. The shares in the ESOP would be allocated to an employee in the ratio of his salary to the corporation's total eligible payroll.

If it is assumed, for example, that Chrysler has an eligible domestic payroll of $2½ billion and that the ESOP has 25 million shares, then one share would be allocated to an employee for each $100 of salary. Thus a $20,000 per year worker would be allocated 200 shares, worth, at issuance, $1,200.

I understand several proposals respecting a Chrysler ESOP would allocate shares equally among the employees without regard to compensation levels.

Under rules taking effect January 1, 1980, for leveraged ESOPs, public corporations such as Chrysler must pass through voting rights to the employee participants. In order to determine the impact that an ESOP might have in the Chrysler aid plan, it is necessary to view the ESOP from the perspective of the various interest groups concerned, the Government, the corporation and its shareholders, the creditors, and the employees.

The principal disadvantage of an ESOP to the Government is that if the aid package succeeds in returning Chrysler to the ranks of viable tax-paying corporations, the Government may lose substantial tax revenue as the loan is repaid. This may be seen from the above example.

Since Chrysler will be contributing $150 million to the ESOP for payments by the ESOP on the principal of the loan, and since these contributions are tax deductible to Chrysler, approximately $75 million of lost revenue to the Government may result by using an ESOP as part of the aid package.

Two mitigating factors regarding the possible Government loss of revenues through an ESOP should be mentioned.

The first is the substantial operating loss carryforwards that will be available to Chrysler to offset future taxes due. Under the tax law, the ESOP contributions will add to the tax losses of the corporation and will not result in any loss of Government revenue unless future Chrysler taxable income is sufficient to offset both the carryforwards and the ESOP contribution.

A second limitation on the size of the potential lost tax revenue is that employees will have to pay an income tax, when the Chrysler shares are distributed to them, equal to the value of the shares when they were purchased by the ESOP trust.

Of course, from the above, one can postulate a set of circumstances under which the Government can actually benefit from the ESOP. If Chrysler is unable to utilize its tax carryforwards, then the Government loses no revenue on the contributions to the ESOP, but collects taxes when the shares are distributed from the ESOP to the employees. . . .

One possible benefit is that the workers of Chrysler, armed with their new proprietary interest in the corporation, will be motivated to work harder and, by so doing, will increase productivity, profits and cash flow. Increased cash flow will make the Government more secure in its position as guarantor on the ESOP debt.

Surely, there is evidence that in many instances ESOPs have led to greater productivity by workers. On the other hand, the case might be made that Chrysler workers already own 13 percent of the stock through various employer-sponsored plans. And further, with their jobs dependent on the success of their troubled employer, their stake in increasing productivity is already high.

Finally, the question must be asked as to whether employee productivity is an essential reason for Chrysler's problems in the first place?

A further intangible benefit of an ESOP as part of the Chrysler bailout, is that it will give the Government an opportunity to monitor the effectiveness of the ESOP concept in a highly visible, well-publicized case. . . .

If it is assumed that Chrysler can get a tax benefit from its contributions to the ESOP that are used to repay the Government loan, then the corporation will be the beneficiary of the cash-flow savings. In other words, the company will be able to deduct what are essentially loan repayments against their taxable income.

In my example, these cash-flow benefits should equal $75 million. Despite this apparent windfall, an executive vice president of Chrysler testified before the House Banking Committee last week that the company would be "concerned" about an employee stock ownership plan requirement because it might "dilute" Chrysler stock.

This, in a nutshell, presents both sides of the financial argument respecting ESOP's. While the value of the company should increase by the tax saving generated by the ESOP, the number of shares outstanding will also increase and perhaps by a larger percentage.

The whole pie is bigger, but there are more shareholder mouths to feed. This dilution in earnings per share usually has a negative impact on the corporation's stock price.

Further, accounting rules require that the corporation reflect the ESOP debt on its books if the corporation has committed to make contributions to the ESOP sufficient to meet the debt service requirements.

Thus, ESOP financing, from an accounting point of view, contains the worst of both worlds, the burden of debt and that dilution of equity.

From the creditor's viewpoint, as we have seen, Government financial aid to Chrysler, funded partially through a Government-guaranteed loan to an ESOP, may increase the cash flow of the corporation by the amount of the tax savings generated by contributions to the plan. To the extent that the cash flow is increased, the funds available to repay other debt becomes available. . . .

At first glance, it would appear that the domestic employees of Chrysler Corp. could be the major beneficiaries of an ESOP. This is true, of course, if an ESOP is looked upon as something for nothing.

To the extent that the employees are asked to give up increases in wages or contributions to pension plans, or to make cash contributions to the plan because a portion of the Government-guaranteed loan has been channeled through an ESOP, they have a real cost for the ESOP.

If, for example, workers agree to a reduction in annual contributions to their pension plan in favor of annual contributions in the same amount in the ESOP, they have sacrificed an interest in a diversified portfolio of blue chip securities for an "all your eggs in one basket" plan funded with stock in a troubled corporation. . . .

On the other hand, it can be argued that without some "give-ups" by the employees, they will be unjustly receiving the windfall benefits of a Government-supported ESOP loan program.

A sound case can be made that whenever the Government supports a corporate aid program, such as that suggested in the instant case, the shareholders will benefit unduly. If that is true, then it is not unreasonable, it seems to me, for the workers to benefit to some extent as well.

In conclusion, it would appear that the question of whether an ESOP should be part of the Chrysler aid picture involves a complex analysis of financial considerations, such as potential Treasury revenue losses or gains, and fairness considerations among such interest groups as shareholders and employees. While detailed analysis of Chrysler financial projections, particularly with respect to the company's ability to utilize operating loss carryforwards will be necessary in measuring potential tax revenue losses, no such objective standards exist for allocating the benefits of windfall gains among competing groups, none of whom, in the opinion of many, deserve them.[5]

Some of the preceding caveats as to ESOP benefits are unique to Chrysler, and some are characteristic of any company that is nearly insolvent and poorly managed. Most of these points were cited in the previously reported testimony of the U.S. Railway Association concerning a proposed ESOP for Conrail. The fundamental criticism remains the dilution of equity and earnings per share, which may or may not be offset by increases in working capital, net earnings, and productivity.

Committee testimony by consumer advocate Ralph Nader reflects the criticism of economist Paul Samuelson, reported in chapter 2 on the economic analysis of ESOPs. Nader's statement was made in response to a question by the committee chairman, Senator William Proxmire of Wisconsin, and reads as follows:

The CHAIRMAN. How would you feel about an ESOP for the employees that was funded through concessions of Chrysler employees? In other words, they would take a freeze on their wages and get in return stock in the market which would make up for the difference that they suffered through taking that reduction. That would increase the cash flow for Chrysler and it would mean the additional equity would serve an immediate and useful purpose.

Mr. NADER. In general, I don't favor that approach, Mr. Chairman.

The CHAIRMAN. Why not?

Mr. NADER. If it is the usual ESOP approach, I concur with Paul Samuelson, who thinks it is primarily a tax-reduction scheme.

Second, I think hooking the fate of workers to the fate of management, which can decide things on its own, is not a proper way of furthering healthy countervailing powers between labor and management at arms length. I think if the UAW wanted in the past to straighten this Chrysler problem out, they would have worked more on the kind of product that Chrysler was producing....[6]

THE SMALL BUSINESS EMPLOYEE OWNERSHIP ACT OF 1980

During the summer of 1980 an omnibus small business bill, S. 2698, became law. Title V thereof is known as the Small Business Employee Ownership Act (SBEOA) of 1980, and it amends several sections of the Small Business Act of 1953 relative to the loan guarantee program of the Small Business Administration (SBA). The act cites a number of findings and declarations of Congress respecting ESOPs and the loan program. These include:

1. Employee ownership of firms provides a means for preserving jobs and business activity;

2. Employee ownership of firms provides a means for keeping a small business small when it might otherwise be sold to a conglomerate or other large enterprise;

3. Employee ownership of firms provides a means for creating a new small business from the sale of a subsidiary of a large enterprise;

4. Unemployment insurance programs, welfare payments and job creation programs are less desirable and more costly for both the government and program beneficiaries than loan programs to maintain employment in firms that would otherwise be closed, liquidated or relocated;

5. By guaranteeing loans to qualified employee trusts and similar employee organizations, the SBA can provide feasible and desirable methods for the transfer of all or part of the ownership of a small business concern to its employees.[7]

Senator Donald Stewart of Alabama, one of the primary advocates of the act, offered the following remarks in support of the legislation during committee hearings:

...the Employee Stock Ownership Act...is a major step in clarifying Small Business Administration regulations which currently impede the SBA from financing employee ownership of business. The bill, which gives SBA the legislative mandate to guarantee loans to employee owned businesses and to employee organizations seeking to purchase their firms, provides an alternative means of promoting small and independent business ownership.

We are all familiar with the serious lack of equity capital currently available [for] our small, growth-oriented businesses which have provided the cornerstone of our nation's economy. This bill would allow SBA to guarantee loans to small businesses with qualified employee stock ownership plans (ESOPs) so that employees can buy the business, thereby, preventing possible closing, relocation, or selling to outside interests. At the same time, new capital would be available to finance needed expansion and growth.

By clarifying SBA's legislative mandate, we are also protecting the fundamental spirit of the free market system enabling small business to remain independent, competitive and productive.[8]

The statements cited from the act and the statement of Senator Stewart reflect a high degree of congressional recognition of the economic and employment viability of ESOPs. Such recognition, whether correct or not, was clearly absent in the legislation of the early and mid 1970s. Perhaps of equal significance is the apparent congressional recognition of the critical economic and employment role of small business and the rising cost and inefficiency of government transfer payment programs.

The SBEOA amends Sections 3 and 7(a) of the Small Business Act to provide that an IRC Section 401(a) qualified trust shall be eligible for loan guarantees with a specific emphasis on a trust representing at least 51 percent of the employees and holding or seeking to acquire at least 51 percent of a company's securities. A trust maintained by an employee organization representing at least 51 percent of the employees may also be eligible for a loan guarantee in the purchase of small business stock.

The trust must be part of an ESOP as defined by IRC Section 4975(e)(7) and must invest primarily in employee securities as defined by IRC Section 409A(1). Thus, the guarantee will cover only purchases of employer common or readily convertible preferred stock. Participants must be given the right to direct the plan as to the voting of such stock with respect to any matter that by law or charter must be decided by majority vote. Among other matters, a company may exclude such voting as to membership on the board of directors, since a majority vote is usually not required for selection thereof.

The trust need not hold any company stock at the time the loan is obtained, but all proceeds therefrom must be used to purchase such stock. The loan is to be repaid by the company, and participants must be fully vested as to their allocations upon repayment. The plan must also provide a put or repurchase option upon distribution if the stock has no established market.

The loan guarantee may be granted where the company is not yet formed or where it is formed but has no assets. This situation frequently arises when an employee group is formed to acquire a division or subsidiary of a conglomerate or parent company. Unlike the usual practice, the act prohibits the SBA from using the assets or business experience of the employee owners as criteria for the loan guarantee except that business experience of those who will manage the new company may be considered. The SBA is also directed to study the use of installment sales with guarantees made directly to the seller of a small business.

NOTES

1. Joint Economic Committee, U.S. Congress, *Employee Stock Ownership Plans (ESOPs), Hearings* (Washington, D.C.: U.S. Government Printing Office, 1976), pt. 1, pp. 545-646.

2. Committee on Finance, U.S. Senate, *Employee Stock Ownership Plans and General Stock Ownership Trusts, Hearings* (Washington, D.C.: U.S. Government Printing Office, 1978), and *Report of the Senate Finance Committee*, H.R. 13511 (P.L. 95-600), October 1, 1978.

3. Chrysler Corporation Loan Guarantee Act of 1979, P.L. 96-185, 15 USC 1861-1901.

4. Committee on Banking, Housing and Urban Affairs, U.S. Senate, *Chrysler Corporation Loan Guarantee Act, Hearings* (Washington, D.C.: U.S. Government Printing Office, 1979), pp. 1079-80.

5. Ibid., pp. 1081-85.

6. Ibid., p. 1265.

7. Section 502 of S. 2698.

8. Select Committee on Small Business, U.S. Senate, *The Small Business Employee Ownership Act, Hearings* (Washington, D.C.: U.S. Government Printing Office, 1979), p. 3.

CHAPTER

6

Applications and Uses:
Benefits v. Costs

This chapter will present and explain the basic procedures and effects of the various applications of an ESOP to a variety of business, economic, and employment situations. These examples are composites of actual cases, but do not present the detailed legal requirements involved or the complete financial consequences. For the legal requirements, the reader is referred to chapter 9 on ESOP planning and implementation. For the financial and managerial consequences, the reader is referred to the comparative analysis of ESOPs in chapters 3 and 4 and the case studies in chapter 7. For employment and labor relations consequences, the reader is referred to chapter 7 and to labor unions positions discussed in chapter 8.

The basic assumptions for all transactions explained in this chapter include a 50 percent overall corporate income tax rate, an 8 percent interest rate, a 6 percent dividend rate, a 20 percent ratio of gross income to total assets, and generally stable prices. Thus, the tax, interest, and dividend rates are net over inflation. In most examples dividends will be ignored and all stock will be considered common stock unless otherwise designated.

INCREASING WORKING CAPITAL AND CASH FLOW

Perhaps the two major reasons for small business failures are poor management and lack of effective access to capital markets. While some ESOP advocates might claim to have found a cure for both business pathogens, a more modest policy would focus upon some comparative tangible evidence. Here the focus will be upon working capital and cash flow.

The tax reduction accruing from contributions of stock or purchase money for stock made to the ESOP trust may be converted into increased short-run working capital and cash flow. The amount deductible is determined by IRC Section 404 at a maximum normal annual rate of 15 percent (25 percent for a leveraged ESOP or LESOP) of annual employee compensation. Carryforward provisions exist for both unused and excess deductions. Since, in this instance, the increased cash is not being used to purchase the company or finance a capital addition or expansion, an equity ESOP is recommended over a leveraged ESOP. Thus, new stock is issued to the ESOP trust, but no new debt is incurred either by the company or the trust. An equity ESOP is simply a tax-leveraged ESOP.

The sequence of events in this instance is as follows:

1. Set up and qualify ESOP and trust.
2. Issue and transfer stock to ESOP trust at up to 15 percent of payroll.
3. Deduct fair market value of contribution from gross income.
4. Pay taxes reduced by 50 percent of contribution.
5. Allocate tax savings to working capital.
6. Repurchase redeemed shares, if necessary, with deductible cash contributions.

Table 6.1 illustrates a simple cash flow, tax, and repurchase work-up before and after an equity ESOP. The value of the initial stock contribution at 15

TABLE 6.1
Working Capital Before and After ESOP
(end of first year)

	Before ESOP[a]	After ESOP[b]
Gross Income	$20,000	$20,000
Contribution (Stock)	-	$10,000
Repurchase Money	-	$1,000
Taxable Income	$20,000	$9,000
Federal and State Taxes	$10,000	$4,500
Net Income	$10,000	$14,500
Outstanding Shares	10,000	11,000
Working Capital	$10,000	$14,500
Book Value per Share	$11.00	$10.41

[a]Refer to table 3.1.

[b]Refer to tables 3.4 and 3.10.

percent of payroll is $10,000 (1,000 shares valued at $10 per share). The second contribution is $1,000 in cash paid to the ESOP trust to repurchase the shares distributed to employees who have separated, retired, or deceased during the year.

The stock contributions increased working capital by $5,000, but the repurchase money contribution reduced this gain by $500, leaving a net advantage of $4,500 over the conventional company. An increase in shares outstanding of 1,000 added a net of $4,500 to equity or $4.50 per share. On a book value basis the differential in share prices is $0.59, or 5.4 percent. On a market value basis the dilution may be less significant for a private company than for a public company. Contributions of preferred stock will reduce net income and working capital without alleviating dilution since dividends will be higher and must be expended from net income.

EMPLOYEE ACQUISITION OF AN EMPLOYER COMPANY OR SUBSIDIARY

In 1979, the Select Committee on Small Business of the U.S. Senate reported that during the 1970s between fifty and sixty companies that were scheduled to close down were purchased by employees.[1] In most cases an ESOP was used, and in about 70 percent of the cases the companies were subsidiaries of conglomerates. In a number of other cases an ESOP company was formed as an alternative to a planned divestiture by a parent company to an outside company. An essential feature of this application is strong employee opposition to the planned shutdown or divestiture, which induces the employees to acquire the company through the use of an ESOP.

This application is equally viable as an alternative to a merger or take-over of a smaller company, public or private, by an unacceptable outside company. In this instance the owners and management of the pre-ESOP company may wish to maintain some equity and management role after the merger or take-over, but the acquiring company may have less favorable plans in mind. It may also be possible that the take-over bid is viewed with considerable hostility.

If the transaction involves a subsidiary, the stock purchase is made from the parent company. If a public company, the stock purchases may be made on the public market if any one day's purchase does not exceed 15 percent of the average daily exchange volume of the preceding four weeks. The company can repurchase without the volume limitation if it does so privately and with no broker or dealer involvement, or it may make a tender offer. If the company is private or close-held, the purchase will be made from the several and relevant stockholders.

A hypothetical ten-year financial analysis of this application is presented in tables 3.7, 3.8, and 3.9. The sequence of steps is as follows:

1. Set up and qualify ESOP and trust for company or subsidiary.
2. Obtain $50,000 of $100,000 purchase price from other sources (e.g., from key or highly compensated employees, from special employee fund, from roll-over of employee profit-sharing or stock bonus plan).
3. ESOP trust (or company) obtains loan of $50,000 from bank with parent company guarantee and/or trust pledge of employer stock as security.
4. Company stock is purchased at fair market value on public market or from parent company or from selling stockholder(s).
5. Transfer of 5,000 shares to trust (to company as treasury stock if company obtained loan) and remaining 5,000 shares to key employees and other direct purchasers.
6. If profit-sharing or stock bonus plan rolled over into ESOP for stock purchase, transfer such shares to trust.
7. Company amortizes loan with pretax dollars by making annual payments to ESOP trust at up to 15 percent (25 percent if loan to trust) of employee compensation (if company loan, 1,000 shares per annum to trust to offset principal with interest deducted separately).
8. Taxes are reduced by 50 percent of company contributions.
9. Tax savings increases net income and working capital.
10. Proceeds of sale to seller(s) are eligible for capital gains treatment on stock sale to ESOP trust.

Table 6.2 presents the financial characteristics of this sequence of events in relation to the effects of the same events upon two other methods of financing the buy-out. The alternatives are identical in all material respects except that in one a conventional company obtains a $50,000 loan through the company to pay half of the $100,000 purchase price of the stock. In the third alternative an ESOP is used; the company again obtains the loan, but offsets the $10,000 per annum principal payments with an equivalent stock contribution to the ESOP trust. In all cases the interest at 8 percent on the loan is a tax-deductible expense.

The advantage of an ESOP is its ability to deduct loan principal payments from taxable income. The effect is that a capital acquisition, whether assets or stock, can be treated as an expense. In all cases the $4,000 first-year interest (8 percent per annum on $50,000 loan) may be expensed. In the company-financed ESOP, the trust receives an annual contribution of 1,000 shares of treasury stock valued at $10 per share. In the trust-financed ESOP, the company makes loan payments to the trust, which transmits the same to the lender. In all cases key employees raised $50,000 to purchase 5,000 shares directly although a roll-over of a profit-sharing or stock bonus (if any cash assets) plan could be used for the same purchase.

TABLE 6.2

Alternative Acquisitions of Employer Company Stock
(end of first year)

	CONVENTIONAL[a]	ESOP[b]	ESOP[c]
	Loan to Company	*Loan to Trust*	*Loan to Company*
Purchase (5,000 shares)	$50,000	$50,000	$50,000
Gross Income	$20,000	$20,000	$20,000
Contribution (Stock)	-	-	$10,000
Contribution (Cash)	-	$10,000	-
Interest	$4,000	$4,000	$4,000
Taxable Income	$16,000	$6,000	$6,000
Federal and State Taxes	$8,000	$3,000	$3,000
Net Income	$8,000	$3,000	$3,000
Outstanding Shares	5,000	10,000	6,000
Debt Reduction	$10,000	-	-
Working Capital	$ (2,000)	$3,000	$3,000
Book Value per Share	$20.00	$10.00	$16.67

NOTE: Loans at 8 percent interest; price per share of $10.00.

[a]Refer to table 3.2.

[b]Refer to table 3.7.

[c]Refer to table 3.8.

At the end of the first year the conventional company holds 5,000 shares of treasury stock, the trust-financed ESOP company holds no treasury stock, and the company-financed ESOP company holds 4,000 shares of treasury stock that will be completely contributed over the next four years. The conventional company, while having the highest share book value, cannot meet its debt burden from current earnings. Its working capital has been reduced by $2,000 at the end of the first year, while both ESOP companies enjoy working capital increases of $3,000 for the same period.

There are certain practical and legal advantages if the loan in this instance is made by the ESOP trust rather than by the company. First, the key employees involved in the buy-out may not have sufficient ownership and control to enable the company to take out a direct loan. The ESOP trust, as an affiliate of the company or subsidiary, may be more acceptable to existing stockholders or the parent company. Second, stockholders wishing to sell their shares in a private or over-the-counter public company may face restrictions on transfers to individuals and may face dividend and ordinary income treatment on a sale to the company. Capital gains treatment is more likely if the sale is to the ESOP trust. Third, it may happen that the company may not be able to deduct the full price it paid for its own shares under the "adequate consideration" rule of ERISA Section 408(e).

Both the company and the ESOP trust may face additional problems of valuation under ERISA and the IRC, restrictions on the transfer or purchase of certain securities by the Securities and Exchange Commission (SEC) and state agencies, and SEC restrictions on tender offers and the volume of purchases on public securities markets. Chapter 9 discusses these matters in greater detail.

IN-HOUSE MARKET FOR EMPLOYER SECURITIES

An ESOP trust is frequently used to provide an in-house market for the existing shareholders of a private or close-held corporation. This helps to resolve two serious problems endemic to shareholders of such corporations: finding a buyer for restricted or minority share interests and finding a means of providing capital gains rates upon liquidation.

Many private companies with historically good earnings, growth, and management may face a very limited or nonexistent market for their securities. Federal and state securities laws may impose restrictions upon both issuance and transfer, and similar restrictions may exist in corporate articles or bylaws. Further, many public companies traded over-the-counter may have a relatively small number of shares publicly held and traded. Sales on the public market may be infrequent and low in volume. The market price may be significantly lower than the book value or earnings value of the shares. Both the stockholder and the company bear the economic burden of this liquidity deficiency, which may restrict small business investment and viability in the economy.

If a controlling stockholder partially liquidates his/her stock holdings with the corporation as the purchaser, the distribution may be considered a dividend and taxed as ordinary income under IRC Sections 301 and 302. Since purchase by the company may carry with it a severe tax penalty, the controlling stockholder looks to the outside market. But, as indicated in the previous paragraph, the outside market has a penalty of its own—lack of sufficient effective demand such that the market price is significantly lower than what is warranted by the earnings and book value of the outstanding shares.

The controlling stockholder may then turn to key employees as a market. However, they may be unable and/or unwilling to raise sufficient funds to buy out the partial interest, and no lender may be willing to lend the funds secured by stock of a corporation for which there is no significant market. Key employees may be willing to buy out a substantial majority of the controlling stockholder's interest (e.g., 8,000 shares, or 80 percent of total shares, outstanding) if a willing lender can be found.

The controlling shareholder may be willing to sell 5,000 shares to these employees who already hold 20 percent or 2,000 shares. He/she is not willing to terminate his/her holdings, however, and this cannot qualify for capital gains treatment under IRC Section 302 if the company buys the stock. Since he/she owns more than 50 percent of the voting stock, the Section 302 capital gain alternative is also foreclosed upon a company purchase.

An ESOP can solve most of the problems cited in the preceding paragraphs to a substantial degree as follows:

1. An ESOP helps to create a market for a private, close-held, or thinly traded company, thereby increasing the effective demand and market price of that company's stock on a subsequent private or public sale.

2. Both the IRC and ERISA permit an ESOP trust to pledge employer securities as security for a loan, which may be further guaranteed by the company since the trust is an affiliate of the company.

3. As an alternative to a loan, the ESOP trust may purchase the shares on an installment basis with tax-deductible annual contributions made to it by the company not to exceed 15 percent of payroll.

4. Since the ESOP trust is merely an affiliate of the company, the controlling shareholder may generally sell a partial interest to the trust at capital gain rates. The IRS has issued Revenue Procedure 77-30 to define the circumstances under which it will issue an advance ruling that such a proposed sale to any qualified defined contribution plan or deferred compensation plan will be considered a sale of stock rather than a dividend distribution.

5. The company may amortize the loan, deducting *both* principal and interest from gross income in annual installments not exceeding 15 percent (25 percent if trust financed) of employee compensation.

6. Or, the ESOP trust may purchase stock in five equal installments of 1,000 shares per annum using deductible annual cash contributions from the company.

7. The ESOP trust will hold 5,000, or 50 percent, of outstanding shares.

8. The former controlling stockholder can liquidate at capital gain rates and may defer recognition of gain under IRC Section 453 if an installment sale is used.

9. The normal principal and interest of $62,000 ($50,000 if installment) can be made for a cash cost to company of only $31,000 ($25,000 if installment) with a 50 percent tax rate.

Table 6.3 illustrates the first-year financial effect of the transaction outlined above. Three alternatives are presented, but for the tax reasons cited above, any direct purchase by the company is not a viable alternative. Thus, the choice centers on using a leveraged ESOP trust or the basic ESOP installment method. Borrowing in this instance does not increase assets and earnings since the purchase concerns only the internal transfer of equity. The interest payment for the leveraged ESOP will not result in increased earnings, leaving the installment ESOP in a preferable position with respect to net income and net income per share.

TABLE 6.3
Alternative In-House Stock Purchases
(end of first year)

	By Company[a]	Leveraged ESOP Trust[b]	Installment ESOP Trust[c]
Purchase (5,000 shares)		$50,000	$50,000
Gross Income		$20,000	$20,000
Contribution (Cash)		$10,000	$10,000
Interest		$4,000	-
Taxable Income		$6,000	$10,000
Federal and State Taxes		$3,000	$5,000
Net Income		$3,000	$5,000
Outstanding Shares		10,000	10,000
Income per Share		$0.30	$0.50

NOTE: Sale of 5,000 of 8,000 shares of controlling stockholder at $10.00 per share.

[a]Not viable for tax reasons.

[b]Trust financed. Refer to table 3.7.

[c]1,000 shares per year for five years. Refer to table 3.9.

Precautions should be taken to assure an arm's-length transaction at prices not in excess of "adequate consideration" for stocks valued not in excess of "fair market value." Both the ERISA and IRS provisions involved here will be discussed in greater detail in chapter 9. As discussed previously, a secondary benefit of the in-house market is the possibility of improving both the private and public markets for company stock. Shares to be sold on the public market should be registered on SEC Form S-8. This may also reduce the repurchase burden of the company.

ACQUISITION BY EMPLOYER COMPANY USING CASH

The acquisition of the stock or assets of another company under present tax laws is a capital transaction with the result that the acquisition must be paid for with after-tax dollars. The payments are not deductible as expense items to the buyer, but capital gains rates and deferred recognition of gain may be available to the seller. If assets are purchased, the purchase price is allocated among the various assets such as plant, equipment, inventory, and goodwill. If stock is purchased, there is no such allocation, but additional liabilities are involved.

Generally the seller favors a stock sale for capital gains availability and the transfer of liabilities. Plant and equipment may provide both capital gains and recapture, while inventory and goodwill provide neither. The buyer wishes to purchase depreciable property, such as plant and equipment, or property that can later be expensed, such as inventory. Stocks and goodwill provide no depreciation, and the former may carry substantial liabilities.

The acquisition may be leveraged by the company or by the ESOP trust or paid from internal sources by either of the preceding. The payment may be in a lump sum or in installments (e.g., 25 percent down and notes payable over five subsequent years). Combinations of the various alternatives are frequently utilized and may include stock or asset exchanges. An acquisition for cash, as described here, is a taxable event to the seller, an event that may or may not be followed by a liquidation and further requires that no merger results (i.e., the acquired company continues as an ongoing subsidiary). ESOP usefulness and availability should be comparable with either an acquisition or a merger.

The sequence of events, with various alternatives included, for the acquisition of a subsidiary valued at $50,000 would be as follows:

1. A qualified ESOP and trust are established for the acquiring company.

2. If leveraged, the company or the ESOP trust obtains a $50,000 loan secured by company stock and/or guaranteed by the company.

3. Or, the company, directly or through the ESOP trust, makes installment payments for five years of $10,000 per annum, which may equal not more than 15 percent (25 percent for a leveraged ESOP or LESOP) of employee compensation (plus reasonable interest, if notes are included and all subsidiary stock is transferred to the parent).

4. The $50,000 payment is made to the subsidiary in exchange for 5,000 shares of its stock transferred to the company if company financed (payment from and stock to trust if trust financed).

5. Or, if installments, the cash and stock are exchanged in equal amounts over five years (plus reasonable interest if notes are included and all subsidiary stock is transferred to the parent).

6. If the purchase is made through the ESOP trust, either leveraged or installment, subsidiary stock is immediately transferred to the parent company in exchange for parent stock.

7. The loan is amortized in five annual installments by the company with principal amount not to exceed 15 percent (25 percent if trust financed) of employee compensation. If company financed, the principal amount is offset with an equivalent stock transfer to the ESOP trust.

8. Or, if assets are acquired, the assets go to the company and company stock is transferred to the ESOP trust to offset principal payments for the assets, whether leveraged or installment.

9. If a leveraged acquisition or installment with notes and interest, the cash cost to the company with an ESOP is half the $62,000 paid ($50,000 principal and $12,000 interest), or $31,000 at 50 percent federal and state tax rates.

10. If an interest-free acquisition, the cash cost to the company with an ESOP is half the $50,000 paid, or $25,000 at 50 percent federal and state tax rates. The cash cost to a conventional company is $50,000.

Table 6.4 reveals the financial consequences at the end of the first year of an acquisition of a $50,000 subsidiary using three financing alternatives. The first is a purchase by a conventional corporation that takes a deduction for the interest, but not for the principal. Working capital is increased by only $3,000 since the principal payment must be made from net income. Income per share is calculated prior to the debt reduction payment, at $1.30 before as compared to $0.30 after. Since the company issues no new stock, the book value per share is now $15 on assets of $150,000.

The second alternative represents an ESOP company where the trust acts as the intermediary between the parent company and the subsidiary. Either the trust obtains the loan for the lump-sum payment of $50,000 to the subsidiary stockholders or, if paid in installments, the trust issues the notes necessary to make the purchase while installment payments are contributed by the company

TABLE 6.4
Acquisition Alternatives Using Cash or Cash and Notes
(end of first year)

	CONVENTIONAL COMPANY[a] Loan or Notes	ESOP TRUST FINANCED[b] Loan or Notes	ESOP COMPANY FINANCED[c] Loan or Notes
Purchase Price	$50,000	$50,000	$50,000
Gross Income	$30,000	$30,000	$30,000
Contribution (Cash)	-	$10,000	-
Contribution (Stock)	-	-	$10,000[d]
Interest	$41,000	$4,000	$4,000
Taxable Income	$26,000	$16,000	$16,000
Federal and State Taxes	$13,000	$8,000	$8,000
Net Income	$13,000	$8,000	$18,000
Debt Reduction	$10,000	-	$10,000
Working Capital	$3,000	$8,000	$8,000
Outstanding Shares	10,000	15,000	11,000
Book Value per Share	$15.00	$10.00	$13.64
Net Income per Share	$1.30	$0.53	$1.64

[a]Refer to table 3.2.

[b]Refer to table 3.5.

[c]Refer to table 3.6.

[d]1,000 shares of common at $10.00 per share.

and passed on to the seller. In either case, the ESOP trust incurs the obligation and receives the full 5,000 shares of newly issued parent company stock in exchange for the stock or assets of the subsidiary. The parent company stock may be used to secure the obligation and/or the parent company may guarantee the same.

The end result is that 15,000 shares of parent stock are now outstanding. Even though the company's contributions to pay off the loan or notes, and the interest thereon, are tax deductible, the dilution of equity and income is significant. Working capital, however, increases by $8,000, substantially more than for the conventional company, and per share working capital is higher than for the conventional company at $0.53 versus $0.30.

The company-financed ESOP has several advantages over the ESOP-trust-financed alternative. The most apparent is the per share net income of the former at $1.64 versus only $0.53 for the latter. Increases in working capital are equal, as are actual tax advantages. An acquisition with an ESOP where the company directly assumes the loan or note obligation means that the cash and notes go directly to the seller, who transfers the stock or assets to the parent company. As the company makes principal payments on the loan or notes, an equivalent amount of parent company stock is contributed to the trust. At the end of five years the trust will hold 5,000 shares. Both the principal payments and the interest are, in effect, tax-deductible expenses even though the company makes debt reduction payments of principal from net income.

In addition to the usual ERISA and IRS provisions, an acquisition—particularly a stock acquisition—may involve SEC and state blue sky law restrictions as to notices and procedures, the transfer or purchase of certain types of securities, and provisions for dissenting shareholders of the seller. Further SEC restrictions may apply to tender offers and the volume of purchases on public securities markets. Chapter 9 discusses these matters in greater detail. There is also a remote possibility that an exchange of parent stock for subsidiary stock between the company and the ESOP trust could be considered a reorganization under IRC Section 368(a).

FINANCING COMPANY EXPANSION OR GROWTH

Frequently a company may encounter the relatively pleasant problem of financing an expansion to meet actual or anticipated market opportunities. This involves internal growth and expansion rather than an outside acquisition as described in the preceding section. The funds to be raised are to be applied primarily to a significant net increase in plant and equipment rather than to cover depreciation or other accumulated or current expenses. Thus, new debt and/or equity financing may be appropriate and productive.

Table 6.5 indicates how such an expansion might be financed using four alternative financing vehicles: borrowing by a conventional company; issuing new stock by a conventional company; issuing new stock by an ESOP company to the trust; borrowing by an ESOP company. Only the third alternative is internally financed, but such financing is limited to 15 percent of employee compensation per year. If a money purchase plan is combined with the ESOP, this ratio could be increaed to 25 percent. Here, a 15 percent limit is maintained such that the expansion and growth rate of the equity ESOP is less than it could be.

The procedure to be followed in setting up the ESOPs is similar to the steps presented in the four previous sections. The same basic assumptions apply: Gross income for the current year is 20 percent of the total assets at the end of the previous year. All increases in working capital are reinvested. Net income is allocated first to debt reduction (if any) and then to working capital. The combined federal and state tax rate is 50 percent. The amount borrowed is $50,000 at 8 percent interest for five years. Stock prices are constant at $10 per share. Starting total assets are $100,000 with no liabilities.

The greatest expansion and growth are achieved with the conventional equity-financed company—provided that an inexpensive and effective outside market exists for its stock. The equity ESOP matches this growth as long as it contributes new stock to the trust and applies the tax saving to new investment. Both of the leveraged companies suffer decreased new investment because of debt service. The leveraged ESOP, while obtaining a tax deduction on principal payments, also must contribute an additional 5,000 shares to the trust over the five-year amortization period. Both ESOPs may be required to make additional cash contributions to repurchase shares distributed by the trust as employees terminate, retire, or decease.

An investment tax credit of up to 1.5 percent may also be available in this application by using a tax credit employee stock ownership plan (TCESOP). This would further reduce the cash cost of the expansion or investment (see "Increasing the Investment Tax Credit," below).

EMPLOYEE COMPENSATION AND INCENTIVE PLAN

A qualified ESOP must be for the general and exclusive benefit of all employees and must not favor managerial, supervisory, and highly compensated employees. Contributions to the plan are based upon up to 15 percent (25 percent with a LESOP) of the first $100,000 of employee compensation such that

TABLE 6.5
Alternative Financing of Company Expansion or Growth

End of 1st Year	Conventional— Debt Financed[a]	Conventional— Equity Financed[b]	ESOP— Equity Financed[c]	ESOP— Debt Financed by Company[d]
Prior Investment	$50,000[e]	$50,000[f]	-	$50,000[e]
Gross Income	$30,000	$30,000	$20,000	$30,000
Contribution (Cash)	-	-	-	-
Contribution (Stock)	-	-	$10,000	$10,000
Interest	$4,000	-	-	$4,000
Taxable Income	$26,000	$30,000	$10,000	$16,000
Federal and State Taxes	$13,000	$15,000	$5,000	$8,000
Net Income	$13,000	$15,000	$15,000	$18,000
Debt Reduction	$10,000	-	-	$10,000
Working Capital	$3,000	$15,000	$15,000	$8,000
New Investment	$3,000	$15,000	$15,000	$18,000
Total Assets	$153,000	$165,000	$115,000	$158,000
Outstanding Shares	10,000	15,000	11,000	11,000

END OF 5TH YEAR				
New Investment	$6,249	$21,961	$21,961	$13,569
Total Assets	$172,736	$241,576	$191,577	$203,261
Outstanding Shares	10,000	15,000	15,000	15,000
END OF 10TH YEAR				
New Investment	$25,290	$35,369	$28,052	$29,760
Total Assets	$278,192	$389,061	$308,579	$327,354
Outstanding Shares	10,000	15,000	15,000	15,000

[a]Refer to table 3.2.

[b]Refer to table 3.3.

[c]Refer to table 3.4.

[d]Refer to table 3.6.

[e]Bank loan.

[f]New stock issue of 5,000 shares at $10.00 per share.

higher-paid employees have a greater allocation. Thus, an ESOP can be used to substitute for a stock option, stock bonus, or profit-sharing plan or it can be used in tandem with any one of them. Since the ESOP allocates on the basis of compensation, little selectivity is available among employees with equal compensation.

Because both the amount of a current contribution and the value of accumulated allocations depend upon company performance, an ESOP has a logical application as an employee incentive plan. A study sponsored by the Economic Development Administration (EDA), Department of Commerce, indicated that employee incentive was the dominant reason given for ESOP adoption among the ESOP companies surveyed.[2] As previously reported in chapter 2, the study results indicate that ESOPs are very effective for this purpose. This finding is supported by a survey of ESOP companies conducted by the Committee on Finance of the U.S. Senate also cited in chapter 2.

Unlike a profit-sharing plan, an ESOP may invest primarily in employer securities, and contributions are not dependent upon profits. The lack of diversity may also involve a higher risk of loss or diminution of plan assets. The value of employer company stock may also be subject to considerable fluctuation if the company stock is listed on a national exchange even when sales and earnings may be relatively stable.

A stock bonus plan may also invest largely in employer securities, and contributions may also be made without respect to profits. An ESOP is distinguished in that: it may engage in financing, it must hold common voting stock or readily convertible preferred, and it must provide substantial pass-through of voting rights to participants. It is likely that at least the last two provisions would make an ESOP preferable to a stock bonus plan from the employee perspective.

An ESOP may also be drafted such that partial distributions to participants may be made upon vesting but prior to retirement. This provision and the voting pass-through may be especially attractive to younger employees who may have little interest in retirement benefits. Since an ESOP is intended more as an incentive plan than as a retirement plan, caution and prudence are called for before an ESOP is substituted for a pension or retirement plan.

As explained in chapter 3, a qualified pension plan is a defined benefit plan subject to both the prudence and diversity requirements of ERISA. The probability of fixed and continuous benefits upon retirement is higher for a pension plan than for an ESOP. ESOP benefits are more likely to fluctuate such that the risk of gain or loss should be weighed against the fixed benefits of a pension plan. The latter is more subject to erosion by inflation than an ESOP, however, and insurance may be available to protect ESOP participants and beneficiaries from losses resulting from declining or worthless stock.

The procedural steps and financial effects of this application are similar to several of the applications and uses presented in the previous sections of this chapter. Reference should be made to the section that most closely approximates the type of ESOP contemplated and to the corresponding financial analysis in chapter 3.

GOING PRIVATE OR PURCHASING SHARES ON THE PUBLIC MARKET

As discussed in a previous section, many smaller public companies, especially those traded over-the-counter, have a small public market or "float" relative to the total shares outstanding and to company assets and earnings. The result can be share prices substantially below what is warranted on the basis of book value and earnings per share. The public market can be both costly and ineffective as a financing vehicle for such a company and for controlling stockholders who may wish to liquidate. Or, as an alternative, perhaps the company is attempting to prevent a take-over bid.

In either situation, the company may seek to "go private." The company could acquire its stock at a bargain discounted price and perhaps reduce the number of outstanding shares. It could avoid the costs and restrictions of being listed on an exchange as well as those associated with SEC jurisdiction. Two major impediments to such a move would be the loss of working capital from a stock acquisition and the loss of a public market, though defective, for existing shareholders or future financing attempts.

The use of an ESOP can remove at least part of these impediments. Earlier sections of this chapter explained how an ESOP can be used to increase working capital and to finance company expansion and growth and concerned the use of an ESOP as an in-house market for company securities. These sections should be consulted for the basic procedural steps and financial effects in the use of an ESOP to go private or purchase shares on the public market. Additional matters warrant further explanation.

The major national exchanges have criteria for delisting a company. For the New York Stock Exchange these include any of the following: less than 1,200 shareholders of at least 100 shares, or less than 600,000 public shares, or a market value under $5 million, or a value of all shares outstanding of less than $8 million and a net income averaging under $600,000 over the past three years.

For the American Stock Exchange, any of the following is sufficient: net assets under $2 million and negative earnings for the past two years, or public shares number under 200,000, or fewer than 400 total shareholders, or insiders hold 90 percent of outstanding shares, or a market value of public shares of less than $1 million. The National Association of Securities Dealers Automated Quotations (NASDAQ) uses any of the following: fewer than two market makers for the stock, or a bid price below $1.00, or fewer than 100,000 public shares, or total assets of less than $500,000, or fewer than 300 total shareholders.

Even if delisted, a company with over 500 stockholders must register with the SEC and file Form 10-K and other disclosure reports. To avoid these requirements, the company must have fewer than 300 shareholders and make an application to the SEC to deregister. In addition, state corporation and securities laws may impose additional requirements. Usually these involve a business purpose test and a fiduciary obligation to minority or dissenting shareholders. Some states may require a redemption of the shares of a dissenting minority stockholder at fair market value.

The ESOP trust can thus be used to make the necessary stock purchases with pretax dollars. Shares can be purchased from existing shareholders in a private sale or on the public market or by tender offer. Public market purchases on any one day should not exceed 15 percent of the average daily volume of the stock during the preceding four weeks, and the bid price should not exceed the highest current or last sale independent bid. The trust purchase may not violate the SEC 10b-5 insider trading rule such that the purpose of the purchase is to manipulate the stock price to the benefit of the company or insiders.

As an affiliate of the company, stock purchased by the trust becomes "tainted," and unless registered on SEC Form S-8, such stock is subject to a holding period and other distribution restrictions as unregistered stock. ERISA Section 406(a) prohibits certain transactions of a qualified plan with a party in interest. This includes stock purchases to increase the price for the benefit of controlling stockholders or the trust fiduciary.

If the stock purchase is by tender offer through the ESOP trust or by the company, the company must register the same on SEC Form 13d. A tender offer is viable when the company seeks a quick purchase to take advantage of a low market price or to prevent a take-over attempt. If the latter, the company may seek voting control of the stock.

ERISA Section 408(e) may limit the premium over market price that the trust can pay in a tender offer, since a purchase from a party in interest may not be in excess of market price. In addition, the listing exchange may require shareholder approval if the purchase exceeds 20 percent of the outstanding shares.

ESTATE PLANNING

This use is similar to the in-house market for employer securities, as explained above. It is especially significant in the case of the sale of stock by the estate of a controlling shareholder of a close-held corporation. A partial redemption by the company may be treated as ordinary income to the estate under IRC Section 302. If the value of the stock exceeds 50 percent of the gross estate, reduced by certain deductions, IRC Section 303 permits certain amounts of the distribution to be treated as capital gains. This amount is limited to estate or similar taxes and the amount of the funeral and administrative expenses of the estate.

Thus, net proceeds to increase the liquidity of the estate may be taxed as ordinary income up to a maximum rate of 70 percent. Further, the redemption by the company must be made with after-tax dollars. The use of an ESOP trust to repurchase the stock will involve the use of pretax dollars contributed by the company and will permit the estate capital gains treatment on the proceeds of the partial liquidation in excess of the Section 303 allowance. If there is stepped-up basis treatment of the stock included in the estate, the entire transaction may be tax free if the value of the stock does not increase from the date of death of the stockholder to the date of repurchase by the trust.

In addition to a qualified ESOP, the essential components of the estate planning function include a buy/sell agreement between the company and the stockholder and the fair and accurate valuation of the company stock at the time of death and at the time of repurchase by the trust. The agreement may not be made with the trust, and the trust will not be legally obligated to repurchase the shares. The ESOP trust may, however, be granted an option to purchase such shares at or below their fair market value.

The purchase money may be accumulated by the company free of the accumulated earnings tax in the year of death of the shareholder or any year thereafter. It is not likely that any significant cash reserve fund will be permitted to accumulate in the ESOP trust since ERISA and IRS require investment primarily in employer securities. At the time of death or thereafter, a significant tax-deductible contribution by the company to the trust is possible to execute the repurchase. The normal 15 percent of employee compensation may be supplemented with an additional 15 percent unused prior-year carryforward or an additional 10 percent from a combined ESOP and money purchase plan or from a leveraged ESOP.

Or, in the alternative, the ESOP trust may purchase life insurance on the controlling stockholder and, upon his/her death, use the proceeds for the stock purchase. Funds borrowed by the trust may not be used to pay life insurance premiums, but any funds contributed by the company may be so used.

Despite the available tax savings, the net effect of the repurchase may reduce company net income and earnings per share. This effect will be greater if the repurchase is leveraged using either the company or the trust. Reference should be made to tables 6.3, 3.7, and 3.9 to evaluate the financial effects of these transactions.

ECONOMIC REDEVELOPMENT AND EMPLOYMENT MAINTENANCE

An ESOP may significantly increase the ability of a business entity to survive and even prosper in situations and under conditions in which a conventional independent company or subsidiary would be shut down, liquidated, abandoned, divested, or dismembered. The data cited previously in chapter 2 and in this chapter from the EDA report, the Senate Finance Committee, the Senate Small Business Committee, and the National Center for Economic Alternatives tend to indicate that ESOPs have both the past record and the future potential to play a significant role in the economic redevelopment of certain local and regional economies. An essential parallel role would concern employment maintenance and upgrading.

An economic development function for ESOPs has been an implicit element of the ESOP philosophy of Louis Kelso as expressed in *The Capitalist Manifesto*, *Two Factor Theory*, and numerous articles, speeches, and congressional appearances since the late 1950s. This may not be shared by most ESOP critics and some ESOP advocates. However, there seems to be little disagreement that the industrial-based economies of the northeastern and north central United States have been experiencing a relative decline since the late 1950s and an absolute decline since the late 1960s. ESOPs have frequently been used in these regions as last-ditch efforts to save companies, jobs, and local economies.

The Economic Development Administration of the U.S. Department of Commerce sponsored a study on changes in company growth (or decline) and employment in the Great Lakes states during the period 1970-1975. (This is a separate study from the study on ESOPs carried out by the University of Michigan in 1978.) The *Great Lakes Report* was carried out by the Academy of Contemporary Problems in 1977 and covered the economies of Illinois, Indiana, Michigan, Ohio, and Wisconsin. One part of the report series, focusing upon Ohio, opened with this introduction (citations omitted):

The evidence continues to mount that the Northeastern region of the United States presently confronts serious economic difficulties. From 1970 to 1975, the employment performance of the three regional economies of the Northeast (New England), Middle Atlantic, and East North Central was substantially below that of the nation. The employment growth rates of this region were lower than the national average, while its unemployment rates were well above that of the nation. In large measure these two economic problems were responsible for the emergence of the coalitions among both Northeastern governors and members of the House of Representatives.

Yet the area's current employment problems and their underlying causal factors are not of recent origin. Since before World War II, the three regional economies have experienced rates of employment growth below the national average.[3]

Table 6.6 presents data from the report concerning increases and decreases in the number of Dun & Bradstreet-rated companies in the Great Lakes states from 1970 to 1975. During this period 157,271 such firms closed, and another 406 emigrated from the region. Only 105,665 new firms opened and 247 immigrated, for a net loss of 51,766. The loss was most pronounced for independent, single-plant companies engaged in wholesaling, retailing, or manufacturing. The largest net gain was for headquarters of multiplant companies. However, this gain resulted from status changes (e.g., from branch to headquarters) of companies already in the region and not from new openings or immigrants.

The great majority of the firms involved was small—less than twenty employees. Since the fatality rate of companies is very high during the first year, many companies could appear on both the closed and opened columns. Among the industrial categories only finance, insurance, real estate, and services indicate any significant increase. Because of both internal and external multiplier effects, the data most damaging to regional economic development and employment are the net loss of 9,208 manufacturing companies.

Table 6.7 concerns the same data base as the previous table except that employment figures instead of the number of companies are used. Thus, from 1970 to 1975 regional employment declined by 27,403, the largest single category of loss—345,067—occurring in manufacturing. Multi-unit headquarter companies in the region show an employment increase of 477,975, but, again, this is due to branches in the region becoming headquarters and not through net openings and immigration.

The employment loss from plant and company closings was substantial—902,644 alone for companies of 100 or more employees. The largest net employment increases occurred in miscellaneous services, transportation, and utilities. The region strongly reflects and perhaps leads the national employ-

TABLE 6.6

Changes in the Number of Companies in Great Lakes States by Type and Industry, 1970-75
(Dun & Bradstreet rated)

By Type	In Region 1970	Firms Opened (Gain)	Firms Closed (Loss)	In-migrant Firms (Gain)	Out-migrant Firms (Loss)	In Region 1975	Net Change[b]
Total Companies	480,248	105,665	157,271	247	406	428,482	(51,766)
Subsidiary	8,281	2,617	3,209	64	82	8,524	243
Not Subsidiary	471,967	103,048	154,062	183	324	419,958	(52,007)
Not Multi-unit	407,508	97,883	135,506	115	246	362,054	(45,454)
Multi-unit							
Headquarters	35,549	7,570	9,439	117	151	40,650	5,101
Multi-unit Branch	37,191	212	12,326	15	9	25,778	(11,413)
By Number of Employees[a]							
1-19		96,618	108,110	157	205		
20-50		5,302	7,996	39	60		
51-99		843	1,564	8	12		
100 or more		649	2,295	33	49		

By Industry[a]

Agriculture	4,561	736	1,144	1	4,290	(271)
Mining	2,648	347	853	9	2,156	(492)
Construction	65,425	14,053	19,214	36	59,870	(5,555)
Manufacturing	72,744	12,536	21,083	143	63,536	(9,268)
Transportation and and Utilities	16,049	2,631	4,462	24	14,085	(1,964)
Wholesale/Retail	264,525	60,341	96,000	127	226,063	(37,562)
Finance, Real Estate and Insurance	4,286	2,314	1,202	16	6,435	2,140
Services	49,198	12,679	13,210	47	50,379	1,161
Public Administration	75	22	14	0	82	7
Unclassified	238	6	74	1	198	(40)

SOURCE: Carol Jusenius and Larry Ledebur, *The Migration of Firms and Workers in Ohio, 1970- 1975: A Great Lakes Regional Report* (Columbus, Ohio: Academy for Contemporary Problems, 1977).

[a]Does not equal total companies due to nonresponses.

[b]Differences between 1970 and 1975 figures do not equal the sum of components of change due to changes in firm status.

TABLE 6.7

Employment Changes in Great Lakes States by Type of Company and Industry, 1970-75

By Type	In Region 1970	Firms Opened (Gain)	Firms Closed (Loss)	In-migrant Firms (Gain)	Out-migrant Firms (Loss)	In Region 1975	Net Change[b]
Total Employment	9,088,565	827,158	1,720,775	35,515	26,149	9,061,162	(27,403)
Not Multi-unit	4,300,494	709,812	1,009,012	13,652	9,257	4,194,743	(185,751)
Multi-unit							
Headquarters	1,528,678	112,862	162,314	18,519	16,369	2,006,653	477,975
Multi-unit Branch	3,179,393	4,484	549,449	344	335	2,859,766	(319,627)
By Number of Employees[a]							
1-19		410,865	466,757	1,066	1,305		
20-50		156,104	241,277	1,265	1,906		
51-99		57,307	110,077	508	827		
100 or more		202,882	902,644	29,676	22,111		

By Industry[a]

Agriculture	26,880	3,779	5,513	50	1	31,244	4,364
Mining	50,143	3,141	14,428	6,642	77	51,851	1,708
Construction	635,750	73,952	153,758	164	438	561,564	(74,186)
Manufacturing	5,160,107	221,765	847,052	19,954	14,921	4,815,040	(345,067)
Transportation and Utilities	429,954	39,938	69,342	576	3,907	491,623	61,669
Wholesale/Retail	1,849,850	354,547	496,714	2,231	2,757	1,985,096	(135,246)
Finance, Real Estate and Insurance	286,225	37,796	20,911	599	1,925	302,943	16,718
Services	463,361	91,268	106,702	2,299	2,123	584,970	121,609
Public Administration	181,676	972	5,542	0	0	231,723	50,047
Unclassified	895	0	713	0	0	183	(712)

Source: Jusenius and Ledebur, *The Migration of Firms and Workers in Ohio, 1970-1975.*

[a]Does not equal total employment due to nonresponses.

[b]Differences between 1970 and 1975 figures do not equal the sum of components of change due to changes in firm status.

ment trend from manufacturing to services. Perhaps of special significance is the overwhelming ratio of employment loss to gain from branches of multi-unit companies in the region: 549,449 to 4,484.

To summarize both tables, the primary cause of the region's losses of companies and employment is the closing rate or death rate of smaller independent companies and branches of larger companies located in the region. No major Sun Belt exodus had taken place in the region from 1970 to 1975. As indicated previously in this chapter, many ESOPs were given birth by the impending shutdowns of branch operations and close-held companies.

A shutdown, closing, or relocation can have a severe impact upon a local or regional economy. A series of the same can have a devastating impact. In 1976 the Associates Corporation of North America moved its corporate headquarters from South Bend, Indiana, to Dallas, Texas. The immediate and direct loss involved 550 jobs and payroll and benefits of $9,625,000. A follow-up study one year after the move determined that the regional (five-county) economic impact involved income losses of $50-60 million and employment losses of about 3,000 jobs.[4]

In September 1977, Youngstown Sheet and Tube, a subsidiary of Lykes Corporation, announced its intention to close its Campbell Works in Youngstown, Ohio. The annual payroll of the 4,100 workers was $72.98 million plus an additional $7.29 million in secondary payrolls.[5] State, county, and local tax losses as a result thereof were estimated at $14.8 to $17.7 million from September 1977 to December 1980.[6] State and county program payments for Aid to Dependent Children and general relief would add another $800,000 to $1.7 million. Federal tax losses and program expenditures were estimated at $12.0-15.1 million and $33.6-36.0 million, respectively.

While the economic and social costs of company and plant closings may be high in the short run, the long-run effect thereof may be beneficial (i.e., a net economic and, most likely, social gain if less efficient companies and industries are not permitted to survive through subsidy or protection). It may be the policy of some conglomerates to milk a subsidiary for other purposes and then dump it rather than try to develop it.[7] Such a company may not be a viable ESOP candidate. Other factors weighing against viability would include obsolete product, plant, or equipment, depletion of raw materials and resources, geographic migration of the market, and prohibitive regulatory constraints.

INCREASING THE INVESTMENT TAX CREDIT

Section 301 of the Tax Reduction Act of 1975, as amended by Section 803 of the Tax Reform Act of 1976, provided a basic additional 1 percent investment tax credit for equivalent company stock contributions made to an ESOP. Voluntary employee contributions matched by the company could qualify the company for another 0.5 percent for a possible total of 11.5 percent. IRC Section 409A(n), added by the revenue act of 1978, superseded these acts and extended the termination date of the provisions from December 31, 1980, to December 31, 1983. The Economic Recovery Tax Act of 1981 (ERTA) advanced this termination date by one year and provided for a payroll-based tax credit starting with 0.5 percent of employee compensation for 1983 and reaching 0.75 percent for the termination year of 1987.

The following are the procedural steps required for a pure TCESOP:

1. A qualified IRC Section 409A(n) TCESOP and trust are established.
2. The company makes an investment in qualified plant and equipment of $50,000 financed by a bank loan (or by a stock issue of 5,000 shares).
3. Interest on the loan is deducted from gross income.
4. Income tax liability is calculated.
5. Normal investment tax credit (ITC) of 10 percent of qualified investment, or $5,000, is deducted.
6. The basic ESOP percentage of 1 percent of qualified investment, or $500, is deducted.
7. The company contributes 50 shares of stock valued at $10 per share to the ESOP trust to equal a $500 deduction.
8. The company contributes an additional 25 shares to the trust to qualify for the additional 0.5 percent ITC.
9. Employees match the company's 0.5 percent with a $250 contribution to the trust to purchase 25 shares from the company. Proceeds go to working capital.
10. A matching ESOP percentage of 0.5 percent, or $250, is deducted from tax liability.
11. Net income is increased by $750 over a conventional company.
12. Working capital is increased $1,000 over a conventional company.
13. Shares outstanding are increased by 100 over a conventional company.

Table 6.8 indicates the investment tax credit available after a qualified investment of $50,000. The normal ITC under present law is 10 percent of such investment and is deducted from the normal tax liability. To this is added the 1 percent basic and 0.5 percent matching TCESOP rate, or $750, which requires an equivalent stock contribution to the trust (75 shares at $10 per share). Initial assets for all companies (prior to investment) are $100,000. With a pure TCESOP there is no dilution of equity or earnings per share. Most TCESOP users are capital-intensive companies such as oil and gas and utilities.

BUILDING CONSUMER EQUITY
IN PUBLIC UTILITIES OR RAILROADS

This version of an ESOP is known as a consumer stock ownership plan (CSOP) and could have similarities to a cooperative in that the equity interest of

TABLE 6.8
Investment Tax Credit: Conventional v. TCESOP Companies

	CONVENTIONAL— DEBT FINANCED	TCESOP— DEBT FINANCED	CONVENTIONAL— EQUITY FINANCED	TCESOP— EQUITY FINANCED
Qualified Investment	$50,000	$50,000	$50,000	$50,000
Gross Income	$30,000	$30,000	$30,000	$30,000
Interest	$4,000	$4,000	-	-
Taxable Income	$26,000	$26,000	$30,000	$30,000
Tax Liability	$13,000	$13,000	$15,000	$15,000
Tax Credit	$5,000	$5,750	$5,000	$5,750
Net Taxes	$8,000	$7,250	$10,000	$9,250
Contribution (Stock)	-	$750	-	$750
Net Income	$18,000	$18,750	$20,000	$20,750
Debt Reduction	$10,000	$10,000	-	-
Working Capital	$8,000	$9,000	$20,000	$21,000
Total Assets	$158,000	$158,750	$170,000	$170,750
Outstanding Shares	10,000	10,100	15,000	15,100
Net Income per Share	$1.80	$1.86	$1.33	$1.38

NOTE: Normal ITC of 10 percent. TCESOP addition of 1.5 percent includes basic and matching contribution. Capital-based ITC for TCESOP's to be replaced by payroll-based ITC beginning in 1983.

the consumer or customer could be a function of account billings of the company to the same. The greater the purchases the consumer makes from the company, the greater would be the stock allocations and dividend distributions made to that consumer by the company. Company stock contributions are made to the CSOP trust or escrow agent, which allocates the same to participating consumer accounts. Dividend income would be applied first to pay the fair market value of the allocated stock, and such dividend income would not be taxed to the consumer until after such payment. Thereafter, the dividend income would give consumers an offset to their utility bills and a voice in company policy through stock ownership.

The stock contributions by the company would be in anticipation of its capital needs, which would require a subscription agreement with the participating consumer. The subscription agreement in turn must be "marketable" or "bankable" commercial paper to enable the company to obtain the required financing. In the alternative, or in addition, the CSOP could be leveraged whereby the trust would obtain the bank loan to purchase the company securities, which in turn would be pledged as security for the loan. The dividend payments could then be used to help repay the principal and at least part of the interest with the subsequent transfer of the stock to the appropriate consumer accounts in the trust as the subscription agreements are paid. The CSOP could be part of a dividend reinvestment plan or stock purchase plan.

If the CSOP qualifies as a cooperative under IRC Sections 1382(a) and 1388(a), dividends would be tax-deductible expenses as "patronage dividends." If so, generous dividends could be made such that the usual IRC 401(a) type of ESOP would not be necessary. The end result could be fewer and lower rate increases and more efficient utility (or transit) companies. The financial characteristics of a qualified CSOP, nonleveraged or leveraged, would be similar to those for a nonleveraged and leveraged ESOP described in tables 6.4 and 6.5. The procedural steps would also be similar except to the extent that cooperative tax status is sought to permit deductions for patronage dividends.

Thus, the procedural steps for a cooperative CSOP are as follows:

1. Approval of CSOP subscription agreements and the capital financing plan is obtained from necessary regulatory agencies.
2. CSOP and trust are established in conformance with cooperative requirements under IRC Sections 1382(a)-1388(a).
3. Written subscription agreements are executed with consumer members as per IRC Section 1388(a).
4. CSOP trust may execute a secondary note or obtain a bank loan, if leveraged.
5. Stock is transferred to the CSOP trust as per plan and subscription agreements. If

the CSOP is leveraged, agreements or company stock or both are given as security for the loan with loan proceeds going to the company in exchange for stock.

6. The company may discount subscription agreements or the CSOP trust note on a secondary market or may use same as security for a loan as per capital financing requirements.
7. Generous dividends are applied to the purchase of stock and deducted from gross income by the company as a patronage dividend. No income is earned by the consumer subscriber.
8. Or, if the CSOP is leveraged, dividends are applied to the loan principal first and then to interest. (The company may pay interest to extent necessary.)
9. Fully paid shares are allocated to consumer subscriber accounts in trust.
10. The company continues to deduct the patronage dividend as paid, and the consumer subscriber has an offset to utility bills.

BUILDING CONSUMER EQUITY IN GOVERNMENT ENTERPRISES

This is a CSOP similar to the one described in the previous section except that the utility or service company involved is a municipal corporation or other public entity. Likely candidates would be municipal water and sewer companies, light and power companies, or local or regional transportation and transit authorities. Perhaps there exists a quantum jump in the level of difficulty to apply a CSOP to the Tennessee Valley Authority, Conrail, or the post office.

Again, the equity interest of the consumer or customer would be based upon account billings to the same by the entity involved. A municipal CSOP could also be leveraged such that less reliance could be placed on bond issues as a source of capital financing. An added attraction is that dividends from the same would probably be exempt from federal income taxes, although the question of municipal versus consumer ownership could be a determinative and complex issue.

Limits on the percentage of consumer ownership would be necessary to keep the enterprise in the public sector. Any contribution by the enterprise to the trust would bring no tax advantage to the enterprise. Thus, the consumer participant would have to rely on dividends and the secondary market to pay off the stocks acquired under the subscription agreement. A certain percentage of the proceeds obtained from discounting the agreements, or the note of the trust in a leveraged CSOP, could go toward share payments.

As the shares are paid, dividends would be paid to the consumer participant. A supplementary plan could be made available for employees of such enterprises, whereby account allocations would be based upon individual or enterprise performance outside the usual wage and promotion schedules. Such an enterprise could have increased patronage, increased community support, fewer strikes and labor problems, and increased operating efficiency.

MISCELLANEOUS USES

The applications and uses of ESOPs may be subject to constraints of imagination as much as those of finance and law. Debt refinance, tax refund, franchises, cooperatives, consumer or community enterprises (CSOPs) are uses and forms that may be as viable, though not as general, as those explained in the previous sections of this chapter. However, the same basic procedures and financial effects are applicable.

SUMMARY OF MAJOR COSTS AND PROBLEMS

There are a number of costs and problems common to many ESOPs that warrant specific enumeration. Most, and perhaps all, of these have been cited in this and in preceding chapters. Some of these costs and problems are inherent in the ESOP concept, and some can be prevented or corrected through rigorous and prudent screening, planning, drafting, administering, and legislating. The most significant include the following:

1. Dilution of equity, earnings, and control.
2. Cashing out by controlling shareholders when a decline in company sales and profits seems imminent.
3. Stripping and dumping of a plant or subsidiary by a parent company or conglomerate whereby profits are diverted to other corporate purposes, rather than being reinvested, and the plant or subsidiary is then disposed of by use of an ESOP.
4. Planning and implementation costs of the ESOP and trust—usually in the $20,000-40,000 range.
5. Loss of alternative plan benefits when a pension plan, stock bonus plan, profit-sharing plan, or similar plan is converted or rolled over into an ESOP.
6. Substitution of an ESOP for more definite employee benefits such as wages, fringe benefits, or pension benefits.
7. Cashing out by participating employees who use the proceeds to compete with or otherwise damage the ESOP company.
8. Inadequate commitment and communication by management in obtaining the necessary degree of employee understanding and participation.
9. Divisive or discriminatory application of the plan among employees (e.g., union versus nonunion, highly versus lowly compensated, managerial versus non-managerial, blue collar versus white collar).

10. Control of trust assets and voting rights of trust securities.
11. Compliance with technical, reporting, and administrative requirements.
12. An excessive repurchase burden resulting from poor planning and/or excessive stock contributions to the trust.
13. Improper or inadequate valuation of employer securities such that the securities are purchased by the ESOP trust for an amount in excess of fair market value.

NOTES

1. Select Committee on Small Business, U.S. Senate, *The Role of the Federal Government and Employee Ownership of Business* (Washington, D.C.: U.S. Government Printing Office, 1979), p. iv.

2. Summarized in Michael Conte and Arnold S. Tannenbaum, "Employee-Owned Companies: Is the Difference Measurable?" *Monthly Labor Review*, vol. 10 (July 1978), p.47.

3. Carol Jusenius and Larry Ledebur, *The Migration of Firms and Workers in Ohio, 1970-1975: A Great Lakes Regional Research Report* (Columbus, Ohio: Academy for Contemporary Problems, 1977), p. 1 (hereafter referred to as *The Great Lakes Report*).

4. Wayne Bartholomew, Paul Joray, and Paul Kockanowski, "Corporation Relocation Impact," *Indiana Business Review*, January 1979, p. 2.

5. Policy and Management Associates, "Socioeconomic Costs and Benefits of the Community-Worker Ownership Plan to the Youngstown-Warren SMSA" [April 1978] in *Youngstown Demonstration Planning Project* (Washington, D.C.: National Center for Economic Alternatives, September 1978), p. 98 (hereafter referred to as *The Youngstown Project*).

6. Ibid., p. 192.

7. See, among other sources, Barry Bluestones and Bennett Harrison, "Capital and Communities: The Causes and Consequences of Private Disinvestment," an unpublished study released in 1980 and prepared for the Progressive Alliance.

CHAPTER

7

Case Studies

The cases and reports on ESOP companies presented herein concern mostly success stories. Several are remarkable, even spectacular, successes. Not all ESOP companies are successes, but the preconditions or latent conditions for success seem to include most of the following: moderate firm size (100-800 employees or $5-50 million in sales); skilled and highly interactive work force; acceptable to good relations between labor and management; moderate if not democratic management style; flat company hierarchy; job shop or project type of production; moderate or cooperative local union(s) leadership [if union(s) are present]; limited employee alternatives or mobility.

E SYSTEMS; DALLAS, TEXAS

In 1972, E Systems, an electronics and aerospace firm, was spun out of LTV, a Dallas-based conglomerate. In the following year, with Louis Kelso as its consultant, an ESOP was established and acquired the company using a tender offer. An earlier contributory employee savings and investment plan at LTV had failed, but by 1976 over 173,000 shares of E Systems' stock was owned by the ESOP trust and allocated to 6,900 of its 9,000 employees. During this same three-year (1973-76) period, turnover reportedly dropped by 50 percent, employee suggestions increased 40 percent, absenteeism declined, and profits increased by over 65 percent per year.[1]

Net income, according to *Moody's*, showed strong early growth in these years with a recent flattening: 1975, $7.2 million; 1976, $14.5 million; 1977, $19.0 million; 1978, $12.7 million; 1979, $18.6 million.

Chairman and president John W. Dixon, an advocate of both the ESOP philosophy and technique, has maintained that the United States will ultimately be socialist if labor and management are on opposite sides of the table.[2] Prior to adopting the ESOP, an extensive employee education program was utilized to explain the nature and benefits of the plan. Plan participants include many members of the locals of the United Auto Workers and the Machinists' unions. The evaluation of one union shop steward with thirty years of service was that workers regarded the ESOP as a "good thing," but that they "don't understand stocks."[3]

THE MILWAUKEE JOURNAL; MILWAUKEE, WISCONSIN

The Milwaukee Journal has been employee owned for over forty years by means of direct employee ownership (DEOC) rather than an ESOP. Employees own 80 percent of the stock with voting rights, and six workers usually sit among the seventeen members of the board of directors.[4] In addition, there is a twenty-four-member shareholder council; its members serve rotating two-year terms and are elected directly by the employees. Thus, many employees at the *Journal* get management perspectives and experience. One observer of the company has commented that the key to its success seems to be in getting workers to think (and act) like "bosses."[5]

Labor relations, as a result, may not fit the pattern of a conventional company, although the *Journal* did have a strike in 1961. Generally, both labor relations and growth have been good. The company has acquired a radio and television station, several smaller printing companies, and a communication signal relay firm. One of the officers of the company local of the Printing and Graphic Communications Workers has reported that *Journal* stock is a "very good investment."[6]

SULLAIR CORP.; MICHIGAN CITY, INDIANA

Sullair manufactures air compressors and related industrial equipment without foremen or belted assembly lines. Founded in 1966 by Donald Hoodes, the current president, the company had captured 30 percent of the U.S. market by 1974.[7] In the same year an ESOP was adopted, and both sales and net income increased by more than 40 percent. Sullair has neither a union nor a pension plan, but fringe benefits include health and life insurance, an Olympic-size swimming pool, and low-priced gasoline from company pumps.

The company experienced remarkable growth during the 1970s, going from 350 employees in early 1976 to 1,200 employees by the end of 1978. *Moody's* reveals the following increases in net sales and net income, respectively (in millions): 1974, $41.9 and $2.4; 1975, $49.1 and $2.4; 1976, $54.7 and $2.1; 1977, $74.6 and $5.9; 1978, $103.0 and $6.7. From 1974 to 1978, net sales increased an average of 36.5 percent per year, and net income increased an average of 44.8 percent per year.

All employees are salaried, are eligible for a bonus plan, and have the option of switching job duties and voting on work schedules. About 80 percent of the employees participate in the ESOP, and employee turnover was reported to be 1 percent per year as of 1976. The company and its operation seem to reflect the philosophy and personality of Hoodes, but some employees consider some of the benefits as a substitute for adequate wages.[8] It is likely that dividends and equity appreciation could more than negate reduced wages. In 1978, net sales per employee reached $85,800, and net income per employee was $5,545.

TEMBEC FOREST PRODUCTS; TEMISCAMING, QUEBEC

In 1972, International Paper Company closed its Canadian subsidiary in Temiscaming, Quebec. A year later the latter opened as Tembec Forest Products, Inc., with workers contributing 38 percent of the equity and the management of the former subsidiary putting up 62 percent. Workers had to give up $0.70 per hour in wages, but this was more than compensated for in equity earnings after the first year alone.[9]

The local union head is the worker representative on the board of directors, and employees sit on committees for hiring, grievances, and safety. Although a minority of workers complained of less discipline, most also reported less rigid work rules, fewer management perks, and better working conditions. Management reported a drop in absenteeism from 3.9 percent to 1.7 percent, more worker suggestions, less pilfering, fewer grievances, and a 30-40 percent increase in productivity since the operation has become employee owned.[10] Tembec is a direct employee-owned company rather than an ESOP.

CHICAGO & NORTH WESTERN TRANSPORTATION COMPANY; CHICAGO

In 1972 the Chicago & North Western Railroad was sold to the C&NWTC for $0.835 per share.[11] Late in 1980 it was trading at over $50. The C&NWTC

is directly owned by about 1,000 of the railroad's 13,400 employees and has shown consistent profitability while other midwestern railroads have edged closer to insolvency. After sustaining a loss in 1975, the company posted the following net income data, according to *Moody's*: 1976, $8.2 million; 1977, $18.1 million; 1978, $15.7 million.

The management and employees of C&NWTC carried over from the preceding company, but management practice and policy changed significantly. Special efforts at communication with workers were implemented, including informal meetings with top management at various company facilities. The company has diversified into chemicals and coal transportation.

SOUTH BEND LATHE; SOUTH BEND, INDIANA

In 1959, Amsted Industries, a Chicago-based conglomerate, acquired South Bend Lathe, a producer of machine tools and small lathes. After fifteen years Amsted decided to sell the division because of its poor profit performance. The South Bend Lathe story was eloquently told by its president, J. R. Boulis, to the Senate Finance Committee in 1978. Boulis had been transferred from another Amsted division to take over at South Bend in 1969. His testimony included the following:[12]

I am Dick Boulis, chairman and president of South Bend Lathe and this is Jerry Vogel. Jerry is one of our skilled machinists. He is vice president of our Union, Local 1722 of the Steelworkers, and he is a member of the board of directors.

I think it is important to note, at the outset, that Jerry is not here representing the United Steelworkers of America, but representing our local and our employees....

Unfortunately, in early 1975, I was advised that the company would be sold at substantially less than book value, and it appeared that the prospective purchaser would quite evidently *liquidate* the division and put some 500 employees on the streets of South Bend.

At this point, I started searching for a way to buy the company. I have no private funds myself. I could not do it. I tried to get our distributors together, I talked to many of our employees, and it looked like we were about to strike out.

Along about this time, a friend of mine in South Bend, the president of a local foundry, asked me if I had ever heard of ESOP. Frankly, I had not, but in a matter of 3 or 4 days, I had become somewhat conversant with employee stock ownership plans and the benefit you could gain from it. I commenced working with John Gibson of the Chicago Office of the Economic Development Administration, a local bank, and many other people who are too numerous to give credit to at this time, but I thank all of them for their efforts. As a result of these efforts, in a matter of about 3 months, we put the deal together and on July 3, 1975, we acquired our division from Amsted Industries and established a 100-percent employee stockownership plan whereby our employees immediately became the beneficial owners of South Bend Lathe.

This acquisition was accomplished by a $5 million grant from the Economic Development Administration to the city of South Bend. This grant then flowed through our employee stockownership trust and was loaned to the new corporation at 3-percent interest repayable over 25 years. Well, some people have said—well, 3-percent interest; that was some gift. But you have to remember that we were really not a financeable company at that time, and this $5 million was not all that was required. We had to go out and borrow another $5 million. We raised that through conventional financing sources, not at 3 percent, but a major portion of it was at 7 points over prime.

So our average rate that we had to pay to acquire the company was more than normal.

From a financial point of view, our employee stockownership has been a *resounding success*, and I would like to give you just a brief summary of the financial position of our company at the end of the current fiscal year, which just ended June 30.

We have had 3 profitable years after a series of unsatisfactory years under Amsted. Profits have improved each year, and for the year just ended, the profits were approximately 10 percent before taxes. . . .

Sales for the year just ended was $18.5 million which represented a 34-percent increase over the first fiscal year.

We started off completely in debt—we simply had nothing to start with, except the debt that we leveraged—but we worked hard at it, and we presently have no bank debt whatsoever. We paid off all of our bank loans and the total commercial debt which was approximately $4.5 million. That was completely paid off in May 1977, and I may remind you, that was only 22 months after we had started our operations.

Our current banking arrangements provide for a $3 million line of credit, should we need the funds, at the national prime rate of interest. We are not using this line of credit, at all. We have a quite liquid position. I think we currently have around $600,000 or $700,000 in cash or short-term investments.

Our current ratio has steadily improved and, at June 30, was 3.2 to 1. Earnings per share have increased from *$20.30* the first year to $52.24 the second year and *$69.48* in the third year.

I think it is important to note that these financial accomplishments were not achieved at the expense of our employee stockholders. Since we acquired our company, our employee's earnings have steadily increased and for the fiscal year just ended averaged over $15,000 a year.

With the general increase to be put into effect on August 1, our average employee's earnings will have increased by *45 percent* since our ESOP was established and since we acquired the company.

Of course, these increases included bonuses that we have distributed. Since acquiring the company, we have distributed seven bonuses, the last six of which were equal to a week's pay. Three of these were distributed in this past fiscal year.

The maximum tax-deductible contribution of 15 percent was made to our ESOP for each of these 3 years, and our employee stockowners will now have an average of *$6,000* in company stock, credited to their ESOP account.

From our analysis of statistics in our industry, it appears that our contribution to our employee stockownership plan is approximately twice the average contribution to pension plans for companies in our industry. We do not have a conventional pension plan or retirement plan at South Bend Lathe. Unfortunately, when we acquired our company, it did not appear that we could be financially successful if we had to assume the costs and legal liabilities for the pension plans in effect at that time.

All of our employees were aware of this and agreed to work for the new corporation for an employee stockownership plan in lieu of the pension plan in existence at that time.

In terms of employee *motivation*, our *productivity* increased very, very substantially in all areas of our company for the first several months after the acquisition. Unfortunately, the fact that our people had agreed to work for an employee stockownership plan rather than the previous pension plan created problems with the International Steelworkers that still have not been resolved. There is a suit pending in Federal court that has been pending there for 2 years wherein the steelworkers are attempting to have us named as the successor to Amsted which, in reality, means we would have to assume the pension liabilities and reinstate the pension plan that was in effect at that time.

We have accomplished a lot in South Bend. The job is not yet finished. We still have many things that have to be done in order that each of our employee stockowners can be secure, but we are confident. Thanks to ESOP, we believe that we have a bright future.

Now, we do not profess to be experts in the economic theories of ESOP. As I said earlier in my testimony, in early 1975 when a friend told me about ESOP I did not know what it was, and I had to start reading on it. I am still not an economic expert on ESOP. But it works. It works in our company.

There definitely is a better rapport, *better morale*; regardless of the problems that we have had with the Steelworkers, we get along better.

I think one reason why I personally support employee stock ownership is I am concerned about the decline of the American industry that is facing our country. At one time, and for many, many years, America led the world in the production of machine tools. We no longer do. We have been replaced by West Germany and Japan. Much of that has to be attributed to a decline in productivity....

...And we think that employee stockownership is the answer. We really sincerely believe that this is a way to revitalize American industry and to put us back on top of the heap, if you will.[12]

The statements of Mr. Boulis concerning earnings, productivity, morale, and employee relations tend to be supported by a 1978 report prepared for the Economic Development Administration (the agency that put up the $5 million grant for the company). The report measured the movement of eight indicators of company and employee performance over a period of about eighteen months from the time the ESOP became operational in late 1975. The results included the following:

1. Profits: Stable, positive, and consistent, following consistent losses from 1970 to 1975.
2. Productivity: Increased as measured by time standards and customer return rates.
3. Equipment costs: Improvement in the use rate of perishable tools per sales dollar.
4. Labor costs: No significant change as a percent of sales dollars. Increases in incentive pay were a factor.
5. Grievances: Favorable change (records only on salaried employees).
6. Turnover: Favorable change (records only on salaried employees).
7. Absenteeism: No change as measured by person-days lost (does not measure late arrivals or early departures from work).
8. Accident rates: No change, but insurance rates dropped.[13]

Despite such favorable reports, employee and union dissatisfaction intensified over major economic and ESOP issues, culminating in a nine-week strike at the company called by Local 1722, International Steelworkers, on August 25, 1980. Local president John Deak, who helped form the ESOP, alleged that instead of a "piece of the action" the workers got a "misunderstanding," while Boulis alleged that workers were unwilling to "think and act like owners."[14] The major issues included improved cost-of-living allowances, the right to have more than one worker on the board of directors, greater stock voting rights, and a revised stock allocation formula.

LOWE'S COMPANIES, INC.; NORTH WILKESBORO, NORTH CAROLINA

H. C. Buchan, one of the founders of this building supply chain, established a profit-sharing plan in 1957. In 1961, one year after his death, Lowe's went public, and the employees, through the plan, acquired 48 percent of the company. Like an ESOP, nearly all of the plan assets (about 90 percent) are invested in employer securities. Few companies of any type can match Lowe's growth record over the sixteen years from 1962 to 1978, when earnings increased by about 20 percent per year.

In November 1979, Lowe's chairman, Robert L. Strickland, submitted testimony to the Senate Committee on Banking, Housing, and Urban Affairs, then conducting hearings on the Chrysler Corporation Loan Guarantee Act and the use of an ESOP therein. His testimony included the following (citations omitted):

My name is Robert L. Strickland, Chairman of Lowe's Companies, Inc. I welcome this opportunity to vigorously endorse the unique intrinsic value of Employee Stock Ownership.

I am a businessman who believes deeply in motivation and productivity, and through 18 years with Lowe's, I have watched employee stock ownership work, and work well! From salesmen to truck drivers, from secretaries to store managers, the motivation, productivity, and achievements of Lowe's employees are a matter of historical fact and documented public record.

Lowe's is a group of retail stores, selling building materials to home builders and home owners in the Southeastern quadrant of our nation, from Indiana to Pennsylvania to Florida to Texas, and with one-fourth our stores in North Carolina.

In 1957, when Lowe's had six stores doing about $18,000,000, I went to visit the company for a job interview....

Today, those six stores have grown to 205 in 19 states. Our $18,000,000 annual sales volume has grown to $900,000,000. The stock, adjusted for splits and dividends, sold for $1.02 in 1961. It's trading now for about $18.00. Many of our employees became wealthy in the process, and the success of Lowe's employee stock ownership began making news.

FORTUNE magazine in 1972 quoted our former Chairman, "We are convinced that profit sharing (and its employee stock ownership) gives our employees a direct, personal self-interest in improving the company's earnings." FORTUNE went on to say "The bounty springs from the fund's portfolio, 90% of which is invested in Lowe's common stock."

NEWSWEEK magazine in 1975 featured Charles Valentine, a $125 a week warehouseman, who retired after 17 years with $660,000 worth of Lowe's stock and cash. NEWSWEEK said "90% of the money is invested in Lowe's stock—and that's the secret."

The CHARLOTTE OBSERVER headlined Ferrell Bryant, a truck driver who "Retired Rich."

In Lowe's own report to employees, we featured Mrs. Mary Marsh, a secretary, who stated, "because it is based on Lowe's stock, it's really an incentive to the employees to help make the company prosper," and also our first six figure man, Mr. Spence Bumgarner who worked for our lumber company subsidiary for 13 years. When he retired, his $150,000 fund balance was greater than the book value of the lumber company!

The Profit Sharing Research Council ran this Cover Story, "Why Lowe's Grows" and also featured a Store Manager, a Salesman, and a Warehouseman, all three of whom retired with balances ranging from $400,000 to $2,000,000. The store manager says "It wasn't until the Plan began buying Lowe's stock that we paid attention." And we were delighted when in 1976 the Honorable Louis Kelso testified before the Senate Finance Committee and told the Lowe's story of employee stock ownership success.

Mr. Kelso is the creator of the Employee Stock Ownership concept, and has said on many occasions that Lowe's Profit-Sharing Plan was in reality an Employee Stock Ownership Plan because 80 to 90% of the fund's assets were invested in company stock.

Mr. Chairman, these success stories were created by:

- A. Employee Stock Ownership.
- B. The motivation and productivity which was thereby created.
- C. The growth in profitability which thereby ensued.
- D. The increase in the price of Lowe's stock as Lowe's incentives and growth pattern were recognized by the stock market and financial community.

But what about those shareholders who are not employees? Do they benefit from employee stock ownership? The evidence is a convincing "yes." Mr. Bert Metzger is President of the Profit Sharing Research Foundation, and his comprehensive study "Does Profit Sharing Pay" authoritatively details how all shareholders are served by employee stock ownership. I quote, "What we need today are organizational incentives—programs which can motivate all factors contributing to corporate growth—stockholders, management, and employees. Employee profit sharing (and stock ownership) is multimotivational because it focuses attention on a common goal and rewards all factors." And this has been Lowe's experience....

Mr. Chairman, the Washington Redskins are a team made up of three teams—offensive, defensive, and specialty. Those three teams have a shared goal—to win and be successful. When one considers three important forces in this country—employees, management, and government—it's getting to be a national tragedy that instead of cooperation and teamwork towards accomplishing shared goals, we have developed adversary relationships that are getting increasingly shrill and acrimonious and non-productive. Japan and OPEC are examples of how national and international teamwork can seize economic initiative and translate it into successful, competitive growth.

I believe, sir, that improved economic teamwork must be a priority national strategy, and that increased Employee Stock Ownership is a powerful tactic by which we can implement that strategy.

Well, how do I know it works? How do I know that Lowe's growth wasn't influenced more by geography, or the business we're in, or management skill, etc.

In the late '50's and early '60's, there were at least five companies like ours in the Sunbelt—one in Virginia, one in South Carolina, and one in Florida, and two in North Carolina. Same geography, same business, different management of course, but not bad management. Three of the companies didn't make it on their own and sold out. The fourth company is about one-fourth our size, and they have just adopted an Employee Stock Ownership Plan. Survival of the motivated, and the productive.

We use several productivity measurements, and in our Annual Reports, we compare ourselves to major retailers and competitors in Sales per Employee, and Net Profit per Employee.

When our employee plan acquired the stock in 1961, it had a dramatic effect on both sales and profits. For the four years prior to the stock acquisition, sales per employee per year averaged $81,000 and net profits after taxes averaged $1,891 per employee per year. For the four years after the acquisition, sales declined, to an average of $73,000, but net profit per employee per year increased 19% to $2,245.

Senator Long, in a survey of ESOP companies, asked for a report of taxes paid before and after employee acquisition of stock. Taxes paid on average during these two four-year periods increased from an average of $1,893 per employee per year, to $2,278, for a 20% increase, or from $418,000 to $1,518,000.

The following table lists our progress in these important productivity measurements since then:

	Per Employee Per Year		
	Sales	*Taxes Paid*	*Profits After Taxes*
1966	$ 86,468	$2,801	$3,131
1971	$ 82,952	$3,128	$3,162
1976	$123,665	$4,555	$4,595

For 1978, although our Taxes and Profits figures are not directly comparable to our prior years, due to our change to LIFO accounting, they are comparable to, and were compared with, other major retailers in our Annual Report:

	Per Employee Per Year	
	Sales	*Profits After Taxes*
Sears	$ 40,000	$1,948
K-Mart	$ 48,900	$1,471
Penny	$ 48,500	$1,528
Wickes	$ 97,800	$1,973
Lowe's	$136,500	$4,084

To sum up the Revenue results of a small business that has grown fairly big, and plans to keep on growing, fueled by employee stock ownership; in 1960, we paid $641,000 in taxes—in 1979 we plan to pay $25,000,000 in taxes, and we look forward to remitting $50,000,000 in taxes, and our employees will own a larger percentage of the company than they do now.

Speaking for myself as an individual, I believe:

- The time for renewed national teamwork is now.
- The time for vastly increased employee stock ownership is now.
- The time for Senator Riegle's bill is now.

Mr. Chairman and Members of the Committee, Lowe's people believe in Employee Stock Ownership. We have seen it work to create incentive, productivity motivation, and wealth. We believe it is Creative Capitalism, and we are more firmly committed to the concept than ever before. We thank the Chairman and this Committee for your consideration to help make this great concept more important to this great country.[15]

Very few companies of any type in any industry can match Lowe's record. Perhaps more important than its growth performance is its comparative efficiency as measured by sales and after-tax profits per employee. Its advantage over Wickes, the closest of the comparison group, is 40 percent in sales and 107 percent in profits. The relatively high profits-to-sales ratio at Sears may reflect the effect of its own profit-sharing plan. Unlike an ESOP, a profit-sharing plan need not invest primarily in employer securities. But since contributions are usually made in cash (from actual profits) rather than stock, the cash flow advantage may be less significant.

ALLIED PLYWOOD, INC.; ALEXANDRIA, VIRGINIA

In 1976, Norman Kurland, former associate of Louis Kelso and long-time ESOP advocate, set up a combination ESOP, profit-sharing stock bonus plan to enable the employees to acquire the company by the time the founders retired.[16] The Allied plan, as a combination plan, will permit deductible contributions of 25 percent of employee compensation to be made to the ESOP (the usual is 15 percent), plus a profit-sharing stock bonus (rather than cash) of about 10 percent, depending upon profits. Edward Sanders and his wife, as founders, will gradually divest their holdings at capital gain rates.

A portion of the profit sharing is also taken in monthly cash payments. On the fifteenth of every month the full-time employees share 30 percent of the gross profits of the prior month. Kurland maintains that employee-owned companies should pay regular dividends, but that employees should not be involved in management. He perceives union representation on the board of directors as a conflict of interest.

BATES FABRICS, INC.; LEWISTON, MAINE

Founded in 1852, Bates Fabrics was once the titan of the New England textile industry. From five mills and 6,500 employees, it was at one plant and 1,100 employees and going down when the Farmers' Home Administration agreed to a 90 percent guarantee on an $8 million loan.[17] Bates formed an ESOP that enabled the employees, through the trust, to acquire the company from the parent firm, Bates Manufacturing Company. The ESOP trust obtained a twenty-five-year loan from the First National Bank of Boston and owns 100 percent of the shares.

This is an employee acquisition through a leveraged ESOP. The bank holds all 4 million shares as security, but a portion is released each year as Bates, through the ESOP trust, makes its scheduled loan payments. The plan does not affect the regular pension program. The tax benefits of the ESOP may be the key factor in the ability of the company to survive an upgrade of its equipment to remain competitive with plants in the South. Denis Blais, local president of the Amalgamated Clothing and Textile Workers Union of America, assessed the prospect as follows: "I don't look at it as a financial blessing for the employees. I see it as a better chance for the plant to survive."[18]

AMTROL, INC.; WEST WARWICK, RHODE ISLAND

Amtrol is a privately owned manufacturing company of about 600 employees with a European subsidiary. In 1975 an ESOP was adopted, and as of late 1978 the trust held 20 percent of the outstanding stock.[19] During that period stock distributions have been made to thirteen retiring employees, but only seven have exercised the "put" option of requiring the trust to repurchase the distribution at the then market value.

Stock valuation in 1977 was $14.00 per share, up 56 percent since the ESOP was adopted in 1975. Sales in 1977 were $45 million and net earnings were $1.2 million, up 13 percent and 17 percent respectively, from the prior year. Taxable income in 1977 was $2.4 million with taxes of $1.2 million, or nearly 50 percent.

The ESOP contribution of $910,000 for that year reduced both taxes and net earnings by about $455,000. The following statement was submitted to the Senate Finance Committee for its ESOP and GSOP hearings:

There has been a very definite improvement in the morale of the employees. This is evident in conversations in which the word "THEY" is seldom used when referring to management. Most employees now use the word "WE" when discussing AMTROL.

There has been a definite increase in efficiency as shown by the reduction in manufacturing costs to 71.3% from 72.9%.

There has been improvement in attendance as reported by Personnel. The employees want the Company to prosper and realize that they share in the ESOP contributions as a percentage of their gross pay.

The physical appearance of the Plant, while previously good through the efforts of the management, is now just as good and it is maintained this way at less expense because each employee has a sense of ownership.

We have put a lot of time, money and effort into the ESOP at AMTROL, but I'm convinced that it is paying off in improved morale, increased efficiencies and a general feeling that everyone at AMTROL has a "Piece of the Action."[20]

HALLMARK CARDS; KANSAS CITY, MISSOURI

As one of the nation's largest and most profitable family-owned companies, Hallmark has had numerous purchase offers and numerous invitations by investment bankers to go public over the years.[21] In 1975 the Hall family and the employees agreed to an incremental employee acquisition through an ESOP. About $40 million from the profit-sharing plan was rolled over into the trust, and a $8.3 million stock contribution was put in by the company.

The ESOP will make additional annual purchases from the Hall family and other stockholders and receive additional transfers from the profit-sharing plan. Hallmark will make periodic contributions of authorized but unissued stock. Eventually, the ESOP will acquire 65 percent of the stock of the estate of Joyce Hall, founder and chairman, and his wife. An estimated 7,500 of about 10,000 employees participate in the ESOP, which, according to president Donald Hall, will enable "employees to participate in the ownership of the company and to share more directly in its success and good fortune."[22]

JONES & PRESSNELL; CHARLOTTE, NORTH CAROLINA

W. T. Grant Company, the bankrupt department store chain, acquired Jones & Pressnell (J & P) in 1969 from the founding partners. By 1975, Grant stores made up 60 percent of J & P's clients.[23] In 1976, using a leveraged ESOP, the 345 employees of J & P purchased the unit for $4.5 million from the Grant Company trustee. First Union National Bank of Charlotte put up a $3.5 million loan; $50,000 came from the company and $500,000 from an existing profit-sharing plan.

J & P had record sales of $12.8 million in 1974, most of it coming from Grant stores. The task was to find new clients. Thomas Jones, J & P president and one of the founding partners, spent every day on the road for several weeks early in 1976, finding 1,150 stores from ten chains equal to the Grant loss. Operations and salaries also had to be cut back to 1974 levels to make the venture viable.

MOHAWK VALLEY COMMUNITY CORP.; HERKIMER, NEW YORK

On March 30, 1976, Sperry Rand Corporation, after having attempted for several years to sell its Library Bureau Division, announced that the operation would be phased out and closed over the next twelve months since its products did not fit Sperry's high-technology product lines.[24] The closing would have involved 256 employees in the village of Herkimer, which had an unemployment rate of 13.7 percent at the time. A coalition of employees, government agencies, and local businesses developed the acquisition plan with the assistance of Sperry.

Mohawk Valley Community Corp. (MVCC) was formed in May and operated on funds donated by the Herkimer County Area Development Corporation. The asset acquisition was completed in September 1976 for nearly

$6 million. A loan of $2 million from EDA, a loan of $1.2 million from the Oneida National Bank, a loan of $400,000 from the Savings Bank of Utica, a loan of $870,000 from the New Jersey EDA (location of a subsidiary), and a public intrastate offering of notes and common stock of $1.6 million provided the financing for the venture. An ESOP was established in the month of closing, but the loans were obtained by the company. MVCC is a company-financed leveraged ESOP wherein loan amortization payments are offset with deductible stock contributions to the trust that increase working capital.

At the end of the first plan year in September 1977 the first stock contribution of 100,000 shares at $2 per share increased working capital by $200,000.[25] An additional 50,000 shares were contributed for the second fiscal year with a debt service of $63,000 per month, or $756,000 per year.

During the first fiscal year the company debt service, principal and interest, was $464,000.[26] A stock contribution of 100,000 shares at $2 per share was made to the trust in September 1977. A prepaid contribution of 50,000 shares was also made for fiscal 1978. While principal payments reduced working capital by $161,000, the contributions increased it by $300,000 to a total of $455,000. Net sales fell to $11.2 million in 1977 from $12.6 million in 1976, and net income fell to $315,000 from $321,000. However, the net effect of the ESOP contributions would increase 1977 net income by $139,000.

Both community and union support was critical in the success of the venture in financial and political terms. Carl Vogel, president of Local 344 of the International Union of Electrical, Radio, and Machine Workers, raised much of the down payment from fellow employees. The company continues to operate in conventional management style and with no workers on the board—to the frustration of Vogel and other employees.[27] Employee ownership has not meant employee control.

VERMONT ASBESTOS GROUP; EDEN MILLS, VERMONT

In January 1974, GAF Corporation, one of the nation's 250 largest industrial companies, announced its intention to close its Belvidere Mountain Sheets Operation as a tax write-off rather than comply with a final order from the Environmental Protection Agency (EPA) to meet emissions standards by March 1975.[28] The closing would have affected 178 employees directly and an additional 120 employees in related businesses in an area where unemployment is usually about 15 percent.

The employees, 135 of them union members, formed Vermont Asbestos Group (VAG) and raised $100,000 after GAF agreed to sell the assets at a "salvage price" of $400,000. Area banks loaned the new company $2 million, fully guaranteed by the Vermont Economic Development Agency. The EPA-required improvements cost $250,000. Most of the loan money was not used, and all loans were repaid in 1975, the year of the acquisition.

VAG is directly owned (DEOC) rather than an ESOP. As initially formed, it was both employee owned and controlled with the board of directors composed of seven union members, seven managers, and one outsider. As the only operating asbestos mine in the United States and with only limited Canadian competition, VAG has posted a satisfactory financial performance. The union-negotiated wage increase in late 1975 was almost double any increase granted by GAF.

At the 1978 annual stockholders' meeting, the old board was replaced by a slate dominated by local bankers and businessmen and a few employees led by an outsider who had gained control of 13 percent of VAG stock.[29] Company earnings had declined in 1977 as the asbestos market tightened. But more importantly, many of the employee-owners had become frustrated and dissatisfied with their own lack of influence and with the methods and decisions of the original board of directors.

REPUBLIC HOSE MANUFACTURING CORP.; YOUNGSTOWN, OHIO

Aeroquip Corporation of Jackson, Michigan, a subsidiary of Libby Owens Ford of Toledo, closed its rubber hose plant in Youngstown in 1978.[30] At that time the plant had 338 employees, down from 4,100 in 1971. Frank Ciarniello, a foreman, approached Aeroquip about an employee acquisition. The company resisted, but Ciarniello, Local 102 of the United Rubber Workers, and C. O. Broadwater, a former operations manager and now president of Republic Hose, were not to be denied.

Broadwater and five other former Aeroquip executives put up $100,000 as the initial working capital. City officials assisted to obtain federal guarantees for local bank loans used to finance the purchase. Union members agreed to wage reductions to $5 an hour and to reduced trade jurisdictional restrictions. A profit-sharing plan replaced the pension plan, and supplemental unemployment benefits were eliminated. The company began operating in April 1979 and began turning monthly profits by September.

Under Aeroquip the plant had 29 supervisors, foremen, and quality control inspectors. Now it has one foreman and two planners. Workers determine how to arrange equipment and design assembly lines, some of which had to be built from scrap. With 132 workers back on the job in November 1979, production was up 40 percent, and the rejection rate had been reduced to 1 percent from 8 percent.

Stock is held directly by employees rather than by an ESOP and can be resold only to the company. Ciarniello turned down an offer to move to management and chose to continue as president of Local 102. As such, he is the worker representative on the board of directors.

JUICE BOWL PRODUCTS, INC.; LAKELAND, FLORIDA

In 1973, Juice Bowl had $5 million in sales and two customers: H. J. Heinz and Libby. That same year it instituted an ESOP and introduced its own label. As of 1978, it had $22 million in sales and over 1,800 customers. The trust held 22 percent of the company stock, which was voted by a board-appointed committee with an employee representative. Juice Bowl's president, John P. Grady, gave this testimony at a U.S. Senate hearing on ESOPs:

In a competitive business such as ours, it is people more than financing, more than processing techniques, or more than uniqueness of product that makes for the difference in success or failure. You really have nothing secret when you produce orange juice. There are hundreds of companies doing it.

Here I sat with a growing company, the equity increasing, and becoming wealthy for the first time in my life, and yet here were a group of people who were contributing to that, and how do you share it with them?

How do you recognize the contribution of a shipping clerk who never considers his day done, who takes the same pride at a satisfied customer as the owner does and who worries just as much about a dissatisfied customer?

How do you reward an employee who comes in early to fix a machine that would have cost 50 percent in daily production if he had reported at the regular time?

What about all of the employees who have done things over and beyond the narrow definition of their job? The owner cannot, as a practical matter, pay them more money than his competition pays or his costs and prices will be out of line. You can thank them, but that becomes pretty hollow after awhile, as the company becomes more and more successful and the employee's reward is limited to his paycheck and perhaps a modest pension program.

Stock bonuses can be given, but the employee would pay taxes on them out of his current income and he would get no dividends on a stock which pays no dividends, and he would have no market for it.

We thought initially we had solved the problem at Juice Bowl with a profit-sharing trust, but it did not really work out. There was no direct connection between the company growth and the employee's interest in the trust. Also, the investment of the trust assets was a problem.

What happened to the money was dependent upon outside factors and the employees themselves had no influence on it. . . .

Besides ownership itself, the value of the shares that they have acquired have appreciated considerably since the initial transaction. Trust assets have increased from $150,000 to over $1 million at this point: 75 percent of the assets of our trust are invested in company stock and the balance is in cash and other equity. The stock is reappraised annually and the growth of the employees' balances have amounted, between company contribution and appreciation, to over 23 percent of their total earnings each year.

We do not have a formal retirement plan at Juice Bowl. However, the projections indicate that ESOP's will end up doing a much superior job for our people.

At the present time, the average balance for the 100 employees that are in this plan from the beginning—and these people whose earnings have probably never exceeded $15,000—have $35,000 and $36,000 in their balances.

The opportunity to develop team effort through ESOP appears to me to be endless. There is no employee who is not in a position to make the company better if he is really motivated to do so. There is no one, from the bottom up, who cannot improve his contribution if he is constantly on the lookout for opportunities.

The key is to unleash the extra thought and extra effort that is hidden away in every employee. We think ESOP does this.

The areas of cost, quality control, cost reduction, customer service, and in all of the places where it takes effort on the part of everybody to get the job done, we see tangible progress.

When a careless forklift truck driver spoils $15 worth of product, everyone who witnesses it knows that they too, share in the loss.

Downtime on a high-speed production line is no longer a chance for an extra break. Instead, it is lost earnings which affect everyone's investment.

Recently we had a campaign to elicit cost savings ideas and received over 200 sound suggestions. There were no prizes offered; only the recognition of a good idea.

We feel that most of our people are genuinely interested in their company and in its progress, and that kind of an attitude is good for them, good for our customers, and good for our stockholders.

Perhaps the biggest weakness in the ESOP program as it currently exists, and one to which the current bill addresses itself, is that the material rewards are too far in the future for younger employees, particularly, to become excited about them. We have thought and experimented with quarterly bonuses which would somehow be tied to the shares of stock held by the trust in order to give our employees the feeling of benefits of ownership right now. Our tax accountants have discouraged this for fear that the IRS would treat such payments as dividends.[31]

HARCO CORP.; MEDINA, OHIO

When the owner and president of Harco sought to sell out and retire in 1971, a group of twenty employees attempted to buy the company, but came up short.[32] A financial "angel" stepped in and purchased 45 percent of the stock. Later, the angel wished to liquidate his interest, and in 1976 an ESOP was formed as the new angel. The ESOP trust is administered by three employees and two officers who also vote the 45 percent interest held by the trust. As the remaining twenty individual employee-owners retire, the ESOP will also acquire their shares. Harco is now 100 percent employee owned with 100 percent (full-time) employee participation in the ESOP. Eventually it will also be 100 percent ESOP owned.

Unlike some other ESOPs and DEOCs, Harco had no prior financial difficulty. The present chairman, W. Joseph McDade, did observe substantial growth after the first employee stock purchase in 1971. Sales increased from $5 million in that year to about $25 million in 1978. The company produces and installs corrosion protection systems, mainly for natural gas and oil pipelines. Harco now has 450 employees and 18 offices, including a major office in Houston and a recent opening in Saudi Arabia.

VALLEY NITROGEN PRODUCERS, INC.; HELM, CALIFORNIA

In 1957 a number of farmers from the San Joaquin Valley, led by a small independent fertilizer distributor, Carl Hoas, approached Louis Kelso concerning a double squeeze being put on them by the government and the major nitrogenous fertilizer producers.[33] Under the government's cotton allotment program the number of acres eligible for support allotments was being reduced each year. Thus, the only way to increase output was to use progressively more nitrogenous fertilizers each year. The basic ingredient for the manufacture of such fertilizers was anhydrous ammonia, which the major petrochemical producers sold at about $250 per ton. The price was both prohibitive and unreasonable to the farmers who sought to build and operate their own plant as a cooperative.

Kelso set up a cooperative consumer stock ownership plan (CSOP) in which the consumer-owners executed stock subscription agreements and product requirement contracts. The agreements were used as security for the loans needed to finance the new plants. All corporate net income was paid out as dividends, which were applied to the stock purchase and which were tax deductible by the company as a patronage dividend. So long as dividends were applied to the stock purchase, neither the company nor the consumer-owners incurred tax liabilities.

As the new plants came on line, the "majors" dropped their prices of anhydrous ammonia from $250 to $66 per ton. About 9,000 farmers have become consumer-owners of a company that in 1978 had sales of $139 million and 878 employees. Kelso estimated that Valley Nitrogen saved California farmers over $1 billion in fertilizer costs over a fifteen-year period.[34]

TAX CREDIT EMPLOYEE STOCK OWNERSHIP COMPANIES

A 1978 survey of 493 companies in the *Fortune* 1,000 revealed that nearly 29 percent had TCESOPs in operation or were developing the same.[35] Such plans are most popular with companies in capital-intensive industries: utilities, 84 percent; oil and coal companies, 77 percent; paper and fiber companies, 63 percent.

These companies include Dow Chemical Company, General Motors Corporation, AT&T, Mobil Oil Company, and Atlantic Richfield Company. Generally the amount allocated to the account of an employee is small since the basic TCESOP credit of 1 percent (1.5 percent if an employee-matched plan) of qualified investment must be distributed among a large number of employees.

NOTES

1. Charles Burck, "There's More to ESOP than Meets the Eye," *Fortune*, March 1976, p. 171.

2. Ibid., p. 170.

3. Ibid., p. 171.

4. Lee Smith, "When Workers are Bosses," *Dun's Review*, June 1977, p. 84.

5. Ibid.

6. Ibid., p. 88.

7. "Employment: The Joy of Work," *Newsweek*, January 12, 1976, p. 61.

8. Ibid.

9. David Clutterbuck, "Employee Takeover Saves Doomed Paper Mill," *International Management*, July 1977, p. 39.

10. Ibid.

11. David Pauly and Frank Maier, "Railroads: Rags to Riches," and "Making Railroaders Rich," *Newsweek*, January 2, 1978, p. 50, and November 17, 1980, p. 80.

12. Committee on Finance, U.S. Senate, *Employee Stock Ownership Plans and General Stock Ownership Trusts, Hearings* (Washington, D.C.: U.S. Government Printing Office, 1978), pp. 93-99 (emphasis added).

13. Survey Research Center, University of Michigan, *Employee Ownership* (Washington: The Economic Development Administration, U.S. Department of Commerce, 1978), p. 63. (Unpublished report).

14. "When Workers Strike the Company They Own," *Business Week*, September 22, 1980, p. 39.

15. Committee on Banking, Housing and Urban Affairs, U.S. Senate, *Chrysler*

Corporation Loan Guarantee Act, Hearings (Washington, D.C.: U.S. Government Printing Office, 1979), pp. 1104-10.

16. "Employees Taking Over Allied Plywood Through ESOP," *Washington Post*, November 27, 1977, p. L1.

17. "Federal Loan Guarantee Helps Employees to Buy Bates Fabrics' Last Mill," *Washington Post*, October 16, 1977, p. L10.

18. Ibid.

19. Committee on Finance, *ESOPs and GSOTs*, pp. 504-19.

20. Ibid., p. 506.

21. "Hallmark to Share Stock Ownership with Workers," *Kansas City Star*, March 12, 1975, p. 1A.

22. Ibid.

23. "Jones & Presnell, A Grant Unit, Survives Via Leveraged Employee Ownership Plan," *Wall Street Journal*, July 22, 1976, p. 6.

24. This section is taken from the Mohawk Valley offering prospectus and various other documents reproduced in Select Committee on Small Business, U.S. Senate, *The Small Business Employee Ownership Act, Hearings* (Washington, D.C.: U.S. Government Printing Office, 1979), pp. 290-348.

25. Ibid., p. 337.

26. Ibid., p. 339.

27. Daniel Zwerdling, *Democracy at Work* (Washington, D.C.: Association for Self Management, 1978), pp. 75-77.

28. Richard Cluster, "Workers Become Owners," *Mother Jones*, April 1976, p. 42.

29. Richard Cluster, "Asbestos Mine Gets New Management," *Dollars and Sense*, May-June 1978, p. 6.

30. "Rebirth: Youngstown Workers Rescue Plant, Turn a Profit," *Akron Beacon Journal*, November 18, 1979, p. A1.

31. Committee on Finance, *ESOPs and GSOTs*, pp. 112-15.

32. "ESOP No Fable; Workers Own Firms," *Cleveland Plain Dealer*, October 28, 1979, p. F1.

33. Statement submitted by Louis Kelso to Committee on Finance, U.S. Senate, *Employee Stock Ownership Plans for Railroads, Hearings* (Washington, D.C.: U.S. Government Printing Office, 1979), pp. 105-7.

34. Ibid., p. 107.

35. Committee on Finance, *ESOPs and GSOTs*, statement of Jeffrey Gates of Hewitt Associates, p. 135.

8

Labor Union Positions

National and international unions have tended to avoid taking official and public positions on ESOPs. Frequently, however, union policy is revealed through informal statements, in internal memoranda, or on a case-by-case basis. Such positions, when taken, are usually nonsupportive, if not negative, and tend to be directed toward ESOPs but not DEOCs. As of this writing, only the United Auto Workers (UAW) has made a significant effort to analyze the ESOP concept and the legislation and to develop a written policy with respect to the same. Without significant union initiatives and support, widespread ESOP success is not likely, as the case studies of the preceding chapter seem to infer.

THE UNITED AUTOMOBILE WORKERS

The UAW has published two written documents concerning ESOPs. The first was an interoffice communication issued in November 1975, from the then president, Leonard Woodcock, to the international staff in the United States; and the second is a more lengthy report published by the UAW Social Security Department in March 1977. The 1975 statement cited numerous areas of concern, including the following:

1. The employers' unilateral control in most cases in establishing, administering, and terminating ESOPs.

2. The lack of sufficient company financial data for the union to determine intelligently the proper contribution to the ESOP, the eligibility and allocations for participants, and the final benefit entitlements.
3. The possible loss of benefits if company stock is overvalued or if the price of the stock falls or if vesting is delayed.
4. The preferability of a guaranteed pension plan or other definite and concrete benefits for which an ESOP may be used as a substitute.
5. Restrictions on the right of employees to vote shares of stock allocated to them under an ESOP.
6. The possible raiding of the trust by management insiders who wish to cash out.
7. The possible anti-union effect of unilateral management determination of allocations to employees, especially in multiplant companies, which could be an unfair labor practice under the National Labor Relations Act (NLRA).
8. The fact that ESOPs are conditions of employment, must be the subject of negotiations with the union (including both local and international representatives), and fall within the purview of the NLRA.

The second publication identifies three basic types of ESOPs: the Kelso ESOP (a leveraged ESOP, trust financed); the buy-out ESOP (an ESOP used to liquidate the holdings of a controlling stockholder); and the TRASOP (now TCESOP). This booklet outlines the operation of the first two basic types, the tax and other benefits to the company and controlling stockholders, a summary of ERISA requirements, and the advantages and disadvantages to employees. The union's interest is stated as follows:

Of primary importance to the Union is the right to bargain over ESOP's. Under the terms of the National Labor Relations Act and various NLRB rulings which have followed its enactment, the establishment or amendment of an ESOP is a mandatory subject of bargaining. In addition, most UAW contracts contain a "zipper clause" stating that the contract covers all agreements between the parties. It is a violation of a "zipper clause" for the employer to unilaterally reopen the contract. Thus, it must be emphasized to the employer involved that any ESOP provisions which would affect bargaining unit members must be the subject of negotiations with the Union (including Local and International Representatives). If the contract would not otherwise be open for bargaining, the Union has the right to refuse to enter into such negotiations. Also, the discussion of ESOP's may be tied to the discussion of other interests of the workers.

Prior to the enactment of ERISA, a union could refuse to permit its members to be covered by a pension plan. The union's action effectively prohibited the employer from adopting a pension plan, qualified by the IRS for tax purposes, because the plan failed to cover a fair cross section of all employees. Under ERISA the union's refusal to permit its members to be covered under a pension plan will not prevent a company from adopting a retirement plan, provided that there is evidence that retirement benefits were the subject of good-faith bargaining. Although ESOP's are not pension plans, there is evidence that the same principle applies to them. Therefore, any indication of non-bargaining unit ESOP activity should be carefully investigated.

The union's refusal to join in an ESOP with non-union employees may limit the utility of an ESOP to the employer. The reason is that employer contributions are limited in most cases to 15% of covered payroll. By taking the union group's payroll out of the total payroll for ESOP purposes, the maximum contribution the employer can make is lowered. As a result, the maximum permissible contribution may be too low to make the ESOP worthwhile to the employer.

In certain circumstances an ESOP may be a valuable benefit to our membership. But the terms of the plan should be as carefully bargained as the terms of any other negotiated benefit.

The right to bargain gives the union an important voice in the determination of the terms of the ESOP. Unlike pension plans, ESOP's are not covered by many of the important protections of ERISA. In fact, ERISA leaves these plans in virtually the same status enjoyed prior to its enactment. Another section of this booklet will describe in detail the areas of ERISA under which ESOP's are exempt.

As a result, the company's lawyers have a considerable amount of latitude in the drafting of ESOP provisions. This latitude can result in unregulated abuses. The number and types of abuses will undoubtedly increase as the number of ESOP's adopted grows. It is the union's task to mold the plans in such a way that potential abuses can be avoided and the maximum benefit can be obtained for our membership.[1]

A number of practical technical and administrative problems are cited by the report. Several of these, including voting rights, were treated as per the UAW recommendation by IRC Section 409A, added by the Revenue Act of 1978. The report listed the following as problem areas:

As was pointed out earlier, the body of regulations governing ESOP's is relatively loose. Thus, it is possible to mold the plan in directions that increase our membership's security. The following subjects have been developed with our experience on ESOP's and should give you an idea as to how the plan should be set up through the negotiation process.

Voting Rights—Regulations have been recently proposed governing ESOP's which are set up to take advantage of the lending feature (Kelso ESOP's) and those set up to take advantage of special tax credits in the 1975 and 1976 Tax Reduction Acts (these are commonly called TRASOP's—for Tax Reduction Act Stock Ownership Plans). These proposed regulations governing Kelso ESOP's and TRASOP's state that the voting rights in the stock must pass through to the participants. Employees must be allowed to vote their shares (including fractional shares) by notifying a fiduciary of the plan—presumably one of the members of the board governing the ESOP—how they want their shares voted.

These regulations do not affect Buy-Out ESOP's. It is possible for a Buy-Out ESOP to be established and non-voting stock be transferred to the participants. Another alternative is to give the employees voting stock but set up a committee composed of management appointed employees who will vote the ESOP stock in a block.

In a case like this the union should demand first, that the stock be voting stock and second, that the voting rights pass through to the individual participants. If this is impossible, the committee that votes the stock should have union representation; preferably the joint board arrangement familiar to our pension plans, with equal company and union representation and an impartial tie breaker.

Investments—Although an ESOP is set up primarily to invest in the stock of the company, it's possible that the ESOT would hold some cash that is not tied up in company stock. The amount of cash that can be held must generally be less than 25% of the assets in the ESOT. The investment of this loose cash should be only in the safest form of short term investments like U.S. Treasury bonds or notes. ESOP proposals have been presented to the UAW with such wide open investments as oil and natural gas leases and speculative real estate. Loose language of this type should be removed.

Dividends—As was previously stated, the company stock may or may not pay dividends. But any dividends that are paid should accrue directly to or be retained for the participants—not reduce company contributions. Again for Kelso ESOP's and TRASOP's the proposed IRS Regulations would include this requirement, but not for Buy-Out ESOP's.

Insurance—It is possible to purchase so-called key-man insurance through an ESOP. The insurance policy is bought for a high paid employee who has many shares of company stock in his account. In the event of his death the policy proceeds are payable to the ESOT to provide enough cash to buy back the stock from the deceased employee's estate. The premiums for the insurance are typically taken on a pro-rata basis from each employee's account held in the ESOT.

The trouble with this arrangement is that employees who leave before the key-man's death get no benefit of the insurance they have paid for. It should be the union's position that insurance premiums should be paid by the company on top of the regular contributions it must make.

Compensation—Stock is usually allocated to the employees' account on the basis of compensation. High paid employees automatically get a bigger piece of the action under this arrangement. Steps can be taken to keep their share from being any larger than it already is. For example, bonuses, commissions or other special forms of compensation can be excluded from the compensation base. At the same time, overtime, shift differential, vacation, holidays and other compensated hours that mainly benefit union members should be included in the compensation base.

There is no reason why stock must be allocated to the employees' accounts on the basis of compensation only. A "point system" could be devised that takes into account both compensation and credited service. In such a system each year of credited service and each dollar of compensation would be worth a certain number of points. Stock would then be allocated on the basis of the total number of points an employee has to his credit. In general, the point system just described allocates more stock to an average worker's account than would a system based on compensation alone.

Contributions—There should be no employee contributions required. Employer contributions should be spelled out as specifically as possible in the ESOP itself. Many ESOP's simply state that the company "shall make contributions to the Trust in such amounts as may be determined by its Board of Directors." Language to this effect is totally unacceptable.

If a Kelso ESOP is established, the term of the loan, the interest rate, the time of payments and the disposition of the stock held as collateral that is released upon payment should all be spelled out in the document.

If a Buy-Out ESOP is established, the number of years in which the Buy-Out will be completed should be set out in the ESOP as well as the amount of the contribution to effect the Buy-Out.

Gains and Losses—For one reason or another, investment losses may occur. A common practice is to allocate these losses over all employees' accounts in proportion to the size of their accounts. This method automatically puts the greatest burden on the older employee who has possibly accumulated a sizeable account over his working lifetime. Losses should be allocated on the basis of compensation—just as contributions are allocated.

Of course, gains can also occur. The method described above for losses will have the opposite effect for gains—short service high paid employees would get the lion's share of the gains. Thus, gains should be allocated to the employees' accounts in proportion to the size of the account.

Termination of employment—It is common to find in ESOP's a vesting schedule that is graded to allow, say, 20% vesting in one year, 40% vesting after two years, etc. This raises the possibility that employees could terminate with less than 100% interest in their account. If they later return to work they must be allowed to buy back into the ESOP. Plans with a provision of this type should allow for the reinstatement of the non-vested portion of the account whether or not the employee buys back into the ESOP.

Administrative Committee—Union representation on this committee is a must. It should be set up along the lines of our typical joint pension committee. Moreover, as was stated in the section on voting of stock, if the plan is a Buy-Out ESOP, and the committee votes the stock, it is important for union members to have at least equal representation on this committee.

The union members of the committee should have access to basic financial data governing the plan's operations like: appraisal reports, trustee statements, company contribution records, stock allocation proceedings, company financial records, etc.

Financial information—In order for the union to be able to make an intelligent decision on an ESOP proposal it must examine the financial statements of the company. This is the only way the workers can get a feel for the financial health and future profitability of the company they are being asked to be stockholders of.[2]

The report concludes with a brief policy statement:

UAW Policy

The following guidelines are to apply in connection with any employer proposal regarding an ESOP:

1. Any such program can apply to bargaining unit workers *only after negotiations* with the Union. This is true whether the employer raises the subject during regular collective bargaining or as a special item while a contract is in effect.
2. If the subject is raised while a contract is in effect, the Union may but does not have to enter into such negotiations. Decisions regarding that, as well as whether the employer should be reminded (before he makes any announcement) of the bargaining requirement, should be determined on the basis of local circumstances.
3. The burden of proof should be on the employer to demonstrate that the ESOP will benefit the workers. While there are situations in which such programs may be satisfactory, the Union must carefully evaluate all aspects of the program—*and of alternative compensation arrangements that might be negotiated in place of the ESOP*—in arriving at a decision regarding the proposal.
4. Before any final agreement is reached to accept an ESOP proposal, *detailed* plan provisions are to be referred to the UAW Social Security Department for analysis. It is probable that the Social Security Department may require additional data about the unit, as well as financial and other company data so that the Research Department can examine the possible future results of the program. Thus, the request for review must be made in advance of bargaining deadlines, in order to provide sufficient time for analysis.

It is emphasized that the UAW does *not* have any policy opposing ESOP's. However, there is considerable reason to be concerned about the manner in which bargaining unit members will be affected by such plans. Each proposal must be analyzed on its own merits and reviewed with your Regional Office or National Servicing Department. If it appears that such a program could be beneficial to the workers, detailed plan provisions and other data should be referred to the UAW Social Security Department for analysis before any final agreement is reached.[3]

The UAW did negotiate a companywide TCESOP with General Motors in 1979 (see chapter 7). Of substantially greater significance is the mandated ESOP for Chrysler Corporation as part of its Loan Guarantee Act of 1979. UAW president Douglas Fraser will become a member of the board, and the employees will own 25 percent of the company through the ESOP (see chapter 5).

THE INTERNATIONAL ASSOCIATION OF MACHINISTS (IAM)

The IAM has gone on record in opposition to ESOPs even though members of locals participate in several of the same, including a DEOC at HPM Corporation in Mount Gilead, Ohio. In a policy memorandum issued in July 1976 to its U.S. lodge and business representatives, IAM president Floyd Smith stated that "Kelsoism is a fraud and a hoax." The memorandum continues as follows:

Rather than a prescription for, "people's capitalism," Kelsoism is a formula for ripping off the working people. Corporations that are growing and profitable (a condition essential to the success of ESOP's) do not need to peddle stock to their own employees. Bankers, insurance companies and mutual funds snap up all that's available.

ESOP's are really a method of shifting the losses of corporate turkeys like Penn-Central from the financial community to the working people. Moreover, as BAR-RON'S Magazine (a business publication) stated not long ago, "the financial games corporations play with employee stock ownership plans can be ingenious and far-reaching." A corporation could, for example, use an employee trust in combination with the loss carry back provisions of the tax laws to become eligible for a refund of all taxes paid the three prior years.

Union members should recognize that employee profit-sharing and stock ownership schemes are not new. They were popular in the boom years of the 1920's. They were considered a fine way to keep unions out and to get workers to accept lower wages in return for a theoretical share of future profits. When the Great Depression hit in 1930, millions of workers were left holding worthless stock.

What is new is that the U.S. Government is now aiding and abetting a massive deception of the work force through tax loopholes that actively encourage companies to finance themselves with worker earnings and savings.

If workers want to buy stock in any corporation as individuals, they should. But the move to substitute ESOP's for a broadly-based pension plan should be resisted.

IAM members are advised to view employee stock ownership plans (ESOP's) with extreme skepticism and IAM representatives are warned to resist employer attempts to foist them upon our members.[4]

THE AMERICAN FEDERATION OF LABOR AND CONGRESS OF INDUSTRIAL ORGANIZATIONS (AFL-CIO)

An internal memorandum of the AFL-CIO issued in October 1976 to member international presidents and research directors warned of the "many potential pitfalls for workers of such plans'' and suggested that ESOPs be considered only in a collective bargaining context without sacrificing wages, pensions, and other benefits. While official opposition has not been a significant policy matter, ESOPs are considered suspect as part of the "tax give-away" to business method of stimulating the economy and "high risk" profit sharing for workers. The memorandum included the following:

The AFL-CIO has not taken any official position for or against such plans. The plans themselves as well as the circumstances under which they would be used vary so substantially that it is difficult to give them a blanket condemnation or endorsement.

We do feel however, that there are many potential pitfalls for workers in such plans.

We suggest first of all, that such programs be considered only within the context of the collective bargaining agreement. Such programs are typically initiated by the employer and frequently offered as a means to get something for nothing. We do not feel this is true and such a program should be evaluated critically and viewed as part of the compensation package. It should not be used to divert attention from needed improvements in wages and other benefits—particularly pensions.

These plans represent a relatively risky form of deferred compensation. Their value to the employee is keyed essentially to the market value of the employer's stock and trusts set up under such plans have few of the protections, safeguards, fiduciary standards and so forth that are found in other types of deferred wage programs. Moreover, since the fund's investment portfolio can be totally in the stock of the employer if the company should fail the worker stands to lose his job *and* his equity in the trust.

Secondly, such plans are particularly advantageous to smaller, closely held corporations with limited means to raise capital. Thus in such circumstances adoption of an ESOP can amount to workers being asked to accept a risk that financial institutions, or others with risk capital to invest are unwilling to bear. Again this does not necessarily mean that it will be against the workers' interest but it indicates a need for caution, skepticism, and critical evaluation.

Staff members of the AFL-CIO have been watching developments in these plans rather closely. If you would like further information, please contact the AFL-CIO Research Department. Also, if your union or its local affiliates has any experience with these plans or have knowledge of situations in which these plans have been proposed or negotiated, we would appreciate hearing from you.[5]

THE INTERNATIONAL BROTHERHOOD OF TEAMSTERS

In Philadelphia a teamster local successfully opposed the adoption of an ESOP at a trucking company while another local supported one adopted by Parr, Inc., in Cleveland. The national office, however, has indicated that it does not have extensive knowledge of ESOPs nor has a position been formulated on the matter.[6]

THE INTERNATIONAL STEEL WORKERS (ISW OR USWA)

While no formal policy has been promulgated, the ISW has not considered an ESOP an appropriate mechanism for labor outside the South Bend Lathe (SBL) setting (see chapter 7).[7] In the SBL case an ESOP was necessary to keep the company in operation and maintain employment. ESOP benefits are generally considered lower than additional wage and pension benefits. A further objection is that an ESOP trust is nearly always company controlled.

Concerning SBL, the ISW has filed suit against both SBL and its former parent company, Amsted Industries, to recover pension benefits lost by SBL employees as a result of the ESOP acquisition. Both the president, John Deak, and the vice-president, Gerald Vogel, of Local 1722 of the ISW played significant roles in the changeover and in subsequent operations. Mr. Vogel expressed his sentiments to Senator Russell Long by stating,

However, I feel it is important to convey my feelings and the feelings of the members of Local 1722 and the employees of South Bend Lathe.

ESOP has not only saved five hundred jobs at South Bend, but it has given us a chance to control our economic future. We feel that ESOP can be good for all American workers. Therefore, we lend our support of Bill S-3241.

Remember, Senator, "A worker who has job security is a worker that's happy, and a happier worker is a more productive worker."[8]

During the Senate Finance Committee hearings on the bill cited in the above statement, SBL's president, Richard Boulis, and Mr. Vogel gave the following responses to a question concerning the general lack of union support for ESOPs:

Mr. BOULIS. The only thing I know is when there are enough employee stock-ownership plans in existence and the employees still see fit to belong to the unions, the big unions are going to have to get with it to maintain their place. It is a very difficult question to answer, because, obviously, I have had it said to me that employee stock-ownership is aimed at getting rid of unions. Believe me, that was not the case in South Bend Lathe.

In fact, before we bought the company, we sent the Steelworkers a contract and said, please sign it. Our bankers wanted to make sure we had a stable workforce. Our bankers wanted to make sure we had a union contract.

But they chose not to. We bought the company anyway.

I am afraid I cannot answer that.

Mr. VOGEL. As I said, it has been around for many, many years, but to us it is a brand new concept and I think that maybe the big unions are a little reluctant to get involved in it because it is so new. Therefore, I think the education of it is very important at this time.[9]

Eventually, however, the interests of SBL President Boulis and ISW Local 1722 diverged significantly on cost-of-living adjustments, employee stock allocation, voting rights, and increased employee representation on the board of directors. On August 25, 1980, some 290 members of Local 1722 struck SBL for nine weeks. The local president, John Deak, proclaimed that employees were promised a "piece of the action," but what actually developed was a misunderstanding over implementation of the ESOP.[10] Norman Kurland, the Washington consultant who packaged the SBL ESOP, concluded that the ISW should have been involved in designing and implementing the ESOP.[11]

ISW local representatives were also involved in discussions with Lykes Corporation and its subsidiary, Youngstown Sheet and Tube, in efforts to utilize an ESOP to purchase and reopen the Campbell Works of the subsidiary in Youngstown (see chapter 6). Negotiations extended from late 1977 through much of 1978, but without success. However, representatives from the international did participate in the effort. The experience indicates that the ISW tends to support ESOP efforts if they are essential to preserving union jobs, when there is joint labor-management administration of the ESOP trust, and when government money is available for the purchase.

THE UNITED MINE WORKERS OF AMERICA (UMW)

The UMW was one of the first unions to be involved in negotiations for an industrywide ESOP. During 1974, Norman Kurland, of Kurland and Associates of Washington, was instrumental in initiating and promoting such an ESOP concept with the UMW and the Bituminous Coal Operators Association. The plan was to incorporate the ESOP into the upcoming industrywide collective bargaining contract. The plan failed when the UMW lost interest in the project.[12]

THE NATIONAL MARITIME UNION OF AMERICA (NMU)

In 1972, legislation was introduced in Congress to permit the sale of U.S. flag passenger vessels to foreign buyers. The NMU opposed the sale and offered to make concessions that would have reduced crew sizes and labor costs. The

NMU president, Shannon Wall, together with Norman Kurland, then principal of Kelso-Bangert & Co., and Senator Russell Long, attempted to establish a giant ESOP to salvage the industry. The plan did not materialize, but in the process the NMU developed a favorable posture on ESOPs.

The NMU position has recently been expressed by President Wall in a written communication:

1. While the NMU has no written policy regarding ESOP's, we did testify before a Senate Committee on H.R. 11789 on February 28, 1972, that we felt that the ESOP technique might be an appropriate vehicle for the revitalization of the U.S. passenger fleet. At that time we stated that "employee participation in ownership of capital equipment and profit sharing would be a new approach for our Union and we are not yet committed to it, but we want the possibilities explored. If this makes the difference in the readiness of investors to invest and of the government to support U.S. passenger operations, we want to know it."

2. The NMU informal position is to utilize the ESOP as a means of capital formation. We have pursued the introduction of ESOP's in certain special circumstances such as passenger ship operations and the coastwise trade as a quid pro quo for contractual modifications.

3. The NMU contract with Rich-Seapack in Brunswick, Georgia, contains an ESOP.[13]

THE INTERNATIONAL COMMUNICATIONS WORKERS UNION (ICW)

ICW President Glenn Watts has recently expressed support for a modified version of the West German system of union consolidation and of joint labor, business, and government negotiation on wages and prices.[14] This policy emphasizes cooperation rather than confrontation among the three entities, but he is opposed to codetermination as practiced in Germany. The ICW concept of cooperation would maintain the basic line of cleavage between business and labor since, as Mr. Watts sees it, "there is a conflict of interest in workers sitting on boards of companies they are negotiating with."[15] Mr. Watts proposed the following alternative:

Employers could create a special class of stock that an employee would earn as pension credits. The stock would pay dividends, which would pile up in the employee's account, and if the company did well the value of the stock would presumably rise over the years.

When the employee retired, he wouldn't get the stock itself, but the total value of the shares and the accumulated dividends. This would be the basis for a retirement annuity, and presumably would have at least kept up with the rate of inflation over the years....

The worker would have a retirement fund that presumably kept up with the inflation rate and the company would not have to fund an indexed retirement plan. In addition, it helps accumulate badly needed capital for investment. It also broadens the base of ownership, which is a very healthy thing for society. I want our capitalist system to survive and the best way to do it is to create more capitalists. The plan also helps fight inflation, because it has no immediate impact on costs. . . .

I think that a lot of the younger labor leaders are changing their minds about this. They're so opposed to codetermination—as I am—that they lose sight of the fact that you can give employees a stake in the success of the company they work for without giving them a voice on the board. . . .

Remember, after a worker retires, he wouldn't keep the stock. Besides, one approach might be to create a special issue of nonvoting stock for this plan. I haven't made up my mind on that yet. And I'm willing to listen to any ideas anyone might have on it.

The fact is that most of our big companies have so much stock outstanding, that it would take decades for the workers to accumulate enough to have a big say—even if we gave them voting stock. . . .[16]

Mr. Watt's proposal constitutes a limited ESOP or special stock bonus plan that serves as a retirement plan. Employee participants would have no voting power over the stock, no immediate monetary gain, and no actual share ownership. Since stock would continue to accumulate in the fund, control over the same would be a critical issue. The lack of diversity and the risk of depreciation of fund holdings remain as with conventional ESOPs. These problems could be reduced through the use of multicompany funds or insurance coverage to protect employees against the risk of loss of the liquidated value of their fund allocations.

THE UNITED RUBBER WORKERS OF AMERICA (URW)

The URW, like the UAW and the ISW, has faced numerous plant closings in the northern industrial states. The URW national office is located in Akron, Ohio, long known as the rubber capital of the United States. While the UAW has no formal written policy on ESOPs, its members participate in several, including one in which the URW assisted in obtaining the financing. A recent letter has stated the URW position as follows:

1. The URW does not have a written policy statement respecting ESOP's.
2. URW's informal position is that ESOP's provide an alternative in some cases to plant closure. We prefer to see a more traditional arrangement regarding ownership; however, we understand the desirability of ESOP's in certain cases. Generally, we are skeptical that the worker benefits very much more than under traditional ownership

since in many instances, management continues to manage and since benefits are often apportioned on basis of salary and service, management is the major beneficiary of such arrangements.

3. We have three URW Locals currently participating in an ESOP at Okonite Company, based in Ramsey, New Jersey. The union played a part in obtaining the necessary financing along with the Industrial Union Department of the AFL-CIO. The Republic Hose Manufacturing Corporation, Youngstown, Ohio is another example of the URW's participation in an ESOP....

4. The URW has not formulated at this time a position regarding specific rules or requirements relating to ESOP implementation and use.[17]

NOTES

1. UAW Social Security Department, *Employee Stock Ownership Plans (ESOP)*, March 1977, pp. 8-9.

2. Ibid., pp. 17-19.

3. Ibid., pp. 20-21.

4. Memorandum 6—Policy, July 6, 1976, from Floyd E. Smith, International President, International Association of Machinists and Aerospace Workers, Washington, D.C., to all Grand Lodge Representatives, Grand Lodge Auditors, Special Representatives, Business Representatives, and Railroad and Airline General Chairmen in the United States. See also George Weimer, "Employee Ownership Takes on a New Approach," *Iron Age*, January 17, 1977, p. 23; and "The Quiet Debate on Co-Determination," *Iron Age*, November 29, 1976, p. 17.

5. Memorandum, October 22, 1976, from Research Department, American Federation of Labor and Congress of Industrial Organizations, Washington, D.C., to International Union Presidents and Research Directors concerning Employee Stock Ownership (ESOP).

6. From communication with Teamster International Research Director Norman Weintraub in 1976 and 1980.

7. From communication with ISW Legal Director Bernard Kleiman in 1976 and 1980.

8. Committee on Finance, U.S. Senate, *Employee Stock Ownership Plans and General Stock Ownership Trusts, Hearings* (Washington, D.C.: U.S. Government Printing Office, 1978), p. 477.

9. Ibid., p. 98.

10. "When Workers Strike the Company They Own," *Business Week*, September 22, 1980, p. 39.

11. Ibid., p. 40.

12. From communications among Kurland, the UMW, and the BCOA in 1974.

13. From communication with NMU President Shannon Wall in 1980.

14. Gerald Rosen, "Breaking the Wage-Price Spiral," *Dun's Review*, November

1979, pp. 74-81. Reprinted with the special permission of *Dun's Review*, November 1979, Copyright 1979, Dun & Bradstreet Publications Corporation.

15. Ibid., p. 78.

16. Ibid., (author's questions omitted).

17. From communication with Steve Clem, URW research director, during July 1980.

CHAPTER

9

Planning, Implementation,
and Administration

This chapter consists primarily of legal requirements under the Internal Revenue Code (Title 26 of the U.S. Code) and the Employee Retirement Income Security Act (Title 29 of the U.S. Code—Labor). The former is administered by the Internal Revenue Service, Department of Treasury, and the latter by the Bureau of Labor-Management Services (BL-MS), Department of Labor. This chapter will treat basics and essentials. It is not intended as a detailed or comprehensive treatment of ESOP-related statutes, regulations, and rulings. To attempt the same would result in a dated and obsolete product in the hands of the reader.

At the end of the chapter a checklist of steps and procedures for implementing a standard ESOP is presented for the reader. It is intended as a guide and should not be used as a substitute for an attorney or CPA qualified in the ESOP area when ESOP implementation is being planned or undertaken. Many companies have unusual market, management, financial, or labor characteristics that may require innovative solutions involving the company, its suppliers and customers, government, and the financial community.

Appendix I reproduces the more significant ESOP-related provisions of the IRC and ERISA. These include IRC Sections 46(a)(2)(E), 46(f)(9), 48(n) and (o), 401(a), 409A, 415(c)(6), 1391-97, 4975, and 6699. IRS Regulation Sections 54.4975-7, 11, and 12 have been added to provide more specific ESOP requirements. Also included are ERISA Sections 406, 407, and 408, IRS Revenue Ruling 59-60, and Sections 331-39 of the Economic Recovery Tax Act of 1981.

BASIC QUALIFICATIONS: IRC

All ESOPs—such as the basic or "statutory" ESOP, the leveraged ESOP or LESOP, the tax credit ESOP or TCESOP (formerly TRASOP), and combination plans—must meet the requirements of IRC Section 401(a). Special legislated ESOP hybrids, such as GSOPs, may be excepted. Section 401(a) applies to deferred compensation plans such as pension, profit-sharing, stock bonus, and money purchase plans. A stock bonus plan could be considered a quasi-ESOP and has several less stringent requirements such as those applying to voting rights and employer securities.

The full text of Section 401(a) is reproduced in the statutory appendix. Among the twenty-two requirements listed for qualification, the following merit citation here:

1. The plan must be for the exclusive benefit of employees or their beneficiaries.
2. Employees or their beneficiaries must receive both the corpus and income from the plan fund.
3. It must be impossible to divert plan assets to purposes other than the exclusive benefit of employees or beneficiaries.
4. Benefits under the plan must not discriminate in favor of employees who are officers, shareholders, or the highly compensated, although "wage" or union employees may be excluded.
5. Plan benefits may not be diminished or defeated by merger, consolidation, or transfer to another plan.
6. Benefits may not be assigned or alienated subject to minor exceptions.
7. Distributions to a participant shall commence within two months after the latest of the participant's sixty-fifth birthday or normal retirement age, the tenth anniversary of participation, or the termination of the participant's employment.
8. No forfeiture penalties may be devised against a participant's withdrawing self-contributions to the plan except within certain limits.
9. Contributions may be based solely on the additional investment tax credit allowable under Section 46(a) if the appropriate stock transfer to the plan trust is made as per Section 48(n)(1).
10. Voting rights must be granted as per Section 409A(e) where a closely held company establishes a defined contribution plan (e.g., ESOP, stock bonus, . . . etc.) and more than 10 percent of the assets of such plan consist of employer securities with the exception of a profit-sharing plan.

A qualified plan enables the employer company to deduct the value of qualifying contributions from taxable income and exempts the trust from taxation on income when earned under Section 501(a). Further, the participant is also exempt from earnings on allocations until distributions are made or dividends are paid under Section 402(a). Capital gains treatment is available for a portion of a lump-sum distribution.

IRC Section 4975(c) prohibits certain types of transactions between the trust of a qualified plan and a "disqualified person." The latter is defined under Subsection (e) as a fiduciary, a person providing services to the plan, an employer, an employee organization, or the beneficial owner of 50 percent or more of the combined voting power of all classes of stock. The prohibited transactions include the selling or leasing of property, the lending of money or extending of credit, the furnishing of goods or services, the transferring of trust assets or personal gain by a fiduciary from trust transactions.

Subsection (d) exempts certain types of plan loans and (d)(3) exempts any loan to an employee stock ownership plan if the loan is primarily for the benefit of plan participants and beneficiaries, if the rate of interest is reasonable and if only "qualifying employer securities" can be given to such person as collateral. Subsection (e)(7) defines an "employee stock ownership plan" as a defined contribution plan that:

1. Is a Section 401(a) qualified stock bonus or stock bonus and money purchase plan;
2. Is designed to invest primarily in qualifying employer securities as defined in Section 409A(l);
3. Meets distribution and "put" option requirements as per Section 409A(h);
4. Meets the voting rights requirements of Section 409A(e) if it is a company with publicly registered and traded stock.

The references to Section 409A will be discussed further in subsequent sections treating those specific topics. Section 4975(a) and (b) impose a tax of 5-100 percent (if not corrected) on prohibited transactions. The entire provision was added by ERISA and is cross referenced thereto concerning violations and penalties. The next section will discuss the relevant ERISA provisions with respect to ESOPs.

The final IRS regulations on ESOPs were issued in two stages in September 1977 and November 1978. The former preceded the Revenue Act of 1978, and the latter preceded the Technical Corrections Act of 1979 (the 1979 act corrected the 1978 act). Regulations Sections 54.4975-7 and 11 remain substantially intact, while 54.4975-12 has been redefined by Section 4975(e)(7) and 409A(1).

Regulation 54.4975-11 states that to be an ESOP a plan must be designated as such in the plan document and must meet the provisions of the section. Regulation 54.4975-7 states that an ESOP is not synonymous with stock bonus plan, but that the latter must be an ESOP to engage in an "exempt loan." The latter is then referred to as a loan made to an ESOP by a disqualified person or a loan to an ESOP that is guaranteed by a disqualified person. The balance of the provisions of the ESOP regulations will be discussed in the subsequent sections of this chapter.

Section 409A was originally intended to apply to tax credit employee stock ownership plans (TCESOPs), but many of the provisions thereof now apply to publicly held and (SEC) registered ESOP companies and some apply to private ESOP companies. A TCESOP is defined as a defined contribution plan that meets the requirements of Section 401(a), is designed to invest primarily in employer securities, and meets the requirements of various subsections. Prior to the Revenue Act of 1978, adding Section 409A to the IRC, the plan, then called a TRASOP or TRAESOP, was not required to be a Section 401(a) qualified plan.

The 1978 act also amended IRC Section 46(a)(2) by lengthening the term for which an additional 1 percent investment tax credit may be taken for equivalent stock contributions to an ESOP trust. This period was increased by three years from January 21, 1975, and ending on December 31, 1983. The additional 0.5 percent investment tax credit available for matching employee contributions was extended from January 1, 1977, to December 31, 1983.

However, the Economic Recovery Tax Act of 1981 (ERTA) set a termination date of December 31, 1982, for both the property-based 1 percent tax credit and the employee matching credit. ERTA substitutes a 0.5 percent to 0.75 percent phased in payroll-based tax credit for the calendar years 1983 through 1987.

The matching percentage requires a second employer contribution equal to 50 percent of the first (e.g., another contribution of 50 shares in addition to the original contribution of 100 shares), plus an employee purchase money contribution matching the second employer contribution. This requirement is explained in IRC Section 48(n) as added by the 1978 act. An employer must make an election for a TCESOP even if an ESOP is in operation. Contributions must be made not later than thirty days after the normal or extended due date for tax return filing for the taxable year, and such contributions will be applied first to the basic TCESOP percentage and then to the matching percentage. The employee matching percentage must be paid in cash to the employer or plan administrator not later than twenty-four months after the close of the taxable year and be invested forthwith in employer securities. The additional tax credit is subject to recapture, but the contributions must remain in the trust.

IRC Section 6699, also added by the Revenue Act of 1978, provides for 100 percent penalties for the failure of an employer company to comply with

Sections 409A and 48(n) if such employer seeks the benefits of a TCESOP election. Final IRS Regulations Sections 1.46-7 and 8, respecting TCESOPs, were published in January 1979 and are coordinated with the sections and amendments added by the Revenue Act.

BASIC QUALIFICATIONS: ERISA

To a significant degree the qualifications and requirements under ERISA and the Department of Labor are coordinated with those of the IRS. In 1974, ERISA added Section 4975 to the IRC plus numerous sections to the Labor Code. The most significant of the labor provisions, vis-à-vis ESOPs, are Sections 406, 407, and 408. With certain exceptions, these sections place restrictions on employee retirement plans as to the types of transactions they can engage in, the parties to those transactions, and the types and extent of assets such plans can hold.

These restrictions are similar to those found in IRC Section 4975 and, to a lesser extent, to those of Section 401(a), except that ERISA uses "party in interest" and IRC uses "disqualified person." The former also uses "adequate consideration" and "qualified employer securities," while the latter uses "fair market value" and "employer securities."

ERISA Section 406 prohibits the fiduciary of a plan from permitting the plan to engage in a transaction with a party in interest involving a sale, lease, exchange, loan, extension of credit, furnishing of goods or services, or transfer of plan assets. The same restrictions apply to the fiduciary on his/her own account. Section 404(a) states the duties of such fiduciary shall be "care, skill, prudence, and diligence" that a "prudent man" in a like capacity would practice, including "diversifying" plan investments and assets except as provided by Section 407(d).

Section 407(a) prohibits a plan from holding more than 10 percent of plan assets in the form of employer securities and real property, and any so held must be qualified. Certain "eligible individual account plans" are exempt from the 10 percent rule and the Section 404(a) diversification rule. Section 407(d) defines such as a profit-sharing, stock bonus, employee stock ownership, or, with limitations, a money purchase plan. The term "employee stock ownership plan" means an individual account plan that is an IRC Section 401(a) qualified stock bonus or stock bonus and money purchase plan and that is designed to "invest primarily in qualifying employer securities."

Section 408(b)(3) states that the prohibited transactions of Section 406 shall not apply to a loan to an ESOP if such loan is primarily for the benefits of plan participants and beneficiaries and if the interest on such loan is reasonable.

Further, any collateral given to a party in interest may consist only of qualifying employer securities. Section 3(14) defines a "party in interest" as any fiduciary, plan employee or counsel, any person providing services to the plan, the employer, or an employee organization, or any direct or indirect owner of 50 percent or more of the stock voting power or value. Thus, where the trust obtains a bank loan and the bank also serves as trust administrator or fiduciary, the trust may give only qualifying employer securities as collateral. This does not prohibit the company from providing a guarantee or additional loan security.

Section 408(e) states that the "prohibited transactions" of Sections 406 and 407 with a party in interest do not apply to the purchase or sale of qualifying employer securities or real property if such purchase or sale is for "adequate consideration," with no commissions, for an eligible individual account plan as defined in Section 407(d). Such a plan includes an ESOP. This provision permits the ESOP trust to purchase such securities from a fiduciary, controlling stockholder, the employer, or an employee organization.

It is important to recognize that the ERISA requirements of care, skill, prudence, and diligence apply to an ESOP, to the employer company, and to the trust fiduciary. Diversification is not required, but an ESOP may not be used to avoid diversification when to do so would clearly violate the prudence provisions.

CONTRIBUTIONS AND ELIGIBLE SECURITIES

Section 401(a)(5) provides that a plan shall not be considered discriminatory merely because contributions or benefits bear uniform relationship to total or regular employee compensation. Section 401(a)(17) requires that the annual compensation of each employee taken into account for the purposes of determining contributions and benefits may not exceed $100,000 for certain types of small company plans. Section 409A(b) states that for purposes of contribution allocations to a TCESOP, employee compensation in excess of $100,000 shall be disregarded. Further, the allocation to each participant must be proportional to the eligible compensation paid to each participant.

IRC Section 404(a)(3) limits employer deductions for contributions to a profit-sharing plan, stock bonus plan, or ESOP to 15 percent of employee compensation for all employees covered by the plan. If, in any year, less than 15 percent is paid in to any such plan, the difference creates a carryforward that can be contributed and deducted in subsequent years. Such amount again may not exceed 15 percent of covered employee compensation for the year when made, and the total contribution, when combined with the regular current year contribution, may not exceed 25 percent of covered employee compensation for such year. If the employer has more than one qualified plan (e.g., an ESOP, a pension plan, and profit-sharing), then the regular current contribution may not exceed 25 percent of covered employee compensation.

ERTA changed the basic 15 percent deduction limitation to 25 percent for leveraged ESOPs (LESOPs). In addition, it provided for an unlimited deduction for employer contributions used by an ESOP to pay interest on a loan used to purchase employer stock.

Since Sections 401(a) and 404(a) consider ESOPs, profit-sharing plans, and stock bonus plans to be comparable, the carryforward exists under a profit-sharing plan, and if the same is converted into an ESOP or frozen and replaced by an ESOP, such carryforward may be used by the ESOP.

Unlike a pension plan, an ESOP requires no fixed or actuarially correct formula for determining the level of contributions. Unlike a profit-sharing plan, it may make contributions during a loss year and use the same to create a net operating loss carryback to the taxable income of the three prior years. IRS Regulation Section 1.401-1(b), however, requires that contributions be "recurring and substantial" in contrast to "single or occasional."

Contributions to an ESOP trust may be made in the form of cash, employer securities or nonemployer securities, or real property. If the latter two, the employer will be subject to capital gains taxes to the extent that the fair market value of the property exceeds its basis therein. In addition, IRC Sections 4975(e)(7) and 409A(a) and Regulation Section 54.4975-11(b) require that an ESOP be invested primarily in employer securities. Cash or employer securities are the viable forms of contributions to an ESOP, including nonvoting common and preferred stock. A stock bonus plan has more latitude in this respect.

ERISA Sections 407(d)(5) and (e) define a "qualified employer security" as stock or a marketable obligation such as a bond, debenture, note, certificate, or other evidence of indebtedness. IRC Section 409A(1) defines "employer securities" as common stock issued by the employer that is readily tradable on an established securities market or, if not so tradable, common stock that has a combination of voting power and dividend rights no less than the highest class of such stock of the employer. Noncallable preferred stock shall be treated as employer securities if it is convertible at any time into the preceding types of stock at a price that is reasonable. Section 4975(e)(8) refers to "qualifying employer security" as defined in Section 409A(1). Regulations Section 54.4975-12 uses the ERISA definition that has been superseded by the 409A(1) rule now followed by the IRS as per the Technical Corrections Act of 1979.

Employee contributions are permitted, but not required, with both ESOPs and TCESOPs. Such contributions should be made in the form of cash and invested in employer securities. Such contributions are subject to strict limitations and nondiscrimination provisions. Since benefits are generally distributed in the form of employer securities, the result may be an "offer" or "sale" under Section 2(3) of the Securities Act of 1933. A large plan may warrant registration on Form S-8, and a small plan may be exempt as an "intrastate" offering. The benefits from employee contributions may not be warranted by the added administrative and regulatory problems except for large TCESOPs.

PARTICIPATION, ALLOCATION, AND VESTING

IRC Section 401(a)(3) requires that a plan meet the minimum participation standards of Section 410 if it is to be qualified. Section 410(a) states that age and service conditions for plan participation by an employee may not extend beyond one year of service or twenty-five years of age, whichever is the later. An ESOP, being a defined contribution plan, may not exclude employees from participation on the basis of age. Provisions are also made for breaks in service.

Under Section 410(b) the plan must benefit (a) 70 percent or more of all employees or (b) 80 percent or more of eligible employees if at least 70 percent of all employees are eligible or (c) such employees as qualify under a classification established by the employer and found not to be discriminatory in favor of employees who are officers, shareholders, or highly compensated. Union employees covered by a collective bargaining agreement may be excluded if retirement benefits were the subject of "good faith" bargaining between the employer and the union. For most companies the last eligibility test would be the easiest to meet since a plan that is discriminatory will not qualify under Section 401(a) anyway.

Employer contributions to an ESOP trust are usually allocated to the accounts of participating employees on the basis of the first $100,000 of covered employee compensation. Except for a TCESOP, combination or alternate criteria may be used such as service units or performance. All allocation formulas must meet the nondiscrimination test, and leveraged ESOPs are prohibited by Regulation Section 54.4975-11 from integrating allocations with social security.

Under ERISA Section 415(c) the "annual additions" or new allocations to an employee account may not exceed the lesser of 25 percent of total compensation or $25,000 as adjusted for inflation. The $25,000 ceiling was effective as of October 1, 1974, and annual adjustments thereto may be made on the basis of the consumer price index as per Subsection (d). Section 415(d)(6) provides a special limitation for ESOPs by combining the $25,000, as adjusted, with the lesser of the amount of employer securities contributed to the plan or the

$25.000. A leveraged ESOP (LESOP) may disregard forfeitures and contributions applied to loan interest in calculating allocation limitations provided that certain contribution conditions are met.

An additional difficulty may be encountered in the case of a LESOP where the employer security is held by a bank as loan collateral and released only as the loan principal is paid. Shares are allocated to employee accounts upon payment and release. Usually a bank is not willing to issue shares pro rata for both principal and interest payments. Few shares would be allocated to early-year participants and many shares to later-year participants. The employer company can avoid this inequity by providing a substitute guarantee or pledge to the bank to release shares for interest paid or borrow shares for allocation from the plan or plan participants. Both IRS Regulation Section 54.4975-7 and Labor Regulation Section 2550.408b-3 require shares to be released from encumbrance as principal and interest are paid.

Section 411(a) sets the minimum vesting standards necessary for plan qualification. An employee's own contributions must be nonforfeitable. As to employer contributions there are three options available:

1. Complete vesting after ten full years of service with such increments as the employer chooses.
2. At least 25 percent vesting after the fifth year of service and the requirement of reaching 100 percent vesting after the fifteenth year in increments of 5 percent per year.
3. The rule of forty-five, wherein an employee with at least five years of service has the service years added to his/her age for a total of forty-five or more. Such employee must be 30 percent vested and reach 100 percent vesting at ten years of service if the combined age and service years total fifty-five. The minimum vesting schedule under this option is 50 percent at ten years of service with 10 percent increments for each service year thereafter.

Certain limited forfeitures and suspensions are provided for in cases involving breaks in service and accrued benefits. In the case of a TCESOP, Section 409A(c) mandates that each participant have a nonforfeitable right to any employer security allocated to his/her account. Thus, there is complete vesting of stock contributions to a TCESOP when the allocations are made.

A further allocation and vesting consideration involves IRS Revenue Ruling 77-30. An ESOP is frequently used to buy out a retiring owner or controlling stockholder or to otherwise provide an in-house market for company stock. The ruling prohibits any such selling stockholder from being allocated more than 20 percent of such stock sold to the ESOP trust.

VOTING RIGHTS

In many ESOPs adopted prior to 1980, the voting rights of employer securities held by the trust were vested in the trustee. The trustee, or the administrative committee directing the trustee, was usually appointed or controlled by the board of directors. Direct voting rights pass-through to employee shareholders was usually encountered only with DEOCs or TCESOPs. In many regular ESOP companies, however, employees or workers are represented on the administrative committee or on the board of directors. Since ESOPs and voting rights were and are the subject of collective bargaining, unions have influenced the makeup of the administrative committee or the degree of pass-through when an ESOP has included members of the bargaining unit.

IRC Section 401(a)(22), added by the Revenue Act of 1978, requires that a defined contribution plan holding more than 10 percent of total plan assets in the form of employer securities must provide voting rights as per Section 409A(e) if the employer stock is not publicly traded. The provision applies to stock bonus plans and ESOPs, but ERTA exempted profit-sharing plans. Section 4975(e)(7) provides that a plan shall not be treated as an ESOP unless it meets Section 409A(e) if it has the registration type of securities as defined by Section 409A(e)(4).

Section 409A(e) applies also to all TCESOPs. The term "registration-type class of securities" means any securities required to be registered under Section 12 of the Securities Exchange Act of 1934 or any that would be so required except for certain exemptions. Generally, this will include any company that is publicly traded where the plan covers 300 or more employees. In such cases Section 409A(e) mandates that each plan participant shall be entitled to direct the plan as to the voting of shares allocated to his/her account.

Where the employer does not have "registration-type class of securities" but the stock is publicly traded (e.g., small intrastate company with a thin float)—as with a Section 401(a)(22) plan—such voting rights need be provided to each participant only with respect to corporate matters that, by law or charter, must be decided by more than a majority vote of the outstanding common shares. Such supramajority matters are usually mandated by state law and frequently involve mergers, reorganizations, dissolutions, or basic changes in the corporate articles or charter.

It should be noted that the voting rights provisions, except those pertaining to TCESOPs, are not retroactive and apply only to securities issued or contributed to an ESOP as of the effective date of the provisions—January 1, 1980. For nonleveraged ESOPs it may be possible to avoid voting rights problems through the use of nonvoting common traded on an established securities market or through the use of noncallable preferred stock readily convertible into qualified common stock at a reasonable price. The reader should refer to the discussion of eligible employer securities discussed earlier in this chapter.

Voting rights pass-through is usually not a major problem for larger TCESOP and ESOP companies where the trust holds a relatively small percentage of the total shares outstanding and where participating employees either support management or tend to have little interest in directing the voting of their shares. In smaller public or in private companies the voting rights provisions could easily involve struggles for control and even the viability of the business. Proper planning, employee education, and judicious management are essential if such problems are to be avoided.

The voting rights provisions of Section 409A(e) were intended for TCESOPs, but Section 401(a)(22) applied them to all private company "defined contribution" plans and Section 4975(e)(7) applied them to all public company ESOPs. Subject to further IRS determination, only the nonleveraged defined contribution plans of publicly traded companies and the profit-sharing plans of closely held companies may be exempt from the pass-through of voting rights.

INVESTMENTS, LOANS, AND INSURANCE

As previously discussed in this chapter, ERISA Section 404(a) requires a fiduciary to diversify the investments of a qualified plan to minimize the risk of loss within the constraints of prudence and diligence. Section 407(a) prohibits a plan from acquiring qualifying employer securities or real property if immediately thereafter the aggregate fair market value of the employer securities and real property exceeds 10 percent of the fair market value of the plan assets. Section 404(a)(2), Section 407(b)(1), and Section 407(d)(3) exempt ESOPs and other eligible individual account plans from the diversification requirement if the plan specifically provides for a greater or primary holding of qualifying employer securities or real property.

The statutory purpose of an ESOP is to invest primarily in employer securities, and both IRS and Department of Labor regulations require that it be specifically designated as such (i.e., as an ESOP). ERISA Section 404(a) also directs that a fiduciary shall discharge his/her duties

with the care, skill, prudence, and diligence under the circumstances then prevailing that a prudent man acting in a like capacity and familiar in such matters would use in the conduct of an enterprise of a like character and with like aims.

The special statutory purpose of an ESOP permits it to invest in employer securities to a degree and under circumstances that would be prohibited with a stock bonus or profit-sharing plan.

For the latter two plans, prudence and the "prudent-man" rule limit the allowable diversification exemption within the constraints of a fair rate of return. An ESOP may acquire employer securities even though the stock does not pay dividends that provide a fair rate of return.[1] An ESOP may be invested entirely in employer securities, whereas such is possible but more difficult with any other type of qualified plan.

The fiduciary of an ESOP trust may not invest in employer securities when it would be clearly imprudent to do so. Such would be the case where the trust has cash assets that the fiduciary uses to purchase company stock when the company is insolvent at the time of the purchase. The prudence rule is also violated where, in similar circumstances, a profit-sharing plan is converted into an ESOP to buy the stock of an insolvent company.[2] While the exact delineation between the prudence rule and the purpose rule for an ESOP is not known, it is known that the permitted zone of conduct is wider for ESOPs than for other qualified plans.

ERISA Section 404(a) also requires that the fiduciary act "for the exclusive purpose of providing benefits to participants and beneficiaries," while IRC Section 401(a) requires a qualified plan to be for the exclusive benefit of "employees or their beneficiaries." Under the code the investment of funds in a qualified plan must meet the four following investment criteria:

1. The cost of the investment must not exceed its fair market value at the time of purchase.
2. A fair rate of return commensurate with the prevailing rate must be attainable.
3. Sufficient liquidity to permit distributions in accordance with the terms of the plan must be available.
4. The safeguards and diversification that would be adhered to by a prudent investor must be observed.[3]

The company or controlling stockholders or other parties may be incidental beneficiaries. One of the more common examples is where an ESOP is established and obtains a loan to acquire a subsidiary from a parent or to liquidate the holdings of a controlling shareholder. Such transactions would normally be taxed under IRC Section 4975 as a prohibited transaction with a disqualified person. Also, ERISA Section 406 would be applicable as to prohibited transactions with a party in interest (both sections are discussed earlier in this chapter).

An ESOP is the only type of qualified Section 401(a) plan specifically exempt from the prohibited transaction rule as applied to loans by IRC Section 4975(d)(3) and ERISA Section 408(b)(3), provided that the primary benefit test is met, that the interest rate is reasonable, and that any collateral given to such disqualified person or party in interest consists only of qualifying employer securities. An ESOP or LESOP may, for the purpose of investing primarily in employer securities, obtain credit from the company, obtain credit from a bank with a company guarantee, obtain credit on behalf of the company, and give qualifying employer securities as collateral in any credit or loan transactions.

Both IRS Regulation Section 54.4975-7 and Labor Regulation Section 2550.408 affirm the primary benefit rule for any loans to ESOPs and advance additional rules for the net effect on plan assets, arm's-length dealing, use of loan proceeds, reasonable interest rate, release of employer securities from encumbrance, and a caution of plan disqualification for exceeding IRC Section 415 allocation limitations. Both specifically state that loan and credit transactions will be subject to "special scrutiny."

ERISA Section 407(e) places an additional prohibition on investments in a "marketable obligation" of the employer company where such are defined as bonds, notes, debentures, certificates, or other evidence of indebtedness. All eligible account plans, ESOPs included, must acquire such a marketable obligation at the price prevailing on a national securities exchange registered with the SEC or, if not applicable, at a price not less favorable than the offering price in a market independent of the issuer, or from an underwriter at a price not in excess of the public offering price as per a prospectus or offering circular, or directly from the issuer at a price no less favorable than the current price paid by persons independent of the issuer.

After such investment, the plan may not hold more than 25 percent of such obligations issued and outstanding. At least 50 percent must be held by persons independent of the issuer, and not more than 25 percent of plan assets may be invested in such obligations. Such prohibitions do not apply to "employer securities" as defined by IRC Section 409A(1).

While an ESOP is required to invest primarily in employer securities, it need not be invested 100 percent therein. Depending on the circumstances, "primarily" could involve a small amount or a large amount over 50 percent and could be construed to involve longer or shorter time periods. Generally, ESOPs may hold a diversified portfolio provided that the prudence and "primarily" rules are met. This could include life insurance on key participants or stockholders, or risk insurance on the possible loss of value in plan securities or assets. However, both IRS Regulation Section 54.4975 and Labor Regulation Section 2550.408 prohibit a LESOP from using borrowed funds for purchasing life insurance or securities other than qualifying employer securities.

If an ESOP takes out a life insurance policy on a controlling stockholder or a key employee and names the trust as the policy beneficiary, it is protected from a possible loss that could result when such an important person dies. Further, it may be assured of the necessary funds to purchase the stock from the estate of such a person and thus help assure that such will not be used in a way detrimental to the company or the plan assets. IRS Regulation Section 54.4975-11(a) prohibits an ESOP trust from entering into a mandatory buy/sell agreement for the purchase of such stock, but the ESOP may execute an option to purchase the stock such that it will have the right of first refusal at fair market value.

Employer securities and qualified employer securities also include the securities of an affiliate or controlled group of companies. Under ERISA Section 407(d)(7), an ''affiliate'' is a member of any ''controlled group'' of corporations, including a parent-subsidiary where the latter is at least 50 percent owned by the former and brother-sister companies where at least 50 percent of each is owned by the same group of five or fewer persons. IRC Section 409A(1) includes as an employer company a corporation ''which is a member of the same controlled group.'' IRC Section 4975(e)(8) refers to Section 409A(1) in discussing ''qualified employer security.''

LABOR LAW AND COLLECTIVE BARGAINING

The National Labor Relations Act (NLRA), 29 U.S.C. 141, et seq., requires mandatory union-management bargaining with respect to wages, hours, conditions of employment, and matters relating to pension, profit-sharing, and other retirement plans. The provision applies to all companies having employees whose activities ''affect interstate commerce.'' Both the union and the company have a duty to bargain in good faith to reach an agreement and to refrain from unfair practices. Neither party is compelled to reach an agreement on any specific proposal and the union may waive its right to bargain on certain issues, such as retirement plans, either by an express agreement or by actions constituting acquiescence. Such a waiver may apply specifically to implementation of or participation in an ESOP.

IRC Sections 401(a)(4) and 410(b)(2)(A) permit excluding from a qualified plan those employees ''who are included in a unit of employees covered by an agreement which the Secretary of Labor finds to be a collective bargaining agreement between employee representatives and one or more employers, if there is evidence that retirement benefits were the subject of good faith bargaining.'' Section 413 specifically provides that qualified 401(a) plans may be established and maintained ''pursuant to an agreement which the Secretary of

Labor finds to be a collective-bargaining agreement between employee representatives and one or more employers.''

In essence, a union may not have the unilateral ability to determine whether or not a company adopts an ESOP, but it does have the ability to determine member participation as well as other substantive matters of the plan. A company may not include in an ESOP some or all of the members of a bargaining unit without submitting the issue to the union for collective bargaining or obtaining the union's waiver with respect thereto. If collective bargaining does take place, and if the company and the union are unable to reach an agreement on the matter despite good-faith efforts on both sides, then the company may proceed with a plan that excludes union members provided that such is not prohibited by a currently operative contractual limitation.

Good-faith collective bargaining may exclude union members from participation in the plan, but nonunion members who are plan participants may not be terminated automatically therefrom if they subsequently become members of the bargaining unit, lacking an agreement with the union on the issue. If an agreement or waiver is obtained such that union members are included in the plan, the plan may not discriminate against union member participants nor penalize nonunion member participants who subsequently become part of the collective bargaining unit. Also, the company may not use plan participation or plan benefits to subvert an ongoing union organization campaign within the company.

CONVERSIONS, COMBINATIONS, AND MULTIPLE PLANS

If a company has an existing qualified plan and wishes to convert or replace the same with an ESOP, several alternatives are available. The existing plan may be continued on a nominal basis while an ESOP is separately established and maintained. The existing plan may be terminated while proceeding with an ESOP, as in the preceding alternative. If this course is taken, the result will be immediate vesting of all accounts of the plan participants. The plan assets may be distributed immediately, held in special accounts until participants retire or terminate, or, in certain circumstances, rolled over into the ESOP. As a third alternative, the company can redesignate the existing plan as an ESOP, which, for vesting purposes, will be treated as a continuation rather than as a termination of the existing plan.

In most circumstances the third alternative is preferable, especially if the prior plan is a profit-sharing or stock bonus plan. Except as to loans and company financing, IRC Sections 401(a) and 4975 and ERISA Sections 407 and 408 generally treat ESOPs, profit-sharing, and stock bonus plans as comparable plans. The unique features of ESOPs in obtaining "exempt" loans, engaging in company financing, and investing in employer securities are more specifically treated in IRS Regulation Sections 54.4975-7 and 11, Sections 1.46-7 and 8, and Labor Regulation Sections 2550.407d-7 and 2550.408b-3. Regulation Sections 54.4975-11 and 2550.407d-7 specifically provide for the conversion of an existing plan into an ESOP or the combination of an ESOP with other plans. IRS Regulation Section 1.401-6(b) also treats ESOPs, profit-sharing plans, and stock bonus plans as comparable plans.

Assuming that a conversion to an ESOP is made without termination of the prior plan, the assets of the prior plan may either be transferred to a special trust account or rolled over into the ESOP trust. If the amendment and restatement are properly drawn, the entire plan will be treated as an ESOP rather than as a combination ESOP-profit-sharing plan or ESOP-stock bonus plan. Since any of these alternatives, plus others, are available, the reader is advised to make a thorough determination as to what type of plan or combination of plans is most appropriate under the circumstances. If employee participants are given a choice of account investments as part of the conversion, additional SEC problems may be encountered since an investment decision may be involved that could require a registration statement.

The least complicated approach would be a combined ESOP-profit-sharing or ESOP-stock bonus plan using a single plan document and trust. Assets in the prior plan would be "frozen," and all future contributions would be made to the ESOP. Distributions would be made from the frozen plan as participants terminate or decease. SEC problems are avoided, but more importantly the prudence and diligence requirements of ERISA Section 404(a) could more easily be met without a conversion from a diversified portfolio into one invested primarily in employer securities. Even though the IRS and Department of Labor might approve the latter approach, participants or beneficiaries under the prior plan may bring suit against the company and fiduciary claiming that such conversion was an imprudent investment.

Any Section 401(a) qualified plan may be used in combination with another such plan, or a multiple of a single type of plan may be used. An ESOP, as a special type of stock bonus plan, may be used in combination with a stock bonus, profit-sharing, money purchase, or pension trust plan, or multiple ESOPs may be used. IRC Section 404(a) permits employer contributions in total of up to 25 percent of covered compensation with combination plans, but total multiple plan contributions are restricted to 15 percent of covered compensations.

However, an ESOP may have to be combined with a money purchase or pension plan to obtain the 25 percent deduction. In the case of the former, the entire 25 percent may be invested in employer securities. A defined-benefit pension plan may not invest more than 10 percent of the value of its assets in employer securities. The 25 percent limit for unused contribution carryforward also applies to the sum of all plans used in combination or multiples. Leveraged ESOPs standing alone qualify for the 25 percent deductions following the Economic Recovery Tax Act of 1981.

SECURITIES LAW PROBLEMS

Any company having securities subject to registration under the Securities Act of 1933 should carefully consider and attempt to avoid any securities problems involving an ESOP. If any such transaction does involve registration under the 1933 act, it is also likely that registration will be required under the Securities Exchange Act of 1934. If so, and if the ESOP has 300 or more participants, then the annual financial reporting under the 1934 act may also be required.

Any company having securities that are offered, sold, traded, or exchanged in a public market in interstate commerce is subject to Securities and Exchange registration, disclosure, and reporting requirements. The major exemptions involve a completely private transaction as determined by Section 4(2) of the 1933 act (Rule 146) and a completely intrastate transaction as determined by Section 3(a)(11) of the act (Rule 147). If the securities of a public company held by the ESOP trust are not registered on Form S-8 as per the 1933 act, such securities acquired by employees or beneficiaries upon distribution may not be resold on the public market without compliance with SEC Rule 144.

In general, contributions only by the employer company of employer securities to a qualified ESOP are exempt from the registration requirements of the 1933 act. The same is true of a cash contribution used to purchase employer securities. An interest in an IRC Section 401(a) qualified plan has not been construed to involve a "sale" or an "offer to sell" a "security" within Section 2(3) of the act so long as contributions are provided entirely by the employer company and so long as no cash allocation option is provided to plan participants. A certificate of interest of participation in a qualified plan does involve a "security" within the meaning of Section 2(1) of the act.

If a qualified plan provides for voluntary employee contributions, Section 3(a)(2) of the act provides an exemption from registration of any interest of participation therein if the contributions are held in a single and separate trust account administered by a bank or insurance company for the employer company. This exemption may not apply to securities distributed to plan participants.

Where employee contributions are either permitted or required, or where a qualified plan is established as a result of collective bargaining, it is possible, if not probable, that the SEC would consider such a transaction to involve an investment decision on the part of the participating employees and, thus, a "sale" or an "offer" to buy or sell as defined by the act. The SEC exemption is premised on the "bonus" concept rather than on the rationale that the plan participants have an investment choice or an investment decision or that they have bargained for the securities as consideration in exchange for specific services.

In *International Brotherhood of Teamsters* v. *Daniel*, 439 U.S. 551. 99 S.Ct. 790 (1979), the SEC argued that a noncontributory compulsory pension plan established by collective bargaining was an "investment contract" within Section 2(1) of the 1933 act and Section 3(a)(10) of the 1934 act and, thus, a security. Further, a sale under Section 2(3) and Section 3(a)(14) of the two respective acts was involved since fraud was involved as per Section 17(a) and Section 10(b) of the respective acts. The Supreme Court, in reversing the two lower courts, held that such a plan is not an investment contract and, therefore, not a security since to be so there must be an "investment of money" in a "common enterprise" with "profits . . . solely from the efforts of others." The Court further stated that ERISA had preempted the pension area. It is likely that noncontributory ESOPs fall within the scope of this decision.

If an ESOP trust purchases employer securities on the public market and such securities have previously been registered, then no offer or sale of an unregistered security is involved regardless of whether the bonus or sale theory is followed. If the purchase is made from controlling stockholders, the transaction is exempt from registration as a private placement as per Section 4(2) of the 1933 act or SEC Rule 146. But since the SEC considers the trust of a qualified plan to be an affiliate of the issuer company, the securities so purchased become "tainted" and may not be resold on the public market except in accordance with SEC Rule 144. These restrictions apply only to a public company in which the plan trustee is not truly and sufficiently independent of the issuer company. The restrictions include a two-year holding period of the tainted securities, a sale pursuant to a "brokers transaction," and timely reporting and filing by the issuing company.

There are several means available for a public employer company to avoid Rule 144 consequences. One, listed above, is to meet the independent trustee test. Another is to provide plan participants with a put option or a right of first refusal such that the securities can be resold to the company or the ESOP trust upon distribution. Rule 144 restrictions on tainted securities apply both to the trust and to the distributees—but only for sales on the public market. A third alternative involves registration of the plan on an SEC Form S-8, which is used to register qualified and nonqualified stock option and stock purchase plans. With such a registration perfected, a normal public sale may be effected.

Rule 144 does not apply to the stock of a private or close-held company. However, state blue sky laws and corporate articles or charters generally require legend stock, a buy/sell agreement, or an investment letter, all of which may severely restrict any resale or secondary distribution of such stock. Thus, in most instances, the plan will provide either a put option to the distributee of the stock, so that it must be repurchased by the company or the ESOP trust at the option of the distributee, or a right of first refusal, such that the company or trust has the option to make the purchase.

If a qualified plan is not exempt from registration under the 1933 act, then it must also be registered under Section 12(g) of the 1934 act, using the same filing. If the plan covers 300 or more employees, a separate 1934 act filing is necessary, and the company must also file regular financial reports on SEC Form 11-K.

If the company has any outstanding convertible securities or warrants or is in the process of making a distribution, the ESOP trust, as an affiliate of the company, may not purchase company securities without prior SEC approval as required by Rule 10(b)(6). If a company officer, director, or beneficial owner of over 10 percent of any class of a company equity security realizes any profit on a purchase or sale of such security within a six-month period, such profit may be recovered by the company under Section 16(d) of the 1934 act unless the plan has been approved by a majority vote of the shareholders.

The rule does not apply if the stock is distributed to the insider upon or after retirement. Further, Rule 10(b)(5) prohibitions against manipulative and deceptive acts in connection with the purchase or sale of company securities apply to the ESOP trust as well as to the company, company insiders, and controlling stockholders.

VALUATION OF COMPANY STOCK AND FAIR MARKET VALUE

The accurate valuation of employer company securities involving the ESOP is necessary for plan qualification under both IRS and ERISA provisions. IRS uses the term "fair market value" primarily as defined by Revenue Ruling 59-60. ERISA uses the term "adequate consideration" as defined by Section 3(18) of the act. These are operative at all times during the existence of the ESOP and specifically whenever employer securities are contributed to the trust, whenever such securities are purchased by the trust, whenever such securities are used or released as loan collateral, each year in which such securities are held by the trust, and whenever a distribution is made from the trust.

Section 3(18) of ERISA defines "adequate consideration" as follows:

(A) in the case of a security for which there is a generally recognized market, either (i) the price of the security prevailing on a national securities exchange which is registered under section 6 of the Securities Exchange Act of 1934, or which has been listed for more than one month (at the time of such sale or purchase) on an electronic quotation system and administered by a national securities association registered under such act, or (ii) if the security is not traded on such a national securities exchange, or so listed on such an electronic quotation system, a price not less favorable to the plan than the offering price for the security as established by the current bid and ask prices quoted by persons independent of the issuer or any party-in-interest.
(B) in the case of an asset other than a security for which there is a generally recognized market, the fair market value of the asset as determined in good faith by the trustee or named fiduciary pursuant to the terms of the plan and in accordance with regulations promulgated by the Secretary.

Subsection (A) applies to public companies, and Subsection (B) applies to private companies. As to the former, an ESOP trust may not pay more or receive less for the security than the going price on a national stock exchange or on the over-the-counter market. It is possible that this price does not represent the fair market value since stocks frequently sell below that which is warranted by the book value of company stock or by company earnings. Conversely, the going price of a stock may also be inflated by favorable stories or rumors concerning a company or an industry regardless of the truth of such matters. Subsection (A) *does not* prohibit a purchase by the trust below fair market value or a sale or exchange in excess of fair market value.

Subsection (B), applying to private companies, does use a fair-market-value test, but presents no criteria nor procedures to be used by the trustee or fiduciary in determining the same. Pending Department of Labor regulations relating to the same, the "good faith" trustee or fiduciary will probably utilize the criteria of Revenue Ruling 59-60. Section 4 of the ruling states the following:

It is advisable to emphasize that in the valuation of the stock of closely held corporations or the stock of corporations where market quotations are either lacking or too scarce to be recognized, all available financial data, as well as all relevant factors affecting the fair market value, should be considered. The following factors, although not all-inclusive are fundamental and require careful analysis in each case:

(a) The nature of the business and the history of the enterprise from its inception.

(b) The economic outlook in general and the condition and outlook of the specific industry in particular.

(c) The book value of the stock and the financial condition of the business.

(d) The earnings capacity of the company.

(e) The dividend-paying capacity.

(f) Whether or not the enterprise has goodwill or other intangible value.

(g) Sales of the stock and size of the block of stock to be valued.

(h) The market price of stocks of corporations engaged in the same or a similar line of business having their stocks actively traded in a free and open market, either on an exchange or over the counter.

The eight factors listed are neither equally available nor equally valid for most companies. For capital- or real-estate-intensive companies, the book value approach is both widely used and fairly accurate. Special attention should be given to the method employed in the appraisal of real estate, in the determination of depreciation, and in the valuation of inventory. In most cases a complete asset appraisal will be necessary to provide authority independent of the company records.

If the company is "thin" on assets, such as a service or retail company, it may be more appropriate to use an earnings-dividend approach or a capitalization of earnings formula. A simple capitalized value (*CV*) is the product of current net income (*NI*) and the earnings multiple (*EM*) or the price/earnings ratio (*P/E*); or it is the quotient of the NI divided by the capitalization rate (*CR*). Usually the *P/E* of a close-held company will be neither accurate nor reliable, and an *EM* or *CR* will be little better. The company under consideration could be compared with similar or comparable private or public companies to obtain a reasonable *EM* or *CR*.

However, the simple *CV* does not account for the company's residual value (of assets), the discounts to future earnings, stock nonliquidity, opportunity cost (interest), inflation, and risk. A simple discounted capitalized value would include the following:

$$DCV = \frac{(NI_1)}{(1+dr)^1} + \frac{(NI_2)}{(1+dr)^2} + \ldots \frac{(NI_2) + R}{(1+dr)^n}$$

where *DCV* is the discounted capitalized value; *NI* is net income where values are given for the first (1), second (2), and *n*th years that income is projected; *dr* is the discount rate for those respective years; and R is the salvage or residual value of company assets.

In many valuations of private companies an alternative or combination book value, discounting, and comparative method is employed as weighted by the characteristics of the company and industry. The first two approaches assume stable, but not stagnant, company characteristics and are less viable when there are recent sales of company stock or capitalization changes. The comparative approach is widely used for private companies and usually involves evaluating at least the following factors relative to the public reference companies:

1. Product characteristics such as quality, mix, growth, market penetration, and technical development.

2. Management quality, including production, finance, and marketing.

3. Labor-management relations and owner-management relations.

4. Industry growth and competition considerations.

5. Economic ratios (e.g., rate of return on stockholder equity, rate of return on assets, rate of return on sales, price/earnings ratio, ratio of current assets to current liabilities, ratio of debt to equity, dividend yield ratio).

Consideration should be given to the effect of stock or cash contributions to the ESOP trust or distributions from the same. It is also appropriate to discount close-held, minority, unregistered, or nonvoting common stock. Revenue Ruling 59-60 also permits the assignment of weights to the various valuation factors and methods, but discourages the mathematical averaging of factors.

It is not IRS policy to evaluate or review the validity of a valuation when a request is made for a determination letter as part of the plan qualification process. The plan may be subsequently audited, and the company will have the opportunity to defend its valuation on its merits if the valuation is questioned. If the IRS does not approve the valuation thereafter, the company may appeal to the tax court. It is in the long-run interest of the company and the trust fiduciaries to assure that timely and accurate valuations are performed by competent and independent appraisers.

The IRS will apply special scrutiny where the ESOP trust engages in a transaction with a disqualified person such as the company, a fiduciary, or a controlling stockholder. Such transactions would include the use of trust cash or other assets to purchase employer securities from the company or the use of the trust as an in-house market to acquire all or part of the employer securities held by a controlling stockholder or held by the estate of the same. Regulation Section 54.4975-11(d)(5) comments on valuation as follows:

For purposes of Sect. 54.4975-7(b)(9) and (12) and this section, valuations must be made in good faith and based on all relevant factors for determining the fair market value of securities. In the case of a transaction between a plan and a disqualified person, value must be determined as of the date of the transaction. For all other purposes under this subparagraph (5), value must be determined as of the most recent valuation date under the plan. An independent appraisal will not in itself be a good faith determination of value in the case of a transaction between a plan and a disqualified person. However, in other cases, a determination of fair market value based on at least an annual appraisal independently arrived at by a person who customarily makes such appraisals and who is independent of any party to a transaction under Sect. 54.4975-7(b)(9) and (12) will be deemed to be a good faith determination of value.

The reader is advised that this section merely introduces valuation issues and procedures and that no company should determine its own fair market value for ESOP purposes. Recently the IRS has increased its audit review of employee benefit plans. IRS Form 6080, an audit form, is usually used in such reviews but it is intended for internal IRS use only.

DISTRIBUTIONS AND DIVIDENDS

Distributions from an ESOP trust are usually made in the form of employer securities. IRS Regulation Section 54.4975-11(f)(1) requires that benefits distributable from the portion of an ESOP consisting of a stock bonus plan may be distributed only in the form of stock of the employer. Benefits distributable from the money-purchase portion of the ESOP may be distributed in the form of employer securities or cash. IRS Regulation Section 1.401-1(b)(1) also requires a stock bonus plan to distribute benefits in stock of the employer company. Since most ESOP's are primarily stock-bonus type plans (i.e., employer contributions are made in the form of employer securities rather than cash), cash distributions and call options have not been significant ESOP features. However, IRC Section 409A(h)(2), relating to TCESOPS, permits distributions to be made in the form either of cash or of employer securities if the plan so provides.

It is also general ESOP practice to provide a put option whereby the participants may require the company (not the trust) to repurchase the distributed employer securities at fair market value as discussed in the previous section. IRS Regulation Section 54.4975-7(b)(10) and Labor Regulation Section 2550.408 b-3(j) require a put option of a leveraged ESOP if the employer security is not publicly traded or if it is subject to "trading limitations" when distributed.

IRC Section 409A(h)(1) requires a put option of TCESOPs if the employer securities are not "readily tradable" on an established market.

The usual put option period is twelve to eighteen months following distribution. The option may not obligate the ESOP trust, but the put provision may grant the trust the option to assume the rights and responsibilities of the employer company at the time the put option is exercised. The distributee may exercise such option within the stated period and receive a lump sum or installment cash payments. The use of the put option increases the fair market value of the employer securities by providing an in-house market, assures the participants of distribution liquidity, and provides the company or the trust with a source of employer securities for future participants.

A right of first refusal option may be used as a substitute for or a supplement to the put option. Its use is common in close-held corporations where continuity and compatability may be essential to survival. Either the company or the ESOP trust may be given a one-time option to purchase the distributed securities at fair market value subject to a time limit or option period. The usual practice is to grant the company and/or the trust the option for a ten- to twenty-day period within one or two years of the date of distribution if the distributee has arranged a sale of the stock.

IRS Regulation Section 54.4975-7(b)(9) and Labor Regulation Section 2550.408b-3(i) permit, but do not require, a right of first refusal option for LESOPs where the employer securities are not publicly traded at the time the option is to be exercised. The purchase price must be the greater of the fair market value, as discussed in the previous section, or the price and terms offered by another buyer making a good-faith offer to purchase the securities.

The benefits of a first right of refusal option are similar to those discussed above concerning the put option. Neither the company nor the ESOP trust, however, may demand or mandate the right to repurchase distributed employer securities. This would constitute a call option and would both restrict the free marketability of such securities and effectively result in a cash distribution from which the stock-bonus type of ESOPs may be excluded.

IRC Section 402 concerns the taxation of distributions from a Section 401(a) qualified trust that is exempt from tax under Section 501(a). Distributions may be made and taken in a lump sum or in installments. If in lump sum, the distribution may be rolled over into an eligible retirement plan within sixty days of receipt of the proceeds and thereby avoid taxation. Such a plan may include a qualified individual retirement account or annuity. The amount so transferred shall not exceed the fair market value of all the property the employee receives from the distribution as reduced by the employee contributions.

A distribution is a lump-sum distribution if it constitutes the entire amount allocated to the participant's account; if it is made within one taxable year (as determined by the recipient); if it is made because of the participant's death, termination, separation, total disability, or election after age 59.5; if the participant or beneficiary has made no previous lump-sum election under the age-59.5 rule; if the participant has been in the plan five or more taxable years prior to the tax year of distribution (excluding unrealized appreciation on employer securities); and if the participant or beneficiary elects lump-sum tax treatment of the distribution.

There is no tax on distributions of an employee's own contributions nor on any unrealized appreciation on distributed employer stock. The tax basis for such stock shall be the fair market value or cost when acquired by the ESOP trust. If the stock is subsequently sold, the appreciation between the cost basis and the fair market value at the time of distribution will be taxed as a long-term capital gain regardless of the holding period. Any appreciation occurring after distribution will be subject to long-term or short-term capital gains treatment depending upon the holding period.

Thus, the total taxable amount of a lump-sum distribution includes the fair market value of the distribution excluding employee contributions and unrealized capital gains. Or, it consists of the participant's earnings from the plan and the cost basis of the employer securities. The cost basis is the employer cash contribution used for the purchase by the ESOP trust or the fair market value if the employer contributed stock. The ordinary income share of the amount is subject to ten-year forward averaging.

The total taxable amount is further reduced by a minimum distribution allowance of the lesser of $10,000 or 50 percent of the total taxable amount as reduced by 20 percent of the amount (if any) by which such amount exceeds $20,000. The balance, or net taxable amount, is taxed as ordinary income using the rates for unmarried individuals not heads of households, with one exception: the amount having the same ratio to the net taxable amount as an individual's pre-1974 participation has to his/her total years of participation shall be subject to capital gains treatment. The tax on 10 percent of the net taxable amount is calculated on the table, then multiplied by ten, and then multiplied by the post-1973/pre-1974 ratio.

The pre-1974 taxable amount is added to the pro rata amount of the pre-1974 minimum distribution allowance. This total is equal to the total taxable amount multiplied by the pre-1974/post-1973 ratio and is taxed as a long-term capital gain. If the employee has previously elected a lump-sum distribution at age 59.5, any subsequent distribution will be taxed as ordinary income to the participant, any beneficiary, or an estate. If the participant dies after receipt of the lump-sum distribution, but before resale of the employer securities therein, proceeds from the subsequent sale will be taxed as capital gains without the benefit of step-up basis.

Installment and other distributions that do not qualify as lump-sum distributions are not eligible for the pre-1974 capital gains proration or for the exclusion of unrealized appreciation on employer securities. Only unrealized appreciation on stock distributions resulting from employee contributions is tax exempt. All other distributions are taxed as ordinary income as though in the form of annuity distributions. The basis of distributed employer stock is the fair market value at the time of the distribution, and upon any subsequent sale a long-term or short-term capital gain will be realized, depending upon the holding period.

If the participant dies prior to receiving all the installment distributions, the undistributed amount is excluded from the estate of such participant for federal estate tax purposes provided that there is a named beneficiary other than the estate. Upon distribution of the balance of the account to the beneficiary, the installments will be taxed in the same manner as they would have been taxed to the participant.

While the installment method involves greater ordinary income treatment of distributions compared to lump-sum, it does permit deferral of taxation and possible use of lower marginal rates as well as partial exclusion for federal estate tax purposes. However, portions of a lump-sum distribution may also be excluded from the gross estate under IRC Section 2039(f) where the recipient elects not to apply ten-year averaging.

IRS Regulation Section 54.4975-11(f)(3) permits an ESOP trust to distribute dividends and other earned income to participants to whom such securities have been allocated. In the case of a stock-bonus type of ESOP, such income must be distributed in employer securities if held for two years or longer. Any current cash distributions of dividends or earnings are treated as ordinary income to plan participants.

REPORTING, DISCLOSURE, AND ACCOUNTING

The administrator of the ESOP trust has three separate reporting and disclosure responsibilities: to the employee participants; to the secretary of the treasury (applicable IRS service center); to the secretary of labor (Labor-Management Services). The principal reporting and disclosure requirements, as well as plan drafting and construction requirements, are contained in IRS

Regulation Section 1.401-1 and ERISA Sections 102, 104, 402, and 403. Copies of all relevant documents are reproduced in the appendixes.

The employer company must communicate the nature, benefits, and limitations of the plan to the employee participants by both oral and written means. An ESOP manual or handbook or summary plan description (SPD) must be prepared and distributed to the employees, and an employee meeting must be held to explain the same. The SPD must be written such that it can be understood by the average plan participant and must contain all the essential information concerning plan type, eligibility, benefits, vesting, voting, distributions, administration, and trustee(s).

Within 120 days of implementation of the plan the SPD must also be filed with Labor-Management Services (L-MS). A plan description, or EBS-1, is not presently required by L-MS; but when it was used, the same filing date applied. The information from the EBS-1 and the SPD is similar except that the former is essentially a data form, while the latter is a written booklet. Any plan modifications must be reported within 60 days of the change(s).

Within seven months of the close of the company's tax year the administrator must file IRS Form 5500 (5500-C if less than 100 employee participants) with both the IRS and L-MS. Form 5500 is identified as the summary annual report (SAR), or EBS-2, by L-MS. The following information is required thereon:

1. A financial statement, certified by a public accountant, listing plan assets and liabilities, changes in net assets, and an enumeration of revenues and expenses.

2. A listing and description of agreements and transactions with parties in interest, including the assets and prices involved in any such transactions.

3. A schedule of assets held by the plan for investment.

The plan administrator must also file an annual registration statement (ARS) with the IRS, reporting participants who have terminated with vested benefits and the nature, amount, and form of the deferred benefit to which each such participant is vested. A copy of the SAR must also be distributed to employee participants and beneficiaries receiving benefits under the plan within nine months of the close of the plan fiscal year. A copy of the ARS must be furnished to each participant who terminates during the year with a deferred vesting benefit.

The plan administrator must also file the exempt organization tax returns (Forms 4848 and 4849) with the IRS. SEC reporting or disclosure requirements, if any, are discussed in the previous section on securities law problems.

An employee participant in an ESOP trust will usually have three types of accounts: an employer stock account, an income or profit-sharing account, and an account of other assets or cash. The trust itself will usually have similar accounts to hold unallocated assets, securities, or cash. A leveraged ESOP trust will also have a loan amortization account. The employee participant account will usually show an income or profit-sharing balance and reallocated forfeitures from the same; contributions of employer securities and the account balance of the same, including forfeiture reallocations; and other asset contribution account balances and forfeitures.

SELECTION OF THE TRUSTEE AND ADMINISTRATOR

The reporting, accounting, administrative, and fiduciary requirements of an ESOP trust are both stringent and complex. It is recommended that a competent and respected professional or institution be selected as the plan trustee and administrator. A commercial bank is a frequent and appropriate choice, even where the bank assisted in financing the ESOP.

Having a bank as a trustee helps to assure arm's-length and independent transactions involving a disqualified person or party in interest. The only unusual liability involves the accurate valuation of stock of a close-held company. A properly drafted trust document can assure that qualified and independent appraisals will be obtained whenever necessary and that the bank will be indemnified against any liability thereof, excepting its own negligent or unlawful acts.

From the position of the company and the employees, it is generally advisable to have a representative plan committee that determines overall plan policy. It may also direct the trustee as to the voting of shares held by the trust to the extent that such voting rights exist and are not passed through to employee participants. It may be advisable for the committee to include union representatives if union members are included in the plan or if the plan is the product of collective bargaining. Serious planning and fair representation can prevent much of the friction and dispute that frequently develop concerning control of the trustee, plan policies, and voting rights.

CHECKLIST AND PROCEDURE GUIDE

1. Determine company qualifications.
   a. Market, financial, and tax analysis.
   b. Labor-management relations and commitment to an ESOP.
   c. Shareholder attitudes toward and effects of an ESOP.

2. Design tentative plan and trust incorporating all the technical and administrative requirements treated in this chapter.

3. Submit tentative plan to the relevant company decision centers for evaluation and comment.

4. Obtain board of directors resolution adopting tentative ESOP and trust as amended.

5. Announce plan trust to employees and conduct meetings with same to explain and discuss plan and trust.

6. Draft final plan and trust with recommendation of trustee and submit to board of directors.

7. Obtain board of directors resolution approving plan, trust, plan committee, and trustee.

8. Obtain execution of plan and trust documents by company officers and plan trustee.

9. Open trust bank account and announce final ESOP and trust to employees.

10. Prepare and distribute summary plan description (SPD) to employee participants.

11. Prepare IRS Form 5302 (employee census) and Form 5301 (application for determination letter) or, if applicable, Form 5303 (collective bargaining plan) or Form 5309 (for TCESOP).

12. File the preceding with the applicable IRS service center together with a copy of the board resolutions, the plan and trust documents, the employee announcement, and the SPD.

13. Make and file the necessary amendments as directed by IRS to obtain a determination letter.

14. Obtain proper valuation of company stock to determine fair market value thereof.

15. Obtain SEC "no action" letter and state consent (if necessary) for transfer of employer securities to trust.

16. Make contribution to ESOP trust prior to filing the company income tax return. If cash contribution, also purchase company stock for no more than fair market value from the company or shareholders.

17. If financed by company or ESOP trust, prepare necessary loan documents, grant applications, promissory notes, and security agreements.

18. Obtain board of directors resolution authorizing the financing plan.

19. Close the financing transaction, obtaining the proper execution of documents and transfer of funds.

20. Design and implement a communication and participation program for participating employees, including periodic meetings, reporting, and the SPD.

21. File SPD and summary annual report (EBS-2) with Labor-Management Services, Department of Labor.

22. File SAR (Form 5500 or 5500-C), exempt organization tax return (Forms 4848 and 4849), and annual registration statement (ARS) with IRS.

23. Distribute copies of SAR and ARS to employee participants or beneficiaries.

NOTES

1. Revenue Ruling 69-65 (1969-1CB 114).

2. *Usery* v. *Penn*, 426 F. Supp. 830 (1976); affirmed, *Marshall* v. *Penn*, 587 F. 2d. 453 (1978).

3. Revenue Ruling 69-494 (1969-2CB 88).

CHAPTER

10

Economic Philosophy and Public Policy

As indicated in chapter 2, ESOPs and similar employee or wage-earner investment plans must ultimately be evaluated according to their long-run impact upon aggregate savings, capital formation, productivity, and wealth distribution. If ESOPs, and variations thereof, have a significant and long-term positive effect upon the rate of savings from current national income, upon the rate of investment or capital formation, upon productivity (either quantitative or qualitative), and upon the broadened ownership of capital, then American capitalism should experience its most significant transformation since the age of Keynes and Roosevelt.

The ESOP concept has evolved into a nascent social movement. It has a central organizing body—the ESOP Association of America—and several satellite organizations. It has its high priest—Louis Kelso—and its patron in chief—Senator Russell Long. The basic economic philosophy developed by Kelso and Adler in *The Capitalist Manifesto* has advanced considerably more at the legislative and operational level than at the intellectual or theoretical level. To adherents of this economic philosophy, ESOP is a generic term that includes most of the general policies and specific proposals advanced by Kelso and Adler as cited in chapter 1 herein.

The ultimate extent of the success or failure of universal capitalism will depend upon private-sector initiatives in interaction with the dominant economic forces of the times. It is the announced purpose of those who believe in the ESOP concept, and even more so of those who believe in the economic philosophy of universal capitalism, to shape, bend, tilt, or otherwise influence public policy in numerous substantive areas of legislation and administration and at all levels of government. Several matters relating to legislation, public policy, and economic forces merit additional comment to supplement the treatment given thereto in previous chapters.

PURE CREDIT AND TWO-TIERED DISCOUNTING

Leveraging is a major factor in corporate finance. It can make the difference between survival and bankruptcy or between growth and stagnation. At the microeconomic level the ultimate restraints on credit involve the value of the assets (collateral) and the net earnings (return on investment) of the company. At the macroeconomic level the ultimate restraint on nominal (money) credit is the Federal Reserve System (monetary policy), while the ultimate restraints on real credit (usable resources) are the savings rate and the productivity rate. "Pure credit" involves a subsidy to differentiate the cost of monetary credit through "two-tier" discounting by the Federal Reserve System such that the allocation of real credit is altered and then consequently increased.

Under the proposed legislation the Federal Reserve would establish a two-tiered interest rate for its discounting operations.[1] The first tier would be the normal discount rate on the eligible commercial paper or borrowing of eligible banks. The second tier would discount the eligible paper involving loans or credit extension to ESOPs, ISOPs (individual stock ownership plans), and CSOPs (consumer stock ownership plans) at pure-credit rates. Such rates, estimated at between 2 percent and 3 percent, would be composed of Federal Reserve administrative costs (0.5 percent), government-sponsored risk insurance (0.5 percent), and bank profits and administrative expense (1-2 percent).[2]

Eligible commercial lenders would have both a low-cost source of reserves and a low-risk type of loan with a moderate, but guaranteed, profit. All loans would be nonrecourse to the eligible plan and its participants and would be self-liquidating in that both principal and interest would be repaid with pretax profits. ESOP type credit would be the beneficiary of a triple subsidy: the principal and interest deduction for loan amortization; the government-sponsored risk insurance; and the pure credit discount rate.

With the opportunity cost of conventional loans and credit substantially higher, lending institutions could be expected to reallocate loan portfolios to favor ESOP, ISOP, and CSOP credit (SOP credit). Heavy discounting of SOP (stock ownership plan) paper could be expected and, therefore, a net increase in loanable bank reserves could be expected. This should tend to lessen the blow to conventional credit markets, which should have experienced increased interest rates and lower bond prices resulting from the rush to SOP credit. In fact, the net effect could be an increase in total new credit—both private and public.

Unless and until this new SOP-initiated credit expansion yields increased investment and production, the consequences will be inflationary without corrective measures by the Federal Reserve. This can be illustrated in monetary terms using a simple money multiplier and equation of exchange. Using approximate mid-1980 data, an M-1B of $600 billion and an annual circulation velocity (V) of 4 will yield a GNP in current prices of $2,400 billion.[3] Assuming the $2,400 billion the GNP involves 120 billion units of goods (Q), the average unit price (P) would be $20. Thus, $M \times V = P \times Q = $ GNP or $600 \times 4 = $20 \times 120 = $2,400$ billion.

With a constant monetary and fiscal policy, assume that the SOP credit program adds new money and credit (ΔM-1B) of $5 billion. Then, because of low-cost discounting, the lenders discount these loans at the Federal Reserve for 2-3 percent and thereby create nearly $5 billion in additional reserves (AR), which are subsequently used to make additional loans. With a modest money multiplier (m) of 3, the secondary increase in M-1B would be $15 billion ($\Delta$M-1B $= AR \times m$). Thus, whereas under normal circumstances the money supply increase would be only about $5 billion, SOP credit and two-tier discounting result in both more initial loans and more total discounting for secondary and tertiary loans, resulting in an increase of $20 billion in M-1B.

With a constant real output (Q), the effect is merely to increase the rate of price increases (ΔP) from 0.8 percent to 3.3 percent. Normal expansion: $605 \times 4 = $20.17 \times 120 = $2,420$ billion GNP, where the $20 billion GNP increase is inflation, or $\Delta P = $20/$2,400 = 0.8$ percent. SOP credit expansion: $620 \times 4 = $20.67 \times 120 = $2,480$ billion where the $80 billion GNP increase is inflation, or $\Delta P = $80/$2,400 = 3.3$ percent.

However, if the Federal Reserve restricts other forms of credit using conventional quantitative and qualitative controls, and if the SOP credit does increase investment and output, then the equation of exchange could read as follows: $615 \times 4 = $20 \times 123 = $2,460$ billion GNP, where the $60 billion GNP increase is real. Or, $\Delta Q = $60/$2,400 = 2.5$ percent. Thus, the SOP credit strategy has lowered the cost of monetary credit for SOPs while increasing it for other uses (i.e., credit for consumption or speculation) such that monetary credit, real credit (usable resources), and real output have all been increased.

Consideration must also be given to the fiscal effects of SOP credit expansion. The pure-credit discount rate would involve minor revenue losses for the Federal Reserve, but the tax revenue losses of SOP financing could have significant monetary and fiscal consequences unless offset by increased GNP and tax revenues resulting from such financing. Further, expansive fiscal policy could severely disrupt capital markets already impacted by SOP financing. Thus, SOP financing may require both monetary and fiscal restraint.

Since SOP financing reduces the cost of capital, investments with lower-than-average returns to capital would be encouraged. It would be necessary for the Federal Reserve to monitor both the expected and the actual investment performance so as to prevent a declining marginal efficiency of capital and the inflationary effect thereof. This could involve a screening process as well as variable discounting rates and, if necessary, discounting disqualification.

INDIVIDUAL STOCK OWNERSHIP PLANS (ISOPs)

The proposed ISOP would replace the ESOP as the basic tool of new capital formation and diversified capital ownership. It would be IRC Section 401(a) qualified such that assets and incomes could be accumulated within the plan tax-free and distributions would receive preferable tax treatment.The ISOP is an individual account plan with a diversified portfolio wherein a bank or similar institution could serve as trustee. Accounts from ESOPs, CSOPs, or GSOPs could be rolled over into an ISOP without tax consequences.

Under one legislative proposal, each adult American would be provided with an ISOP account with a credit allocation quota such that any time an SEC-registered company issued new stock, the account holder could purchase a corresponding quota of such stock.[4] Low-interest bank loans, nonrecourse to the participant, would be available through pure-credit discounting. The loans would be amortized by dividend earnings that would be paid generously, for such dividends would be tax deductible to the corporations.

To discourage speculators, no secondary speculative sales would be allowed to ISOPs. Only the newly issued stock of SEC-registered companies would be eligible. Any ISOP stock purchases in excess of the pure-credit allocation to that account would be made by conventional means.

THE CAPITAL DIFFUSION INSURANCE CORPORATION (CDIC)

The CDIC would have functions similar to the Federal Deposit Insurance Corporation (FDIC) or the Pension Guarantee Insurance Corporation (PGIC). Part of the interest payment involved in SOP financing (e.g., 0.5 percent) would go to the CDIC as an annual premium payment to protect the lending institutions against full losses in cases of loan default. Premium rates could be differentiated, based upon *Moody's, Standard & Poor*, or similar ratings of company financial integrity.

A secondary function could be to insure the asset value of ESOPs, GSOPs, ISOPs, and CSOPs. Again, premium rates could be differentiated based upon company and plan characteristics. Perhaps the need for such insurance is greatest in the case of ESOPs because little or no portfolio diversification exists and because plan participants are also employees of the sponsoring company. As indicated in chapters 6 and 9, such portfolio-risk insurance is presently available through some private insurance companies and may be purchased by ESOPs.

GENERAL POLICY ON INDIVIDUAL AND CORPORATE TAXES

The basic tax scheme of universal capitalism is a uniform and integrated flat-rate income tax applicable to all persons and business entities.[5] The basic premise is that property, ownership, and profits are inseparable. For tax purposes, corporations would be treated like partnerships in that profits would be taxable at the uniform integrated flat rate to the stockholders on a per share basis. To encourage dividend pay-outs, tax deductions would be allowed for distributions, including those dividend distributions applied to the amortization of a stock purchase of any qualified SOP.

A wealth tax would replace the existing estate and gift tax such that capital or property estates could be accumulated up to a certain limit (e.g., up to $500,000 under one legislative proposal), but beyond that limit a periodic tax would be levied on the excess so as to prevent the concentration of wealth and economic power. The wealth tax could be avoided by transferring the excess accumulation to family members, charities, employees, or others. Since the basis of the wealth tax is the total value of accumulated property, it would be levied without regard to the income tax and it could be progressive to increase its effectiveness.

State and local laws would need revision to conform to the income and wealth tax. This would involve dramatic adjustments for county and state governments, which tend to derive most of their operating revenues from general property and sales taxes, respectively. The capital gains and other tax preferences would also be subject to revision to discourage speculation in and turnover of qualified property and to promote the long-run accumulation of the same.

THE GAO REPORT

In August 1978 and again in July 1979, Senator Russell Long, as chairman of the Senate Committee on Finance, requested that the comptroller general of the United States, General Accounting Office (GAO), review the ESOPs of federal contractors to determine if there are problems that require corrective legislation and to attempt to determine whether ESOPs affect productivity or employee motivation.[6] GAO reviewed sixteen ESOP companies with federal contracts in Alabama, California, Florida, Maryland, New York, Oklahoma, Texas, and Virginia. Three of the companies were public and SEC registered and thirteen were close-held with the number of participants ranging from 25 to 6,100.

No TCESOPs were included in the review, which was not and did not purport to be a representative sample of all ESOP companies. Using data from the Department of Labor (Labor) and the Senate Select Committee on Small Business, the report indicated that about 2,500 ESOPs existed in 1978 and 3,000 in 1979.[7] The Department of Treasury (Treasury) provided GAO with an estimated tax revenue loss from ESOPs during fiscal 1979 of between $1.5 billion and $2.3 billion.[8]

Despite the report's limited and nonrepresentative methodology, its findings represent the most significant government criticism of ESOPs at the policy level as of this writing. Specifically, it charged that close-held companies tended to sell stock to the ESOP trusts based upon improper valuations, failed to assure participants of a market for such stock, did not pass through voting rights to participants, and failed to provide the required communication and reporting to participants.[9] The report called for legislative changes by Congress and for additional regulations and increased scrutiny by Labor and Treasury to address the areas of criticism.

The report includes the following statements:

We reviewed the operations of ESOPs in 3 publicly traded and 13 closely held companies. Our analysis of transactions in the 13 closely held companies showed that the plans generally were not being operated in the best interest of participants. Specifically, one or more of the following problems which could affect participants' benefits were present in each of the closely held company plans:

—Plan fiduciaries acquired employer stock without taking the steps necessary to assure that the transactions were not for more than fair market value.

—Plan documents did not contain provisions requiring the employer or the ESOP to repurchase employer stock when distributed to participants.

—Companies did not pass voting rights to participants for employer stock acquired by the ESOP.

In the absence of specific guidelines and ESOP regulations and in view of the pervasive nature of the problems with ESOPs at the 13 companies whose plans we reviewed, similar problems with ESOPs at other closely held companies are likely.

The problems identified with stock valuation, marketability, and voting in closely held companies were not observed in the publicly traded companies because their stock was:

—Traded in an established market at prices determined by willing buyers and sellers (this procedure overcame the valuation and marketability problems noted in closely held companies).

—Registered with the Securities and Exchange Commission, which made all transactions in the stock subject to the Commission's reporting and disclosure requirements. Additionally, these companies passed full voting rights directly to ESOP participants for shares of company stock allocated to their account....

Although ERISA's fundamental policy is to protect employees' pension plan interests, and a major congressional intent behind ESOPs is diffusion of ownership of the company to employees, the plans of the closely held companies we reviewed

—invested ESOP assets in employer stock that may be unmarketable when distributed to participants and

—with one exception, had not passed voting rights to ESOP participants for stock conveyed to the plan.

Companies have used ESOPs largely for their own advantage, such as for tax benefits and to give the company a market for its stock, rather than for the primary benefit of participants and beneficiaries.[10]

The report clearly identifies the improper valuation of close-held employer securities as the dominant defect of ESOPs. Treasury, in responding to the report, stated that this problem and others raised by the report are generally applicable to all eligible individual account plans excepted from the limitations on investment in employer securities (diversity rule) under ERISA Section 407.[11] Such plans include profit-sharing, stock bonus, ESOP, and money purchase pension plans.

While accepting the Treasury conclusion as accurate, GAO made the following points on stock valuation:

Each of the 13 closely held companies whose ESOP we reviewed sold or contributed company common stock to its ESOP at questionable prices. The prices were based on appraisal valuations that lacked the independence required for good faith determinations and/or did not consider all relevant factors necessary in determining the fair market value. These circumstances resulted primarily because plan fiduciaries had not taken the steps required by ERISA and its implementing regulations to assure that ESOP pay no more than fair market value for employer stock.

Additionally, Labor had not developed regulations, as contemplated by ERISA, for valuing company stock. The only guidelines Labor or IRS cited for valuing stock of closely held companies were very general and subject to broad interpretations. These conditions resulted in stock appraisers using significantly different approaches in considering the same appraisal factors. Contributing or selling overvalued stock to an ESOP is to the advantage of the company or individual making the contribution or sale because of the increased tax deduction or cash proceeds involved. Furthermore, transactions involving overvalued stock could be detrimental to the plan and its participants because such transactions

—are prohibited by ERISA and are subject to an excise tax,

—could mislead the participants about the value of their ESOP accounts, and

—could increase the amount on which participants would ultimately pay income tax. . . .

Some factors relevant to determining fair market values are outlined and discussed in Revenue Ruling 59-60. According to this ruling, the following factors, although not all inclusive, are fundamental and require careful analysis.

1. The nature of the business and the history of the enterprise from its inception.

2. The economic outlook in general and the condition and outlook of the industry in particular.

3. The book value of the stock and the financial condition of the business.

4. The earning capacity of the company.

5. The dividend-paying capacity.

6. Whether or not the enterprise has goodwill or other intangible value.

7. Sales of the stock and the size of the block of stock to be valued.

8. The market price of stocks of corporations engaged in the same or a similar line of business having their stocks actively traded in a free and open market, either on an exchange or over the counter.

Other factors, according to industry valuation experts and/or IRS, that could affect the fair market value of stock that should be considered include:

1. Potential discounts for lack of marketability.

2. Potential discounts for minority interests.

3. Obligations to repurchase ESOP stock from terminating participants. . . .

Valuation guidance contained in Revenue Ruling 59-60 is inadequate because it recognizes various approaches to stock valuation with no restrictions against annually selecting the approach that will yield the highest value. The valuation guidance also does not specify whether:

—Pretax or posttax earnings are to be used when the capitalization of earnings approach is used to value stock.

—Pre-ESOP contribution or post-ESOP contribution earnings should be used in capitalizing earnings.

—ESOP loan obligations guaranteed by the company should be recognized as a company liability (which results in a corresponding reduction of book value) when stock values are based on book value.

—Calculated stock values should be discounted because of lack of marketability and, if so, by how much.

—Calculated stock values should be discounted for minority interest or failure to pass voting rights.[12]

The final area of the GAO review concerned productivity and employee motivation. The scope of this review included the sixteen sample companies and three studies: the Conte and Tannenbaum survey for EDA (cited in chapters 2, 6, and 7, herein); a 1977 University of California, Los Angeles, questionnaire survey; the 1975 report to the U.S. Railway Association (cited in chapter 5 herein). While the EDA-sponsored study was the only one of the three that specifically addressed profitability, the GAO summarized its review as follows:

One widely discussed theory underlying ESOPs is that employee participation results in improved worker motivation and increased productivity. However, available published research data on this theory are largely inconclusive, and we were unable to develop substantive evidence in our review of 16 ESOPs to support this theory. Our review showed, however, that some companies may have precluded any potential for positively motivating employees because they had not involved employees in the ESOP or effectively communicated details about the plan—factors that we believe are essential if such plans are to motivate employees and improve productivity.

Discussions with company officials and review of plan documents disclosed that companies established the ESOP for such purposes as providing an employee pension plan, generating cash flow for the company, giving the company a market for its stock, and providing tax advantages to the company. Officials at only 4 of the 16 companies cited improved employee motivation and productivity as a reason for establishing the

ESOP, and only 2 cited this as the primary reason for establishing the ESOP. None of the companies whose plans we reviewed had assessed the effects of their ESOP on employees.

Although there has been some research addressing ESOP effects on motivation and productivity, the published studies we reviewed were tentative in their conclusions. These studies cite a lack of industry experience with ESOPs and a limited number of plans available for analysis as their basis for qualifying their conclusions on ESOPs and suggesting a need for further study.

As discussed in previous chapters, several aspects of ESOP operations in closely held companies we reviewed adversely affect workers' interests. These adverse effects, coupled with the fact that the operational details of ESOPs have not been effectively communicated to employees, would tend to lessen the potential for favorable morale and productivity effects at companies where such conditions exist.[13]

The GAO report fails to give serious consideration to the sociological basis recommendations, while neither representative nor comprehensive, have public policy implications. It is not likely that the various proposals presented in this chapter will gain general congressional approval until the major problems raised by the GAO report are resolved. The voting rights problem has been largely resolved by the Technical Corrections Act of 1979 in that such rights must be granted to a substantial degree.[14] And, as the report indicates, more intense scrutiny and auditing by the IRS may do much to resolve the valuation problem.[15] The put option and the option to take distributions in cash, rather than employer company stock, should do much to resolve the lack of marketability problem cited by the report.[16]

The GAO report fails to give serious consideration to the sociological basis for plan success or failure. It may not be sufficient to cite a lack of knowledge or understanding among employees as to the nature and operation of an ESOP. Knowledge and understanding must be linked both to belief and commitment and to plan success or failure. Chapter 7, on case studies, raises the inference that there is a strong causal link between commitment and plan success.

Stringent regulation may reduce the abuse and misuse of ESOPs while having little effect upon plan success at either the plant (micro) or aggregate (macro) level. Supportive public policy may mean more ESOPs while doing little to minimize abuses at the micro level.

Success is primarily a function of economic and social circumstance where success is measured by a positive impact upon productivity, profits, savings, capital formation, and dispersion of capital ownership. The evidence presented in this book indicates that success is likely if economic self interest and commitment are combined with knowledge and understanding.

NOTES

1. The matters discussed in the first four sections of this chapter are treated in part 2 of a two-part article by Norman G. Kurland, "Beyond ESOP: Steps Toward Tax Justice," *Tax Executive*, July 1977, pp. 386-402. Kurland was formerly the Washington, D.C., counsel for Kelso-Bangert & Co. and now heads his own ESOP investment banking and consulting group in Washington.

2. Ibid., p. 389.

3. As per Federal Reserve definition, M-1B is equal to currency and coins in circulation, plus demand deposits at banks and other financial depositories, plus bank savings deposits.

4. Kurland, "Beyond ESOP," p. 388.

5. Ibid., p. 398.

6. The comptroller general, United States General Accounting Office, *Employee Stock Ownership Plans: Who Benefits Most in Closely Held Companies?* (Washington, D.C.: U.S. General Accounting Office, 1980), p. 1.

7. Ibid., p. 3.

8. Ibid. Compare this with the tax revenue loss estimated in chapter 2, "Comparative Analysis."

9. Ibid., Digest, pp. i, ii, and iii.

10. Ibid., pp. 6, 22.

11. Ibid., p. 49. See also chapter 9, "Investments, Loans, and Insurance" and "Valuation of Company Stock and Fair Market Value."

12. Ibid., pp. 8-10 and 18.

13. Ibid., p. 37.

14. See chapter 9, "Voting Rights."

15. See also chapter 9, "Valuation of Company Stock and Fair Market Value."

16. See chapter 9, "Distributions and Dividends."

APPENDIX

I

Statutes, Regulations, and Rules

CONTENTS

INTERNAL REVENUE CODE (IRC)

SEC. 46 AMOUNT OF CREDIT

(a)(2) (E) Employee plan percentage.—For purposes of this paragraph, the employee plan percentage is—

   (i) with respect to the period beginning on January 21, 1975, and ending on December 31, 1983, 1 percent, and

   (ii) with respect to the period beginning on January 1, 1977, and ending on December 31, 1983, an additional percentage (not in excess of ½ of 1 percent) which results in an amount equal to the amount determined under section 48(n)(1)(B).

This sub-paragraph shall apply to a corporation only if it meets the requirements of section 409A and only if it elects (at such time, in such form, and in such manner as the Secretary prescribes) to have this subparagraph apply.

(f) (9) **Special rule for additional credit.**—If the taxpayer makes an election under subparagraph (E) of subsection (a)(2), for a taxable year beginning after December 31, 1975, then, notwithstanding the prior paragraphs of this subsection, no credit shall be allowed by section 38 in excess of the amount which would be allowed without regard to the provisions of subparagraph (E) of subsection (a)(2) if—

(A) the taxpayer's cost of service for ratemaking purposes or in its regulated books of account is reduced by reason of any portion of such credit which results from the transfer of employer securities or cash to a tax credit employee stock ownership plan which meets the requirements of section 409A;

(B) the base to which the taxpayer's rate of return for ratemaking purposes is applied is reduced by reason of any portion of such credit which results from a transfer described in subparagraph (A) to such employee stock ownership plan; or

(C) any portion of the amount of such credit which results from a transfer described in subparagraph (A) to such employee stock ownership plan is treated for ratemaking purposes in any way other than as though it had been contributed by the taxpayer's common shareholders.

SEC. 48 DEFINITIONS; SPECIAL RULES

(n) Requirements for Allowance of Employee Plan Percentage.—
(1) In general.—

(A) Basic employee plan percentage.—The basic employee plan percentage shall not apply to any taxpayer for any taxable year unless the taxpayer on his return for such taxable year agrees, as a condition for the allowance of such percentage—

(i) to make transfers of employer securities to a tax credit employee stock ownership plan maintained by the taxpayer having an aggregate value equal to 1 percent of the amount of the qualified investment (as determined under subsections (c) and (d) of section 46) for the taxable year, and

(ii) to make such transfers at the times prescribed in subparagraph (C).

(B) Matching employee plan percentage.—The matching employee plan percentage shall not apply to any taxpayer for any taxable year unless the basic employee plan percentage applies to such taxpayer for such taxable year, and the taxpayer on his return for such taxable year agrees, as a condition for the allowance of the matching employee plan percentage—

(i) to make transfers of employer securities to a tax credit employee stock ownership plan maintained by the employer having an aggregate value equal to the lesser of—

(I) the sum of the qualified matching employee contributions made to such plan for the taxable year, or

(II) one-half of 1 percent of the amount of the qualified investment (as determined under subsections (c) and (d) of section 46) for the taxable year, and

(ii) to make such transfers at the times prescribed in subparagraph (C).

(C) Times for making transfers.—The aggregate of the transfers required under subparagraphs (A) and (B) shall be made—

(i) to the extent allocable to that portion of the employee plan credit allowed for the taxable year or allowed as a carryback to a preceding taxable year, not later than 30 days after the due date (including extensions) for filing the return for the taxable year, or

(ii) to the extent allocable to that portion of the employee plan credit which is allowed as a carryover in a succeeding taxable year, not later than 30 days after the due date (including extensions) for filing the return for such succeeding taxable year.

The Secretary may by regulations provide that transfers may be made later than the times prescribed in the preceding sentence where the amount of any credit or carryover or carryback for any taxable year exceeds the amount shown on the return for the taxable year (including where such excess is attributable to qualified matching employee contributions made after the close of the taxable year).

(D) Ordering rules.—For purposes of subparagraph (C), the portion of the employee plan credit allowed for the current year or as a carryover or carryback shall be determined—

(i) first by treating the credit or carryover or carryback as attributable to the regular percentage,

(ii) second by treating the portion (not allocated under clause (i) of such credit or carryover or carryback as attributable to the basic employee plan percentage, and

(iii) finally by treating the portion (not allocated under clause (i) or (ii) as attributable to the matching employee plan percentage.

(2) Qualified Matching Employee Contribution Defined.—

(A) In general.—For purposes of this subsection, the term "qualified matching employee contribution" means, with respect to any taxable year, any contribution made by an employee to a tax credit employee stock ownership plan maintained by the taxpayer if—

(i) each employee who is entitled to an allocation of employer securities transferred to the tax credit employee stock ownership plan under paragraph (1)(A) is entitled to make such a contribution,

(ii) the contribution is designated by the employee as a contribution intended to be taken into account under this subparagraph for the taxable year,

(iii) the contribution is paid in cash to the employer or plan administrator not later than 24 months after the close of the taxable year, and is invested forthwith in employer securities, and

(iv) the tax credit employee stock employee plan meets the requirements of subparagraph (B).

(B) Plan requirements.—For purposes of subparagraph (A), a tax credit employee stock ownership plan meets the requirements of this subparagraph if—

(i) participation in the tax credit employee stock employee plan is not required as a condition of employment and the tax credit employee stock employee plan does not require matching employee contributions as a condition of participation in the tax credit employee stock employee plan, and

(ii) the tax credit employee stock employee plan provides for allocation of all employer securities transferred to it or purchased by it (because of the requirements of paragraph (1)(B) to the account of each participant in an amount equal to such participant's matching employee contributions for the year.

(3) Certain contributions of cash treated as contributions of employer securities.—For purposes of this subsection, a transfer of cash shall be treated as a transfer of employer securities if the cash is, under the tax credit employee stock ownership plan, used within 30 days to purchase employer securities.

(4) Adjustments if employee plan credit recaptured.—If any portion of the employee plan credit is recaptured under section 47 or the employee plan credit is reduced by a final determination—

(A) the employer may reduce the amount required to be transferred to the tax credit employee stock ownership plan under paragraph (1) for the current taxable year or any succeeding taxable year by an amount equal to such portion (or reduction), or

(B) notwithstanding the provisions of paragraph (5) and to the extent not taken into account under subparagraph (A), the employer may deduct an amount equal to such portion (or reduction), subject to the limitations of section 404.

(5) Disallowance of deduction.—No deduction shall be allowed under section 162, 212, or 404 for amounts required to be transferred to a tax credit employee stock ownership plan under this subsection.

(6) Definitions.—For purposes of this subsection—

(A) Employer securities.—The term "employer securities" has the meaning given to such term by section 409A(*l*).

(B) Value.—The term "value" means—

(i) in the case of securities listed on a national exchange, the average of closing prices of such securities for the 20 consecutive trading days immediately preceding the due date for filing the return for the taxable year (determined with regard to extensions), or

(ii) in the case of securities not listed on a national exchange, the fair market value as determined in good faith and in accordance with regulations prescribed by the Secretary.

(*o*) Certain Credits Defined.—For purposes of this title—

(1) Regular investment credit.—The term "regular investment credit" means that portion of the credit allowable by section 38 which is attributable to the regular percentage.

(2) Energy investment credit.—The term "energy investment credit" means that portion of the credit allowable by section 38 which is attributable to the energy percentage.

(3) Employee plan credit.—The term "employee plan credit" means the sum of—

(A) the basic employee plan credit, and

(B) the matching employee plan credit.

(4) Basic employee plan credit—The term "basic employee plan credit" means that portion of the credit allowable by section 38 which is attributable to the basic employee plan percentage.

(5) Matching employee plan credit.—The term "matching employee plan credit" means that portion of the credit allowable by section 38 which is attributable to the matching employee plan percentage.

(6) Basic employee plan percentage.—The term "basic employee plan percentage" means the 1-percent employee plan percentage set forth in section 46(a)(2) (E)(i).

(7) Matching employee plan percentage.—The term "matching employee plan percentage" means the additional employee plan percentage (not to exceed ½ of 1 percent) set forth in section 46(a)(2)(E)(ii).

SEC. 401. QUALIFIED PENSION, PROFIT-SHARING, AND STOCK BONUS PLANS.

(a) Requirements for Qualification.—A trust created or organized in the United States and forming part of a stock bonus, pension, or profit-sharing plan of an employer for the exclusive benefit of his employees or their beneficiaries shall constitute a qualified trust under this section—

(1) if contributions are made to the trust by such employer, or employees, or both, or by another employer who is entitled to deduct his contributions under section 404(a)(3)(B) (relating to deduction for contributions to profit-sharing and stock bonus plans), for the purpose of distributing to such employees or their beneficiaries the corpus and income of the fund accumulated by the trust in accordance with such plan;

(2) if under the trust instrument it is impossible, at any time prior to the satisfaction of all liabilities with respect to employees and their beneficiaries under the trust, for any part of the corpus or income to be (within the taxable year or thereafter) used for, or diverted to, purposes other than for the exclusive benefit of his employees or their beneficiaries;

(3) if the plan of which such trust is a part satisfies the requirements of section 410 (relating to minimum participation standards); and

(4) if the contributions or the benefits provided under the plan do not discriminate in favor of employees who are—

(A) officers,

(B) shareholders, or

(C) highly compensated.

For purposes of this paragraph, there shall be excluded from consideration employees described in section 410(b)(2)(A) and (C).

(5) A classification shall not be considered discriminatory within the meaning of paragraph (4) or section 410(b) (without regard to paragraph (1)(A) thereof) merely because it excludes employees the whole of whose remuneration constitutes "wages" under section 3121(a)(1) (relating to the Federal Insurance Contributions Act) or merely because it is limited to salaried or clerical employees. Neither shall a plan be considered discriminatory within the meaning of such provisions merely because the contributions or benefits of or on behalf of the employees under the plan bear a uniform relationship to the total compensation, or the basic or regular rate of compensation, of such employees, or merely because the contributions or benefits based on that part of an employee's remuneration which is excluded from "wages" by section 3121(a)(1) differ from the contributions or benefits based on employee's remuneration not so excluded, or differ because of any retirement benefits created under State or Federal law. For purposes of this paragraph and paragraph (10), the total compensation of an individual who is an employee within the meaning of subsection (c)(1) means such individual's earned income (as defined in subsection (c)(2)), and the basic or regular rate of compensation of such an individual shall be determined, under regulations prescribed by the Secretary, with respect to that portion of his earned income which bears the same ratio to his earned income as the basic or regular compensation of the employees under the plan bears to the total compensation of such employees. For purposes of determining whether two or more plans of an employer satisfy the requirements of paragraph (4) when considered as a single plan, if the amount of contributions on behalf of the employees allowed as a deduction under section 404 for the taxable year with respect to such plans, taken together, bears a uniform relationship to the total compensation, or the basic or regular rate of compensation, of such employees, the plans shall not be considered discriminatory merely because the rights of employees to, or derived from, the employer contributions under the separate plans do not become nonforfeitable at the same rate. For the purposes of determining whether two or more plans of an employer satisfy the requirements of paragraph (4) when considered as a single plan, if the employees' rights to benefits under the separate plans do not become nonforfeitable at the same rate, but the levels of benefits provided by the separate plans satisfy the requirements of regulations prescribed by the Secretary to take account of the differences in such rates, the plans shall not be considered discriminatory merely because of the difference in such rates. For purposes of determining whether one or more plans of an employer satisfy the requirements of paragraph (4) and of section 410(b), an employer may take into account all simplified employee pensions to which only the employer contributes.

(6) A plan shall be considered as meeting the requirements of paragraph (3) during the whole of any taxable year of the plan if on one day in each quarter it satisfied such requirements.

(7) A trust shall not constitute a qualified trust under this section unless the plan of

which such trust is a part satisfies the requirements of section 411 (relating to minimum vesting standards).

(8) A trust forming part of a pension plan shall not constitute a qualified trust under this section unless the plan provides that forfeitures must not be applied to increase the benefits any employee would otherwise receive under the plan.

(9) In the case of a plan which provides contributions or benefits for employees some or all of whom are employees within the meaning of subsection (c)(1), a trust forming part of such plan shall not constitute a qualified trust under this section unless, under the plan, the entire interest of each employee—

(A) either will be distributed to him not later than his taxable year in which he attains the age of 70½ years, or, in the case of an employee other than an owner-employee (as defined in subsection (c)(3)), in which he retires, whichever is the later, or

(B) will be distributed, commencing not later than such taxable year, (i) in accordance with regulations prescribed by the Secretary, over the life of such employee or over the lives of such employee and his spouse, or (ii) in accordance with such regulations, over a period not extending beyond the life expectancy of such employee or the life expectancy of such employee and his spouse.

A trust shall not be disqualified under this paragraph by reason of distributions under a designation, prior to the date of enactment of this paragraph, by any employee under the plan of which such trust is a part of a method of distribution which does not meet the terms of the preceding sentence.

(10) In the case of a plan which provides contributions or benefits for employees some or all of whom are owner-employees (as defined in subsection (c)(3)—

(A) paragraph (3), the first and second sentences of paragraph (5), and section 410 shall not apply, but—

(i) such plan shall not be considered discriminatory within the meaning of paragraph (4) merely because the contributions or benefits of or on behalf of employees under the plan bear a uniform relationship to the total compensation, or the basic or regular rate of compensation, of such employees, and

(ii) such plan shall not be considered discriminatory within the meaning of paragraph (4) solely because under the plan contributions described in subsection (e) which are in excess of the amounts which may be deducted under section 404 for the taxable year may be made on behalf of any owner-employee; and

(B) a trust forming a part of such plan shall constitute a qualified trust under this section only if the requirements in subsection (d) are also met.

(11) (A) A trust shall not constitute a qualified trust under this section if the plan of which such trust is a part provides for the payment of benefits in the form of an annuity unless such plan provides for the payment of annuity benefits in a form having the effect of a qualified joint and survivor annuity.

(B) Notwithstanding the provisions of subparagraph (A), in the case of a plan which provides for the payment of benefits before the normal retirement age (as defined in section 411 (a)(8)), the plan is not required to provide for the payment of annuity benefits in a form having the effect of a qualified joint and survivor annuity during the period beginning on the date on which the employee enters into the plan as a participant and ending on the later of—

(i) the date the employee reaches the earliest retirement age under the plan, or

(ii) the first day of the 120th month beginning before the date on which the employee reaches normal retirement age.

(C) A plan described in subparagraph (B) does not meet the requirements of subparagraph (A) unless, under the plan, a participant has a reasonable period during which he may elect the qualified joint and survivor annuity form with respect to the period beginning on the date on which the period described in subparagraph (B) ends and ending on the date on which he reaches normal retirement age (as defined in section 411(a)(8)) if he continues his employment during that period. A plan does not meet the requirements of this subparagraph unless, in the case of such an election, the payments under the survivor annuity are not less than the payments which would have been made under the joint annuity to which the participant would have been entitled if he made an election described in this subparagraph immediately prior to his retirement and if his retirement had occurred on the day before his death and within the period within which an election can be made.

(D) A plan shall not be treated as not satisfying the requirements of this paragraph solely because the spouse of the participant is not entitled to receive a survivor annuity (whether or not an election described in subparagraph (C) has been made under subparagraph (C) unless the participant and his spouse have been married throughout the 1-year period ending on the date of such participant's death.

(E) A plan shall not be treated as satisfying the requirements of this paragraph unless, under the plan, each participant has a reasonable period (as prescribed by the Secretary by regulations) before the annuity starting date during which he may elect in writing (after having received a written explanation of the terms and conditions of the joint and survivor annuity and the effect of an election under this subparagraph) not to take such joint and survivor annuity.

(F) A plan shall not be treated as not satisfying the requirements of this paragraph solely because under the plan there is a provision that any election described in subparagraph (C) or (E), and any revocation of any such election, does not become effective (or ceases to be effective) if the participant dies within a period (not in excess of 2 years) beginning on the date of such election or revocation, as the case may be. The preceding sentence does not apply unless the plan provision described in the preceding sentence also provides that such an election or revocation will be given effect in any case in which—

(i) the participant dies from accidental causes,

(ii) a failure to give effect to the election or revocation would deprive the participant's survivor of a survivor annuity, and

(iii) such election or revocation is made before such accident occurred.

(G) For purposes of this paragraph—

(i) the term "annuity starting date" means the first day of the first period for which an amount is received as an annuity (whether by reason of retirement or by reason of disability),

(ii) the term "earliest retirement age" means the earliest date on which, under the plan, the participant could elect to receive retirement benefits, and

(iii) the term "qualified joint and survivor annuity" means an annuity for the life of the participant with a survivor annuity for the life of his spouse which is not less than one-half of, or greater than, the amount of the annuity payable during the joint lives of the participant and his spouse and which is the actuarial equivalent of a single life annuity for the life of the participant.

For purposes of this paragraph, a plan may take into account in any equitable manner (as determined by the Secretary) any increased costs resulting from providing joint and survivor annuity benefits.

(H) This paragraph shall apply only if—

(i) the annuity starting date did not occur before the effective date of this paragraph, and

(ii) the participant was an active participant in the plan on or after such effective date.

(12) A trust shall not constitute a qualified trust under this section unless the plan of which such trust is a part provides that in the case of any merger or consolidation with, or transfer of assets or liabilities to, any other plan after September 2, 1974, each participant in the plan would (if the plan then terminated) receive a benefit immediately after the merger, consolidation, or transfer which is equal to or greater than the benefit he would have been entitled to receive immediately before the merger, consolidation, or transfer (if the plan had then terminated). This paragraph shall apply in the case of a multiemployer plan only to the extent determined by the Pension Benefit Guaranty Corporation.

(13) A trust shall not constitute a qualified trust under this section unless the plan of which such trust is a part provides that benefits provided under the plan may not be assigned or alienated. For purposes of the preceding sentence, there shall not be taken into account any voluntary and revocable assignment of not to exceed 10 percent of any benefit payment made by any participant who is receiving benefits under the plan unless the assignment or alienation is made for purposes of defraying plan administration costs. For purposes of this paragraph a loan made to a participant or beneficiary shall not be treated as an assignment or alienation if such loan is secured by the participant's accrued nonforfeitable benefit and is exempt from the tax imposed by section 4975 (relating to tax on prohibited transactions) by reasons of section 4975(d)(1). This paragraph shall take effect on January 1, 1976 and shall not apply to assignments which were irrevocable on September 2, 1974.

(14) A trust shall not constitute a qualified trust under this section unless the plan of which such trust is a part provides that, unless the participant otherwise elects, the

payment of benefits under the plan to the participant will begin not later than the 60th day after the latest of the close of the plan year in which—

(A) the date on which the participant attains the earlier of age 65 or the normal retirement age specified under the plan,

(B) occurs the 10th anniversary of the year in which the participant commenced participation in the plan, or

(C) the participant terminates his service with the employer.

In the case of a plan which provides for the payment of an early retirement benefit, a trust forming a part of such plan shall not constitute a qualified trust under this section unless a participant who satisfied the service requirements for such early retirement benefit, but separated from the service (with any nonforfeitable right to an accrued benefit) before satisfying the age requirement for such early retirement benefit, is entitled upon satisfaction of such age requirement to receive a benefit not less than the benefit to which he would be entitled at the normal retirement age, actuarially reduced under regulations prescribed by the Secretary.

(15) A trust shall not constitute a qualified trust under this section unless under the plan of which such trust is a part—

(A) in the case of a participant or beneficiary who is receiving benefits under such plan, or

(B) in the case of a participant who is separated from the service and who has nonforfeitable rights to benefits,

such benefits are not decreased by reason of any increase in the benefit levels payable under title II of the Social Security Act or any increase in the wage base under such title II, if such increase takes place after September 2, 1974, or (if later) the earlier of the date of first receipt of such benefits or the date of such separation, as the case may be.

(16) A trust shall not constitute a qualified trust under this section if the plan of which such trust is a part provides for benefits or contributions which exceed the limitations of section 415.

(17) In the case of a plan which provides contributions or benefits for employees some or all of whom are employees within the meaning of subsection (c)(1), or are shareholder-employees within the meaning of section 1379(d), only if the annual compensation of each employee taken into account under the plan does not exceed the first $100,000 of such compensation.

(18) In the case of a trust which is part of a plan providing a defined benefit for employees some or all of whom are employees within the meaning of subsection (c)(1), or are shareholder-employees within the meaning of section 1379(d), only if such plan satisfies the requirements of subsection (j).

(19) A trust shall not constitute a qualified trust under this section if under the plan of which such trust is a part any part of a participant's accrued benefit derived from employer contributions (whether or not otherwise nonforfeitable), is forfeitable solely because of withdrawal by such participant of any amount attributable to the benefit

derived from contributions made by such participant. The preceding sentence shall not apply to the accrued benefit of any participant unless, at the time of such withdrawal, such participant has a nonforfeitable right to at least 50 percent of such accrued benefit (as determined under section 411). The first sentence of this paragraph shall not apply to the extent that an accrued benefit is permitted to be forfeited in accordance with section 411(a)(3)(D)(iii) (relating to proportional forfeitures of benefits accrued before September 2, 1974, in the event of withdrawal of certain mandatory contributions).

(20) A trust forming part of a pension plan shall not be treated as failing to constitute a qualified trust under this section merely because the pension plan of which such trust is a part makes a payment or distribution described in section 402(a)(5)(A)(i) or 403 (a)(4)(A)(i). This paragraph shall not apply to a defined benefit plan unless the employer maintaining such plan files a notice with the Pension Benefit Guaranty Corporation (at the time and in the manner prescribed by the Pension Benefit Guaranty Corporation) notifying the Corporation of such payment or distribution and the Corporation has approved such payment or distribution or, within 90 days after the date on which such notice was filed, has failed to disapprove such payment or distribution.

(21) A trust forming part of an ESOP shall not fail to be considered a permanent program merely because employer contributions under the plan are determined solely by reference to the amount of credit which would be allowable under section 46(a) if the employer made the transfer described in section 48(n)(1).

(22) If a defined contributions plan—

(A) is established by an employer whose stock is not publicly traded, and

(B) after acquiring securities of the employer, more than 10 percent of the total assets of the plan was securities of the employer,

any trust forming part of such plan shall not constitute a qualified trust under this section unless the plan meets the requirements of subsection (e) of section 409A.

SEC. 409A. QUALIFICATIONS FOR TAX CREDIT EMPLOYEE STOCK OWNERSHIP PLANS.

(a) **Tax Credit Employee Stock Ownership Plan Defined.**—Except as otherwise provided in this title, for purposes of this title, the term "tax credit employee stock ownership plan" means a defined contribution plan which—

(1) meets the requirements of section 401(a),

(2) is designed to invest primarily in employer securities, and

(3) meets the requirements of subsections (b), (c), (d), (e), (f), (g), and (h) of this section.

(b) **Required Allocation of Employer Securities.—**

(1) **In general.**—A plan meets the requirements of this subsection if—

(A) the plan provides for the allocation for the plan year of all employer securities transferred to it or purchased by it (because of the requirements of section 48(n)(1)(A)) to the accounts of all participants who are entitled to share in such allocation, and

(B) for the plan year the allocation to each participant so entitled is an amount which bears substantially the same proportion to the amount of all such securities allocated to all such participants in the plan for that year as the amount of compensation paid to such participant during that year bears to the compensation paid to all such participants during that year.

(2) Compensation in excess of $100,000 disregarded.—For purposes of paragraph (1), compensation of any participant in excess of the first $100,000 per year shall be disregarded.

(3) Determination of compensation.—For purposes of this subsection, the amount of compensation paid to a participant for any period is the amount of such participant's compensation (within the meaning of section 415(c)(3)) for such period.

(4) Suspension of allocation in certain cases.—Notwithstanding paragraph (1), the allocation to the account of any participant which is attributable to the basic employee plan credit may be extended over whatever period may be necessary to comply with the requirements of section 415.

(c) Participants Must Have Nonforfeitable Rights.—A plan meets the requirements of this subsection only if it provides that each participant has a nonforfeitable right to any employer security allocated to his account.

(d) Employer Securities Must Stay in the Plan.—A plan meets the requirements of this subsection only if it provides that no employer security allocated to a participant's account under subsection (b) (or allocated to a participant's account in connection with matched employer and employee contributions) may be distributed from that account before the end of the 84th month beginning after the month in which the security is allocated to the account. To the extent provided in the plan, the preceding sentence shall not apply in the case of separation from service, death, or disability.

(e) Voting Rights.—

(1) In general.—A plan meets the requirements of this subsection if it meets the requirements of paragraph (2) or (3), whichever is applicable.

(2) Requirements where employer has a registration-type class of securities.—If the employer has a registration-type class of securities, the plan meets the requirements of this paragraph only if each participant in the plan is entitled to direct the plan as to the manner in which employer securities which are entitled to vote and are allocated to the account of such participant are to be voted.

(3) Requirement for other employers.—If the employer does not have a registration-type class of securities, the plan meets the requirements of this paragraph only if each participant in the plan is entitled to direct the plan as to the manner in which voting rights under employer securities which are allocated to the account of such participant are to be exercised with respect to a corporate matter which (by law or charter) must be decided by more than a majority vote of outstanding common shares voted.

(4) Registration-type class of securities defined.—For purposes of this subsection, the term "registration-type class of securities" means—

(A) a class of securities required to be registered under section 12 of the Securities Exchange Act of 1934, and

(B) a class of securities which would be required to be so registered except for the exemption from registration provided in subsection (g)(2)(H) of such section 12.

(f) Plan Must Be Established Before Employer's Due Date.—

(1) In general.—A plan meets the requirements of this subsection only if it is established on or before the due date (including any extension of such date) for the filing of the employer's tax return for the first taxable year of the employer for which an employee plan credit is claimed by the employer with respect to the plan.

(2) Special rule for first year.—A plan which otherwise meets the requirements of this section shall not be considered to have failed to meet the requirements of section 401(a) merely because it was not established by the close of the first taxable year of the employer for which an employee plan credit is claimed by the employer with respect to the plan.

(g) Transferred Amounts Must Stay in Plan Even Though Investment Credit is Redetermined or Recaptured.—A plan meets the requirements of this subsection only if it provides that amounts which are transferred to the plan (because of the requirements of section 48(n)(1)) shall remain in the plan (and, if allocated under the plan, shall remain so allocated) even though part or all of the employee plan credit is recaptured or redetermined.

(h) Right to Demand Employer Securities; Put Option.—

(1) In general.—A plan meets the requirements of this subsection if a participant who is entitled to a distribution from the plan—

(A) has a right to demand that his benefits be distributed in the form of employer securities, and

(B) if the employer securities are not readily tradable on an established market, has a right to require that the employer repurchase employer securities under a fair valuation formula.

(2) Plan may distribute cash in certain cases.—A plan which otherwise meets the requirements of this section or of section 4975(e)(7) shall not be considered to have failed to meet the requirements of section 401(a) merely because under the plan the benefits may be distributed in cash or in the form of employer securities.

(i) Reimbursement for Expenses of Establishing and Administering Plan.—A plan which otherwise meets the requirements of this section shall not be treated as failing to meet such requirements merely because it provides that—

(1) Expenses of establishing plan.—As reimbursement for the expenses of establishing the plan, the employer may withhold from amounts due the plan for the taxable year for which the plan is established (or the plan may pay) so much of the amounts paid or incurred in connection with the establishment of the plan as does not exceed the sum of—

(A) 10 percent of the first $100,000 which the employer is required to transfer to the plan for that taxable year under section 48(n)(1), and

(B) 5 percent of any amount so required to be transferred in excess of the first $100,000; and

(2) **Administrative expenses.**—As reimbursement for the expenses of administering the plan, the employer may withhold from amounts due the plan (or the plan may pay) so much of the amounts paid or incurred during the taxable year as expenses of administering the plan as does not exceed the lesser of—

(A) the sum of—

(i) 10 percent of the first $100,000 of the dividends paid to the plan with respect to stock of the employer during the plan year ending with or within the employer's taxable year, and

(ii) 5 percent of the amount of such dividends in excess of $100,000 or

(B) $100,000.

(j) Conditional Contributions to the Plan.—A plan which otherwise meets the requirements of this section shall not be treated as failing to satisfy such requirements (or as failing to satisfy the requirements of section 401(a) of this title or of section 403(c)(1) of the Employee Retirement Income Security Act of 1974) merely because of the return of a contribution (or a provision permitting such a return) if—

(1) the contribution to the plan is conditioned on a determination by the Secretary that such plan meets the requirements of this section,

(2) the application for a determination described in paragraph (1) is filed with the Secretary not later than 90 days after the date on which an employee plan credit is claimed, and

(3) the contribution is returned within 1 year after the date on which the Secretary issues notice to the employer that such plan does not satisfy the requirements of this section.

(k) Requirements Relating to Certain Withdrawals.—Notwithstanding any other law or rule of law—

(1) the withdrawal from a plan which otherwise meets the requirements of this section by the employer of an amount contributed for purposes of the matching employee plan credit shall not be considered to make the benefits forfeitable, and

(2) the plan shall not, by reason of such withdrawal, fail to be for the exclusive benefit of participants or their beneficiaries,

if the withdrawn amounts were not matched by employee contributions or were in excess of the limitations of section 415. Any withdrawal described in the preceding sentence shall not be considered to violate the provisions of section 403(c)(1) of the Employee Retirement Income Security Act of 1974.

(l) Employer Securities Defined.—For purposes of this section—

(1) In General.—The term "employer securities" means common stock issued by the employer (or by a corporation which is a member of the same controlled group) which is readily tradable on an established securities market.

(2) Special rule where there is no readily tradable common stock.—If there is no common stock which meets the requirements of paragraph (1), the term "employer securities" means common stock issued by the employer (or by a corporation which is a member of the same controlled group) having a combination of voting power and dividend rights equal to or in excess of—

(A) that class of common stock of the employer (or of any other such corporation) having the greatest voting power, and

(B) that class of common stock of the employer (or of any other such corporation) having the greatest dividend rights.

(3) Preferred stock may be issued in certain cases.—Noncallable preferred stock shall be treated as employer securities if such stock is convertible at any time into stock which meets the requirements of paragraph (1) or (2) (whichever is applicable) and if such conversion is at a conversion price which (as of the date of the acquisition by the tax credit employee stock ownership plan) is reasonable. For purposes of the preceding sentence, under regulations prescribed by the Secretary, preferred stock shall be treated as noncallable if after the call there will be a reasonable opportunity for a conversion which meets the requirements of the preceding sentence.

(4) Controlled group of corporations defined.—

(A) In general.—For purposes of this subsection, the term "controlled group of corporation" has the meaning given to such term by section 1563(a) (determined without regard to subsections (a)(4) and (e)(3)(C) of section 1563).

(B) Common parent may own only 50 percent of first tier subsidiary.—For purposes of subparagraph (A), if the common parent owns directly stock possessing at least 50 percent of the voting power of all classes of stock and at least 50 percent of each class of nonvoting stock in a first tier subsidiary, such subsidiary (and all other corporations below it in the chain which would meet the 80 percent test of section 1563(a) if the first tier subsidiary were the common parent) shall be treated as includible corporations.

(m) Nonrecognition of Gain or Loss on Contribution of Employer Securities to Tax Credit Employee Stock Ownership Plan.—No gain or loss shall be recognized to the taxpayer with respect to the transfer of employer securities to a tax credit employee stock ownership plan maintained by the taxpayer to the extent that such transfer is required under subparagraph (A) or (B) of section 48(n)(1).

(n) Cross References.—

(1) For requirements for allowance of employee plan credit, see section 48(n).

(2) For assessable penalties for failure to meet requirements of this section,

or for failure to make contributions required with respect to the allowance of an employee plan credit, see section 6699.

SEC. 415. LIMITATIONS ON BENEFITS AND CONTRIBUTIONS UNDER QUALIFIED PLANS

(c)(6) Special limitation for employee stock ownership plan.—

(A) In the case of an employee stock ownership plan (as defined in subparagraph (B)), under which no more than one-third of the employer contributions for a year are allocated to the group of employees consisting of officers, shareholders owning more than 10 percent of the employer's stock (determined under subparagraph (B)(iv)), or employees described in subparagraph (B)(iii), the amount described in paragraph (c)(1)(A) (as adjusted for such year pursuant to subsection (d)(1)) for a year with respect to any participant shall be equal to the sum of (i) the amount described in paragraph (c)(1)(A) (as so adjusted) determined without regard to this paragraph and (ii) the lesser of the amount determined under clause (i) or the amount of employer securities contributed to the employee stock ownership plan.

(B) For purposes of this paragraph—

(i) the term "employee stock ownership plan" means a [an] employee stock ownership plan (within the meaning of section 4975(e)(7)) or a tax credit employee stock ownership plan,

(ii) the term "employer securities" has the meaning given to such term by section 409A,

(iii) an employee described in this clause is any participant whose compensation for a year exceeds an amount equal to twice the amount described in paragraph (1)(A) for such year (as adjusted for such year pursuant to subsection (d)(1)), determined without regard to subparagraph (A) of this paragraph, and

(iv) an individual shall be considered to own more than 10 percent of the employer's stock if, without regard to stock held under the employee stock ownership plan, he owns (after application of section 1563(e)) more than 10 percent of the total combined voting power of all classes of stock entitled to vote or more than 10 percent of the total value of shares of all classes of stock.

SEC. 1391. DEFINITIONS.

(a) **General Stock Ownership Corporation.**—For purposes of this subchapter, the term "general stock ownership corporation" (hereinafter referred to as a "GSOC" means a domestic corporation which—

(1) is not a member of an affiliated group (as defined in section 1504), and

(2) is chartered and organized after December 31, 1978, and before January 1, 1984;

(3) is chartered by an act of a State legislature or as a result of a State-wide referendum;

(4) has a charter providing—

(A) for the issuance of only 1 class of stock,

(B) for the issuance of shares only to eligible individuals (as defined in subsection (c));

(C) for the issuance of at least one share to each eligible individual, unless such eligible individual elects within one year after the date of issuance not to receive such share;

(D) that no share of stock shall be transferable—

(i) by a shareholder other than by will or the laws of descent and distribution until after the expiration of 5 years from the date such stock is issued by the GSOC except where the shareholder ceases to be a resident of the State;

(ii) to any person other than a resident individual of the chartering State;

(iii) to any individual who, after the transfer, would own more than 10 shares of the GSOC;

(E) that such corporation shall qualify as a GSOC under the Internal Revenue Code;

(5) is empowered to invest in properties (but not in properties acquired by it or for its benefit through the right of eminent domain).

For purposes of this subsection, section 1504(a) shall be applied by substituting "20 percent" for "80 percent" wherever it appears.

(b) Electing GSOC.—For purposes of this subchapter, the term "electing GSOC" means a GSOC which files an election under section 1392 which, under section 1392, is in effect for such taxable year.

(c) Eligible Individuals.—For purposes of subsection (a), the term "eligible individual" means an individual who is, as of a date specified in the State's enabling legislation for the GSOC, a resident of the chartering State and who remains a resident of such State between that date and the date of issuance.

(d) Treated as Private Corporation.—For purposes of this title, a GSOC shall be treated as a private corporation and not as a governmental unit.

(e) Study of General Stock Ownership Corporation.—The staff of the Joint Committee on Taxation shall prepare a report on the operation and effects of this subchapter relating to GSOC's. An interim report shall be filed within two years after the first GSOC is formed and a final report shall be filed by September 30, 1983.

SEC. 1392. ELECTION BY GSOC.

(a) Eligibility.—Except as provided in section 1393, any GSOC may elect, in accordance with the provisions of this section, not to be subject to the taxes imposed by this chapter.

(b) Effect.—If a GSOC makes an election under subsection (a) then—

(1) with respect to the taxable years of the GSOC for which such election is in effect, such corporation shall not be subject to the taxes imposed by this chapter and, with respect to such taxable years and all succeeding taxable years, the provisions of section 1396 shall apply to such GSOC, and

(2) with respect to each such taxable year, the provisions of sections 1393, 1394, and 1395 shall apply to the shareholders of such GSOC.

(c) **Where and How Made.**—An election under subsection (a) may be made by a GSOC at such time and in such manner as the Secretary shall prescribe by regulations.

(d) **Years for Which Effective.**—An election under subsection (a) shall be effective for the taxable year of the GSOC for which it is made and for all succeeding taxable years of the GSOC, unless it is terminated under subsection (f).

(e) **Taxable Year.**—The taxable year of a GSOC shall end on October 31 unless the Secretary consents to a different taxable year.

(f) **Termination.**—The election of a GSOC under subsection (a) shall terminate for any taxable year during which it ceases to be a GSOC and for all succeeding taxable years. The election of a GSOC under subsection (a) may be terminated at any other time with the consent of the Secretary, effective for the first taxable year with respect to which the Secretary consents and for all succeeding taxable years.

SEC. 1393. GSOC TAXABLE INCOME TAXED TO SHAREHOLDERS

(a) **General Rule.**—The taxable income of an electing GSOC for any taxable year shall be included in the gross income of the shareholders of such GSOC in the manner and to the extent set forth in this subsection.

(1) **Amount included in gross income.**—Each shareholder of an electing GSOC on any day of a taxable year of such GSOC shall include in his gross income for the taxable year with or within which the taxable year of the GSOC ends the amount he would have received if, on each day of such taxable year, there had been distributed pro rata to its shareholders by such GSOC an amount equal to the taxable income of the GSOC for its taxable year divided by the number of days in the GSOC's taxable year.

(2) **Taxable income defined.**—For purposes of this section, the term "taxable income" of a GSOC shall be determined without regard to the deductions allowed by part VIII of subchapter B (other than deductions allowed by section 248, relating to organizational expenditures).

(b) **Special Rule for Investment Credit.**—The investment credit of an electing GSOC for any taxable year shall be allowed as a credit to the shareholders of such corporation in the manner and to the extent set forth in this subsection.

(1) **Credit.**—There shall be apportioned among the shareholders a credit equal to the amount each shareholder would have received if, on each day of such taxable year, there had been distributed pro rata to the shareholders the electing GSOC's net investment credit divided by the number of days in the GSOC's taxable year.

(2) **Net investment credit.**—For purposes of this paragraph the term "net

investment credit'' means the investment credit of the electing GSOC for its taxable year less any tax from recomputing a prior year's investment credit in accordance with section 47.

(3) **Recapture.**—There shall be apportioned among the shareholders of a GSOC, in the manner described in paragraph (1), an additional tax equal to the excess of any tax resulting from recomputing a prior year's investment credit in accordance with section 47 over the investment credit of the GSOC for its taxable year.

SEC. 1394. RULES APPLICABLE TO DISTRIBUTIONS OF AN ELECTING GSOCs.

(a) **Shareholder Income Account.**—An electing GSOC shall establish and maintain a shareholder income account which account shall be—

(1) increased at the close of the GSOC's taxable year by an amount equal to the GSOC's taxable income for such year, and

(2) decreased, but not below zero, on the first day of the GSOC's taxable year by the amount of any GSOC distribution to the shareholders of such GSOC made or treated as made during the prior taxable year.

(b) **Taxation of Distribution.**—Distributions by an electing GSOC shall be treated as—

(1) a distribution of previously taxed income to the extent such distribution does not exceed the balance of the shareholder income account as of the close of the taxable year of the GSOC, and

(2) a distribution to which section 301(a) applies but only to the extent such distribution exceeds the balance of the shareholder income account as of the close of the taxable year of the GSOC.

(c) **Distributions Not Treated as a Dividend.**—Any amounts includible in the gross income of any individual by reason of ownership of stock in a GSOC shall not be considered as a dividend for purposes of section 116.

(d) **Regulations.**—The Secretary shall have authority to prescribe by regulation, rules for treatment of distributions in respect of shares of stock of the GSOC that have been transferred during the taxable year.

SEC. 1395. ADJUSTMENT TO BASIS OF STOCK OF SHAREHOLDERS.

The basis of a shareholder's stock in an electing GSOC shall be increased by the amount includible in the gross income of such shareholder under section 1393, but only to the extent to which such amount is actually included in the gross income of such shareholder.

SEC. 1396. MINIMUM DISTRIBUTIONS.

(a) **General Rule.**—A GSOC shall distribute at least 90 percent of its taxable income for any taxable year by January 31 following the close of such taxable year. Any distribution made on or before January 31 shall be treated as made as of the close of the preceding taxable year.

(b) Imposition of Tax in Case of Failure to Make Minimum Distributions.—If a GSOC fails to make the minimum distribution requirements described in subsection (a), there is hereby imposed a tax equal to 20 percent of the excess of the amount required to be distributed over the amount actually distributed.

SEC. 1397. SPECIAL RULES APPLICABLE TO AN ELECTING GSOC.

(a) General Rule.—The current earnings and profits of an electing GSOC as of the close of its taxable year shall not include the amount of taxable income for such year which is required to be included in the gross income of the shareholders of such GSOC under section 1393(a).

(b) Special Rule For Audit Adjustments.—

(1) Taxable income.—Taxable income of an electing GSOC shall, in the year of final determination, be increased or decreased, as the case might be, by any adjustment to taxable income for a prior taxable year.

(2) Investment credit.—The net investment credit of an electing GSOC shall, in the year of final determination, be increased or decreased, as the case might be, by any adjustment to the net investment credit for a prior taxable year.

(3) Method of making adjustments.—An electing GSOC shall include in gross income for the year of an adjustment the amount described in paragraph (1) and shall take into account the adjustment described in paragraph (2), and shall be liable for payment of interest in the amount that would have been payable by the GSOC under section 6601 (relating to interest on underpayment, nonpayment or extensions of time for payment, of tax) or receivable by the GSOC under section 6611 (relating to interest on overpayments) if such GSOC had been a corporation other than an electing GSOC.

SEC. 4975. TAX ON PROHIBITED TRANSACTIONS.

(a) Initial Taxes on Disqualified Person.—There is hereby imposed a tax on each prohibited transaction. The rate of tax shall be equal to 5 percent of the amount involved with respect to the prohibited transaction for each year (or part thereof) in the taxable period. The tax imposed by this subsection shall be paid by any disqualified person who participates in the prohibited transaction (other than a fiduciary acting only as such).

(b) Additional Taxes on Disqualified Person.—In any case in which an initial tax is imposed by subsection (a) on a prohibited transaction and the transaction is not corrected within the correction period, there is hereby imposed a tax equal to 100 percent of the amount involved. The tax imposed by this subsection shall be paid by any disqualified person who participated in the prohibited transaction (other than a fiduciary acting only as such).

(c) Prohibited Transaction.—

(1) General rule.—For purposes of this section, the term "prohibited transaction" means any direct or indirect—

(A) sale or exchange, or leasing, of any property between a plan and a disqualified person;

(B) lending of money or other extension of credit between a plan and a disqualified person;

(C) furnishing of goods, services, or facilities between a plan and a disqualified person;

(D) transfer to, or use by or for the benefit of, a disqualified person of the income or assets of a plan;

(E) act by a disqualified person who is a fiduciary whereby he deals with the income or assets of a plan in his own interest or for his own account; or

(F) receipt of any consideration for his own personal account by any disqualified person who is a fiduciary from any party dealing with the plan in connection with a transaction involving the income or assets of the plan.

(2) Special exemption.—The Secretary shall establish an exemption procedure for purposes of this subsection. Pursuant to such procedure, he may grant a conditional or unconditional exemption of any disqualified person or transaction, or class of disqualified persons or transactions, from all or part of the restrictions imposed by paragraph (1) of this subsection. Action under this subparagraph may be taken only after consultation and coordination with the Secretary of Labor. The Secretary may not grant an exemption under this paragraph unless he finds that such exemption is—

(A) administratively feasible,

(B) in the interests of the plan and of its participants and beneficiaries, and

(C) protective of the rights of participants and beneficiaries of the plan.

Before granting an exemption under this paragraph, the Secretary shall require adequate notice to be given to interested persons and shall publish notice in the Federal Register of the pendency of such exemption and shall afford interested persons an opportunity to present views. No exemption may be granted under this paragraph with respect to a transaction described in subparagraph (E) or (F) of paragraph (1) unless the Secretary affords an opportunity for a hearing and makes a determination on the record with respect to the findings required under subparagraphs (A), (B), and (C) of this paragraph, except that in lieu of such hearing the Secretary may accept any record made by the Secretary of Labor with respect to an application for exemption under section 408(a) of title I of the Employee Retirement Income Security Act of 1974.

(3) Special rule for individual retirement accounts.—An individual for whose benefit an individual retirement account is established and his beneficiaries shall be exempt for the tax imposed by this section with respect to any transaction concerning such account (which would otherwise be taxable under this section) if, with respect to such transaction, the account ceases to be an individual retirement account by reason of the application of section 408(e)(2)(A) or if section 408(e)(4) applies to such account.

(d) Exemptions.—The prohibitions provided in subsection (c) shall not apply to—

(1) any loan made by the plan to a disqualified person who is a participant or beneficiary of the plan if such loan—

(A) is available to all such participants or beneficiaries on a reasonably equivalent basis,

(B) is not made available to highly compensated employees, officers, or shareholders in an amount greater than the amount made available to other employees,

(C) is made in accordance with specific provisions regarding such loans set forth in the plan,

(D) bears a reasonable rate of interest, and

(E) is adequately secured;

(2) any contract, or reasonable arrangement, made with a disqualified person for office space, or legal, accounting, or other services necessary for the establishment or operation of the plan, if no more than reasonable compensation is paid therefor;

(3) any loan to an [a] leveraged employee stock ownership plan (as defined in subsection (e)(7)), if—

(A) such loan is primarily for the benefit of participants and beneficiaries of the plan, and

(B) such loan is at a reasonable rate of interest, and any collateral which is given to a disqualified person by the plan consists only of qualifying employer securities (as defined in subsection (c)(8));

(4) the investment of all or part of a plan's assets in deposits which bear a reasonable interest rate in a bank or similar financial institution supervised by the United States or a State, if such bank or other institution is a fiduciary of such plan and if—

(A) the plan covers only employees of such bank or other institution and employees of affiliates of such bank or other institution, or

(B) such investment is expressly authorized by a provision of the plan or by a fiduciary (other than such bank or institution or affiliates thereof) who is expressly empowered by the plan to so instruct the trustee with respect to such investment;

(5) any contract for life insurance, health insurance, or annuities with one or more insurers which are qualified to do business in a State if the plan pays no more than adequate consideration, and if each such insurer or insurers is—

(A) the employer maintaining the plan, or

(B) a disqualified person which is wholly owned (directly or indirectly) by the employer establishing the plan, or by any person which is a disqualified person with respect to the plan, but only if the total premiums and annuity considerations written by such insurers for life insurance, health insurance, or annuities for all plans (and their employers) with respect to which such insurers are disqualified persons (not including premiums or annuity considerations written by the employer maintaining the plan) do not exceed 5 percent of the total premiums and annuity considerations written for all lines of insurance in that year by such insurers (not including premiums or annuity considerations written by the employer maintaining the plan);

(6) the provision of any ancillary service by a bank or similar financial institution supervised by the United States or a State, if such service is provided at not more than reasonable compensation, if such bank or other institution is a fiduciary of such plan, and if—

(A) such bank or similar financial institution has adopted adequate internal safeguards which assure that the provision of such ancillary service is consistent with sound banking and financial practice, as determined by Federal or State supervisory authority, and

(B) the extent to which such ancillary service is provided is subject to specific guidelines issued by such bank or similar financial institution (as determined by the Secretary after consultation with Federal and State supervisory authority), and under such guidelines the bank or similar financial institution does not provide such ancillary service—

(i) in an excessive or unreasonable manner, and

(ii) in a manner that would be inconsistent with the best interests of participants and beneficiaries of employee benefit plans;

(7) the exercise of a privilege to convert securities, to the extent provided in regulations of the Secretary, but only if the plan receives no less than adequate consideration pursuant to such conversion;

(8) any transaction between a plan and a common or collective trust fund or pooled investment fund maintained by a disqualified person which is a bank or trust company supervised by a State or Federal agency or between a plan and a pooled investment fund of an insurance company qualified to do business in a State if—

(A) the transaction is a sale or purchase of an interest in the fund,

(B) the bank, trust company, or insurance company receives not more than reasonable compensation, and

(C) such transaction is expressly permitted by the instrument under which the plan is maintained, or by a fiduciary (other than the bank, trust company, or insurance company, or an affiliate thereof) who has authority to manage and control the assets of the plan;

(9) receipt by a disqualified person of any benefit to which he may be entitled as a participant or beneficiary in the plan, so long as the benefit is computed and paid on a basis which is consistent with the terms of the plan as applied to all other participants and beneficiaries;

(10) receipt by a disqualified person of any reasonable compensation for services rendered, or for the reimbursement of expenses properly and actually incurred, in the performance of his duties with the plan, but no person so serving who already receives full-time pay from an employer or an association of employers, whose employees are participants in the plan, or from an employee organization whose members are

participants in such plan shall receive compensation from such fund, except for reimbursement of expenses properly and actually incurred;

(11) service by a disqualified person as a fiduciary in addition to being an officer, employee, agent, or other representative of a disqualified person;

(12) the making by a fiduciary of a distribution of the assets of the trust in accordance with the terms of the plan if such assets are distributed in the same manner as provided under section 4044 of title IV of the Employee Retirement Income Security Act of 1974 (relating to allocation of assets); or

(13) any transaction which is exempt from section 406 of such Act by reason of section 408(e) of such Act (or which would be so exempt if such section 406 applied to such transaction).

The exemptions provided by this subsection (other than paragraphs (9) and (12)) shall not apply to any transaction with respect to a trust described in section 401(a) which is part of a plan providing contributions or benefits for employees some or all of whom are owner-employees (as defined in section 401(c)(3)) in which a plan directly or indirectly lends any part of the corpus or income of the plan to, pays any compensation for personal services rendered to the plan to, or acquires for the plan any property from or sells any property to, any such owner-employee, a member of the family (as defined in section 267(c)(4) of any such owner-employee, or a corporation controlled by any such owner-employee through the ownership, directly or indirectly, of 50 percent or more of the total combined voting power of all classes of stock entitled to vote or 50 percent or more of the total value of shares of all classes of stock of the corporation. For purposes of the preceding sentence, a shareholder-employee (as defined in section 1379), a participant or beneficiary of an individual retirement account, individual retirement annuity, or an individual retirement bond (as defined in section 408 or 409), and an employer or association of employees which establishes such an account or annuity under section 408(c) shall be deemed to be an owner-employee.

(e) Definitions.—

(1) **Plan.**—For purposes of this section, the term "plan" means a trust described in section 401(a) which forms a part of a plan, or a plan described in section 403(a) or 405(a), which trust or plan is exempt from tax under section 501(a), an individual retirement account described in section 408(a) or an individual retirement annuity described in section 408(b) or a retirement bond described in section 409 (or a trust, plan, account, annuity, or bond which, at any time, has been determined by the Secretary to be such a trust, plan, account, or bond).

(2) **Disqualified person.**—For purposes of this section, the term "disqualified person" means a person who is—

(A) a fiduciary;

(B) a person providing services to the plan;

(C) an employer any of whose employees are covered by the plan;

(D) an employee organization any of whose members are covered by the plan;

(E) an owner, direct or indirect, of 50 percent or more of—

(i) the combined voting power of all classes of stock entitled to vote or the total value of shares of all classes of stock of a corporation,

(ii) the capital interest or the profits interest of a partnership, or

(iii) the beneficial interest of a trust or unincorporated enterprise,

which is an employer or an employee organization described in subparagraph (C) or (D);

(F) a member of the family (as defined in paragraph (6)) of any individual described in subparagraph (A), (B), (C), or (E);

(G) a corporation, partnership, or trust or estate of which (or in which) 50 percent or more of—

(i) the combined voting power of all classes of stock entitled to vote or the total value of shares of all classes of stock of such corporation,

(ii) the capital interest or profits interest of such partnership, or

(iii) the beneficial interest of such trust or estate, is owned directly or indirectly, or held by persons described in subparagraph (A), (B), (C), (D), or (E);

(H) an officer, director (or an individual having powers or responsibilities similar to those of officers or directors), a 10 percent or more shareholder, or a highly compensated employee (earning 10 percent or more of the yearly wages of an employer) of a person described in subparagraph (C), (D), (E), or (G); or

(I) a 10 percent or more (in capital or profits) partner or joint venturer of a person described in subparagraph (C), (D), (E), or (G).

The Secretary, after consultation and coordination with the Secretary of Labor or his delegate, may by regulation prescribe a percentage lower than 50 percent for subparagraphs (E) and (G) and lower than 10 percent for subparagraphs (H) and (I).

(3) Fiduciary.—For purposes of this section, the term "fiduciary" means any person who—

(A) exercises any discretionary authority or discretionary control respecting management of such plan or exercises any authority or control respecting management or disposition of its assets.

(B) renders investment advice for a fee or other compensation, direct or indirect, with respect to any moneys or other property of such plan, or has any authority or responsibility to do so, or

(C) has any discretionary authority or discretionary responsibility in the administration of such plan.

Such term includes any person designated under section 405(c)(1)(B) of the Employee Retirement Income Security Act of 1974.

(4) Stockholdings.—For purposes of paragraphs (2)(E)(i), and (G)(i) there shall be taken into account indirect stockholdings which would be taken into account under section 267(c), except that, for purposes of this paragraph, section 267(c)(4) shall be treated as providing that the members of the family of an individual are the members within the meaning of paragraph (6).

(5) Partnerships; trusts.—For purposes of paragraphs (2)(E)(ii) and (iii), (G)(ii) and (iii), and (I) the ownership of profits or beneficial interests shall be determined in accordance with the rules for constructive ownership of stock provided in section 267(c) (other than paragraph (3) thereof), except that section 267(c)(4) shall be treated as providing that the members of the family of an individual are the members within the meaning of paragraph (6).

(6) Member of family.—For purposes of paragraph (2)(F), the family of any individual shall include his spouse, ancestor, lineal descendant, and any spouse of a lineal descendant.

(7) Employee stock ownership plan.—The term "employee stock ownership plan" means a defined contribution plan—

(A) which is a stock bonus plan which is qualified, or a stock bonus and a money purchase plan both of which are qualified under section 401(a), and which are designed to invest primarily in qualifying employer securities; and

(B) which is otherwise defined in regulations prescribed by the Secretary.

A plan shall not be treated as an employee stock ownership plan unless it meets the requirements of section 409A(h) and, if the employer has a registration-type class of securities (as defined in section 409A(e)(4)), it meets the requirements of section 409A(e).

(8) Qualifying employer security.—The term "qualifying employer security" means any employer security within the meaning of section 409A(1). If any moneys or other property of a plan are invested in shares of an investment company registered under the Investment Company Act of 1940, the investment shall not cause that investment company or that investment company's investment adviser or principal underwriter to be treated as a fiduciary or a disqualified person for purposes of this section, except when an investment company or its investment adviser or principal underwriter acts in connection with a plan covering employees of the investment company, its investment adviser, or its principal underwriter.

(f) Other Definitions and Special Rules.—For purposes of this section—

(1) Joint and several liability.—If more than one person is liable under subsection (a) or (b) with respect to any one prohibited transaction, all such persons shall be jointly and severally liable under such subsection with respect to such transaction.

(2) Taxable period.—The term "taxable period" means, with respect to any prohibited transaction, the period beginning with the date on which the prohibited transaction occurs and ending on the earlier of—

(A) the date of mailing of a notice of deficiency pursuant to section 6212, with respect to the tax imposed by subsection (a), or

(B) the date on which correction of the prohibited transaction is completed.

(3) Sale or exchange; encumbered property.—A transfer of real or personal property by a disqualified person to a plan shall be treated as a sale or exchange if the property is subject to a mortgage or similar lien which the plan assumes or if it is subject to a mortgage or similar lien which a disqualified person placed on the property within the 10-year period ending on the date of the transfer.

(4) Amount involved.—The term "amount involved" means, with respect to a prohibited transaction, the greater of the amount of money and the fair market value of the other property given or the amount of money and the fair market value of the other property received; except that, in the case of services described in paragraphs (2) and (10) of subsection (d) the amount involved shall be only the excess compensation. For purposes of the preceding sentence, the fair market value—

(A) in the case of the tax imposed by subsection (a), shall be determined as of the date on which the prohibited transaction occurs; and

(B) in the case of the tax imposed by subsection (b), shall be the highest fair market value during the correction period.

(5) Correction.—The terms "correction" and "correct" mean, with respect to a prohibited transaction, undoing the transaction to the extent possible, but in any case placing the plan in a financial position not worse than that in which it would be if the disqualified person were acting under the highest fiduciary standards.

(6) Correction period.—The term "correction period" means, with respect to a prohibited transaction, the period beginning with the date on which the prohibited transaction occurs and ending 90 days after the date of mailing of a notice of deficiency with respect to the tax imposed by subsection (b) under section 6212, extended by—

(A) any period in which a deficiency cannot be assessed under section 6213(a), and

(B) any other period which the Secretary determines is reasonable and necessary to bring about the correction of the prohibited transaction.

(g) Application of Section.—This section shall not apply—

(1) in the case of a plan to which a guaranteed benefit policy (as defined in section 401(b)(2)(B) of the Employee Retirement Income Security Act of 1974) is issued, to any assets of the insurance company, insurance service, or insurance organization merely because of its issuance of such policy;

(2) to a governmental plan (within the meaning of section 414(d)); or

(3) to a church plan (within the meaning of section 414(e)) with respect to which the election provided by section 410(d) has not been made.

In the case of a plan which invests in any security issued by an investment company registered under the Investment Company Act of 1940, the assets of such plan shall be deemed to include such security but shall not, by reason of such investment, be deemed to include any assets of such company.

(h) Notification of Secretary of Labor.—Before sending a notice of deficiency with respect to the tax imposed by subsection (a) or (b), the Secretary shall notify the Secretary of Labor and provide him a reasonable opportunity to obtain a correction of the prohibited transaction or to comment on the imposition of such tax.

(i) Cross Reference.—

For provisions concerning coordination procedures between Secretary of Labor and Secretary of Treasury with respect to application tax imposed by

this section and for authority to waive imposition of the tax imposed by subsection (b), see section 3003 of the Employee Retirement Income Security Act of 1974.

SEC. 6699. ASSESSABLE PENALTIES RELATING TO TAX CREDIT EMPLOYEE STOCK OWNERSHIP PLAN.

(a) In General.—If a taxpayer who has claimed an employee plan credit for any taxable year—

(1) fails to satisfy any requirement provided by section 409A, or

(2) fails to make any contribution which is required under section 48(n) within the period required for making such contribution,

the taxpayer shall pay a penalty in an amount equal to the amount involved in such failure.

(b) No Penalty Where There Is Timely Correction of Failure.—Subsection (a) shall not apply with respect to any failure if the employer corrects such failure (as determined by the Secretary) within 90 days after the Secretary notifies him of such failure.

(c) Amount Involved Defined.—

(1) In general.—For purposes of this section, the term "amount involved" means an amount determined by the Secretary.

(2) Maximum and minimum amount.—The amount determined under paragraph (1)—

(A) shall not exceed the amount determined by multiplying the qualified investment of the employer for the taxable year to which the failure relates by the employee plan percentage claimed by the employer for such year, and

(B) shall not be less than the product of one-half of 1 percent of the amount referred to in subparagraph (A), multiplied by the number of months (or parts thereof) during which such failure continues.

Economic Recovery Tax Act of 1981 (ERTA)

Subtitle D—Employee Stock Ownership Provisions

SEC. 331. PAYROLL-BASED CREDIT FOR ESTABLISHING EMPLOYEE STOCK OWNERSHIP PLAN.

(a) IN GENERAL.—Subpart A of part IV of subchapter A of chapter 1 (relating to credits allowed), as amended by section 221 of this Act, is further amended by inserting immediately after section 44F the following new section:

"SEC. 44G. EMPLOYEE STOCK OWNERSHIP CREDIT.

"(a) GENERAL RULE.—

"(1) CREDIT ALLOWED.—In the case of a corporation which elects to have this section apply for the taxable year and which meets the requirements of subsection (c)(1), there is allowed as a credit against the tax imposed by this chapter for the taxable year an amount equal to the amount of the credit determined under paragraph (2) for such taxable year.

"(2) DETERMINATION OF AMOUNT.—

"(A) IN GENERAL.—The amount of the credit determined under this paragraph for the taxable year shall be equal to the lesser of—

"(i) the aggregate value of employer securities transferred by the corporation for the taxable year to a tax credit employee stock ownership plan maintained by the corporation, or

"(ii) the applicable percentage of the amount of the aggregate compensation (within the meaning of section 415(c)(3)) paid or accrued during the taxable year to all employees under a tax credit employee stock ownership plan.

"(B) APPLICABLE PERCENTAGE.—For purposes of applying subparagraph (A)(ii), the applicable percentage shall be determined in accordance with the following table:

"For aggregate compensation
paid or accrued during
a portion of the tax-
able year occurring
in calendar year: The applicable percentage is:

1983	0.5
1984	0.5
1985	0.75
1986	0.75
1987	0.75
1988 or thereafter	0

"(b) LIMITATION BASED ON AMOUNT OF TAX.—

"(1) LIABILITY FOR TAX.—

"(A) IN GENERAL.—The credit allowed by subsection (a) for any taxable year shall not exceed an amount equal to the sum of—

"(i) so much of the liability for tax for the taxable year as does not exceed $25,000, plus

"(ii) 90 percent of so much of the liability for tax for the taxable year as exceeds $25,000.

"(B) LIABILITY FOR TAX DEFINED.—For purposes of this paragraph, the term 'liability for tax' means the tax imposed by this chapter for the taxable year, reduced by the sum of the credits allowed under a section of this subpart having a lower number designation than this section, other than credits allowable by sections 31, 39, and 43. For purposes of the preceding sentence, the term 'tax imposed by this chapter' shall not include any tax treated as not imposed by this chapter under the last sentence of section 53(a).

"(C) CONTROLLED GROUPS.—In the case of a controlled group of corporations, the $25,000 amount specified in subparagraph (A) shall be reduced for each component member of such group by apportioning $25,000 among the component members of such group in such manner as the Secretary shall by regulations prescribe. For purposes of the preceding sentence, the term 'controlled group of corporations' has the meaning assigned to such term by section 1563(a) (determined without regard to subsections (a)(4) and (e)(3)(C) of such section).

"(2) CARRYBACK AND CARRYOVER OF UNUSED CREDIT.—

"(A) ALLOWANCE OF CREDIT.—If the amount of the credit determined under this section for any taxable year exceeds the limitation provided under paragraph (1)(A) for such taxable year (hereinafter in this paragraph referred to as the 'unused credit year'), such excess shall be—

"(i) an employee stock ownership credit carryback to each of the 3 taxable years preceding the unused credit year, and

"(ii) an employee stock ownership credit carryover to each of the 15 taxable years following the unused credit year,

and shall be added to the amount allowable as a credit by this section for such years. If any portion of such excess is a carryback to a taxable year ending before January 1, 1983, this section shall be deemed to have been in effect for such taxable year for purposes of allowing such carryback as a *credit under this section. The entire amount of the unused credit for an unused credit year shall be carried to the earliest of the 18 taxable years to which (by reason of clauses (i) and (ii)) such credit may be carried, and then to each of the other 17 taxable years to the extent that, because of the limitation contained in subparagraph (B), such unused credit may not be added for a prior taxable year to which such unused credit may be carried.*

"(B) LIMITATION.—The amount of the unused credit which may be added under subparagraph (A) for any preceding or succeeding taxable year shall not exceed the amount by which the limitation provided under paragraph (1)(A) for such taxable year exceeds the sum of—

"(i) the credit allowable under this section for such taxable year, and

"(ii) the amounts which, by reason of this paragraph, are added to the amount allowable for such taxable year and which are attributable to taxable years preceding the unused credit year.

"(3) CERTAIN REGULATED COMPANIES.—No credit shall be allowed under this section to a taxpayer if—

"(A) the taxpayer's cost of service for ratemaking purposes or in its regulated books of account is reduced by reason of any portion of such credit which results from the transfer of employer securities or cash to a tax credit employee stock ownership plan which meets the requirements of section 409A;

"(B) the base to which the taxpayer's rate of return for ratemaking purposes is applied is reduced by reason of any portion of such credit which results from a transfer described in subparagraph (A) to such employee stock ownership plan; or

"(C) any portion of the amount of such credit which results from a transfer described in subparagraph (A) to such employee stock ownership plan is treated for ratemaking purposes in any way other than as though it had been contributed by the taxpayer's common shareholders.

"(c) DEFINITIONS AND SPECIAL RULES.—

"(1) REQUIREMENTS FOR CORPORATION.—A corporation meets the requirements of this paragraph if it—

"(A) establishes a plan—

"(i) which meets the requirements of section 409A, and

"(ii) under which no more than one-third of the employer contributions for the taxable year are allocated to the group of employees consisting of—

"(I) officers,

"(II) shareholders owning more than 10 percent of the employer's stock (within the meaning of section 415(c)(6)(B)(iv)), or

"(III) employees described in section 415(c)(6)(B)(iii), and

"(B) agrees, as a condition for the allowance of the credit allowed by this subsection—

"(i) to make transfers of employer securities to a tax credit employee stock ownership plan maintained by the corporation having an aggregate value of not more than the applicable percentage for the taxable year (determined under subsection (a)(2)) of the amount of the aggregate compensation (within the meaning of section 415(c)(3)) paid or accrued by the corporation during the taxable year, and

"(ii) to make such transfers at the times prescribed in paragraph (2).

"(2) TIMES FOR MAKING TRANSFERS.—The transfers required under paragraph (1)(B) shall be made not later than 30 days after the due date (including extensions) for filing the return for the taxable year.

"(3) ADJUSTMENTS TO CREDIT.—If the credit allowed under this section is reduced by a final determination, the employer may reduce the amount required to be transferred to the tax credit employee stock ownership plan under paragraph (1)(B) for the taxable year in which the final determination occurs or any succeeding taxable year by an amount equal to such reduction to the extent such reduction is not taken into account in any deduction allowed under section 404(i)(2).

"(4) CERTAIN CONTRIBUTIONS OF CASH TREATED AS CONTRIBUTIONS OF EMPLOYER SECURITIES.—For purposes of this section, a transfer of cash shall be treated as a transfer of employer securities if the cash is, under the tax credit employee stock ownership plan, used within 30 days to purchase employer securities.

"(5) DISALLOWANCE OF DEDUCTION.—Except as provided in section 404(i), no deduction shall be allowed under section 162, 212, or 404 for amounts required to be transferred to a tax credit employee stock ownership plan under this section.

"(6) EMPLOYER SECURITIES.—For purposes of this section, the term 'employer securities' has the meaning given such term in section 409A(1).

"(7) VALUE.—For purposes of this section, the term 'value' means—

"(A) in the case of securities listed on a national exchange, the average of closing prices of such securities for the 20 consecutive trading days immediately preceding the date on which the securities are contributed to the plan, or

"(B) in the case of securities not listed on a national exchange, the fair market value as determined in good faith and in accordance with regulations prescribed by the Secretary.".

(b) DEDUCTIBILITY OF UNUSED PORTIONS OF THE CREDIT.—Section 404 is amended by adding at the end thereof the following new subsection:

"(i) DEDUCTIBILITY OF UNUSED PORTIONS OF EMPLOYEE STOCK OWNERSHIP CREDIT.—

"(1) UNUSED CREDIT CARRYOVERS.—There shall be allowed as a deduction (without regard to any limitations provided under this section) for the last taxable year to which an unused employee stock ownership credit carryover (within the meaning of section 44G(b)(2)(A)) may be carried, an amount equal to the

portion of such unused credit carryover which expires at the close of such taxable year.

"(2) REDUCTIONS IN CREDIT.—There shall be allowed as a deduction (subject to the limitations provided under this section) an amount equal to any reduction of the credit allowed under section 44G resulting from a final determination of such credit to the extent such reduction is not taken into account in section 44G(c)(3).".

(c) CONFORMING AMENDMENTS.—

(1) Section 409A (relating to qualifications for tax credit employee stock ownership plans) is amended—

    (A) by inserting "or 44G(c)(1)(B)" after "section 48(n)(1)(A)" in subsection (b)(1)(A),

    (B) by inserting "or the credit allowed under section 44G (relating to the employee stock ownership credit)" after "basic employee plan credit" in subsection (b)(4),

    (C) by inserting "or 44G(c)(1)(B)" after "section 48(n)(1)" in subsection (g),

    (D) by inserting "or the credit allowed under section 44G (relating to employee stock ownership credit)" after "employee plan credit" in subsection (g),

    (E) by inserting "or 44G(c)(1)(B)" after "section 48(n)(1)" in subsection (i)(1)(A),

    (F) by inserting "section 44G(c)(1)(B), or" after "required under" in subsection (m),

    (G) by inserting "or employee stock ownership credit" after "employee plan credit" in subsection (n)(2), and

    (H) by adding at the end of subsection (n) the following new paragraph:

"(3) For requirements for allowance of an employee stock ownership credit, see section 44G.".

(2) Subsection (c) of section 56 (relating to regular tax deductions defined) is amended by striking out "and 43" and inserting in lieu thereof "43, and 44G".

(3) Subsection (a) of section 6699 (relating to assessable penalties relating to tax credit employee stock ownership plan) is amended—

    (A) by inserting "or a credit allowable under section 44G (relating to the employee stock ownership credit)" after "employee plan credit",

    (B) by striking out "section 409A, or" in paragraph (1) and inserting in lieu thereof "section 409A with respect to a qualified investment made before January 1, 1983,",

    (C) by inserting after paragraph (2) the following new paragraphs:

"(3) fails to satisfy any requirement provided under section 409A with respect to a credit claimed under section 44G in taxable years ending after December 31, 1982, or

"(4) fails to make any contribution which is required under section 44G(c)(1)(B) within the period required for making such contribution,".

(4) Paragraph (2) of section 6699 is amended to read as follows:

"(2) MAXIMUM AND MINIMUM AMOUNT.—

"(A) The amount determined under paragraph (1) with respect to a failure described in paragraph (1) or (2) of subsection (a)—

"(i) shall not exceed the amount of the employee plan credit claimed by the employer to which such failure relates, and

"(ii) shall not be less than the product of one-half of 1 percent of the amount referred to in subparagraph (A), multiplied by the number of months (or parts thereof) during which such failure continues.

"(B) The amount determined under paragraph (1) with respect to a failure described in paragraph (3) or (4) of subsection (a)—

"(i) shall not exceed the amount of the credit claimed by the employer under section 44G to which such failure relates, and

"(ii) shall not be less than the product of one-half of 1 percent of the amount referred to in subparagraph (A), multiplied by the number of months (or parts thereof) during which such failure continues.".

(d) TECHNICAL AMENDMENTS RELATED TO CARRYOVER AND CARRY-BACK OF CREDITS.—

(1) CARRYOVER OF CREDIT.—

(A) Subparagraph (A) of section 55(c)(4) (relating to credits), as amended by this Act, is amended by inserting "44G(b)(1)," before "53(b)".

(B) Subsection (c) of section 381 (relating to items of the distributor or transferor corporation), as amended by this Act, is amended by adding at the end thereof the following new paragraph:

"(29) CREDIT UNDER SECTION 44G.—The acquiring corporation shall take into account (to the extent proper to carry out the purposes of this section and section 44G, and under such regulations as may be prescribed by the Secretary) the items required to be taken into account for purposes of section 44G in respect of the distributor or transferor corporation."

(C) Section 383 (relating to special limitations on unused investment credits, work incentive program credits, new employee credits, alcohol fuel credits, foreign taxes, and capital losses), as in effect for taxable years beginning with and after the first taxable year to which the amendments made by the Tax Reform Act of 1976 apply, is amended—

(i) by inserting "to any unused credit of the corporation under section 44G(b)(2)," after "44F(g)(2),", and

(ii) by inserting "EMPLOYEE STOCK OWNERSHIP CREDITS," after "RESEARCH CREDITS," in the section heading.

(D) Section 383 (as in effect on the day before the date of the enactment of the Tax Reform Act of 1976) is amended—

(i) by inserting "to any unused credit of the corporation which could otherwise be carried forward under section 44G(b)(2)," after "44F(g)(2),", and

(ii) by inserting "EMPLOYEE STOCK OWNERSHIP CREDITS," after "RESEARCH CREDITS," in the section heading.

(E) The Table of sections for part V of subchapter C of chapter 1 is amended by inserting "employee stock owner-

ship credits," after "research credits," in the item relating to section 383.

(2) CARRYBACK OF CREDIT.—

(A) Subparagraph (C) of section 6511(d)(4) (defining credit carryback), as amended by this Act, is amended by striking out "and research credit carryback" and inserting in lieu thereof "research credit carryback, and employee stock ownership credit carryback".

(B) Section 6411 (relating to quick refunds in respect of tentative carryback adjustments), as amended by this Act, is amended—

(i) by striking out "or unused research credit" each place it appears and inserting in lieu thereof "unused research credit, or unused employee stock ownership credit";

(ii) by inserting "by an employee stock ownership credit carryback provided by section 44G(b)(2)" after "by a research and experimental credit carryback provided in section 44F(g)(2), in the first sentence of subsection (a);

(iii) by striking out "or a research credit carryback from" each place it appears and inserting in lieu thereof "a research credit carryback, or employee stock ownership credit carryback from"; and

(iv) by striking out "new employee credit carryback)" in the second sentence of subsection (a) and inserting in lieu thereof "new employee credit carryback, or, in the case of an employee stock ownership credit carryback, to an investment credit carryback, a new employee credit carryback or a research and experimental credit carryback)".

(e) OTHER TECHNICAL AND CLERICAL AMENDMENTS.—

(1) Subsection (b) of section 6096 (relating to designation of income tax payments to Presidential Election Campaign Fund), as amended by this Act, is amended by striking out "and 44F" and inserting in lieu thereof "44F, and 44G".

(2) The table of sections for subpart A of part IV of subchapter A of chapter 1 is amended by inserting after the item relating to section 44F the following new item:

"Sec. 44G. Employee stock ownership credit."

(f) EFFECTIVE DATE.—

(1) The amendments made by subsection (a) shall apply to aggregate compensation (within the meaning of section 415(c)(3) of the Internal Revenue Code of 1954), paid or accrued after December 31, 1982, in taxable years ending after such date.

(2) The amendments made by subsections (b) and (c) shall apply to taxable years ending after December 31, 1982.

SEC. 332. TERMINATION OF THE PORTION OF THE INVESTMENT CREDIT ATTRIBUTABLE TO EMPLOYEE PLAN PERCENTAGE.

(a) IN GENERAL.—*Subparagraph (E) of section 46(a)(2) (relating to employee plan percentage) is amended—*

(1) by striking out "December 31, 1983" in clauses (i) and (ii) and inserting in lieu thereof "December 31, 1982",

(2) by striking out "and" at the end of clause (i),

(3) by striking out the period at the end of clause (ii) and inserting in lieu thereof ", and", and

(4) by inserting after clause (ii) the following new clause:

"(iii) with respect to any period beginning after December 31, 1982, zero.".

(b) TECHNICAL AMENDMENT.—*Clause (i) of section 48(n)(1)(A) (relating to requirements for allowance of employee plan percentage) is amended by striking out "equal to" and inserting in lieu thereof "which does not exceed".*

(c) EFFECTIVE DATES.—

(1) The amendments made by subsection (a) shall be effective on the date of enactment of this Act.

(2) The amendment made by subsection (b) shall apply to qualified investments made after December 31, 1981.

SEC. 333. TAX TREATMENT OF CONTRIBUTIONS ATTRIBUTABLE TO PRINCIPAL AND INTEREST PAYMENTS IN CONNECTION WITH AN EMPLOYEE STOCK OWNERSHIP PLAN.

(a) DEDUCTIBILITY.—*Section 404(a) (relating to deductions for employer contributions to an employees' trust) is amended by adding at the end thereof the following new paragraph:*

"(10) CERTAIN CONTRIBUTIONS TO EMPLOYEE STOCK OWNERSHIP PLANS.—

"(A) PRINCIPAL PAYMENTS.—*Notwithstanding the provisions of paragraphs (3) and (7), if contributions are paid into a trust which forms a part of an employee stock ownership plan (as described in section 4975(e)(7)), and such contributions are, on or before the time prescribed in paragraph (6), applied by the plan to the repayment of the principal of a loan incurred for the purpose of acquiring qualifying employer securities (as described in section 4975(e)(8)), such contributions shall be deductible under this paragraph for the taxable year determined under paragraph (6). The amount deductible under this paragraph shall not, however, exceed 25 percent of the compensation otherwise paid or accrued during the taxable year to the employees under such employee stock ownership plan. Any amount paid into such trust in any taxable year in excess of the amount deductible under this paragraph shall be deductible in the succeeding taxable years in order of time to the extent of the difference between the amount paid and deductible in each such succeeding year and the maximum amount deductible for such year under the preceding sentence.*

"(B) INTEREST PAYMENT.—*Notwithstanding the provisions of paragraphs (3) and (7), if contributions are made to an employee stock ownership plan (described in subparagraph (A)) and such contributions are applied by the plan to the repayment of interest on a loan incurred for the purpose of acquiring qualifying employer securities (as described in subparagraph (A)), such contributions shall be deductible for the taxable year with respect to which such contributions are made as determined under paragraph (6).".*

(b) EXCLUSION FROM LIMITATION ON ANNUAL ADDITIONS.—

(1) IN GENERAL.—*Section 415(c)(6) (relating to limitations on benefits and contributions made under qualified plans) is amended by adding at the end thereof the following new subparagraph:*

"(C) In the case of an employee stock ownership plan (as described in section 4975(e)(7)), under which no more than one-third of the employer contributions for a year which are deductible under paragraph (10) of section 404(a) are allocated to the group of employees consisting of officers, shareholders owning more than 10 percent of the employer's stock (determined under subparagraph (B)(iv)), or employees described in subparagraph (B)(iii), the limitations imposed by this section shall not apply to—

"(i) forfeitures of employer securities under an employee stock ownership plan (as described in section 4975(e)(7)) if such securities were acquired with the proceeds of a loan (as described in section 404(a)(10)(A)), or

"(ii) employer contributions to such an employee stock ownership plan which are deductible under section 404(a)(10)(B) and charged against the participant's account.".

(2) EFFECTIVE DATE.—*The amendment made by this subsection shall apply to years beginning after December 31, 1981.*

SEC. 334. CASH DISTRIBUTIONS FROM AN EMPLOYEE STOCK OWNERSHIP PLAN.

Section 409A(h)(2) (relating to right to demand employer securities) is amended—

(1) *by adding at the end thereof the following new sentence: "In the case of an employer whose charter or bylaws restrict the ownership of substantially all outstanding employer securities to employees or to a trust described in section 401(a), a plan which otherwise meets the requirements of this subsection or section 4975(e)(7) shall not be considered to have failed to meet the requirements of section 401(a) merely because it does not permit a participant to exercise the right described in paragraph (1)(A) if such plan provides that participants entitled to a distribution from the plan shall have a right to receive such distribution in cash."; and*

(2) *by striking out "this section" in the first sentence thereof and inserting in lieu thereof "this subsection".*

SEC. 335. PUT OPTION FOR STOCK BONUS PLANS.

Section 401(a)(23) (relating to cash distribution option for stock bonus plans) is amended by striking out "409A(h)(2)" and inserting in lieu thereof "409A(h), except that in applying section 409A(h) for purposes of this paragraph, the term 'employer securities' shall include any securities of the employer held by the plan".

SEC. 336. PUT OPTION REQUIREMENTS FOR BANKS; PUT OPTION PERIOD.

Section 409A(h) (relating to put options for employee stock ownership plans) is amended by adding at the end thereof the following new paragraphs:

"(3) SPECIAL RULE FOR BANKS.—In the case of a plan established and maintained by a bank (as defined in section 581) which is prohibited by law from redeeming or purchasing its own securities, the requirements of paragraph (1)(B) shall not apply if the plan provides that participants entitled to a distri-

bution from the plan shall have a right to receive a distribution in cash.

"(4) PUT OPTION PERIOD.—An employer shall be deemed to satisfy the requirements of paragraph (1)(B) if it provides a put option for a period of at least 60 days following the date of distribution of stock of the employer and, if the put option is not exercised within such 60-day period, for an additional period of at least 60 days in the following plan year (as provided in regulations promulgated by the Secretary).".

SEC. 337. DISTRIBUTION OF EMPLOYER SECURITIES FROM A TAX CREDIT EMPLOYEE STOCK OWNERSHIP PLAN IN THE CASE OF A SALE OF EMPLOYER ASSETS OR STOCK.

(a) IN GENERAL.—Section 409A(d) (relating to distribution of employer securities) is amended by striking out the last sentence thereof and inserting in lieu thereof the following: "To the extent provided in the plan, the preceding sentence shall not apply in the case of—

"(1) death, disability, or separation from service;

"(2) a transfer of a participant to the employment of an acquiring employer from the employment of the selling corporation in the case of—

"(A) a sale to the acquiring employer of substantially all of the assets used by the selling corporation in a trade or business conducted by the selling corporation, or

"(B) the sale of substantially all of the stock of a subsidiary of the employer, or

"(3) with respect to the stock of a selling corporation, a disposition of such selling corporation's interest in a subsidiary when the participant continues employment with such subsidiary.".

(b) EFFECTIVE DATE.—The amendments made by this section shall apply to distributions described in section 409A(d) of the Internal Revenue Code of 1954 (or any corresponding provision of prior law) made after March 29, 1975.

SEC. 338. PASS THROUGH OF VOTING RIGHTS ON EMPLOYER SECURITIES.

(a) IN GENERAL.—Paragraph (22) of section 401(a) (relating to qualified pension, profit-sharing, and stock bonus plans) is amended to read as follows:

"(22) if a defined contribution plan (other than a profit-sharing plan)—

"(A) is established by an employer whose stock is not publicly traded, and

"(B) after acquiring securities of the employer, more than 10 percent of the total assets of the plan are securities of the employer,

any trust forming part of such plan shall not constitute a qualified trust under this section unless the plan meets the requirements of subsection (e) of section 409A."

(b) EFFECTIVE DATE.—The amendment made by this section shall apply to acquisitions of securities after December 31, 1979.

SEC. 339. EFFECTIVE DATE.

Except as otherwise provided, the amendments made by this subtitle shall apply to taxable years beginning after December 31, 1981.

Employee Retirement Income Security Act (ERISA) Title I

SEC. 406. (a) Except as provided in section 408:   29 USC 1106.

(1) A fiduciary with respect to a plan shall not cause the plan to engage in a transaction, if he knows or should know that such transaction constitutes a direct or indirect—

(A) sale or exchange, or leasing, of any property between the plan and a party in interest;

(B) lending of money or other extension of credit between the plan and a party in interest;

(C) furnishing of goods, services, or facilities between the plan and a party in interest;

(D) transfer to, or use by or for the benefit of, a party in interest, of any assets of the plan; or

(E) acquisition, on behalf of the plan, of any employer security or employer real property in violation of section 407(a).

(2) No fiduciary who has authority or discretion to control or manage the assets of a plan shall permit the plan to hold any employer security or employer real property if he knows or should know that holding such security or real property violates section 407(a).

(b) A fiduciary with respect to a plan shall not—

(1) deal with the assets of the plan in his own interest or for his own account,

(2) in his individual or in any other capacity act in any transaction involving the plan on behalf of a party (or represent a party) whose interests are adverse to the interests of the plan or the interests of its participants or beneficiaries, or

(3) receive any consideration for his own personal account from any party dealing with such plan in connection with a transaction involving the assets of the plan.

(c) A transfer of real or personal property by a party in interest to a plan shall be treated as a sale or exchange if the property is subject to a mortgage or similar lien which the plan assumes or if it is subject to a mortgage or similar lien which a party-in-interest placed

88 STAT. 880

on the property within the 10-year period ending on the date of the transfer.

10 PERCENT LIMITATION WITH RESPECT TO ACQUISITION AND HOLDING OF EMPLOYER SECURITIES AND EMPLOYER REAL PROPERTY BY CERTAIN PLANS

29 USC 1107.

SEC. 407. (a) Except as otherwise provided in this section and section 414:

(1) A plan may not acquire or hold—

(A) any employer security which is not a qualifying employer security, or

(B) any employer real property which is not qualifying employer real property.

(2) A plan may not acquire any qualifying employer security or qualifying employer real property, if immediately after such acquisition the aggregate fair market value of employer securities and employer real property held by the plan exceeds 10 percent of the fair market value of the assets of the plan.

(3)(A) After December 31, 1984, a plan may not hold any qualifying employer securities or qualifying employer real property (or both) to the extent that the aggregate fair market value of such securities and property determined on December 31, 1984, exceeds 10 percent of the greater of—

(i) the fair market value of the assets of the plan, determined on December 31, 1984, or

(ii) the fair market value of the assets of the plan determined on January 1, 1975.

(B) Subparagraph (A) of this paragraph shall not apply to any plan which on any date after December 31, 1974; and before January 1, 1985, did not hold employer securities or employer real property (or both) the aggregate fair market value of which determined on such date exceeded 10 percent of the greater of

(i) the fair market value of the assets of the plan, determined on such date, or

(ii) the fair market value of the assets of the plan determined on January 1, 1975.

(4)(A) After December 31, 1979, a plan may not hold any employer securities or employer real property in excess of the amount specified in regulations under subparagraph (B). This subparagraph shall not apply to a plan after the earliest date after December 31, 1974, on which it complies with such regulations.

Regulations.

(B) Not later than December 31, 1976, the Secretary shall prescribe regulations which shall have the effect of requiring that a plan divest itself of 50 percent of the holdings of employer securities and employer real property which the plan would be required to divest before January 1, 1985, under paragraph (2) or subsection (c) (whichever is applicable).

(b)(1) Subsection (a) of this section shall not apply to any acquisition or holding of qualifying employer securities or qualifying employer real property by an eligible individual account plan.

(2) CROSS REFERENCES.—

(A) For exemption from diversification requirements for holding of qualifying employer securities and qualifying employer real property by eligible individual account plans, see section 404(a)(2).

(B) For exemption from prohibited transactions for certain acquisitions of qualifying employer securities and qualifying employer real property which are not in violation of 10 percent limitation, see section 408(e).

(C) For transitional rules respecting securities or real property subject to binding contracts in effect on June 30, 1974, see section 414(c).

September 2, 1974   - 53 -   Pub. Law 93-406

88 STAT. 881

(c)(1) A plan which makes the election, under paragraph (3) shall be treated as satisfying the requirement of subsection (a)(3) if and only if employer securities held on any date after December 31, 1974 and before January 1, 1985 have a fair market value, determined as of December 31, 1974, not in excess of 10 percent of the lesser of—

(A) the fair market value of the assets of the plan determined on such date (disregarding any portion of the fair market value of employer securities which is attributable to appreciation of such securities after December 31, 1974) but not less than the fair market value of plan assets on January 1, 1975, or

(B) an amount equal to the sum of (i) the total amount of the contributions to the plan received after December 31, 1974, and prior to such date, plus (ii) the fair market value of the assets of the plan, determined on January 1, 1975.

(2) For purposes of this subsection, in the case of an employer security held by a plan after January 1, 1975, the ownership of which is derived from ownership of employer securities held by the plan on January 1, 1975, or from the exercise of rights derived from such ownership, the value of such security held after January 1, 1975, shall be based on the value as of January 1, 1975, of the security from which ownership was derived. The Secretary shall prescribe regulations to carry out this paragraph.

(3) An election under this paragraph may not be made after December 31, 1975. Such an election shall be made in accordance with regulations prescribed by the Secretary, and shall be irrevocable. A plan may make an election under this paragraph only if on January 1, 1975, the plan holds no employer real property. After such election and before January 1, 1985 the plan may not acquire any employer real property.

(d) For purposes of this section—   Definitions.

(1) The term "employer security" means a security issued by an employer of employees covered by the plan, or by an affiliate of such employer. A contract to which section 408(b)(5) applies shall not be treated as a security for purposes of this section.

(2) The term "employer real property" means real property (and related personal property) which is leased to an employer of employees covered by the plan, or to an affiliate of such employer. For purposes of determining the time at which a plan acquires employer real property for purposes of this section, such property shall be deemed to be acquired by the plan on the date on which the plan acquires the property or on the date on which the lease to the employer (or affiliate) is entered into, whichever is later.

(3)(A) The term "eligible individual account plan" means an individual account plan which is (i) a profit-sharing, stock bonus, thrift, or savings plan; (ii) an employee stock ownership plan; or (iii) a money purchase plan which was in existence on the date of enactment of this Act and which on such date invested primarily in qualifying employer securities. Such term excludes an individual retirement account or annuity described in section 408 of the Internal Revenue Code of 1954.   Post, p. 959.

(B) Notwithstanding subparagraph (A), a plan shall be treated as an eligible individual account plan with respect to the acquisition or holding of qualifying employer real property or qualifying employer securities only if such plan explicitly provides for acquisition and holding of qualifying employer securities or qualifying employer real property (as the case may be). In the case of a plan in existence on the date of enactment of this Act, this subparagraph shall not take effect until January 1, 1976.

(4) The term "qualifying employer real property" means parcels of employer real property—

(A) if a substantial number of the parcels are dispersed geographically;

(B) if each parcel of real property and the improvements thereon are suitable (or adaptable without excessive cost) for more than one use;

(C) even if all of such real property is leased to one lessee (which may be an employer, or an affiliate of an employer); and

(D) if the acquisition and retention of such property comply with the provisions of this part (other than section 404 (a)(1)(B) to the extent it requires diversification, and sections 404(a)(1)(C), 406, and subsection (a) of this section).

(5) The term "qualifying employer security" means an employer security which is stock or a marketable obligation (as defined in subsection (e)).

(6) The term "employee stock ownership plan" means an individual account plan—

(A) which is a stock bonus plan which is qualified, or a stock bonus plan and money purchase both of which are qualified, under section 401 of the Internal Revenue Code of 1954, and which is designed to invest primarily in qualifying employee securities, and

26 USC 401.

(B) which meets such other requirements as the Secretary of the Treasury may prescribe by regulation.

(7) A corporation is an affiliate of an employer if it is a member of any controlled group of corporations (as defined in section 1563(a) of the Internal Revenue Code of 1954, except that "applicable percentage" shall be substituted for "80 percent" wherever the latter percentage appears in such section) of which the employer who maintains the plan is a member. For purposes of the preceding sentence, the term "applicable percentage" means 50 percent, or such lower percentage as the Secretary may prescribe by regulation. A person other than a corporation shall be treated as an affiliate of an employer to the extent provided in regulations of the Secretary. An employer which is a person other than a corporation shall be treated as affiliated with another person to the extent provided by regulations of the Secretary. Regulations under this paragraph shall be prescribed only after consultation and coordination with the Secretary of the Treasury.

26 USC 1563.

(8) The Secretary may prescribe regulations specifying the extent to which conversions, splits, the exercise of rights, and similar transactions are not treated as acquisitions.

Regulations.

(e) For purposes of subsection (d)(5), the term "marketable obligation" means a bond, debenture, note, or certificate, or other evidence of indebtedness (hereinafter in this subsection referred to as "obligation") if—

"Marketable obligation."

(1) such obligation is acquired—

(A) on the market, either (i) at the price of the obligation prevailing on a national securities exchange which is registered with the Securities and Exchange Commission, or (ii) if the obligation is not traded on such a national securities exchange, at a price not less favorable to the plan than the offering price for the obligation as established by current bid and asked prices quoted by persons independent of the issuer;

(B) from an underwriter, at a price (i) not in excess of the public offering price for the obligation as set forth in a prospectus or offering circular filed with the Securities and

Exchange Commission, and (ii) at which a substantial portion of the same issue is acquired by persons independent of the issuer; or

(C) directly from the issuer, at a price not less favorable to the plan than the price paid currently for a substantial portion of the same issue by persons independent of the issuer;

(2) immediately following acquisition of such obligation—

(A) not more than 25 percent of the aggregate amount of obligations issued in such issue and outstanding at the time of acquisition is held by the plan, and

(B) at least 50 percent of the aggregate amount referred to in subparagraph (A) is held by persons independent of the issuer; and

(3) immediately following acquisition of the obligation, not more than 25 percent of the assets of the plan is invested in obligations of the employer or an affiliate of the employer.

EXEMPTIONS FROM PROHIBITED TRANSACTIONS

Sec. 408. (a) The Secretary shall establish an exemption procedure for purposes of this subsection. Pursuant to such procedure, he may grant a conditional or unconditional exemption of any fiduciary or transaction, or class of fiduciaries or transactions, from all or part of the restrictions imposed by sections 406 and 407(a). Action under this subsection may be taken only after consultation and coordination with the Secretary of the Treasury. An exemption granted under this section shall not relieve a fiduciary from any other applicable provision of this Act. The Secretary may not grant an exemption under this subsection unless he finds that such exemption is—

(1) administratively feasible,

(2) in the interests of the plan and of its participants and beneficiaries, and

(3) protective of the rights of participants and beneficiaries of such plan.

29 USC 1108.

Before granting an exemption under this subsection from section 406 (a) or 407(a), the Secretary shall publish notice in the Federal Register of the pendency of the exemption, shall require that adequate notice be given to interested persons, and shall afford interested persons opportunity to present views. The Secretary may not grant an exemption under this subsection from section 406(b) unless he affords an opportunity for a hearing and makes a determination on the record with respect to the findings required by paragraphs (1), (2), and (3) of this subsection.

Publication in Federal Register.

(b) The prohibitions provided in section 406 shall not apply to any of the following transactions:

Nonapplicability

(1) Any loans made by the plan to parties in interest who are participants or beneficiaries of the plan if such loans (A) are available to all such participants and beneficiaries on a reasonably equivalent basis, (B) are not made available to highly compensated employees, officers, or shareholders in an amount greater than the amount made available to other employees, (C) are made in accordance with specific provisions regarding such loans set forth in the plan, (D) bear a reasonable rate of interest, and (E) are adequately secured.

(2) Contracting or making reasonable arrangements with a party in interest for office space, or legal, accounting, or other services necessary for the establishment or operation of the plan. if no more than reasonable compensation is paid therefor.

88 STAT. 884

(3) A loan to an employee stock ownership plan (as defined in section 407(d)(6)), if—

(A) such loan is primarily for the benefit of participants and beneficiaries of the plan, and

(B) such loan is at an interest rate which is not in excess of a reasonable rate.

If the plan gives collateral to a party in interest for such loan, such collateral may consist only of qualifying employer securities (as defined in section 407(d)(5)).

(4) The investment of all or part of a plan's assets in deposits which bear a reasonable interest rate in a bank or similar financial institution supervised by the United States or a State, if such bank or other institution is a fiduciary of such plan and if—

(A) the plan covers only employees of such bank or other institution and employees of affiliates of such bank or other institution, or

(B) such investment is expressly authorized by a provision of the plan or by a fiduciary (other than such bank or institution or affiliate thereof) who is expressly empowered by the plan to so instruct the trustee with respect to such investment.

(5) Any contract for life insurance, health insurance, or annuities with one or more insurers which are qualified to do business in a State, if the plan pays no more than adequate consideration, and if each such insurer or insurers is—

(A) the employer maintaining the plan, or

(B) a party in interest which is wholly owned (directly or indirectly) by the employer maintaining the plan, or by any person which is a party in interest with respect to the plan, but only if the total premiums and annuity considerations written by such insurers for life insurance, health insurance, or annuities for all plans (and their employers) with respect to which such insurers are parties in interest (not including premiums or annuity considerations written by the employer maintaining the plan) do not exceed 5 percent of the total premiums and annuity considerations written for all lines of insurance in that year by such insurers (not including premiums or annuity considerations written by the employer maintaining the plan).

(6) The providing of any ancillary service by a bank or similar financial institution supervised by the United States or a State, if such bank or other institution is a fiduciary of such plan, and if—

(A) such bank or similar financial institution has adopted adequate internal safeguards which assure that the providing of such ancillary service is consistent with sound banking and financial practice, as determined by Federal or State supervisory authority, and

(B) the extent to which such ancillary service is provided is subject to specific guidelines issued by such bank or similar financial institution (as determined by the Secretary after consultation with Federal and State supervisory authority), and adherence to such guidelines would reasonably preclude such bank or similar financial institution from providing such ancillary service (i) in an excessive or unreasonable manner, and (ii) in a manner that would be inconsistent with the best interests of participants and beneficiaries of employee benefit plans.

September 2, 1974   - 57 -   Pub. Law 93-406 88 STAT. 885

Such ancillary services shall not be provided at more than reasonable compensation.

(7) The exercise of a privilege to convert securities, to the extent provided in regulations of the Secretary, but only if the plan receives no less than adequate consideration pursuant to such conversion.

(8) Any transaction between a plan and (i) a common or collective trust fund or pooled investment fund maintained by a party in interest which is a bank or trust company supervised by a State or Federal agency or (ii) a pooled investment fund of an insurance company qualified to do business in a State, if—

    (A) the transaction is a sale or purchase of an interest in the fund,

    (B) the bank, trust company, or insurance company receives not more than reasonable compensation, and

    (C) such transaction is expressly permitted by the instrument under which the plan is maintained, or by a fiduciary (other than the bank, trust company, or insurance company. or an affiliate thereof) who has authority to manage and control the assets of the plan.

(9) The making by a fiduciary of a distribution of the assets of the plan in accordance with the terms of the plan if such assets are distributed in the same manner as provided under section 4044 of this Act (relating to allocation of assets). Post, p. 1025.

(c) Nothing in section 406 shall be construed to prohibit any fiduciary from—

    (1) receiving any benefit to which he may be entitled as a participant or beneficiary in the plan, so long as the benefit is computed and paid on a basis which is consistent with the terms of the plan as applied to all other participants and beneficiaries;

    (2) receiving any reasonable compensation for services rendered, or for the reimbursement of expenses properly and actually incurred, in the performance of his duties with the plan; except that no person so serving who already receives full-time pay from an employer or an association of employers, whose employees are participants in the plan, or from an employee organization whose members are participants in such plan shall receive compensation from such plan, except for reimbursement of expenses properly and actually incurred; or

    (3) serving as a fiduciary in addition to being an officer, employee, agent, or other representative of a party in interest.

(d) Section 407(b) and subsections (a), (b), (c), and (e) of this section shall not apply to any transaction in which a plan, directly or indirectly—

    (1) lends any part of the corpus or income of the plan to;

    (2) pays any compensation for personal services rendered to the plan to; or

    (3) acquires for the plan any property from or sells any property to;

any person who is with respect to the plan an owner-employee (as defined in section 401(c)(3) of the Internal Revenue Code of 1954), 26 USC 401. a member of the family (as defined in section 267(c)(4) of such Code) 26 USC 267. of any such owner-employee, or a corporation controlled by any such owner-employee through the ownership, directly or indirectly, of 50 percent or more of the total combined voting power of all classes of stock entitled to vote or 50 percent or more of the total value of shares of all classes of stock of the corporation. For purposes of this subsection a shareholder employee (as defined in section 1379 of the Internal

88 STAT. 886

26 USC 1379.

Post, pp. 959, 964.

Revenue Code of 1954) and a participant or beneficiary of an individual retirement account, individual retirement annuity, or an individual retirement bond (as defined in section 408 or 409 of the Internal Revenue Code of 1954) and an employer or association of employers which establishes such an account or annuity under section 408(c) of such code shall be deemed to be an owner-employee.

(e) Sections 406 and 407 shall not apply to the acquisition or sale by a plan of qualifying employer securities (as defined in section 407 (d)(5)) or acquisition, sale or lease by a plan of qualifying employer real property (as defined in section 407(d)(4))—

(1) if such acquisition, sale, or lease is for adequate consideration (or in the case of a marketable obligation, at a price not less favorable to the plan than the price determined under Section 407(e)(1)),

(2) if no commission is charged with respect thereto, and

(3) if—

(A) the plan is an eligible individual account plan (as defined in section 407(d)(3)), or

(B) in the case of an acquisition or lease of qualifying employer real property by a plan which is not an eligible individual account plan, or of an acquisition of qualifying employer securities by such a plan, the lease or acquisition is not prohibited by section 407(a).

TREASURY REGULATION

Sec. 54.4975-7 (T.D. 7506, filed 8-30-77.)
Other statutory exemptions.

(a) [Reserved]

(b) *Loans to employee stock ownership plans*—

(1) *Definitions.* When used in this paragraph (b) and § 54.4975-11, the terms listed below have the following meanings:

(i) *ESOP.* The term "ESOP" refers to an employee stock ownership plan that meets the requirements of section 4975(e)(7) and § 54. 4975-11. It is not synonymous with "stock bonus plan." A stock bonus plan must, however, be an ESOP to engage in an exempt loan. The qualification of an ESOP under section 401(a) and § 54.4975-11 will not be adversely affected merely because it engages in a non-exempt loan.

(ii) *Loan.* The term "loan" refers to a loan made to an ESOP by a disqualified person or a loan to an ESOP which is guaranteed by a disqualified person. It includes a direct loan of cash, a purchase-money transaction, and an assumption of the obligation of an ESOP. "Guarantee" includes an unsecured guarantee and the use of assets of a disqualified person as collateral for a loan, even though the use of assets may not be a guarantee under applicable state law. An amendment of a loan in order to qualify as an exempt loan is not a refinancing of the loan or the making of another loan.

(iii) *Exempt loan.* The term "exempt loan" refers to a loan that satisfies the provisions of this paragraph (b). A "nonexempt loan" is one that fails to satisfy such provisions.

(iv) *Publicly traded.* The term "publicly traded" refers to a security that is listed on a national securities exchange registered under section 6 of the Securities Exchange Act of 1934 (15 U.S.C. 78f) or that is quoted on a system sponsored by a national securities association registered under section 15A(b) of the Securities Exchange Act (15 U.S.C. 78o).

(v) *Qualifying employer security.* The term "qualifying employer security" refers to a security described in § 34.4975-12.

(2) *Statutory exemption*—(1) *Scope.* Section 4975(d)(3) provides an exemption from the excise tax imposed under section 4975(a) and (b) by reason of section 4975 (c)(1)(A) through (E). Section 4975(d)(3) does not provide an

exemption from the imposition of such tax by reason of section 4975(c)(1)(F), relating to fiduciaries receiving consideration for their own personal account from any party dealing with a plan in connection with a transaction involving the income or assets of the plan.

(ii) *Special scrutiny of transaction.* The exemption under section 4975(d)(3) includes within its scope certain transactions in which the potential for self-dealing by fiduciaries exists and in which the interests of fiduciaries may conflict with the interests of participants. To guard against these potential abuses, the Internal Revenue Service will subject these transactions to special scrutiny to ensure that they are primarily for the benefit of participants and their beneficiaries. Although the transactions need not be arranged and approved by an independent fiduciary, fiduciaries are cautioned to exercise scrupulously their discretion in approving them. For example, fiduciaries should be prepared to demonstrate compliance with the net effect test and the arm's-length standard under paragraph (b)(3)(ii) and (iii) of this section. Also, fiduciaries should determine that the transaction is truly arranged primarily in the interest of participants and their beneficiaries rather than, for example, in the interest of certain selling shareholders.

(3) *Primary benefit requirement*—(i) *In General.* An exempt loan must be primarily for the benefit of the ESOP participants and their beneficiaries. All the surrounding facts and circumstances, including those described in paragraph (b)(3)(ii) and (iii) of this section, will be considered in determining whether the loan satisfies this requirement. However, no loan will satisfy the requirement unless it satisfies the requirements of paragraph (b)(4), (5), and (6) of this section.

(ii) *Net effect on plan assets.* At the time that a loan is made, the interest rate for the loan and the price of securities to be acquired with the loan proceeds should not be such that plan assets might be drained off.

(iii) *Arm's-length standard.* The terms of a loan, whether or not between independent parties, must, at the time the loan is made, be at least as favorable to the ESOP as the terms of a comparable loan resulting from arm's-length negotiations between independent parties.

(4) *Use of loan proceeds.* The proceeds of an exempt loan must be used within a reasonable time after their receipt by the borrowing ESOP only for any or all of the following purposes:

(i) to acquire qualifying employer securities.

(ii) To repay such loan.

(iii) To repay a prior exempt loan. A new loan, the proceeds of which are so used, must satisfy the provisions of this paragraph (b).

Except as provided in paragraph (b)(9) and (10) of this section or as otherwise required by applicable law, no security acquired with the proceeds of an exempt loan may be subject to a put, call, or other option, or buy-sell or similar arrangement while held by and when distributed from a plan, whether or not the plan is then an ESOP.

(5) *Liability and collateral of ESOP for loan.* An exempt loan must be without recourse against the ESOP. Furthermore, the only assets of the ESOP that may be given as collateral on an exempt loan are qualifying employer securities of two classes: those acquired with the proceeds of the loan and those that were used as collateral on a prior exempt loan repaid with the proceeds of the current exempt loan. No person entitled to payment under the exempt loan shall have any right to assets of the ESOP other than:

(i) Collateral given for the loan,

(ii) Contributions (other than contributions of employer securities) that are made under an ESOP to meet its obligations under the loan, and

(iii) Earnings attributable to such collateral and the investment of such contributions.

The payments made with respect to an exempt loan by the ESOP during a plan year must not exceed an amount equal to the sum of such contributions and earnings received during or prior to the year less such payments in prior years. Such contributions and earnings must be accounted for separately in the books of account of the ESOP until the loan is repaid.

(6) *Default.* In the event of default upon an exempt loan, the value of plan assets transferred in satisfaction of the loan must not exceed the amount of default. If the lender is a disqualified person, a loan must provide for a transfer of plan assets upon default only upon

and to the extent of the failure of the plan to meet the payment schedule of the loan. For purposes of this subparagraph (6), the making of a guarantee does not make a person a lender.

(7) *Reasonable rate of interest.* The interest rate of a loan must not be in excess of a reasonable rate of interest. All relevant factors will be considered in determining a reasonable rate of interest, including the amount and duration of the loan, the security and guarantee (if any) involved, the credit standing of the ESOP and the guarantor (if any), and the interest rate prevailing for comparable loans. When these factors are considered, a variable interest rate may be reasonable.

(8) *Release from encumbrance—(i) General rule.* In general, an exempt loan must provide for the release from encumbrance under this subdivision (i) of plan assets used as collateral for the loan. For each plan year during the duration of the loan, the number of securities released must equal the number of encumbered securities held immediately before release for the current plan year multiplied by a fraction. The numerator of the fraction is the amount of principal and interest paid for the year. The denominator of the fraction is the sum of the numerator plus the principal and interest to be paid for all future years. See § 54.4975-7 (b) (8)(iv). The number of future years under the loan must be definitely ascertainable and must be determined without taking into account any possible extensions or renewal periods. If the interest rate under the loan is variable, the interest to be paid in future years must be computed by using the interest rate applicable as of the end of the plan year. If collateral includes more than one class of securities, the number of securities of each class to be released for a plan year must be determined by applying the same fraction to each class.

(ii) *Special rule.* A loan will not fail to be exempt merely because the number of securities to be released from encumbrance is determined solely with reference to principal payments. However, if release is determined with reference to principal payments only, the following three additional rules apply. The first rule is that the loan must provide for annual payments of principal and interest at a cumula-

tive rate that is not less rapid at any time than level annual payments of such amounts for 10 years. The second rule is that interest included in any payment is disregarded only to the extent that it would be determined to be interest under standard loan amortization tables. The third rule is that this subdivision (ii) is not applicable from the time that, by reason of a renewal, extension, or refinancing, the sum of the expired duration of the exempt loan, the renewal period, the extension period, and the duration of a new exempt loan exceeds 10 years.

(iii) *Caution against plan disqualification.* Under an exempt loan, the number of securities released from encumbrance may vary from year to year. The release of securities depends upon certain employer contributions and earnings under the ESOP. Under § 54.4975-11(d)(2) actual allocations to participants' accounts are based upon assets withdrawn from the suspense account. Nevertheless, for purposes of applying the limitations under section 415 to these allocations, under § 54.974-11(a) (8)(ii) contributions used by the ESOP to pay the loan are treated as annual additions to participants' accounts. Therefore, particular caution must be exercised to avoid exceeding the maximum annual additions under section 415. At the same time, release from encumbrance in annually varying numbers may reflect a failure on the part of the employer to make substantial and recurring contributions to the ESOP which will lead to loss of qualification under section 401(a). The Internal Revenue Service will observe closely the operation of ESOP's that release encumbered securities in varying annual amounts, particularly those that provide for the deferral of loan payments or for balloon payments.

(iv) *Illustration.* The general rule under paragraph (b)(8)(i) of this section operates as illustrated in the following example:

Example. Corporation X establishes an ESOP that borrows $750,000 from a bank. X guarantees the loan, which is for 15 years at 5% interest and is payable in level annual amounts of $72,256.72. Total payments on the loan are $1,083,850.80. The ESOP uses the entire loan proceeds to acquire 15,000 shares of X stock which is used as collateral for the loan.

The number of securities to be released for the first year is 1,000 shares, *i.e.*, 15,000 shares × $72,256.72/$1,083,850.80 = 15,000 shares × 1/15. The number of securities to be released for the second year is 1,000 shares, *i.e.*, 14,000 shares × $72,256.72/$1,011,594.08 = 14,000 shares × 1/14. If all loan payments are made as originally scheduled, the number of securities released in each succeeding year of the loan will also be 1,000.

(9) *Right of first refusal.* Qualifying employer securities acquired with proceeds of an exempt loan may, but need not, be subject to a right of first refusal. However, any such right must meet the requirements of this subparagraph (9). Securities subject to such right must be stock or an equity security, or a debt security convertible into stock or an equity security. Also, the securities must not be publicly traded at the time the right may be exercised. The right of first refusal must be in favor of the employer, the ESOP, or both in any order or priority. The selling price and other terms under the right must not be less favorable to the seller than the greater of the value of the security determined under § 54.4975-11(d)(5), or the purchase price and other terms offered by a buyer, other than the employer or the ESOP, making a good faith offer to purchase the security. The right of first refusal must lapse no later than 14 days after the security holder gives written notice to the holder of the right that an offer by a third party to purchase the security has been received.

(10) *Put option.* A qualifying employer security acquired with the proceeds of an exempt loan by an ESOP after September 30, 1976, must be subject to a put option if it is not publicly traded when distributed or if it is subject to a trading limitation when distributed. For purposes of this subparagraph (10), a "trading limitation" on a security is a restriction under any Federal or state securities law, any regulation thereunder, or an agreement, not prohibited by this paragraph (b), affecting the security which would make the security not as freely tradable as one not subject to such restriction. The put option must be exercisable only by a participant, by the participant's

donees, or by a person (including an estate or its distributee) to whom the security passes by reason of a participant's death. (Under this subparagraph (10), "participant" means a participant and beneficiaries of the participant under the ESOP.) The put option must permit a participant to put the security to the employer. Under no circumstances may the put option bind the ESOP. However, it may grant the ESOP an option to assume the rights and obligations of the employer at the time that the put option is exercised. If it is known at the time a loan is made that Federal or state law will be violated by the employer's honoring such put option, the put option must permit the security to be put, in a manner consistent with such law, to a third party (*e.g.*, an affiliate of the employer or a shareholder other than the ESOP) that has substantial net worth at the time the loan is made and whose net worth is reasonably expected to remain substantial.

(11) *Duration of put option*—(i) *General rule.* A put option must be exercisable at least during a 15-month period which begins on the date the security subject to the put option is distributed by the ESOP.

(ii) *Special rule.* In the case of a security that is publicly traded without restriction when distributed but ceases to be so traded within 15 months after distribution, the employer must notify each security holder in writing on or before the tenth day after the date the security ceases to be so traded that for the remainder of the 15-month period the security is subject to a put option. The number of days between such tenth day and the date on which notice is actually given, if later than the tenth day, must be added to the duration of the put option. The notice must inform distributees of the terms of the put options that they are to hold. Such terms must satisfy the requirements of paragraph (b)(10) through (12) of this section.

(12) *Other put option provision*—(i) *Manner of exercise.* A put option is exercised by the holder notifying the employer in writing that the put option is being exercised.

(ii) *Time excluded from duration of put option.* The period during which a put option is exercisable does not include any time when a distributee is unable to exercise it because the party bound by the put option is prohibited from honoring it by applicable Federal or state law.

(iii) *Price.* The price at which a put option must be exercisable is the value of the security, determined under § 54.4975-11 (d)(5).

(iv) *Payment terms.* The provisions for payment under a put option must be reasonable. The deferral of payment is reasonable if adequate security and a reasonable interest rate are provided for any credit extended and if the cumulative payments at any time are no less than the aggregate of reasonable periodic payments as of such time. Periodic payments are reasonable if annual installments, beginning with 30 days after the date the put option is exercised, are substantially equal. Generally, the payment period may not end more than 5 years after the date the put option is exercised. However, it may be extended to a date no later than the earlier of 10 years from the date the put option is exercised or the date the proceeds of the loan used by the ESOP to acquire the security subject to the put option are entirely repaid.

(v) *Payment restrictions.* Payment under a put option may be restricted by the terms of a loan, including one used to acquire a security subject to a put option, made before Nov. 1, 1977. Otherwise, payment under a put option must not be restricted by the provisions of a loan or any other arrangement, including the terms of the employer's articles of incorporation, unless so required by applicable state law.

(13) *Other terms of loan.* An exempt loan must be for a specific term. Such loan may not be payable at the demand of any person, except in the case of default.

(14) *Status of plan as ESOP.* To be exempt, a loan must be made to a plan that is an ESOP at the time of such loan. However, a loan to a plan formally designated as an ESOP at the time of the loan that fails to be an ESOP because it does not comply with section 401(a) of the Code or § 54.4975-11 will be exempt as of the time of such loan if the plan is amended retroactively under section 401(b) or § 54.4975-11(a)(4).

(15) *Special rules for certain loans*—(i) *Loans made before January 1, 1976.* A loan made before January 1, 1976, or made afterwards under a binding agreement in effect on January 1, 1976 (or under renewals permitted by the terms of the agreement on that date) is exempt for the entire period of the loan if it otherwise satisfies the provisions of this paragraph (b) for such period, even though it does not satisfy the following provisions of this section: the last sentence of paragraph (b)(4) and all of paragraph (b)(5), (6), (8)(i) and (ii), and (9) through (13), inclusive.

(ii) *Loans made after December 31, 1975, but before Nov. 1, 1977.* A loan made after December 31, 1975, but before Nov. 1, 1977 or made afterwards under a binding agreement in effect on Nov. 1, 1977 (or under renewals permitted by the terms of the agreement on that date) is exempt for the entire period of the loan if it otherwise satisfies the provisions of this paragraph (b) for such period even though it does not satisfy the following provisions of this section: paragraph (b)(6) and (9) and the three additional rules listed in paragraph (b)(8)(ii).

(iii) *Release rule.* Notwithstanding paragraph (b)(15)(i) and (ii) of this section, if the proceeds of a loan are used to acquire securities after Nov. 1, 1977, the loan must comply by such date with the provisions of paragraph (b)(8) of this section.

(iv) *Default rule.* Notwithstanding paragraph (b)(15)(i) and (ii) of this section, a loan by a disqualified person other than a guarantor must meet the requirements of paragraph (b)(6) of this section. A loan will meet these requirements if it is retroactively amended before Nov. 1, 1977 to meet these requirements.

(v) *Put option rule.* With respect to a security distributed before Nov. 1, 1977, the put option provisions of paragraph (b)(10), (11), and (12) of this section will be deemed satisfied as of the date the security is distributed if by December 31, 1977, the security is subject to a put option satisfying such provisions. For purposes of satisfying such provisions, the security will be deemed distributed on the date the put option is issued. However, the put option provisions need not be satisfied with respect to a security that is not owned on Nov. 1, 1977 by a person in whose hands a put option must be exercisable.

Sec. 54-4975-11 (T.D. 7506, filed 8-30-77; amended by T.D. 7571, filed 11-16-78.) **"ESOP" requirements**.

(a) *In general*—(1) *Type of plan*. To be an "ESOP" (employee stock ownership plan), a plan described in section 4975(e)(7)(A) must meet the requirements of this section. See section 4975(e)(7)(B).

(2) *Designation as ESOP*. To be an ESOP, a plan must be formally designated as such in the plan document.

(3) *Continuing loan provisions under plan*—(i) *Creation of protections and rights*. The terms of an ESOP must formally provide participants with certain protections and rights with respect to plan assets acquired with the proceeds of an exempt loan. These protections and rights are those referred to in the third sentence of § 54.4975-7 (b)(4), relating to put, call or other options and to buy-sell or similar arrangements, and in § 54.4975-7(b)(10), (11), and (12), relating to put options.

(ii) *"Nonterminable" protections and rights*. The terms of an ESOP must also formally provide that these protections and rights are non-terminable. Thus, if a plan holds or has distributed securities acquired with the proceeds of an exempt loan and either the loan is repaid or the plan ceases to be an ESOP, these protections and rights must continue to exist under the terms of the plan. However, the protections and rights will not fail to be non-terminable merely because they are not exercisable under § 54.4975-7(b)(11) and (12)(ii). For example, if, after a plan ceases to be an ESOP, securities acquired with the proceeds of an exempt loan cease to be publicly traded, the 15-month period prescribed by § 54.4975-7(b)(11) includes the time when the securities are publicly traded.

(iii) *No incorporation by reference of protections and rights*. The formal requirements of paragraph (a)(3)(i) and (ii) of this section must be set forth in the plan. Mere reference to the third sentence of § 54.4975-7 (b)(4) and to the

provisions of § 54.4975-7(b)(10), (11), and (12) is not sufficient.

(iv) *Certain remedial amendments*. Notwithstanding the limits under paragraph (a)(4) and (10) of this section on the retroactive effect of plan amendments, a remedial plan amendment adopted before December 31, 1979, to meet the requirements of paragraph (a)(3)(i) and (ii) of this section is retroactively effective as of the later of the date on which the plan was designated as an ESOP or November 1, 1977.

(4) *Retroactive amendment*. A plan meets the requirements of this section as of the date that it is designated as an ESOP if it is amended retroactively to meet, and in fact does meet, such requirements at any of the following times:

(i) 12 months after the date on which the plan is designated as an ESOP;

(ii) 90 days after a determination letter is issued with respect to the qualification of the plan as an ESOP under this section, but only if the determination is requested by the time in paragraph (a)(4)(i) of this section; or

(iii) A later date approved by the district director.

(5) *Addition to other plan*. An ESOP may form a portion of a plan the balance of which includes a qualified pension, profit-sharing, or stock bonus plan which is not an ESOP. A reference to an ESOP includes an ESOP that forms a portion of another plan.

(6) *Conversion of existing plan to an ESOP*. If an existing pension, profit-sharing, or stock bonus plan is converted into an ESOP, the requirements of section 404 of the Employee Retirement Income Security Act of 1974 (ERISA) (88 Stat. 877), relating to fiduciary duties, and section 401(a) of the Code, relating to requirements for plans established for the exclusive benefit of employees, apply to such conversion. A conversion may constitute a termination of an existing plan. For definition of a termination, see the regulations under section 411(d)(3) of the Code and section 4011(f) of ERISA.

(7) *Certain arrangements barred*—(i) *Buy-sell agreements*. An arrangement involving an

ESOP that creates a put option must not provide for the issuance of put options other than as provided under § 54.-4975-7(b)(10), (11), and (12). Also, an ESOP must not otherwise obligate itself to acquire securities from a particular security holder at an indefinite time determined upon the happening of an event such as the death of the holder.

(ii) *Integrated plans.* A plan designated as an ESOP after November 1, 1977, must not be integrated directly or indirectly with contributions or benefits under Title II of the Social Security Act or any other State or Federal law. ESOP's established and integrated before such date may remain integrated. However, such plans must not be amended to increase the integration level or the integration percentage. Such plans may in operation continue to increase the level of integration if under the plan such increase is limited by reference to a criterion existing apart from the plan.

(8) *Effect of certain ESOP provisions on section 401(a) status—*(i) *Exempt loan requirements.* An ESOP will not fail to meet the requirements of section 401(a)(2) merely because it gives plan assets as collateral for an exempt loan under § 54.4975-7(b)(5) or uses plan assets under § 54.4975-7(b)(6) to repay an exempt loan in the event of default.

(ii) *Individual annual contribution limitation.* And ESOP will not fail to meet the requirements of section 401(a)(16) merely because annual additions under section 415(c) are calculated with respect to employer contributions issued to repay an exempt loan rather than with respect to securities allocated to participants.

(iii) *Income pass-through.* An ESOP will not fail to meet the requirements of section 401(a) merely because it provides for the current payment of income under paragraph (f)(3) of this section.

(9) *Transitional rules for ESOP's established before Nov. 1, 1977.* A plan established before Nov. 1, 1977 that otherwise satisfies the provisions of this section constitutes an ESOP if it is amended by December 31, 1977, to comply from Nov. 1, 1977 with this section even though before Nov. 1, 1977 the plan did not

satisfy paragraphs (c) and (d)(2), (4), and (5) of this section.

(10) *Additional transitional rules.* Notwithstanding paragraph (a)(9) of this section, a plan established before Nov. 1, 1977 that otherwise satisfies the provisions of this section constitutes an ESOP if by December 31, 1977, it is amended to comply from Nov. 1, 1977 with this section even though before such date the plan did not satisfy the following provisions of this section:

(i) Paragraph (a)(3) and (8)(iii);

(ii) The last sentence of paragraph (d)(3); and

(iii) Paragraph (f)(3).

(b) *Plan designed to invest primarily in qualifying employer securities.* A plan constitutes an ESOP only if the plan specifically states that it is designed to invest primarily in qualifying employer securities. Thus, a stock bonus plan or a money purchase pension plan constituting an ESOP may invest part of its assets in other than qualifying employer securities. Such plan will be treated the same as other stock bonus plans or money purchase pension plans qualified under section 401(a) with respect to those investments.

(c) *Suspense account.* All assets acquired by an ESOP with the proceeds of an exempt loan under section 4975(d)(3) must be added to and maintained in a suspense account. They are to be withdrawn from the suspense account by applying § 54.4975-7(b)(8) and (15) as if all securities in the suspense account were encumbered. Such assets acquired before Nov. 1, 1977, must be withdrawn by applying § 54.4975-7 (b)(8) or the provision of the loan that controls release from encumbrance. Assets in such suspense accounts are assets of the ESOP. Thus, for example, such assets are subject to section 401(a)(2).

(d) *Allocations to accounts of participants—*(1) *In general.* Except as provided in this section, amounts contributed to an ESOP must be allocated as provided under § 1.401-1(b)(ii) and (iii) of this chapter, and securities acquired by an ESOP must be accounted for as provided under § 1.402(a)-1(b)(2)(ii) of this chapter.

(2) *Assets withdrawn from suspense account.* As of the end of each plan year, the ESOP must consistently allocate to the participants' accounts non-monetary units representing participants' interests in assets withdrawn from the suspense account.

(3) *Income.* Income with respect to securities acquired with the proceeds of an exempt loan must be allocated as income of the plan except to the extent that the ESOP provides for the use of income from such securities to repay the loan. Certain income may be distributed currently under paragraph (f)(3) of this section.

(4) *Forfeitures.* If a portion of a participant's account is forfeited, qualifying employer securities allocated under paragraph (d)(2) of this section must be forfeited only after other assets. If interests in more than one class of qualifying employer securities have been allocated to the participant's account, the participant must be treated as forfeiting the same proportion of each such class.

(5) *Valuation.* For purposes of § 54.-4975-7 (b)(9) and (12) and this section, valuations must be made in good faith and based on all relevant factors for determining the fair market value of securities. In the case of a transaction between a plan and a disqualified person, value must be determined as of the date of the transaction. For all other purposes under this subparagraph (5), value must be determined as of the most recent valuation date under the plan. An independent appraisal will not in itself be a good faith determination of value in the case of a transaction between a plan and a disqualified person. However, in other cases, a determination of fair market value based on at least an annual appraisal independently arrived at by a person who customarily makes such appraisals and who is independent of any party to a transaction under § 54.4975-7(b)(9) and (12) will be deemed to be a good faith determination of value.

(e) *Multiple plans*—(1) *General rule.* An ESOP may not be considered together with another plan for purposes of applying section 401(a)(4) and (5) or section 410 (b) unless—

(i) The ESOP and such other plan exist on Nov. 1, 1977; or

(ii) Paragraph (e)(2) of this section is satisfied.

(2) *Special rule for combined ESOP's.* Two or more ESOP's, one or more of which does not exist on Nov. 1, 1977, may be considered together for purposes of applying section 401(a)(4) and (5) or section 410(b) only if the proportion of qualifying employer securities to total plan assets is substantially the same for each ESOP and—

(i) The qualifying employer securities held by all ESOP's are all of the same class; or

(ii) The ratios of each class held to all such securities held is substantially the same for each plan.

(3) *Amended coverage, contribution, or benefit structure.* For purposes of paragraph (e)(1)(i) of this section, if the coverage, contribution, or benefit structure of a plan that exists on Nov. 1, 1977 is amended after that date, as of the effective date of the amendment, the plan is no longer considered to be a plan that exists on Nov. 1, 1977.

(f) *Distribution*—(1) *In general.* Except as provided in paragraph ˙(f)(2) and (3) of this section, with respect to distributions, a portion of an ESOP consisting of a stock bonus plan or a money purchase pension plan is not to be distinguished from other such plans under section 401(a). Thus, for example, benefits distributable from the portion of an ESOP consisting of a stock bonus plan are distributable only in stock of the employer. Also, benefits distributable from the money-purchase portion of the ESOP may be, but are not required to be, distributable in qualifying employer securities.

(2) *Exempt loan proceeds.* If securities acquired with the proceeds of an exempt loan available for distribution consist of more than one class, a distributee must receive substantially the same proportion of each such class. However, as indicated in paragraph (f)(1) of this section, benefits distributable from the portion of an ESOP consisting of a stock bonus plan are distributable only in stock of the employer.

(3) *Income.* Income paid with respect to qualifying employer securities acquired by an ESOP in taxable years beginning after December 31, 1974, may be distributed at any time after receipt by the plan to participants on whose behalf such securities have been allocated. However, under an ESOP that is a stock

bonus plan, income held by the plan for a 2-year period or longer must be distributed under the general rules described in paragraph (f)(1) of this section. (See the last sentence of section 803(h), Tax Reform Act of 1976.)

Section 54.4975-12 (T.D. 7506, filed 8-30-77.) **Definition of the term "qualifying employer security".**

(a) *In general.* For purposes of section 4975 (e) (8) and this section, the term "qualifying employer security" means an employer security which is—

(1) Stock or otherwise an equity security, or

(2) A bond, debenture, note, or certificate or other evidence of indebtedness which is described in paragraphs (1), (2), and (3) of section 503(e).

(b) *Special rule.* In determining whether a bond, debenture, note, or certificate or other evidence of indebtedness is described in paragraphs (1), (2), and (3) of section 503(e), any organization described in section 401(a) shall be treated as an organization subject to the provisions of section 503.

IRS REVENUE RULING 59-60

26 CFR 20.2031-2: Valuation of stocks
and bonds.

> In valuing the stock of closely held corporations, or the stock of corporations where market quotations are not available, all other available financial data, as well as all relevant factors affecting the fair market value must be considered for estate tax and gift tax purposes. No general formula may be given that is applicable to the many different valuation situations arising in the valuation of such stock. However, the general approach, methods, and factors which must be considered in valuing such securities are outlined.
> Revenue Ruling 54-77, C.B. 1954-1, 187, superseded.

SECTION 1. PURPOSE.

The purpose of this Revenue Ruling is to outline and review in general the approach, methods and factors to be considered in valuing shares of the capital stock of closely held corporations for estate tax and gift tax purposes. The methods discussed herein will apply likewise to the valuation of corporate stocks on which market quotations are either unavailable or are of such scarcity that they do not reflect the fair market value.

SEC. 2. BACKGROUND AND DEFINITIONS.

.01 All valuations must be made in accordance with the applicable provisions of the Internal Revenue Code of 1954 and the Federal Estate Tax and Gift Tax Regulations. Sections 2031(a), 2032 and 2512(a) of the 1954 Code (sections 811 and 1005 of the 1939 Code) require that the property to be included in the gross estate, or made the subject of a gift, shall be taxed on the basis of the value of the property at the time of death of the decedent, the alternate date if so elected, or the date of gift.

.02 Section 20.2031-1(b) of the Estate Tax Regulations (section 81.10 of the Estate Tax Regulations 105) and section 25.2512-1 of the Gift Tax Regulations (section 86.19 of Gift Tax Regulations 108) define fair market value, in effect, as the price at which the property would change hands between a willing buyer and a willing seller when the former is not under any compulsion to buy and the latter is not under any compulsion to sell, both parties having reasonable knowledge of relevant facts. Court decisions frequently state in addition that the hypothetical buyer and seller are assumed to be able, as well as willing, to trade and to be well informed about the property and concerning the market for such property.

.03 Closely held corporations are those corporations the shares of which are owned by a relatively limited number of stockholders. Often the entire stock issue is held by one family. The result of this situation is that little, if any, trading in the shares takes place. There is, therefore, no established market for the stock and such sales as occur at irregular intervals seldom reflect all of the elements of a representative transaction as defined by the term "fair market value."

Sec. 3. Approach to Valuation.

.01 A determination of fair market value, being a question of fact, will depend upon the circumstances in each case. No formula can be devised that will be generally applicable to the multitude of different valuation issues arising in estate and gift tax cases. Often, an appraiser will find wide differences of opinion as to the fair market value of a particular stock. In resolving such differences, he should maintain a reasonable attitude in recognition of the fact that valuation is not an exact science. A sound valuation will be based upon all the relevant facts, but the elements of common sense, informed judgment and reasonableness must enter into the process of weighing those facts and determining their aggregate significance.

.02 The fair market value of specific shares of stock will vary as general economic conditions change from "normal" to "boom" or "depression," that is, according to the degree of optimism or pessimism with which the investing public regards the future at the required date of appraisal. Uncertainty as to the stability or continuity of the future income from a property decreases its value by increasing the risk of loss of earnings and value in the future. The value of shares of stock of a company with very uncertain future prospects is highly speculative. The appraiser must exercise his judgment as to the degree of risk attaching to the business of the corporation which issued the stock, but that judgment must be related to all of the other factors affecting value.

.03 Valuation of securities is, in essence, a prophesy as to the future and must be based on facts available at the required date of appraisal. As a generalization, the prices of stocks which are traded in volume in a free and active market by informed persons best reflect the consensus of the investing public as to what the future holds for the corporations and industries represented. When a stock is closely held, is traded infrequently, or is traded in an erratic market, some other measure of value must be used. In many instances the next best measure may be found in the prices at which the stocks of companies engaged in the same or a similar line of business are selling in a free and open market.

Sec. 4. Factors To Consider.

.01 It is advisable to emphasize that in the valuation of the stock of closely held corporations or the stock of corporations where market quotations are either lacking or too scarce to be recognized, all available financial data, as well as all relevant factors affecting the fair market value, should be considered. The following factors, although not all-inclusive are fundamental and require careful analysis in each case:

(a) The nature of the business and the history of the enterprise from its inception.

(b) The economic outlook in general and the condition and outlook of the specific industry in particular.

(c) The book value of the stock and the financial condition of the business.

(d) The earning capacity of the company.

(e) The dividend-paying capacity.

(f) Whether or not the enterprise has goodwill or other intangible value.

(g) Sales of the stock and the size of the block of stock to be valued.

(h) The market price of stocks of corporations engaged in the same or a similar line of business having their stocks actively traded in a free and open market, either on an exchange or over-the-counter.

.02 The following is a brief discussion of each of the foregoing factors:

(a) The history of a corporate enterprise will show its past stability or instability, its growth or lack of growth, the diversity or lack of diversity of its operations, and other facts needed to form an opinion of the degree of risk involved in the business. For an enterprise which changed its from of organization but carried on the same or closely similar operations of its predecessor, the history of the former enterprise should be considered. The detail to be considered should increase with approach to the required date of appraisal, since recent events are of greatest help in predicting the future; but a study of gross and net income, and of dividends covering a long prior period, is highly desirable. The history to be studied should include, but need not be limited to, the nature of the business, its products or services, its operating and investment assets, capital structure, plant facilities, sales records and management, all of which should be considered as of the date of the appraisal, with due regard for recent significant changes. Events of the past that are unlikely to recur in the future should be discounted, since value has a close relation to future expectancy.

(b) A sound appraisal of a closely held stock must consider current and prospective economic conditions as of the date of appraisal, both in the national economy and in the industry or industries with which the corporation is allied. It is important to know that the company is more or less successful than its competitors in the same industry, or that it is maintaining a stable position with respect to competitors. Equal or even greater significance may attach to the ability of the industry with which the company is allied to compete with other industries. Prospective competition which has not been a factor in prior years should be given careful attention. For example, high profits due to the novelty of its product and the lack of competition often lead to increasing competition. The public's appraisal of the future prospects of competitive industries or of competitors within an industry may be indicated by price trends in the markets for commodities and for securities. The loss of the manager of a so-called "one-man" business may have a depressing effect upon the value of the stock of such business, particularly if there is a lack of trained personnel capable of succeeding to the management of the enterprise. In valuing the stock of this type of business, therefore, the effect of the loss of the manager on the future expectancy of the business, and the absence of management-succession potentialities are pertinent factors to be taken into consideration. On the other hand, there may be factors which offset, in whole or in part, the loss of the manager's services. For instance, the nature of the business and of its assets may be such that they will not be impaired by the loss of the manager. Furthermore, the loss may be adequately covered by life insurance, or competent management might be employed on the basis of the consideration paid for the former manager's services. These, or other offsetting factors, if found to exist, should be carefully weighed against the loss of the manager's services in valuing the stock of the enterprise.

(c) Balance sheets should be obtained, preferably in the form of comparative annual statements for two or more years immediately preceding the date of appraisal, together with a balance sheet at the end of the month preceding that date, if corporate accounting will permit. Any balance sheet descriptions that are not self-explanatory, and balance sheet items comprehending diverse assets or liabilities, should be clarified in essential detail by supporting supplemental schedules. These statements usually will disclose to the appraiser (1) liquid position (ratio of current assets to current liabilities); (2) gross and net book value of principal classes of fixed assets; (3) working capital; (4) long-term indebtedness; (5) capital structure; and (6) net worth. Consideration also should be given to any assets not essential to the operation of the business, such as investments in securities, real estate, etc. In general, such nonoperating assets will command a lower rate of return than do the operating assets, although in exceptional cases the reverse may be true. In computing the book value per share of stock, assets of the investment type should be revalued on the basis of their market price and the book value adjusted accordingly. Comparison of the company's balance sheets over several years may reveal, among other facts, such developments as the acquisition of additional production facilities or subsidiary companies, improvement in financial position, and details as to recapitalizations and other changes in the capital structure of the corporation. If the corporation has more than one class of stock outstanding, the charter or certificate of incorporation should be examined to ascertain the explicit rights and privileges of the various stock issues including: (1) voting powers, (2) preference as to dividends, and (3) preference as to assets in the event of liquidation.

(d) Detailed profit-and-loss statements should be obtained and considered for a representative period immediately prior to the required date of appraisal, preferably five or more years. Such statements should show (1) gross income by principal items; (2) principal deductions from gross income including major prior items of operating expenses, interest and other expense on each item of long-term debt, depreciation and depletion if such deductions are made, officers' salaries, in total if they appear to be reasonable or in detail if they seem to be excessive, contributions (whether or not deductible for tax purposes) that the nature of its business and its community position require the corporation to make, and taxes by principal items, including income and excess profits taxes; (3) net income available for dividends; (4) rates and amounts of dividends paid on each class of stock; (5) remaining amount carried to surplus; and (6) adjustments to, and reconciliation with, surplus as stated on the balance sheet. With profit and loss statements of this character available, the appraiser should be able to separate recurrent from nonrecurrent items of income and expense, to distinguish between operating income and investment income, and to ascertain whether or not any line of business in which the company is engaged is operated consistently at a loss and might be abandoned with benefit to the company. The percentage of earnings retained for business expansion should be noted when dividend-paying capacity is considered. Potential future income is a major factor in many valuations of closely-held stocks, and all information concerning past income which will be helpful in predicting the future should be secured. Prior earnings records usually are the most reliable guide as to the future expectancy, but resort to arbitrary five-or-ten-year averages without regard to current trends or future prospects will not produce a realistic valuation. If, for instance, a record of progressively increasing or decreasing net income is found, then greater weight may be accorded the most recent years' profits in estimating earning power. It will be helpful, in judging risk and the extent to which a business is a marginal operator, to consider deductions from income and net income in terms of percentage of sales. Major categories of cost and expense to be so analyzed include the consumption of raw materials and supplies in the case of manufacturers, processors and fabricators; the cost of purchased merchandise in the case of merchants; utility services; insurance; taxes; depletion or depreciation; and interest.

(e) Primary consideration should be given to the dividend-paying capacity of the company rather than to dividends actually paid in the past. Recognition must be given to the necessity of retaining a reasonable portion of profits in a company to meet competition. Dividend-paying capacity is a factor that must be considered in an appraisal, but dividends actually paid in the past may not have any relation to dividend-paying capacity. Specifically, the dividends paid by a closely held family company may be measured by the income needs of the stockholders or by their desire to avoid taxes on dividend receipts, instead of by the ability of the company to pay dividends. Where an actual or effective controlling interest in a corporation is to be valued, the dividend factor is not a material element, since the payment of such dividends is discretionary with the controlling stockholders. The individual or group in control can substitute salaries and bonuses for dividends, thus reducing net income and understating the dividend-paying capacity of the company. It follows, therefore, that dividends are less reliable criteria of fair market value than other applicable factors.

(f) In the final analysis, goodwill is based upon earning capacity. The presence of goodwill and its value, therefore, rests upon the excess of net earnings over and above a fair return on the net tangible assets. While the element of goodwill may be based primarily on earnings, such factors as the prestige and renown of the business, the ownership of a trade or brand name, and a record of successful operation over a prolonged period in a particular locality, also may furnish support for the inclusion of intangible value. In some instances it may not be possible to make a separate appraisal of the tangible and intangible assets of the business. The enterprise has a value as an entity. Whatever intangible value there is, which is supportable by the facts, may be measured by the amount by which the appraised value of the tangible assets exceeds the net book value of such assets.

(g) Sales of stock of a closely held corporation should be carefully investigated to determine whether they represent transactions at arm's length. Forced or distress sales do not ordinarily reflect fair market value nor do isolated sales in small amounts necessarily control as the measure of value. This is especially true in the valuation of a controlling interest in a corporation. Since, in the case of closely held stocks, no prevailing market prices are available, there is no basis for making an adjustment for blockage. It follows, therefore, that such stocks should be valued upon a consideration of all the evidence affecting the fair market value. The size of the block of stock itself is a relevant factor to be considered. Although it is true that a minority interest in an unlisted corporation's stock is more difficult to sell than a similar block of listed stock, it is equally true that control of a corporation, either actual or in effect, representing as it does an added element of value, may justify a higher value for a specific block of stock.

(h) Section 2031(b) of the Code states, in effect, that in valuing unlisted securities the value of stock or securities of corporations engaged in the same or a similar line of business which are listed on an exchange should be taken into consideration along with all other factors. An important consideration is that the corporations to be used for comparisons have capital stocks which are actively traded by the public. In accordance with section 2031(b) of the Code, stocks listed on an exchange are to be considered first. However, if sufficient comparable companies whose stocks are listed on an exchange cannot be found, other comparable companies which have stocks actively traded in on the over-the-counter market also may be used. The essential factor is that whether the stocks are sold on an exchange or over-the-counter there is evidence of an active, free public market for the stock as of the valuation date. In selecting corporations for comparative purposes, care should be taken to use only comparable companies. Although the only restrictive requirement as to comparable corporations specified in the statute is that their lines of business be the same or similar, yet it is obvious that consideration must be given to other relevant factors in order that the most valid comparison possible will be obtained. For illustration, a corporation having one or more issues of preferred stock, bonds or debentures in addition to its common stock should not be considered to be directly comparable to one having only common stock outstanding. In like manner, a company with a declining business and decreasing markets is not comparable to one with a record of current progress and market expansion.

SEC. 5. WEIGHT TO BE ACCORDED VARIOUS FACTORS.

The valuation of closely held corporate stock entails the consideration of all relevant factors as stated in section 4. Depending upon the circumstances in each case, certain factors may carry more weight than others because of the nature of the company's business. To illustrate:

(a) Earnings may be the most important criterion of value in some cases whereas asset value will receive primary consideration in others. In general, the appraiser will accord primary consideration to earnings when valuing stocks of companies which sell products or services to the public; conversely, in the investment or holding type of company, the appraiser may accord the greatest weight to the assets underlying the security to be valued.

(b) The value of the stock of a closely held investment or real estate holding company, whether or not family owned, is closely related to the value of the assets underlying the stock. For companies of this type the appraiser should determine the fair market values of the assets of the company. Operating expenses of such a company and the cost of liquidating it, if any, merit consideration when appraising the relative values of the stock and the underlying assets. The market values of the underlying assets give due weight to potential earnings and dividends of the particular items of property underlying the stock, capitalized at rates deemed proper by the investing public at the date of appraisal. A current appraisal by the investing public should be superior to the retrospective opinion of an individual. For these reasons, adjusted net worth should be accorded greater weight in valuing the stock of a closely held investment or real estate holding company, whether or not family owned, than any of the other customary yardsticks of appraisal, such as earnings and dividend paying capacity.

Sec. 6.   Capitalization Rates.

In the application of certain fundamental valuation factors, such as earnings and dividends, it is necessary to capitalize the average or current results at some appropriate rate. A determination of the proper capitalization rate presents one of the most difficult problems in valuation. That there is no ready or simple solution will become apparent by a cursory check of the rates of return and dividend yields in terms of the selling prices of corporate shares listed on the major exchanges of the country. Wide variations will be found even for companies in the same industry. Moreover, the ratio will fluctuate from year to year depending upon economic conditions. Thus, no standard tables of capitalization rates applicable to closely held corporations can be formulated. Among the more important factors to be taken into consideration in deciding upon a capitalization rate in a particular case are: (1) the nature of the business; (2) the risk involved; and (3) the stability or irregularity of earnings.

Sec. 7.   Average of Factors.

Because valuations cannot be made on the basis of a prescribed formula, there is no means whereby the various applicable factors in a particular case can be assigned mathematical weights in deriving the fair market value. For this reason, no useful purpose is served by taking an average of several factors (for example, book value, capitalized earnings and capitalized dividends) and basing the valuation on the result. Such a process excludes active consideration of other pertinent factors, and the end result cannot be supported by a realistic application of the significant facts in the case except by mere chance.

Sec. 8.   Restrictive Agreements.

Frequently, in the valuation of closely held stock for estate and gift tax purposes, it will be found that the stock is subject to an agreement restricting its sale or transfer. Where shares of stock were acquired by a decedent subject to an option reserved by the issuing corporation to repurchase at a certain price, the option price is usually accepted as the fair market value for estate tax purposes. See Rev. Rul. 54-76, C.B. 1954-1, 194. However, in such case the option price is not determinative of fair market value for gift tax purposes. Where the option, or buy and sell agreement, is the result of voluntary action by the stockholders and is binding during the life as well as at the death of the stockholders, such agreement may or may not, depending upon the circumstances of each case, fix the value for estate tax purposes. However, such agreement is a factor to be considered, with other relevant factors, in determining fair market value. Where the stockholder is free to dispose of his shares during life and the option is to become effective only upon his death, the fair market value is not limited to the option price. It is always necessary to consider the relationship of the parties, the relative number of shares held by the decedent, and other material facts, to determine whether the agreement represents a bonafide business arrangement or is a device to pass the decedent's shares to the natural objects of his bounty for less than an adequate and full consideration in money or money's worth. In this connection see Rev. Rul. 157 C.B. 1953-2, 255, and Rev. Rul. 189, C.B. 1953-2, 294.

APPENDIX

II

Forms

CONTENTS

Form 5301

(Rev. June 1976)

Department of the Treasury
Internal Revenue Service

Application for
Determination for Defined Contribution Plan
For Profit-sharing, Stock Bonus and Money Purchase Plans
(Under sections 401(a), 405(a), 414(l) and 501(a) of the Internal Revenue Code)

This Form is Open to Public Inspection

File in Duplicate
For IRS Use Only
Case number ▶.............................
Issue date ▶.............................
EPMF status code ▶.............................
File folder number ▶

▶ **Church and Governmental Plans.**—All items need not be completed. See instruction "B. What to File."

▶ **Please complete every applicable item on this form. If an item does not apply, enter N/A.**

1 (a) Name, address and ZIP code of employer

Telephone number ▶ ( )

(b) Name, address and ZIP code of plan administrator, if other than employer

(c) Administrator's identification number ▶   Telephone number ▶ ( )

2 Employer's identification number

3 Business code number

4 Date incorporated or business commenced

5 Employer's taxable year ends

6 Determination requested for:
- **(a)** *(i)* ☐ Initial qualification—date plan adopted ▶............................. *(ii)* ☐ Amendment—date adopted ▶.............................
- *(iii)* If (ii) is checked, enter file folder number ▶
- **(b)** Were employees who are interested parties given the required notification of the filing of this application? . ☐ Yes ☐ No
- **(c)** If this application involves a merger or consolidation with another plan, enter the employer identification number(s) and the plan number(s) of such other plan(s) ▶

7 Type of entity: **(a)** ☐ Corporation **(b)** ☐ Subchapter S corporation **(c)** ☐ Sole proprietor **(d)** ☐ Partnership **(e)** ☐ Tax exempt organization **(f)** ☐ Church **(g)** ☐ Governmental organization **(h)** ☐ Other (specify) ▶

8 (a) Name of Plan
- **(b)** Plan number ▶.................. **(c)** Plan year ends ▶..............
- **(d)** Is this a Keogh (H.R. 10) plan? . . . . ☐ Yes ☐ No
- **(e)** If "Yes," is an owner-employee in the plan? . ☐ Yes ☐ No

9 (a) If this is an adoption of a master or prototype plan (other than Keogh) or a district approved pattern plan, enter name of such plan
- **(b)** Letter serial number or notification letter number

10 Type of plan: **(a)** ☐ Profit-sharing **(b)** ☐ Stock bonus **(c)** ☐ Money purchase **(d)** ☐ Target benefit

11 Effective date of plan | **12** Effective date of amendment | **13** Date plan was communicated to employees ▶.................... How communicated? ▶

14 (a) Indicate the general eligibility requirements for participation under the plan and indicate the section and page number of plan or trust where each provision is contained:
- *(i)* ☐ All employees
- *(ii)* ☐ Hourly rate employee only
- *(iii)* ☐ Salaried employee only
- *(iv)* ☐ Other job class (specify) ▶.............................
- *(v)* Length of service (number of years) ▶.....................
- *(vi)* Minimum age (specify) ▶...................
- *(vii)* Maximum age (specify) ▶...................
- *(viii)* Minimum pay (specify) ▶...................
- **(b)** Are the eligibility requirements the same for future employees? . . . . ☐ Yes ☐ No
  If "No," explain ▶.............................
- **(c)** Does the plan recognize service only with this employer? . . . . . . ☐ Yes ☐ No
  If "No," explain ▶

Section and page number * | GOVERNMENT USE ONLY

15 Coverage of plan at (give date) ▶.............................
Enter here the number of self-employed individuals ▶

Number

- **(a)** Total employed (if a Keogh plan, include all self-employed individuals) . . . .
- **(b)** Exclusions under plan (do not count an employee more than once):
  - *(i)* Minimum age or years of service required (specify) ▶.............................
  - *(ii)* Employees included in collective bargaining . . . .
  - *(iii)* Nonresident aliens who receive no earned income from United States sources . . . . .
- **(c)** Total exclusions, sum of (b)(i) through (iii) . . . .
- **(d)** Employees not excluded under the statute, (a) less (c) . . . .

* Of plan or trust or other document constituting the plan.

Under penalties of perjury, I declare that I have examined this application, including accompanying statements, and to the best of my knowledge and belief it is true, correct and complete.

Signature ▶_____ Title ▶_____ Date ▶_____

c70—575-279-1

Form 5301 (Rev. 6–76)   **Page 2**

(Section references are to the Internal Revenue Code)	Number	GOVERNMENT USE ONLY

15 Coverage (continued):

    (e) Ineligible under plan on account of (do not count an employee included in (b)):

        (i)   Minimum pay . . . .

        (ii) Hourly-paid . . . .

        (iii) Maximum age . . . .

        (iv) Other (specify) ▶..

    (f) Employees ineligible, sum of (e)(i) through (iv) . . . .

    (g) Employees eligible to participate, line (d) less line (f) . . . .

    (h) Number of employees participating in plan . . . .

    (i) Percent of nonexcluded employees who are participating, (h) divided by (d) . . .   %

        Complete (j) only if (i) is less than 70% and complete (k) only if (i) is 70% or more.

    (j) Percent of nonexcluded employees who are eligible to participate, (g) divided by (d) . . . .   %

    (k) Percent of eligible employees who are participating, (h) divided by (g) . . . .   %

        If (i) and (j) are less than 70% or (k) is less than 80%, see instructions.

    (l) Total number of participants, include certain retired and terminated employees, see instructions . . . . .

	Yes	No	Section and page number *

16 Employee contributions:

    (a) Are mandatory contributions limited to 6%, or less, of compensation? . . . .

    (b) Are voluntary contributions limited to 10%, or less, of compensation for all qualified plans? .

    (c) Are employee contributions nonforfeitable? . . . .

17 Employer contributions:

    (a) Under a profit-sharing or stock bonus plan, are they determined under—

        (i) ☐ A definite formula   (ii) ☐ An indefinite formula   (iii) ☐ Both

    (b) Under profit-sharing or stock bonus plans are contributions limited to—

        (i) ☐ Current earnings   (ii) ☐ Accumulated earnings   (iii) ☐ Combination

    (c) Money purchase—Enter rate of contribution ▶...

    (d) State target benefit formula, if applicable ▶..

18 Integration:

    Is this plan integrated with Social Security or Railroad Retirement? . . . . . .

    If "Yes," see instructions.

19 Vesting—Check the appropriate box to indicate the vesting provisions of the plan:

    (a) ☐ Full and immediate

    (b) ☐ Full vesting after 10 years of service

    (c) ☐ 5- to 15-year vesting, i.e., 25% after 5 years of service, 5% additional for each of the next 5 years, then 10% additional for each of the next 5 years

    (d) ☐ Rule of 45 (see section 411(a)(2)(C))

    (e) ☐ For each year of employment, commencing with the 4th such year, vesting not less than 40% after 4 years of service, 5% additional for each of the next 2 years, and 10% additional for each of the next 5 years

    (f) ☐ 100% vesting within 5 years after contributions are made (class year plans only)

    (g) ☐ Other (specify and see instructions) ▶

20 Administration:

    (a) Type of funding entity: (i) ☐ Trust   (ii) ☐ Custodial account   (iii) ☐ Non-trusteed

        If you checked (i) or (ii), enter date executed ▶ ....

    (b) Enter name of trustee or custodian, if any ▶..

....

	Yes	No	

    (c) Does trust agreement prohibit reversion of funds to the employer? . . . . .

    (d) Specify the limits placed on the purchase of insurance contracts, if any:

        (i)   Ordinary life ▶..

        (ii) Term insurance ▶..

        (iii) Other (specify) ▶..

    (e) If the trustees may earmark specific investments, including insurance contracts, are such investments subject to the employee's consent, or purchased ratably where employee consent is not required? . . . .

    (f) Are loans to participants limited to their vested interests? . . . .

    (g) If Puerto Rican trust, does it qualify for tax exemption under the laws of Puerto Rico? . . .

* Of plan or trust or other document constituting the plan.   c70—575-279–1

Form 5301 (Rev. 6-76)   Page **3**

	Yes	No	Section and page number *	GOVERNMENT USE ONLY

21 Requirements for benefits—distributions—allocations:

(a) Normal retirement age is ►............... State years of service required ►.............

(b) Early retirement age is ►.................... State years of service required ►.............

(c) If employer's consent is required for early retirement, are benefits limited to vested benefits? .

(d) (i) Does the plan provide that the payment of benefits, unless the employee elects otherwise, will commence not later than the 60th day after the latest of (1) the close of the plan year in which the participant attains the earlier of age 65, or the normal retirement age specified under the plan, (2) the close of the plan year in which occurs the 10th anniversary of the year in which participant commenced participation or (3) the close of the plan year in which the participant terminates his service with the employer? . . . .

(ii) Does plan provide for payment of benefits if claim is not filed? . . . . .

(e) Distribution of account balances may be made in:

(i) ☐ Lump sum   (ii) ☐ Annuity contracts

(iii) ☐ Substantially equal annual installments—not exceeding ►.......... years

(iv) ☐ Other (specify) ►..

(f) If distributions are made in installments, are they credited with:

(i) ☐ Fund earnings

(ii) ☐ Interest at a rate of ►..............% per year

(iii) ☐ Other (specify) ►..

(g) If insurance contracts are distributed, are the modes of settlement contained in the contracts limited to those provided under the plan? . . . .

(h) If plan provides for payment of annuity benefits, does the plan provide a joint and survivor benefit unless participant elects otherwise? . . . .

(i) Are all optional modes of distribution of equal value? . . . .

(j) If this is a stock bonus plan, are distributions made in employer stock? . . .

(k) Other event permitting distribution (specify) ►................................

(l) If participants may withdraw their contributions or earnings, may such withdrawal be made without forfeiting vested benefits based on employer contributions? . . . .

(m) Are contributions allocated on the basis of total compensation? . . . . . .

If "No," see instructions.

(n) Are forfeitures allocated, in case of a profit-sharing or stock bonus plan, on basis of total compensation? . . . .

If "No," explain how allocated.

(o) Are trust earnings and losses allocated on the basis of account balances? . . .

If "No," explain how allocated.

(p) In case of target benefit or other money purchase plan, are forfeitures allocated to reduce employer contributions? . . . .

If "No," explain how allocated.

(q) Does plan provide for maximum limitation under section 415? . . . . . .

(r) In the case of a merger or consolidation with another plan or transfer of assets or liabilities to another plan, will each participant be entitled to the same or greater benefit as if the plan had terminated? . . . .

(s) Does the plan prohibit the assignment or alienation of benefits? . . . . . .

(t) Does the plan preclude divestment for cause? . . . .

(u) Are trust assets valued at current value? . . . .

(v) Are trust assets valued at least annually? . . . .

If "No," explain when valued.

22 Termination:

(a) Is there a provision in the plan for terminating the plan and/or trust? . . . .

(b) Are the amounts credited to participants' accounts nonforfeitable upon termination or partial termination of the plan? . . . .

(c) Upon complete discontinuance of contributions under a profit-sharing or stock bonus plan are the employees' rights under the plan nonforfeitable? . . . . .

* Of plan or trust or other document constituting the plan.   c70—575—279—1

Form 5301 (Rev. 6-76)   Page **4**

		Yes	No	GOVERNMENT USE ONLY
23	Miscellaneous:			
	(a) Has power of attorney been submitted with the application (or previously submitted)? . . .			
	(b) Have you completed and attached Form 5302?			
	(c) Is the adopting employer a member of a controlled group of corporations or under commonly controlled trades or businesses? . . . . If "Yes," see instructions.	▨	▨	
	(d) Is any issue relating to this plan or trust currently pending before the Internal Revenue Service, the Department of Labor, the Pension Benefit Guaranty Corporation or any Court? . . . . If "Yes," attach explanation.			
	(e) Other qualified plans—Enter for each other qualified plan you maintain (do not include plans that were established under union-negotiated agreements that involved other employers):			
	(i) Name of plan ▶..			
	(ii) Type of plan ▶..			
	(iii) Rate of employer contribution, if fixed ▶............................			
	(iv) Benefit formula or monthly benefit ▶.................................			
	(v) Number of participants ▶			

		Yes	No	
24	In the case of a request on an initial qualification, have the following documents been included:			
	(a) Copies of all instruments constituting the plan or joinder agreement?			
	(b) Copy of trust indenture?			
	(c) Evidence that retirement benefits for employees in 15(b)(ii) were the subject of good faith bargaining between employee representatives and employer(s)—where that has occurred and is the basis for excluding certain employees, see section 410(b)(2)(A)?	▨	▨	
25	In the case of a request involving an amendment, after initial qualification, have the following documents been included:	▨	▨	
	(a) A copy of the amendment(s)?			
	(b) A description of the amendment covering the items changed and an explanation of the provisions before and after the amendment?			
	(c) A completely restated plan? †			
	(d) A working copy of the plan in which there has been incorporated all of the previous amendments representing the provisions of the plan as currently in effect? †			
	(e) Copies of all amendments adopted since the date of the last determination letter for which no determination letter has been issued by the Internal Revenue Service? †			

		Yes	No	Section and page number *
26	This section pertains to Keogh (H.R. 10) plans only:			
	(a) Do owner-employees have the option to participate			
	(b) Does plan prohibit distribution of benefits to owner-employees before age 59½, except for disability?			
	(c) Does plan prohibit excess contributions for self-employed individuals? . . .			
	(d) Is a definition of earned income provided?			
	(e) Are distributions of benefits to owner-employees required to commence not later than age 70½?			
	(f) Are the self-employed individual participants covered only under this plan? . .			
	(g) Does plan prohibit the allocation of forfeitures to self-employed individuals? .			

† If plan is being amended for the first time to conform to the participation and vesting standards of the *Employee Retirement Income Security Act of 1974*, or if the plan has been amended at least three times since the last restated plan was submitted, one of the documents specified under (c) or (d) must be attached.

If any item in 24 or 25 is answered "No," please explain.

* Of plan or trust or other document constituting the plan.

If more space is needed for any item, attach additional sheets of the same size.

Form **5303** (Rev. June 1976) Department of the Treasury Internal Revenue Service	**Application for** **Determination for Collectively-Bargained Plan** (Under Sections 401(a) and 501(a) of the Internal Revenue Code) (Section references are to the Internal Revenue Code.) **This Form is Open to Public Inspection**	**File in Duplicate** **For IRS Use Only** Case number ► .... Issue date ► .... EPMF status code ► .... File folder number ►

► **Church and Governmental Plans.**—All items need not be completed. See instruction "B. What to File."

► **Please complete every item on this form. If an item does not apply, enter N/A.**

1 (a) Name, address and ZIP code of employer if a single employer plan	**2** Employer's identification number
	3 Business code number
Telephone number ► ( )	
(b) Name, address and ZIP code of plan administrator, if other than employer	**4** Date incorporated or business commenced
	5 Employer's taxable year ends

(c) Administrator's identification number ►   Telephone number ► ( )

6 (a) Determination requested for:
   (i) ☐ Initial qualification—date plan adopted ► .... **(ii)** ☐ Amendment—date adopted ► ....
   (iii) ☐ If (ii) is checked, enter file folder number ► ....
(b) Were employees who are interested parties given the required notification of the filing of this application? . ☐ Yes ☐ No
(c) If this application involves a merger or consolidation with another plan(s), enter the employer identification number(s) and the plan number(s) of such other plan(s)

7 Check appropriate box to indicate the type of plan entity:
   (a) ☐ Single-employer plan   **(b)** ☐ Plan of controlled group of corporations or common control employers
   (c) ☐ Multiemployer plan   **(d)** ☐ Other multiple-employer plan   **(e)** ☐ Church   **(f)** ☐ Governmental organization
   (g) ☐ Other (specify) ►

8 (a) Name of Plan	**(b)** Plan number ► ....
	(c) Plan year ends ►

9 (a) If this is an adoption of a master or prototype plan (other than Keogh) or a district approved pattern plan, enter name of such plan	**(b)** Letter serial number or notification letter number

10 (a) Defined benefit plan—indicate whether:
    (i) ☐ Unit benefit   **(ii)** ☐ Fixed benefit
    (iii) ☐ Flat benefit   **(iv)** ☐ Other (specify) ►....
 ....
 (b) Defined contribution—indicate whether:
    (i) ☐ Profit-sharing   **(ii)** ☐ Money purchase
    (iii) ☐ Stock bonus
	(c) Does plan provide for variable benefits? . . ☐ Yes ☐ No
	 If "Yes," check appropriate box to indicate type.
	    (i) ☐ Cost of living **(ii)** ☐ Asset fluctuation
	    (iii) ☐ Other (specify) ►

11 Effective date of plan	**12** Effective date of amendment	**13** Date plan was communicated to employees ► .... How communicated ►

14 (a) Indicate the general eligibility requirements for participation under the plan and indicate the section and page number of plan or trust where each provision is contained:
    (i) ☐ All employees   **(v)** Length of Service (number of years) ► ....
    (ii) ☐ Hourly rate employee only   **(vi)** Minimum age (specify) ► ....
    (iii) ☐ Salaried employee only   **(vii)** Maximum age (specify) ► ....
    (iv) ☐ Other job class (specify) ► ....   **(viii)** Minimum pay (specify) ► ....
 (b) Are the eligibility requirements the same for future employees? . . . . . ☐ Yes ☐ No
 If "No," explain ►
 (c) Does the plan recognize service only with this employer(s)? . . . . . ☐ Yes ☐ No
 If "No," explain ►
	Section and page number*	GOVERNMENT USE ONLY

*of plan or other document—trust or collective bargaining agreement.

Under penalties of perjury, I (we) declare that I (we) have examined this application, including accompanying statements, and to the best of my (our) knowledge and belief it is true, correct and complete.

Signature	Title	Date
Signature	Title	Date

Form 5303 (Rev. 6–76)   Page 2

		Number	GOVERNMENT USE ONLY
15 Coverage of plan at (give date) ▶...			
(a) Complete only if you checked 7(a), (b) or (d):			
(i) Total employed			
(ii) Exclusions—		▨▨▨▨▨	
a. Minimum age or years of service required (specify) ▶..............................			
b. Nonresident aliens who receive no earned income from United States sources . .			
c. Not members of bargaining unit			
(iii) Total exclusions			
(iv) Employees not excluded under the statute, (i) less (iii)			
(v) Employees who do not meet plan eligibility requirements			
(vi) Employees eligible to participate, (iv) less (v)			
(vii) Employees participating in the plan			
(viii) Total number of participants (include certain retired and terminated employees) . . .		▨▨▨▨▨	
(b) Complete only if you checked 7(c), (e), (f) or (g):			
(i) Total number of participants (include certain retired and terminated employees) . . .			
(ii) Participants whose benefits or accounts are fully vested			
(iii) Number of contributing employers			
(c) Are employees of the representative labor unions or of the plan included in the plan? . . . . ☐ Yes ☐ No			
If "Yes," attach a completed Form 5302 with respect to the employees of each such union and/or each such plan.			

	Yes	No	Section and page number*	GOVERNMENT USE ONLY
16 Employee contributions:				
(a) Are mandatory contributions limited to 6%, or less, of compensation?				
(b) If voluntary, are contributions limited to 10%, or less, of compensation for all qualified plans?				
(c) Are employee contributions nonforfeitable?				
17 Employer contributions under a defined contribution plan:				
(a) Indicate the method used to determine employer contributions— (i) ☐ Definite formula, (ii) ☐ Indefinite formula, or (iii) ☐ Both				
(b) Indicate whether employer contributions are limited to— (i) ☐ Current earnings, (ii) ☐ Accumulated earnings, or (iii) ☐ Combination				
(c) Money purchase, enter rate of contribution ▶				
18 Is any issue, relating to this plan or trust, currently pending before the Internal Revenue Service, the Department of Labor, the Pension Benefit Guaranty Corporation or any court? . . . . ☐ Yes ☐ No				
If "Yes," explain ▶				

	Section and page number*	GOVERNMENT USE ONLY
19 Vesting—Check the appropriate box to indicate the vesting provisions of the plan:		
(a) ☐ Full and immediate		
(b) ☐ Full vesting after 10 years of service		
(c) ☐ 5- to 15-year vesting, i.e., 25% after 5 years of service, 5% additional for each of the next 5 years, then 10% additional for each of the next 5 years		
(d) ☐ Rule of 45 (see section 411(a)(2)(C))		
(e) ☐ For each year of employment, commencing with the 4th such year, vesting not less than 40% after 4 years of service, 5% additional for each of the next 2 years, and 10% additional for each of the next 5 years		
(f) ☐ 100% vesting within 5 years after contributions are made (class year plans only)		
(g) ☐ Other (specify) ▶		
Note: *If the vesting schedule is less rapid than 19(e), submit a schedule of turnover of employees or provide sufficient facts upon which a determination can be made that the vesting schedule of the plan is satisfactory. See Rev. Proc. 76–11, 1976–9 I.R.B. 22 or its successor, if any.*		
20 Administration:		
(a) Type of funding entity: (i) ☐ Trust (iii) ☐ Non-trusteed (ii) ☐ Custodial account (iv) ☐ Trust with insurance contracts		
If you checked (i) or (ii), enter date executed ▶		
(b) Enter name of trustee or custodian, if any ▶		

	Yes	No
(c) Does trust agreement prohibit reversion of funds to the employer?		
(d) If borrowing on insurance contracts is permitted, is it on a pro-rata basis and only for payment of premiums?		
(e) If Puerto Rican trust, does it qualify for tax exemption under the laws of Puerto Rico?		

* of plan or other document—trust or collective bargaining agreement.

Form 5303 (Rev. 6–76)

Page **3**

	Yes	No	Section and page number*	GOVERNMENT USE ONLY

21 Additional information for all plans:

(a) Normal retirement age is ▶............... State years of service required ▶...............

(b) *(i)* Does the plan provide that the payment of benefits, unless the employee elects otherwise, will commence not later than the 60th day after the latest of (1) the close of the plan year in which the participant attains the earlier of age 65 or the normal retirement age specified under the plan, (2) the close of the plan year in which occurs the 10th anniversary of the year in which participant commenced participation or (3) the close of the plan year in which the participant terminates his service with the employer? . . . .

(ii) Does plan provide for payment of benefits if claim is not filed? . . . . .

(c) Normal form of retirement benefit ▶..

(d) If plan provides for payment of annuity benefits, does the plan provide a joint and survivor benefit unless participant elects otherwise? . . . .

(e) Are all optional modes of distribution of equal value? . . . .

(f) If participants may withdraw their contributions or earnings, may such withdrawal be made without forfeiting vested benefits based on employer contributions? . .

(g) Does the plan prohibit the assignment or alienation of benefits? . . . . . .

(h) Does the plan preclude divestment for cause? . . . .

22 Additional information for defined benefit plans only:

(a) Benefit at normal retirement age is ▶..

(b) Benefit at early retirement age is ▶..

(c) Are benefits computed on the basis of total compensation? . . . .

(d) Is duplication of benefits upon re-entry into the plan prohibited? . . . .

(e) Is there a disability benefit under the plan? . . . .

(f) Does the plan provide for a death benefit, other than survivor annuity, before retirement?

If "Yes," indicate whether such benefits are limited to—

(i) ☐ 100 times the monthly pension or the reserve, if larger.

(ii) ☐ The actuarial equivalent of the benefits accrued to the date of death.

(iii) ☐ Other (explain) ▶................................

(g) Does plan provide for maximum limitation under section 415? . . . .

23 Additional information for defined contribution plans only:

(a) Are contributions allocated on the basis of total compensation? . . . . . .

(b) Forfeitures are allocated—

(i) ☐ On basis of total compensation

(ii) ☐ To reduce employer contributions

(iii) ☐ Other (specify) ▶................................

(c) Trust earnings and losses are allocated on the basis of:

(i) ☐ Account balances

(ii) ☐ Other (specify) ▶................................

(d) Specify the limits placed on the purchase of insurance contracts, if any:

(i) Ordinary life ▶................................

(ii) Term insurance ▶................................

(iii) Other (specify) ▶................................

	Yes	No

(e) Does plan provide for maximum limitation under section 415? . . . .

(f) Are trust assets valued at current value? . . . .

(g) Trust assets are valued:

(i) ☐ Annually   *(ii)* ☐ Semi-annually   *(iii)* ☐ Quarterly

(iv) ☐ Other (specify) ▶

24 Were contributions made to the trust during periods before all essential conditions for qualification of the plan and trust were first met? . . . . ☐ Yes ☐ No

If "Yes," furnish statement of receipts and disbursements and other information bearing on the operation of the plan and trust for each period.

* of plan or other document—trust or collective bargaining agreement.

Form 5303 (Rev. 6-76)   Page **4**

	Yes	No	Section and page number *	GOVERNMENT USE ONLY
25 Termination of plan or trust:				
(a) Is there a provision in the plan for terminating the plan and/or trust?				
(b) Are the participants' rights under the plan nonforfeitable upon termination or partial termination of the plan?				
(c) Upon complete discontinuance of contributions under a profit-sharing or stock bonus plan, are the participants' rights under the plan nonforfeitable?				

	Yes	No	GOVERNMENT USE ONLY
26 In the case of an initial qualification, have the following documents been included:			
(a) Copies of all instruments constituting the plan or joinder agreement?			
(b) Copy of collective bargaining agreement?			
(c) Copies of trust indentures or group annuity contracts?			
(d) A detailed description of all methods, factors and assumptions used in determining costs or actual experience under the plan (including any loading, contingency reserves, or special factors, and the basis of any insured costs or liabilities involved therein) explaining their source and application in detail to permit ready analysis and verification?			
27 In the case of a request involving an amendment, after initial qualification, have the following documents been included:			
(a) A copy of the amendment(s)?			
(b) Copy of collective bargaining agreement?			
(c) A description of the amendment covering the items changed and an explanation of the provisions before and after the amendment?			
(d) A completely restated plan? †			
(e) A working copy of the plan in which there has been incorporated all of the previous amendments representing the provisions of the plan as currently in effect? †			
(f) Copies of all amendments adopted since the date of the last determination letter for which no determination letter has been issued by the Internal Revenue Service? †			

† *If plan is being amended for the first time to conform to the participation and vesting standards of the Employee Retirement Income Security Act of 1974, or if the plan has been amended at least three times since the last restated plan was submitted, one of the documents specified under (d) or (e) must be attached.*

If any item in 26 or 27 is answered "No," please explain.

* of plan or other document—trust or collective bargaining agreement.

If more space is needed for any item, attach additional sheets of the same size.

☆ U.S. GOVERNMENT PRINTING OFFICE : 1976—O-575-281   E.I.36-2717749

Form 5302
(Rev. June 1976)
Department of the Treasury
Internal Revenue Service

Employee Census

▶ Attach to application for determination—defined benefit and defined contribution plans.

Schedule of 25 highest paid participating employees for 12-month period ended ▶

(Round off to nearest dollar)

This Form is NOT Open to Public Inspection

Name of employer

Employer identification number

Line no.	Employee's last name and initials (List in order of compensation) (a)	Check			Age (d)	Years of service (e)	Annual Nondeferred Compensation			Employee contributions under the plan (i)	Amount allocated under each other qualified plan of deferred compensation (j)	Defined Benefit	Defined Contribution		
		Officer or shareholder (b)	Percent of voting stock owned (c)				Used in computing benefits or employee's share of contributions (f)	Excluded (g)	Total (h)			Annual benefit expected (k)	Employer contribution allocated (l)	Number of units, if any (m)	Forfeitures allocated in the year (m)
1															
2															
3															
4															
5															
6															
7															
8															
9															
10															
11															
12															
13															
14															
15															
16															
17															
18															
19															
20															
21															
22															
23															
24															
25															
Totals for above															
Totals for all others (Specify number ▶)															
Totals for all participants															

575–199–2

General Instructions

(References are to the Internal Revenue Code)

Every employer or plan administrator who files an application for determination with respect to a defined benefit or a defined contribution plan is required to attach thereto this schedule, which must be completed in all details.

Prepare the employee census for a current 12-month period. Generally, the 12-month period should be the employer's taxable year, a calendar year or the plan year.

Section 6104(a)(1)(B) provides generally that applications, filed with respect to the qualification of a pension, profit-sharing or stock bonus plan, shall be open to public inspection. However, section 6104(a)(1)(C) provides that information concerning the compensation of any participant shall not be opened to public inspection. Consequently, the information contained in this schedule shall not be made available to the public, including plan participants and other employees of the employer who established the plan.

This schedule is to be used by the Internal Revenue Service in its analysis of an application for determination as to whether a plan of deferred compensation qualifies under section 401(a) or 405(a).

If there are fewer than 25 participants, list all the participants. Otherwise, only the 25 highest-paid participants need be listed.

Specific Instructions

In column (a), list the participants in the order of compensation, starting with the highest-paid participant followed by the next highest-paid participant, and so on.

In column (b), enter a check mark or an "X" to indicate that a participant is either an officer or a shareholder. If a participant is neither an officer nor a shareholder, make no entry in this column for such participant.

In column (c), enter only the percentage of voting stock owned by a participant. For example, participant "P" owns 200 shares of voting stock of the employer's 5,000 shares outstanding. His percentage is 4% (200 ÷ 5,000). If a participant owns only nonvoting stock of the employer, make no entry in this column.

In column (d), enter the attained age of each participant as of the end of the year for which this schedule applies. For example, if a participant reached his 47th birthday on January 7, 1975, and the schedule covers the calendar year 1975, enter 47 for that participant.

In column (e), enter the number of full years of service of each participant with respect to employment with the employer, and any prior employer if such employment is recognized for plan purposes.

In column (f), enter the amount of each participant's compensation that is recognized for plan purposes in computing the benefit (in case of a defined benefit plan) or in computing the amount of employer contribution that is allocated to the account of each participant (in the case of a defined contribution plan). Do not include any portion of the employer contributions to this or any other qualified plan as compensation for any participant.

In column (g), enter the amount of compensation that is not recognized for purposes of column (f). For example, if a participant received $12,500 compensation for the year, $1,000 of which was a bonus and the plan does not recognize bonuses for plan purposes, enter $11,500 in column (f) and $1,000 in column (g).

In column (h), enter the total amount of compensation for the year for each participant. The amount entered in this column will be the sum of the amounts entered in columns (f) and (g) with respect to each participant. Again, do not enter any amount of employer contributions made to this or any other qualified plan.

In column (i), enter the total amount of mandatory and voluntary contributions made by each participant. If the plan does not provide for employee contributions of any kind, leave blank or enter "N/A."

In column (j), enter the portion of the employer's contribution (1) that is attributable to the cost for providing each participant's benefits under all plans other than this plan or (2) that is allocated to each participant's account under all plans other than this plan.

In column (k), enter the amount of benefit each participant may expect to receive at normal retirement age based on current information, assuming no future compensation increases. For example, under a 30% benefit plan, a participant whose benefit is based on annual compensation of $10,000 may expect an annual benefit of $3,000 ($10,000 × 30%) at retirement. In such case enter $3,000.

In column (l), enter the amount of the employer's contribution that is allocated to the account of each participant.

In column (m), enter the number of units, if any, used to determine the amount of the employer contribution that is allocated to each participant.

In column (n), enter the amount of the forfeitures that is allocated to each participant, unless forfeitures are allocated to reduce employer contributions.

Form **5309**
(Rev. April 1978)

Department of the Treasury
Internal Revenue Service

Application for Determination of Employee Stock Ownership Plan

(Under section 301 of the Tax Reduction Act of 1975
as amended by the Tax Reform Act of 1976)

For IRS Use Only
Case number ▶
Issue date ▶
EPMF status code ▶
File folder no. ▶

1 (a) Name, address and ZIP code of employer

Telephone number ▶ ( )

(b) Name, address and ZIP code of plan administrator, if other than employer

(c) Administrator's identification number ▶   Telephone number ▶ ( )

2 Employer's identification number

3 Business code no. (same as that shown on Form 1120)

4 Date incorporated or business commenced

5 Employer's taxable year ends

6 This is an application for
- **(a)** ☐ A plan intended to meet the requirements of section 301 of the Tax Reduction Act of 1975 (the Act).
- **(b)** ☐ A plan intended to meet the requirements of section 301 of the Act and section 401(a) of the Code.
- **(c)** ☐ An amendment to a plan previously qualified under section 401(a) intended to modify such plan to also meet the requirements under section 301 of the Act.

If you checked (b) or (c), complete only questions 7, 8 and 12 below and file this form as an attachment to Form 5301 or 5303; if you checked (a) complete this form in its entirety and file it as directed in the instructions.

7 Plan: (a) Name   **(b)** Number   **(c)** Date plan year ends

8 Type of plan: (a) ☐ Profit-sharing   **(b)** ☐ Stock bonus   **(c)** ☐ Money purchase and stock bonus

9 ☐ Initial qualification   Effective date of plan ▶   **10** ☐ Amendment   Effective date ▶   **11** Date plan was communicated to employees ▶   How communicated ▶

12 Indicate the section and page number where the following plan provisions will be found:

	Section and Page Number
(a) Plan is designed to invest primarily in employer securities (see general information 2.)	
(b) The amount of employer securities or cash transferred to this plan is not less than the amount specified under section 301(d)(6) of the Act of the qualified investment (as determined under section 46(c) and (d) of the Code) of the taxpayer for the taxable year . .	
(c) *(i)* The allocation of the employer securities transferred or purchased because of section 46(a)(2)(B)(i) is in substantially the same proportion that such employee's compensation bears to the total compensation of all participants, and as further specified in section 301(d) of the Act. (See general information 4.)	
(ii) The allocation of the employer securities transferred or purchased because of section 46(a)(2)(B)(ii) is in an amount equal to the matching employee contributions for the year as required under section 301(e)(5) of the Act	
(d) Each participant must be entitled to direct the plan to vote the securities allocated in (c) above in the manner in which the participant chooses	
(e) No allocated employer securities may be distributed to any participant before the end of the 84th month after the month of allocation of such securities except in the case of separation from service, death or disability	
(f) The rights of all participants must be nonforfeitable in the securities allocated to them in (c) above	
(g) Except as provided in section 301(d)(8)(B)(iii), of the Act, if any part of the amount of the credit determined under section 46(a)(2)(B) of the Code is recaptured in accordance with the provisions of such Code the contributions remain in the plan or in participants' accounts, as the case may be, and continue to be allocated in accordance with the original plan agreement . .	
(h) Plan meets the requirements of section 415 of the Code	

13 (a) Indicate the general eligibility requirements for participation under the plan and indicate the section and page number of plan or trust where each provision is contained:

	(i)–(iv)	(v)–(viii)
(i) ☐ All employees *(v)* Length of service (number of years) ▶		
(ii) ☐ Hourly rate employee only *(vi)* Minimum age (specify) ▶		
(iii) ☐ Salaried employee only *(vii)* Maximum age (specify) ▶		
(iv) ☐ Other job class (specify) ▶ *(viii)* Minimum pay (specify) ▶		

(b) Are the eligibility requirements the same for future employees? . . . . ☐ Yes   ☐ No
If "No," explain ▶

14 Coverage of plan at (give date) ▶

	Number
(a) Total employed, see specific instructions	
(b) Exclusions under plan (do not count an employee more than once):	
(i) Minimum age or years of service required (specify) ▶	
(ii) Employees on whose behalf retirement benefits were the subject of collective bargaining	
(iii) Nonresident aliens who receive no earned income from United States sources	
(c) Total exclusions, sum of (b)(i) through (iii)	
(d) Balance, line (a) less line (c)	

Under penalties of perjury, I declare that I have examined this application, including accompanying statements, and to the best of my knowledge and belief it is true, correct and complete.

Signature ▶   Title ▶   Date ▶

Form 5309 (Rev. 4–78)   Page **2**

		Number
(e)	Ineligible under plan on account of (do not count an employee included in (b)):	
(i)	Minimum pay	
(ii)	Hourly-paid	
(iii)	Other (specify) ▶..	
(f)	Total ineligible, sum of (e)(i) through (iii)	
(g)	Number eligible to participate, (d) less (f)	
(h) *(i)*	Number of employees participating in the plan	
(ii)	Percent participating, (h)(i) divided by (d). (If less than 70% complete (i) and (j). If 70% or more, do not complete (i) or (j).)	%
(i)	Percent eligible, (g) divided by (d), if less than 70% see specific instructions	%
(j)	Percent of eligible employees participating, (h)(i) divided by (g)	%
(k)	If percent in (j) is less than 80%, see specific instruction.	

General Information

(All section references are to the Internal Revenue Code of 1954 unless otherwise specified.)

Corporate employers may apply for an advance determination letter for an Employee Stock Ownership Plan which meets the requirements of section 301(d) or 301(d) and (e) of the Tax Reduction Act of 1975 (the Act).

Section 46(a) has been amended to allow corporations to elect an additional investment credit by establishing a plan which meets the requirements of section 301(d) or 301(d) and (e) of the Act.

A plan under section 301(d) or 301(d) and (e) of the Act need not be a plan qualified under section 401(a). In general the requirements of section 301(d) and (e) of the Act are as follows:

1. A corporate employer (employer) must establish a written stock bonus plan, stock bonus and money purchase pension plan, or a profit-sharing plan.

2. The plan must be designed to invest primarily in employer securities. Such securities may only be common stock issued by the employer or a corporation which is a member of a controlled group of corporations which includes the employer (within the meaning of section 1563(a), determined without regard to section 1563(a)(4) and (e)(3)(c)), with voting power and dividend rights no less favorable than voting power and dividend rights of other common stock, or securities convertible into such stock issued by the employer or such corporation.

3. The contribution to the plan for any taxable year for which the additional investment credit is elected may not be less than the amount specified under section 301(d)(6) of the Act, of the qualified investment (as determined under section 46(c) and (d)) of the taxpayer for the taxable year.

4. (a) All employer securities transferred to or purchased by the plan because of section 46(a)(2)(B)(i) must be allocated to the account of each participant (who was a participant at any time during the plan year, whether or not he is a participant at the end of the plan year) as of the close of each plan year in substantially the same ratio that the compensation paid each participant (disregarding any compensation in excess of $100,000) bears to the compensation (disregarding any compensation in excess of $100,000 with respect to any participant) paid to all participants during that year.

(b) All employer securities transferred to or purchased by the plan because of section 46(a)(2)(B)(ii) must be allocated to the account of each participant (who was a participant at any time during the plan year) as of the close of the plan year in an amount equal to the employee's matching employee contributions for the year.

5. Each participant must be entitled to direct the plan to vote his allocated stock in any way he wishes.

6. No allocated stock may be distributed before the end of the 84th month after the month in which the stock is allocated, except in the case of separation from service, death or disability.

7. The rights of all participants in allocated stock must be nonforfeitable.

8. No amount shall be allocated to any participant in excess of the amount which might be allocated if the plan met the requirements of section 401.

9. The plan must meet requirements of sections 410 and 415.

10. Except as provided in section 301(d)(8)(B)(iii) of the Act, any amounts transferred to the plan because of section 46(a)(2)(B) may not revert to the employer if the amount of the investment credit determined under section 46(a)(2)(B) is recaptured in accordance with the provisions of the Code.

General Instructions

A. Who may file.—Any corporate employer, who has elected the additional investment credit under section 46(a)(2)(B) and established a plan intended to meet the requirements under section 301(d) or 301(d) and (e) of the Act may file their application.

B. What to File.—

1. For initial determination or amendment regarding a plan intended to meet the requirements under section 301(d) or 301(d) and (e) of the Act but not section 401(a) of the Code, file Form 5309 plus a copy of the plan or amendment.

2. For initial determination or amendment regarding a plan intended to meet the requirements under section 301(d) or 301(d) and (e) of the Act as well as section 401(a) of the Code, file Forms 5309 and 5301 or 5303 plus a copy of all documents and statements required by such forms.

3. To amend a plan previously qualified under section 401(a) so that it also qualifies as a plan under section 301(d) or 301(d) and (e) of the Act, submit completed Forms 5309 and 5301 or 5303 plus all the documents and statements required by such forms.

C. Where to File.—

1. An employer other than employers described in 2 below must file with the District Director for the district in which the principal place of business of the employer is located.

2. For plans of more than one employer, file with the District Director for the district in which is located the principal place of business of the plan administrator.

D. Signature.—The application must be signed by the principal officer authorized to sign.

Specific Instructions

For initial qualification of a plan intended to qualify under section 401(a) as well as section 301(d) or 301(d) and (e) of the Act or to amend a plan previously qualified under section 401(a) so that it also qualifies as a plan under section 301(d) or 301(d) and (e) of the Act, complete only items 1 through 8 and 12 and file this Form 5309 as an attachment to Form 5301 or 5303. If you check item 6(b) or (c) and also check item 8(c) complete item 7 for each plan, i.e., the money purchase plan and the stock bonus plan. File a Form 5301 or 5303 for each such plan with a Form 5309 attached to each.

7(b). Plan Number.—Enter the three digit serial number you assigned this plan. Numbering starts with 001. If you have any other deferred compensation plans, number this plan in sequence with existing plans.

14. Coverage.—In general, if your plan does not meet the requirements of section 410(b)(1)(A) (70–80% rule), you must submit a schedule using the format below to show that your plan meets the requirements of section 410(b)(1)(B).

1	2		3	4	5	6	7
	* Compensation range		Total employees	Statutory exclusions 410 (b)(2)	Other exclusions	Employees participating (3 minus sum of 4 and 5)	Participants who are officers or shareholders
Group	At least	But not more than					
	Totals						

* The compensation brackets used must reflect the pay pattern of the employer.

14(a). Enter the total number of employees as of the date given on line 14. For a controlled group of corporations item 14 must be completed as though the controlled group constitutes a single entity.

☆ U.S.GPO:1978-0-263-422   E.I.#430814328

Form **5500** Department of the Treasury Internal Revenue Service Department of Labor Pension and Welfare Benefit Programs Pension Benefit Guaranty Corporation	**Annual Return/Report of Employee Benefit Plan** **(With 100 or more participants)** This form is required to be filed under sections 104 and 4065 of the Employee Retirement Income Security Act of 1974 and sections 6057(b) and 6058(a) of the Internal Revenue Code, referred to as the Code.	19**79** Amended ☐ This Form is Open to Public Inspection

For the calendar plan year 1979 or fiscal plan year beginning   , 1979 and ending   19

File original of this form, including schedules and attachments, completed in ink or type.

▶ Keogh (H.R. 10) plans with fewer than 100 participants and with at least one owner-employee participant **do not file this form.** File Form 5500–K instead.

▶ Other pension benefit plans and certain welfare benefit plans with fewer than 100 participants **do not file this form.** File Form 5500–C instead.

▶ Governmental plans and church plans (not electing coverage under section 410(d) of the Code). Do not file this form. File Form 5500–G instead.

▶ Welfare benefit plans with 100 or more participants complete only items 1 through 16 and item 22.

▶ Pension benefit plans, unless otherwise excepted, complete all items. Annuity arrangements of certain exempt organizations and individual retirement account trusts of employers complete only items 1 through 6, 9 and 10.

▶ Plan number—Your 3 digit plan number must be entered in item 5(c); see instruction 5(c) for explanation of "plan number."

▶ If any item does not apply, enter "N/A."

1 (a) Name of plan sponsor (employer if for a single employer plan)	**1 (b)** Employer identification number
Address (number and street)	**1 (c)** Telephone number of sponsor ( )
City or town, State and ZIP code	**1 (d)** If plan year changed since last re- turn/report check here . . ▶ ☐
2 (a) Name of plan administrator (if other than plan sponsor)	**1 (e)** Business code number
Address (number and street)	**2 (b)** Administrator's employer identification no.
City or town, State and ZIP code	**2 (c)** Telephone number of administrator ( )

3 Name, address and identification number of plan sponsor and/or plan administrator as they appeared on the last return/report filed for this plan if not the same as in 1 or 2 above: **(a)** Sponsor ▶

(b) Administrator ▶

4 Check appropriate box to indicate the type of plan entity (check only one box):

(a) ☐ Single-employer plan   **(c)** ☐ Multiemployer plan   **(e)** ☐ Multiple-employer plan (other)

(b) ☐ Plan of controlled group of corporations   **(d)** ☐ Multiple-employer-collec-   **(f)** ☐ Group insurance arrangement (of
     or common control employers   tively-bargained plan   welfare plans)

5 (a) *(i)* Name of plan ▶	**5 (b)** Effective date of plan
(ii) ☐ Check if name of plan changed since last return/report	**5 (c)** Enter three digit plan number ▶

6 Check at least one item in (a) or (b) and applicable items in (c).

(a) Welfare benefit plan: *(i)* ☐ Health insurance   *(ii)* ☐ Life insurance   *(iii)* ☐ Supplemental unemployment

     (iv) ☐ Other (specify) ▶

(b) Pension benefit plan:

     (i)   Defined benefit plan—(Indicate type of defined benefit plan below):

         (A) ☐ Fixed benefit   **(B)** ☐ Unit benefit   **(C)** ☐ Flat benefit

         (D) ☐ Other (specify) ▶

     (ii)   Defined contribution plan—(indicate type of defined contribution plan below):

         (A) ☐ Profit-sharing   **(B)** ☐ Stock bonus   **(C)** ☐ Target benefit   **(D)** ☐ Other money purchase

         (E) ☐ Other (specify) ▶

     (iii) ☐ Defined benefit plan with benefits based partly on balance of separate account of participant (section 414(k) of the Code)

     (iv) ☐ Annuity arrangement of a certain exempt organization (section 403(b)(1) of the Code)

     (v) ☐ Custodial account for regulated investment company stock (section 403(b)(7) of the Code)

     (vi) ☐ Trust treated as an individual retirement account (section 408(c) of the Code)

     (vii) ☐ Other (specify) ▶

Under penalties of perjury and other penalties set forth in the instructions, I declare that I have examined this report, including accompanying schedules and statements, and to the best of my knowledge and belief, it is true, correct, and complete.

Date ▶ ....   Signature of employer/plan sponsor ▶ ....

Date ▶ ....   Signature of plan administrator ▶ ....

Form 5500 (1979)   Page **2**

6 (Continued)

(c) Other plan features: *(i)* ☐ Thrift-savings   *(ii)* ☐ Keogh (H.R. 10) plan

　　　(iii) ☐ Pension plan maintained outside the United States   *(iv)* ☐ Participant-directed account plan

(d) Sponsor's taxable year ends . . . . ▶ Month　　　Day　　　Year

7 Number of participants as of the end of the plan year (welfare plans complete only (a)(iv), (b), (c) and (d)):

(a) Active participants (employed or carried as active)　*(i)* Number fully vested . .

　　　　　　　　　　　　　　　　　　　　　(ii) Number partially vested .

　　　　　　　　　　　　　　　　　　　　　(iii) Number nonvested . . .

　　　　　　　　　　　　　　　　　　　　　(iv) Total . . . .

(b) Retired or separated participants receiving benefits . . . .

(c) Retired or separated participants entitled to future benefits . . . .

(d) Subtotal, sum of (a), (b) and (c) . . . .

(e) Deceased participants whose beneficiaries are receiving or are entitled to receive benefits . . . .

(f) Total, (d) plus (e) . . . .

	Yes	No
(g) *(i)* During this plan year or prior plan year was any participant(s) separated from service with a deferred vested benefit for which a Schedule SSA (Form 5500) is required to be attached to this form?		
(ii) If "Yes," enter the number of separated participants . . . . ▶		

8 Plan amendment information (welfare plans do not complete (b)(ii)):

	Yes	No
(a) Was any amendment to this plan adopted in this plan year?		
(b) If "Yes," *(i)* And if any amendments have resulted in a change in the information contained in a summary plan description or previously furnished summary description of modifications—		
(A) Have summary descriptions of change(s) been sent to participants?		
(B) Have summary descriptions of the change(s) been filed with DOL?		
(ii) Does any such amendment result in the reduction of the accrued benefit of any participant under the plan?		
(c) Enter the date the most recent amendment was adopted . . ▶ Month　　Day　　Year		

9 Plan termination information (welfare plans complete only (a), (b), (c) and (f)):

	Yes	No
(a) Was this plan terminated during ☐ this plan year or ☐ any prior plan year?		
(b) If "Yes," were all trust assets distributed to participants or beneficiaries or transferred to another plan? . .		
(c) Was a resolution to terminate this plan adopted during this plan year or any prior plan year?		
(d) If (a) or (c) is "Yes," have you received a favorable determination letter from IRS with respect to such termination?		
(e) If (d) is "No," has a determination letter been requested from IRS?		
(f) If (a) or (c) is "Yes," have participants and beneficiaries been notified of the termination or the proposed termination?		
(g) If either item 10(a) or (c) is "Yes," and this plan is covered under PBGC termination insurance program has a notice of intent to terminate been filed with PBGC?		

10 (a) In this plan year, was this plan merged or consolidated into another plan or were assets or liabilities transferred to another plan? . . |

If "Yes," identify other plan(s):

(b) Name of plan(s) ▶	(c) Employer identification number(s)	(d) Plan number(s)

(e) Has Form 5310 been filed? . . . . ☐ Yes ☐ No

11 Indicate funding arrangement:

(a) ☐ Trust (benefits provided in whole from trust funds)

(b) ☐ Trust or arrangement providing benefits partially through insurance and/or annuity contracts

(c) ☐ Trust or arrangement providing benefits exclusively through insurance and/or annuity contracts

(d) ☐ Custodial account described in section 401(f) of the Code and not included in (c) above

(e) ☐ Other (specify) ▶ ....

(f) If (b) or (c) is checked, enter the number of Schedule A's (Form 5500) which are attached . . . . . . ▶

12 Did any person who rendered services to the plan receive, directly or indirectly, compensation from the plan in the plan year? . . ☐ Yes ☐ No

If "Yes," furnish the following information:

a. Name	b. Official plan position	c. Relationship to employer, employee organization or person known to be a party-in-interest	d. Gross salary or allowances paid by plan	e. Fees and commissions paid by plan	f. Nature of service code (see Instructions)

13 Plan assets and liabilities at the beginning and the end of the plan year (list all assets and liabilities at current value). A fully insured welfare plan or a pension plan with no trust and which is funded entirely by allocated insurance contracts which fully guarantee the amount of benefit payments should check box and and not complete this item . . . . ☐

Note: *Include all plan assets and liabilities of a trust or separately maintained fund. (If more than one trust/fund, report on a combined basis.) Include all insurance values except for the value of that portion of an allocated insurance contract which fully guarantees the amount of benefit payments. Round off amounts to nearest dollar. Trusts with no assets at the beginning and the end of the plan year enter zero on line 13(h).*

Assets	a. Beginning of year	b. End of year
(a) Cash: *(i)* On hand		
(ii) In bank: (A) Certificates of deposit		
(B) Other interest bearing		
(C) Noninterest bearing		
(iii) Total cash, sum of (i) and (ii)		
(b) Receivables: *(i)* Employer contributions		
(ii) Employee contributions		
(iii) Other		
(iv) Reserve for doubtful accounts		
(v) Net receivables, sum of (i), (ii) and (iii) minus (iv)		
(c) General investments other than party-in-interest investments:		
(i) U.S. Government securities: (A) Long term		
(B) Short term		
(ii) State and municipal securities		
(iii) Corporate debt instruments: (A) Long term		
(B) Short term		
(iv) Corporate stocks: (A) Preferred		
(B) Common		
(v) Shares of a registered investment company		
(vi) Real estate		
(vii) Mortgages		
(viii) Loans other than mortgages		
(ix) Value of interest in pooled fund(s)		
(x) Other investments		
(xi) Total general investments, sum of (i) through (x)		
(d) Party-in-interest investments:		
(i) Corporate debt instruments		
(ii) Corporate stocks: (A) Preferred		
(B) Common		
(iii) Real estate		
(iv) Mortgages		
(v) Loans other than mortgages . . . . : .		
(vi) Other investments		
(vii) Total party-in-interest investments, sum of (i) through (vi)		
(e) Buildings and other depreciable property		
(f) Value of unallocated insurance contracts (other than pooled separate accounts):		
(i) Separate accounts		
(ii) Other		
(iii) Total, (i) plus (ii)		
(g) Other assets		
(h) Total assets, sum of (a)(iii), (b)(v), (c)(xi), (d)(vii), (e), (f)(iii) and (g)		
Liabilities		
(i) Payables: *(i)* Plan claims		
(ii) Other payables		
(iii) Total payables, (i) plus (ii)		
(j) Acquisition indebtedness		
(k) Other liabilities		
(l) Total liabilities, sum of (i)(iii), (j) and (k)		
(m) Net assets, (h) less (l)		
(n) During the plan year what were the:		
(i) Total cost of acquisitions for common stock?		
(ii) Total proceeds from dispositions of common stock?		

Form 5500 (1979)   Page **4**

14 Plan income, expenses and changes in net assets for the plan year:

Note: *Include all income and expenses of a trust(s) or separately maintained fund(s) including any payments made for allocated insurance contracts. Round off amounts to nearest dollar.*

Income	a. Amount	b. Total
(a) Contributions received or receivable in cash from—		
(i) Employer(s) (including contributions on behalf of self-employed individuals)		
(ii) Employees		
(iii) Others		
(b) Noncash contributions (specify nature and by whom made) ▶		
(c) Total contributions, sum of (a) and (b)		
(d) Earnings from investments—		
(i) Interest		
(ii) Dividends		
(iii) Rents		
(iv) Royalties		
(e) Net realized gain (loss) on sale or exchange of assets—		
(i) Aggregate proceeds		
(ii) Aggregate costs		
(f) Other income (specify) ▶		
(g) Total income, sum of (c) through (f)		

Expenses	a. Amount	b. Total
(h) Distribution of benefits and payments to provide benefits—		
(i) Directly to participants or their beneficiaries		
(ii) To insurance carrier or similar organization for provision of benefits		
(iii) To other organizations or individuals providing welfare benefits		
(i) Interest expense		
(j) Administrative expenses—		
(i) Salaries and allowances		
(ii) Fees and commissions		
(iii) Insurance premiums for Pension Benefit Guaranty Corporation		
(iv) Insurance premiums for fiduciary insurance other than bonding		
(v) Other administrative expenses		
(k) Other expenses (specify) ▶		
(l) Total expenses, sum of (h) through (k)		
(m) Net income (expenses), (g) minus (l)		

(n) Change in net assets—	a. Amount	b. Total
(i) Unrealized appreciation (depreciation) of assets		
(ii) Other changes (specify) ▶		
(o) Net increase (decrease) in net assets for the year, (m) plus (n)		
(p) Net assets at beginning of year, line 13(m), column a		
(q) Net assets at end of year, (o) plus (p) (equals line 13(m), column b)		

15 All plans complete (a). Plans funded with insurance policies or annuity contracts also complete (b) and (c):	Yes	No
(a) Since the end of the plan year covered by the last return/report has there been a termination in the appointment of any trustee, accountant, insurance carrier, enrolled actuary, administrator, investment manager or custodian? . If "Yes," explain and include the name, position, address and telephone number of the person whose appointment has been terminated ▶		
(b) Have any insurance policies or annuities been replaced during the plan year? . If "Yes," explain the reason for the replacement ▶		
(c) At any time during the plan year was the plan funded with: *(i)* ☐ Individual policies or annuities, *(ii)* ☐ Group policies or annuities, or *(iii)* ☐ Both.		

Form 5500 (1979)   **Page 5**

	Yes	No
16 Bonding:		
(a) Was the plan insured by a fidelity bond against losses through fraud or dishonesty?		
If "Yes," complete (b) through (f); if "No," only complete (g).		
(b) Indicate number of plans covered by this bond ▶................		
(c) Enter the maximum amount of loss recoverable ▶		
(d) Enter the name of the surety company ▶................		
....		
(e) Does the plan, or a known party-in-interest with respect to the plan, have any control or significant financial interest, direct or indirect, in the surety company or its agents or brokers?		
(f) In the current plan year was any loss to the plan caused by the fraud or dishonesty of any plan official or employee of the plan or of other person handling funds of the plan?		
If "Yes," see specific instructions.		
(g) If the plan is not insured by a fidelity bond, explain why not ▶		
....		

17 Information about employees of employer at end of the plan year. (Plans not purporting to satisfy the percentage tests of section 410(b)(1)(A) of the Code complete only (a) below and see specific instructions):

(a) Total number of employees	
(b) Number of employees excluded under the plan because of:	
(i) Minimum age or years of service	
(ii) Employees on whose behalf retirement benefits were the subject of collective bargaining . . .	
(iii) Nonresident aliens who receive no earned income from United States sources	
(iv) Total excluded, sum of (i), (ii) and (iii)	
(c) Total number of employees not excluded, (a) less (b)(iv)	
(d) Employees ineligible (specify reason) ▶	
....	
(e) Employees eligible to participate, (c) less (d)	
(f) Employees eligible but not participating	
(g) Employees participating, (e) less (f)	

	Yes	No
18 Is this plan an adoption of a:		
(a) ☐ Master/prototype, **(b)** ☐ Field prototype, **(c)** ☐ Pattern, **(d)** ☐ Model plan or **(e)** ☐ Bond purchase plan? .		
If "Yes," enter the four or eight digit IRS serial number (see instructions) ▶		
19 (a) Is it intended that this plan qualify under section 401(a) or 405 of the Code?		
(b) Have you requested or received a determination letter from the IRS for this plan?		
(c) Is this a plan with Employee Stock Ownership Plan (ESOP) features?		
(i) If "Yes," was a current appraisal of the value of the stock made immediately prior to the contribution of the stock or the purchase of the stock by the trust?		
(ii) If (i) is "Yes," was the appraisal made by an unrelated third party?		
(iii) If (ii) is "No," was the appraisal made in accordance with the provisions of Revenue Ruling 59–60? . . .		
20 If plan is integrated, check appropriate box:		
(a) ☐ Social security **(b)** ☐ Railroad retirement **(c)** ☐ Other		
21 (a) Is this a defined benefit plan subject to the minimum funding standards for this plan year?		
If "Yes," attach Schedule B (Form 5500).		
(b) Is this a defined contribution plan, i.e., money purchase or target benefit, subject to the minimum funding standards? (If a waiver was granted, see instructions.)		
If "Yes," complete (i), (ii) and (iii) below:		
(i) Amount of employer contribution required for the plan year under section 412 of the Code . .		
(ii) Amount of contribution paid by the employer for the plan year		
Enter date of last payment by employer . . . . . ▶ Month .... Day .... Year		
(iii) If (i) is larger than (ii) subtract (ii) from (i) and enter the funding deficiency here, otherwise enter zero. (If you have a funding deficiency file Form 5330.)		

	Yes	No
22 The following questions relate to the plan year. If (a)(i), (ii), (iii), (iv) or (v) is checked "Yes," schedules of such items in the format set forth in the instructions are required to be attached to this form.		
(a) *(i)* Did the plan have assets held for investment?		
(ii) Did any non-exempt transaction involving plan assets involve a party known to be a party-in-interest? . .		
(iii) Were any loans by the plan or fixed income obligations due the plan in default as of the close of the plan year or classified during the year as uncollectable?		
(iv) Were any leases to which the plan was a party in default or classified during the year as uncollectable? . .		
(v) Were any plan transactions or series of transactions in excess of 3% of the current value of plan assets? . .		

Form 5500 (1979)   Page **6**

22 *(Continued)*

  (b) The accountant's opinion is ☐ not required or ☐ required, attached to this form, and is—

    (i) ☐ Unqualified

    (ii) ☐ Qualified

    (iii) ☐ Adverse

    (iv) ☐ Other (explain) ▶

23 (a) Is the plan covered under the Pension Benefit Guaranty Corporation termination insurance program? . . . . ☐ Yes ☐ No ☐ Not determined

If "Yes," list employer identification number(s) and/or plan number(s) used in any filing with PBGC if the number was different from the numbers listed in item 1(b) or 5(c) ▶

  (b) If (a) is "Yes," did one or more reportable events or other events requiring notice to the Pension Benefit Guaranty Corporation occur since the last return/report Form 5500, 5500–C or 5500–K which was filed for this plan? . . . .

Yes | No

Check (√)

  (c) If (b) is "Yes," check the applicable box(es) in (i) through (x) below:

    (i) Notification by the Internal Revenue Service that the plan has ceased to be a plan as described in section 4021(a)(2) of ERISA or a determination by the Secretary of Labor of non-compliance with Title I of ERISA .

    (ii) A decrease in active participants to the extent specified in the instructions . . . .

    (iii) A determination by the Internal Revenue Service that there has been a termination or partial termination of the plan within the meaning of section 411(d)(3) of the Code . . . .

    (iv) An inability to pay benefits when due . . . .

    (v) A distribution to a substantial owner to the extent specified in the instructions . . . .

    (vi) An alternative method of compliance has been prescribed for this plan by the Secretary of Labor under section 110 of ERISA . . . .

    (vii) A cessation of operations at a facility to the extent specified in the instructions . . . .

    (viii) A withdrawal of a substantial employer . . . .

    (ix) An amendment to the plan that will result in the reduction of the current or future benefits under the plan .

    (x) Other (see instructions) . . . .

If additional space is required for any item, attach additional sheets the same size as this form.

☆ U.S. GOVERNMENT PRINTING OFFICE : 1980—O-283-193   23 188 5979

Form **5500-C**
Department of the Treasury
Internal Revenue Service

Department of Labor
Pension and Welfare Benefit Programs

Pension Benefit Guaranty Corporation

Annual Return/Report of Employee Benefit Plan
(With fewer than 100 participants)
This form is required to be filed under sections 104 and 4065 of the Employee Retirement Income Security Act of 1974 and sections 6057(b) and 6058(a) of the Internal Revenue Code, referred to as the Code.

1979
Amended ☐

This Form is Open to Public Inspection

For the calendar plan year 1979 or fiscal plan year beginning _____ , 1979 and ending _____ , 19 ___

File original of this form, including schedules and attachments, completed in ink or type. If any item does not apply, enter "N/A."

▶ Do not file this form for Keogh (H.R. 10) plans with fewer than 100 participants and with at least one owner-employee participant. File Form 5500-K instead.

▶ Governmental plans and church plans (not electing coverage under section 410(d) of the Code). **Do not file this form.** File Form 5500-G instead.

▶ Pension benefit plans, unless otherwise excepted, complete all items. Annuity arrangements of certain exempt organizations, and individual retirement account trusts of employers complete only items 1 through 6, 9 and 10.

▶ Certain welfare benefit plans are not required to file this form—see instructions.

▶ Welfare benefit plans required to file this form do not complete items 7(a), 7(c), 17, 18, 20 and 22.

▶ Plan number—Your 3 digit plan number must be entered in item 5(c); see instruction 5(c) for explanation of "plan number."

1 (a) Name of plan sponsor (employer if for a single employer plan)	**1 (b)** Employer identification number
Address (number and street)	**1 (c)** Telephone number of sponsor ( )
City or town, State and ZIP code	**1 (d)** If plan year changed since last return/report check here ▶ ☐
2 (a) Name of plan administrator (if other than plan sponsor)	**1 (e)** Business code number
Address (number and street)	**2 (b)** Administrator's employer identification no.
City or town, State and ZIP code	**2 (c)** Telephone number of administrator ( )

3 Name, address and identification number of plan sponsor and/or plan administrator as they appeared on the last return/report filed for this plan if not the same as in 1 or 2 above: **(a)** Sponsor ▶ ....
(b) Administrator ▶

4 Check appropriate box to indicate the type of plan entity (check only one box):
(b) ☐ Plan of controlled group of corporations or common control employers
(d) ☐ Multiple-employer-collectively-bargained plan
(a) ☐ Single-employer plan
(c) ☐ Multiemployer plan
(e) ☐ Multiple-employer plan (other)

5 (a) *(i)* Name of plan ▶ ....
(ii) ☐ Check if name of plan changed since the last Form 5500-C return/report.

5 (b) Effective date of plan

5 (c) Enter three digit plan number ▶

6 Type of plan: **(a)** ☐ Defined benefit **(b)** ☐ Defined contribution **(c)** ☐ Welfare benefit
(d) ☐ Participant-directed account plan **(e)** ☐ Other (specify) ▶

7 (a) Active participants: *(i)* Fully vested .... *(ii)* Partially vested .... *(iii)* Nonvested .... *(iv)* Total ▶
(b) Total participants: *(i)* Beginning of plan year ▶ .... *(ii)* End of plan year ▶

		Yes	No
(c) *(i)* During the plan year or a prior plan year, was any pension benefit plan participant(s) separated from service with a deferred vested benefit for which a Schedule SSA (Form 5500) is required to be attached?			
(ii) If "Yes," enter the number of separated participants . . . . ▶			
8 Was this plan amended in this plan year?			
9 Plan termination information: **(a)** Was this plan terminated during this plan year or any prior plan year?			
(b) If "Yes," were all trust assets distributed to participants or beneficiaries or transferred to another plan?			
(c) If item 22(a) is to be checked "Yes" and 9(a) is "Yes," has a notice of intent to terminate been filed with PBGC? .			
10 (a) In this plan year, was this plan merged or consolidated into another plan or were assets or liabilities transferred to another plan?			

If "Yes," identify other plan(s):
(b) Name of plan(s) ▶ ....

(c) Employer identification number(s)	**(d)** Plan number(s)

(e) Has Form 5310 been filed? . . . . ☐ Yes ☐ No

Under penalties of perjury and other penalties set forth in the instructions, I declare that I have examined this report, including accompanying schedules and statements, and to the best of my knowledge and belief it is true, correct, and complete.

Date ▶ .... Signature of employer/plan sponsor ▶ ....

Date ▶ .... Signature of plan administrator ▶ ....

Form 5500–C (1979)   Page 2

11 Indicate funding arrangement:
   (a) ☐ Trust **(b)** ☐ Fully insured **(c)** ☐ Combination **(d)** ☐ Other (specify) ▶..
   (e) If (b) or (c) are checked enter number of Schedule A's (Form 5500) which are attached . . . . . ▶

12 Single employer plans enter the taxable year end of the employer . . . . . ▶ Month   Day   Year

13 Plan assets and liabilities at the beginning and the end of the current plan year (list all assets and liabilities at current value). A fully insured welfare plan or a pension plan with no trust and which is funded entirely by allocated insurance contracts which fully guarantee the amount of benefit payments should check the box and **not** complete this item . . . . ▶ ☐

> Note: Include all plan assets and liabilities of a trust or separately maintained fund. If more than one trust/fund, report on a combined basis. Include all insurance values except for the value of that portion of an allocated insurance contract which fully guarantees the amount of benefit payments. Round off amounts to nearest dollar. If you have no assets to report enter zero on line 13(g).

Assets	Beginning of year		End of year	
	a. Party-in-interest	b. Total	c. Party-in-interest	d. Total
(a) Cash				
(b) Receivables				
(c) Investments—(i) Government securities				
(ii) Pooled funds/mutual funds				
(iii) Corporate (debt and equity instruments)				
(iv) Real estate and mortgages				
(v) Other				
(d) Buildings and other depreciable property				
(e) Unallocated insurance contracts				
(f) Other assets				
(g) Total assets, sum of (a) through (f)				
Liabilities and Net Assets				
(h) Payables				
(i) Acquisition indebtedness				
(j) Other liabilities				
(k) Total liabilities, sum of (h) through (j)				
(l) Net assets, (g) minus (k)				

14 Plan income, expenses and changes in net assets during the plan year:

> Note: Include all income and expenses of a trust(s) or separately maintained fund(s) including any payments made for allocated insurance contracts. Round off amounts to nearest dollar.

	a. Amount	b. Total
(a) Contributions received or receivable in cash from—		
(i) Employer(s) (including contributions on behalf of self-employed individuals)		
(ii) Employees		
(iii) Others		
(b) Noncash contributions (specify nature and by whom made) ▶		
(c) Earnings from investments (interest, dividends, rents, royalties)		
(d) Net realized gain (loss) on sale or exchange of assets		
(e) Other income (specify) ▶		
(f) Total income, sum of (a) through (e)		
(g) Distribution of benefits and payments to provide benefits—		
(i) Directly to participants or their beneficiaries		
(ii) To insurance carrier or similar organization for provision of benefits (including prepaid medical plans)		
(iii) To other organizations or individuals providing welfare benefits		
(h) Interest expense		
(i) Administrative expenses (salaries, fees, commissions, insurance premiums)		
(j) Other expenses (specify) ▶		
(k) Total expenses, sum of (g) through (j)		
(l) Net income, (f) minus (k)		
(m) Changes in net assets—(i) Unrealized appreciation (depreciation) of assets		
(ii) Other changes (specify) ▶		
(n) Net increase (decrease) in net assets for the year (l) plus (m)		
(o) Net assets at beginning of year (line 13(l), column b)		
(p) Net assets at end of year, (n) plus (o) (equals line 13(l), column d)		

Form 5500–C (1979)   Page **3**

		Yes	No
15	All plans complete (a). Plans funded with insurance policies or annuity contracts also complete (b) and (c).		

(a) Since the end of the plan year covered by the last return/report has there been a termination in the appointment of any trustee, accountant, insurance carrier, enrolled actuary, administrator, investment manager or custodian? .
If "Yes," explain and include the name, position, address and telephone number of the person whose appointment has been terminated ▶ ....
....
....
....
....
....
....
....

(b) Have any insurance policies or annuities been replaced during the plan year? . . . .
If "Yes," explain the reason for the replacement ▶ ....

(c) At any time during the plan year was the plan funded with:
   (i) ☐ Individual policies or annuities, *(ii)* ☐ Group policies or annuities, or *(iii)* ☐ Both.

16 (a) Is the plan insured by a fidelity bond? . . . .
   (i) If "Yes," enter name of surety company ▶ ....
   (ii) Amount of bond coverage ▶ ....
(b) Was any loss discovered since the last return/report Form 5500, 5500–C or 5500–K was filed for this plan? .

17 Information about employees of the employer at end of the plan year. (Plans not purporting to satisfy the percentage tests of section 410(b)(1)(A) of the Code complete only (a) below and see instructions):
(a) Total number of employees . . . .
(b) Number of employees excluded under the plan because of:
   (i) Minimum age or years of service . . . .
   (ii) Employees on whose behalf retirement benefits were the subject of collective bargaining . . . .
   (iii) Nonresident aliens who receive no earned income from United States sources . . . .
   (iv) Total excluded, sum of (i), (ii) and (iii) . . . .
(c) Total number of employees not excluded, (a) less (b)(iv) . . . .
(d) Employees ineligible (specify reason) ▶ ....
....
(e) Employees eligible to participate, (c) less (d) . . . .
(f) Employees eligible but not participating . . . .
(g) Employees participating, (e) less (f) . . . .

		Yes	No
18	Is this plan an adoption of a:		

(a) ☐ Master/prototype, **(b)** ☐Field prototype, **(c)** ☐ Pattern, **(d)** ☐ Model plan, or **(e)** ☐ Bond purchase plan? . .
If "Yes," enter the four or eight digit IRS serial number (see instructions) . . . ▶

19 Did any person who rendered services to the plan receive, directly or indirectly, compensation from the plan in the plan year? . . . .
If "Yes," see instructions for information required.

20 (a) Is this a defined benefit plan subject to the minimum funding standards for this plan year? . . . .
If "Yes," attach Schedule B (Form 5500).
(b) Is this a defined contribution plan, i.e., money purchase or target benefit, subject to the minimum funding standards (if a waiver was granted see instructions)? . . . .
If "Yes," complete *(i)*, *(ii)* and *(iii)* below:
   (i) Amount of employer contribution required for the plan year . . . . $ ....
   (ii) Amount of contribution paid by the employer for the plan year . . . . . . $
      Enter date of last payment by employer ▶ Month............ Day............ Year.........
   (iii) If (i) is larger than (ii) subtract (ii) from (i) and enter the funding deficiency here.
      Otherwise enter zero. (If you have a funding deficiency file Form 5330.) . . . $

21 (a) Did any non-exempt transaction, involving plan assets, involve a person known to be a party-in-interest? . . . .
If (a) is "Yes," attach a list of such transactions in the same format as is shown in the instructions.
(b) Were any loans by the plan or fixed income obligations due the plan in default as of the close of the plan year or classified during the year as uncollectable? . . . .
(c) Were any leases to which the plan was a party in default or classified as uncollectable during the plan year? . .

Form 5500–C (1979)   Page **4**

22 (a) Is the plan covered under the Pension Benefit Guaranty Corporation termination insurance program? . . . . ☐ Yes ☐ No ☐ Not determined

If "Yes," list employer identification number and/or plan number used in any filing with PBGC if the number was different than the numbers listed in item 1(b) or 5(c) ▶..

		Yes	No
(b) If (a) is "Yes," did one or more reportable events or other events requiring notice to PBGC occur since the last return/report Form 5500, 5500–C or 5500–K which was filed for this plan?			

(c) If (b) is "Yes," check the applicable box(es) in (i) through (x) below:

		Check (√)
(i)	Notification by the Internal Revenue Service that the plan has ceased to be a plan as described in section 4021(a)(2) of ERISA or a determination by the Secretary of Labor of non-compliance with Title I of ERISA .	
(ii)	A decrease in active participants to the extent specified in the instructions	
(iii)	A determination by the Internal Revenue Service that there has been a termination or partial termination of the plan within the meaning of section 411(d)(3) of the Code	
(iv)	An inability to pay benefits when due	
(v)	A distribution to a substantial owner to the extent specified in the instructions	
(vi)	An alternative method of compliance has been prescribed for this plan by the Secretary of Labor under section 110 of ERISA	
(vii)	A cessation of operations at a facility to the extent specified in the instructions	
(viii)	A withdrawal of a substantial employer	
(ix)	An amendment to the plan that will result in the reduction of the current or future benefits under the plan .	
(x)	Other (see instructions)	

		Yes	No
23	Is this a plan with Employee Stock Ownership Plan (ESOP) features?		
(a)	If "Yes," was a current appraisal of the value of the stock made immediately prior to the contribution of the stock or the purchase of the stock by the trust?		
(b)	If (a) is "Yes," was the appraisal made by an unrelated third party?		
(c)	If (b) is "No," was the appraisal made in accordance with the provisions of Revenue Ruling 59–60?		

If additional space is required for any item, attach additional sheets the same size as this form.

☆U.S.GPO:1979-0-283-198   EI# 430814328

APPENDIX

III

Sample Summary Plan Description

YOUR CORPORATION

SUMMARY PLAN DESCRIPTION

February 28, 1978

Name of Plan

THE YOUR CORPORATION
EMPLOYEE STOCK OWNERSHIP PLAN
(ESOP)

Administered by

THE YOUR CORPORATION EMPLOYEE STOCK
OWNERSHIP PLAN COMMITTEE:

Joe Doe
Jane Cane
Jack Black

Trusted By

Any National Bank

Employer Federal ID #xx-xxxxxxx, Plan yyy

PLAN DATES

The anniversary date of the Plan is December 31 of each year. Records of the Plan are maintained on a fiscal year basis from January 1st to December 31st of each year. The company's fiscal year coincides with the plan year.

The effective date of the Plan is January 1,1977.

CONTENTS

SUMMARY PLAN DESCRIPTION
THE YOUR CORPORATION EMPLOYEE
STOCK OWNERSHIP PLAN

INTRODUCTION

This Summary Plan Description explains the basic provisions of the Your Corporation Employee Stock Ownership Plan, which became effective as of January 1, 1977. The terms of the plan provide for you as an employee to share in the ownership of the company as you build capital for your retirement. Contributions will be made, as determined by the company's board of directors, to a trust. Your individual account will be credited with a portion of this contribution based on your pay, and your account will share in the gains and losses of the trust.

Upon your normal retirement at or after age sixty-five, or early retirement at or after age sixty, in the event of disability or death at any time, the *entire* amount of your accumulated account becomes payable to you or your designated beneficiary in installments or in a lump sum. Upon termination for any other reason, you will be entitled to receive the vested interest in your account balances. The vested interest is determined by the years of service with the company.

Through the plan, you will share in the growth of the company. We believe that the plan's benefits can provide a significant reward for a successful career with Your Corporation.

The purpose of this summary is to describe the main features of the plan in general terms so you can understand the benefits it provides. The complete terms of the plan are set forth in the official plan document, which will be provided to you if you so request. In the event of any difference between this summary and the provisions of the plan, the official plan document will govern.

YOUR CORPORATION

1. **WHO IS ELIGIBLE?**

    As an employee of the company, you will be eligible to participate in the plan if you are not covered by a collective bargaining agreement that included retirement benefits as part of the bargaining, unless that bargaining agreement provides for your inclusion in the plan.

2. **WHEN DOES PARTICIPATION START?**

    If you were a participant in the Your Corporation's Employee Retirement and Savings Plan as of January 1, 1977, you are automatically a participant in this plan. Otherwise, your participation in the plan will begin on the July 1 or the January 1 after you have completed 1,000 hours of service or one year of service, whichever occurs earlier. For purposes of participation in the plan, you complete one year of service if you have 1,000 hours of service, whether or not continuous, in a twelve-consecutive-month period beginning with your employment commencement date or an anniversary of that date.

3. **WHO PAYS FOR THE PLAN?**

    Contributions to the plan are made by the company. Each year, the board of directors will determine the amount of the contribution. No employee contributions to the plan are required or permitted.

4. **WHO SHARES IN COMPANY CONTRIBUTIONS?**

    Company contributions are allocated as of each October 31 to the account of each participant who:

    a. Completed at least 1,000 hours of service in the plan year or
    b. Retired, died, or became disabled during the year, regardless of the number of hours of service.

5. **HOW ARE COMPANY CONTRIBUTIONS DIVIDED AMONG INDIVIDUAL PARTICIPANTS?**

    You will share in the company's contributions and plan forfeitures in the same proportion as your compensation bears to the total of all participants' compensation. Compensation means the regular or basic wage and salary, including any overtime compensation paid during the plan year, but excluding bonuses, commissions, expense accounts, irregular compensation, and all deferred compensation paid during the plan year.

6. **WHO HOLDS THE PLAN FUNDS?**

    All amounts contributed to the plan will be deposited in a trust fund with the plan trustee. All benefits provided by the plan are paid from the trust fund.

7. HOW ARE PLAN FUNDS INVESTED?

The trustee will invest and reinvest the trust fund as directed by the administrative committee.

8. HOW DO INVESTMENT RESULTS AFFECT INDIVIDUAL PARTICIPANTS' ACCOUNTS?

The value of the trust fund is determined each year as of December 31. The income of the fund, together with any gains in the value of the investments, is added proportionately to participants' accounts. Any losses in the fund are subtracted from participants' accounts in the same manner. The administrative committee may decide to have the fund valued on any other date in addition to the regular annual valuation date.

9. WHAT DETERMINES THE TOTAL VALUE OF A PARTICIPANT'S ACCOUNT?

The total value of your account will depend on the following factors:

a. Your share in company contributions, which will vary from year to year depending on the overall success of the business.

b. Your share in investment earnings and gains or losses of fund investments.

c. Forfeitures of former employees who leave without being fully vested in their account balances.

10. WHAT IS MEANT BY "VESTED INTEREST"?

The term "vested interest" means the portion of your account that you actually "own" and that will be payable to you or your designated beneficiary as described in questions 11 and 12. After you have three years of service with the company, you will become partially vested in your accounts. You will be entitled to a percentage of what is in your accounts if you leave the company for any reason other than retirement (including both regular and early retirement), disability, or death. The percentage to which you are entitled is computed according to the following formula:

Credited Service	*Nonforfeitable Percentage of Accounts*
Less than 3 years	0.0%
Three years, but less than 4 years	25.0
Four years, but less than 5 years	32.5
Five years, but less than 6 years	40.0
Six years, but less than 7 years	47.5
Seven years, but less than 8 years	55.0
Eight years, but less than 9 years	62.5
Nine years, but less than 10 years	70.0
Ten years, but less than 11 years	77.5

Eleven years, but less than 12 years	85.0
Twelve years, but less than 13 years	92.5
Thirteen years or more	100.0

11. WHEN ARE PAYMENTS MADE FROM THE PLAN?

No amounts are payable prior to your termination of employment, whether for routine causes or for the following:

a. *At Normal Retirement Date* - Your normal retirement date is the first of the month following your sixty-fifth birthday. With the consent of the company, you may continue to work after age sixty-five. If you do, you will continue to share in the plan until your actual retirement.

b. *At Early Retirement* - You may elect to retire the first of the month following your sixtieth birthday.

c. *In the Event of Disability* - Disability means your inability, for physical or mental reasons, to continue with the company as determined by the committee.

d. *Upon Death* - At death, the full amount of your account becomes payable to the beneficiary named by you.

The committee may defer payments of your account in cases of regular termination until your normal retirement date (age sixty-five).

12. HOW ARE PAYMENTS MADE?

Your vested account may be paid in a lump sum or in installments, or in a combination of these methods of payment, as determined by the committee.

Any amounts in your account not paid to you at the time you leave the company will generally be held as an active account in the trust fund.

13. MUST A PARTICIPANT APPLY FOR BENEFITS?

You need not apply for benefits. When you retire, terminate, die, or become disabled, the committee will evaluate your right or your beneficiary's right to benefits and will present the decision in writing. If you or your designated beneficiary disagree with that decision, an appeal may be submitted to the committee.

14. CAN A PARTICIPANT LOSE BENEFITS?

No, you may not lose (forfeit) any part of your vested interest.

15. WHAT HAPPENS IF A PARTICIPANT IS REHIRED AFTER A TERMINATION OF EMPLOYMENT?

After termination if you are reemployed in an eligible employment status (see question 1), you will again become a participant as of the date of reemployment and will share in the allocation of company contributions made as of the last day of that plan year if you have at least 1,000 hours of service for the plan year.

16. CAN A PARTICIPANT MAKE WITHDRAWALS FROM THE PLAN?

Withdrawals from your company contribution account are not permitted.

17. **How Is the Plan Administered?**

The plan is administered by an administrative committee appointed by the company's board of directors.

The plan contains detailed provisions outlining the committee's duties, which include interpretation of the provisions of the plan, determination of eligibility, and responsibility for the general operation of the plan.

The committee maintains a record of all participants' accounts in accordance with the terms of the plan. These records are maintained on a plan-year basis, which runs from January 1 through the following December 31. As soon as practicable after the end of each plan year, the committee will give you a statement of your account under the plan.

18. **How Are Hours of Service Counted?**

You are credited with an hour of service for each hour for which you are compensated by the company or for which you receive back pay from the company. In addition to hours of actual work for which you receive pay, nonwork hours—such as vacation or illness—for which you are compensated are credited. You are also credited with hours of service based on your normally scheduled hours per week for the time while on company-approved leave of absence, on military or jury duty, or on a temporary layoff if you returned to active employment and remain employed for at least thirty days.

If you are not paid on an hourly basis or if the company does not maintain records of your hours, you will be credited with 190 hours for each month for which you have compensation from the company.

19. **Changes in the Plan**

The company expects to maintain the plan indefinitely; however, it reserves the right to amend or terminate the plan at any time should it be considered desirable or necessary. The plan is also subject to approval by the Internal Revenue Service and, although it is not anticipated, changes in details of the plan may be required. Once the plan has been officially approved by the Internal Revenue Service, no amendment may take away from you any vested interest in your account. If the plan is terminated, the company cannot recover any part of the trust fund, and all accounts become 100 percent vested. The trust fund will continue to hold the fully vested accounts, which will become payable as determined by the committee.

20. **Taxation of Accounts**

The plan has been designed to meet Internal Revenue Code requirements for qualification in order to take advantage of special tax treatment for qualified plans. This means that allocations of company contributions and forfeitures to your account and any investment earnings or gains are not currently taxable to you; thus, there is a full before-tax compounding of the company contributions, forfeitures, and investment earnings of your account. You will be taxed only when you actually receive benefits from the plan. The taxation depends on how your account is paid to you.

Due to changes in the tax laws in 1974, 1975, and 1976, the tax treatment on distributions has become quite complex. You should consult your tax advisor regarding treatment of payments made to you.

ADDITIONAL INFORMATION

TYPE OF PLAN

Self-administered employee stock ownership plan. The benefits are not insured by the pension benefit, since that insurance program does not apply to defined contribution plans such as an employee stock ownership plan. The plan may purchase private insurance.

PURPOSE

The purpose of the plan is to enable participating employees to acquire equity ownership interest in Your Corporation. Consequently, the assets in the trust will be invested primarily in company stock. The assets held in the trust are for the exclusive benefit of participants and their beneficiaries.

AGENT

The agent for legal process may be made upon the plan administrator or the plan trustee as listed on the cover page.

FIDUCIARY

The named fiduciary for the plan is the plan committee.

IMPORTANT NOTICE OF PARTICIPANTS' RIGHTS

As a participant in the Your Corporation Employee Stock Ownership Plan, you are entitled to certain rights and protections under the Employee Retirement Income Security Act of 1974 (ERISA). ERISA provides that all plan participants shall be entitled to:

1. Examine, without charge, at the plan administrator's office, all plan documents and copies of all documents filed by the plan with the U.S. Department of Labor, such as annual reports and plan descriptions.

2. Obtain copies of all plan documents and other plan information upon written request to the plan administrator. The plan administrator may make a reasonable charge for the copies.

3. Receive a summary of the plan's annual financial report. The plan administrator is required by law to furnish each participant with a copy of this summary financial report.

4. Obtain, once a year, a statement of their total account balance. The plan administrator may require a written request for this statement, but the statement must be provided free of charge.

5. File suit in a federal court if any materials requested are not received within thirty days of the participant's request, unless the materials were not sent because of matters beyond the control of the plan administrator. The court may require the plan administrator to pay up to $100 for each day's delay until the materials are received.

In addition to creating rights for plan participants, ERISA imposes obligations upon the persons who are responsible for the operation of the plan. These persons are referred to as "fiduciaries" in the law. Fiduciaries must act solely in the interest of the plan participants, and they must exercise prudence in the performance of their plan duties. Fiduciaries who violate ERISA may be removed and required to make good any losses they have caused the plan.

The company, your employer, may not fire you or discriminate against you to prevent you from obtaining a benefit under the plan or exercising your rights under ERISA.

If you are improperly denied a benefit in full or in part, you have a right to file suit in a federal or a state court. If plan fiduciaries are misusing the plan's money, you have a right to file a suit in a federal court or request assistance from the U.S. Department of Labor. If you are successful in your lawsuit, the court may, if it so decides, require the other party to pay your legal costs, including attorney's fees.

If you have any questions about this statement or your rights under ERISA, you should contact the plan administrator or the nearest area office of the U.S. Labor-Management Service Administration, Department of Labor.

APPENDIX

IV

Sample Plan and Trust

CONTENTS

Employee Stock Ownership Plan

Trust Agreement

YOUR CORPORATION

EMPLOYEE STOCK OWNERSHIP PLAN AND TRUST AGREEMENT

February 28, 1978

Name of Plan

THE YOUR CORPORATION EMPLOYEE STOCK OWNERSHIP PLAN AND TRUST

Administered by

THE YOUR CORPORATION EMPLOYEE STOCK OWNERSHIP PLAN COMMITTEE:

Joe Doe
Jane Cane
Jack Black

Trusted By

Any National Bank

Employer Federal ID **#xx-xxxxxxx**, Plan **yyy**

PLAN DATES

The anniversary date of the Plan is December 31 of each year. Records of the Plan are maintained on a fiscal year basis from January 1st to December 31st of each year. The company's fiscal year coincides with the plan year.

The effective date of the Plan is January 1,1977.

THE YOUR CORPORATION
EMPLOYEE STOCK OWNERSHIP PLAN

SECTION 1.   PLAN PURPOSE AND OPERATION

The purpose of this plan is to enable participating employees of the company to share in the development and growth of the company and to provide participants with an opportunity to build capital for their retirement. The plan is designed to do so without any deductions from participants' paychecks and without any cash investment by participants. Since a primary purpose of the plan is to enable participants to acquire an ownership interest in the company, all contributions made to the Trust will be invested primarily in Company stock.

The plan, effective as of January 1, 1977, is intended to qualify as an employee stock ownership plan as defined in Section 4975(e) (7) of the Internal Revenue Code and is designed to qualify under Section 401(a) of the Internal Revenue Code. Assets held in trust under the plan as a result of company contributions, earnings, or other additions will be administered, distributed, forfeited, and otherwise governed by the provisions of the plan, which is administered by a committee and trusteed by Any National Bank for the exclusive benefit of plan participants and their beneficiaries.

SECTION 2.   DEFINITIONS

Accounts: Several accounts are maintained to record the interest of a participant in the plan, primarily a company stock account and another investments account.

Anniversary Date: December 31 of each year.

Annual Additions: The sum of the amounts credited to a participant's accounts from company contributions and forfeitures.

Approved Absence: An absence from work, including absence due to temporary disability, granted to and approved for an employee by the company in a uniform and nondiscriminatory manner, or an absence from work for service in the Armed Forces or other government services.

Beneficiary: The person or persons entitled to receive benefits under the plan in the event of a participant's death.

Break in Service: A plan year during which a participant has not completed more than 999 hours of service, provided, however, that a break in service shall be measured by the eligibility computation period.

Committee: The committee appointed by the board of directors of the company to administer the plan, direct the trustee, and to serve as plan fiduciary.

Company: The Your Corporation

Company Stock: Shares of any class of stock, preferred or common, voting or non-voting, issued by the company. For stock acquired by the plan after December 31, 1979, the term "company stock" means common stock issued by the company having a combination of voting power and dividend rights equal to that class of company common stock having the greatest voting power and having the greatest dividend rights.

Eligible Compensation: The total wages paid or accrued to a participant by the company for each plan year, including overtime, but excluding contributions to this or any other deferred compensation plan, commissions and bonuses, and compensation paid or accrued prior to the entry date on which an employee first becomes eligible to participate.

Eligibility Period: The initial eligibility period is twelve consecutive months or 1,000 hours beginning with the employee's employment commencement date. After such initial period, the subsequent eligibility period shall be the twelve-month period ending on the last day of the plan year. This subsequent period shall begin on the first day of the plan year included within the first twelve months of employment.

Employee: A person employed by the company any portion of whose income is subject to withholding of income tax and/or for whom social security contributions are made by the company, as well as any other person qualifying as a common law employee of the company.

ERISA: The Employee Retirement Income Security Act of 1974, as amended from time to time and administered by the Department of Labor.

Forfeiture: The portion of a participant's accounts that does not become part of his/her plan benefit.

Hour of Service: An hour of service is each hour for which an employee is paid by the company or is entitled to back pay from the company.

Limitation Year: For purposes of the limitations on contributions and benefits imposed by Section 415 of the Internal Revenue Code, the limitation year shall be the company's fiscal year.

Participant: An employee who is participating in the plan.

Plan: The Your Corporation Employee Stock Ownership Plan, which includes the plan and trust documents.

Plan Benefits: The amount(s) of the distribution(s) to which a participant or beneficiary becomes entitled upon termination of participation.

Plan Year: The twelve-month period ending on each anniversary date (December 31 of each year).

Trust: The trust for the plan created by the trust agreement entered into between the company and the trustee.

Trustee: The trustee designated by the company's board of directors, or any successor trustee, which agrees to act by executing the trust agreement.

Valuation Date: The plan anniversary date (December 31 of each year).

Vesting Period: For purposes of vesting under Section 11, all plan years after December 31, 1977, during which a participant has completed 1,000 or more hours of service shall be included. Years of service also include all years of service prior to December 31, 1977.

Year of Service: Any plan year during which an employee is credited with at least 1,000 hours of service.

SECTION 3.   ELIGIBILITY REQUIREMENTS

On any employment commencement anniversary date, any employee of the company who has completed at least one year of service or 1,000 hours during the eligibility period and is still then employed by the company, and is not included in a group of employees covered by a collective bargaining agreement between employee representatives and the company, shall be eligible to become a participant in this plan as of such date. Officers and directors of the company who are also employees shall be eligible to participate in the plan on the same basis as other employees. All doubtful cases of eligibility to participate in the plan shall be resolved by the committee.

Employees whose retirement benefits are subject to collective bargaining are not eligible to participate in the plan unless the collective bargaining agreement provides for such participation. For purposes of eligibility and vesting, years of service shall include years during which an employee is covered by a collective bargaining agreement.

SECTION 4.   PARTICIPATION REQUIREMENTS

(a) Participation: Participation in the plan continues until it is terminated by the participant's break in service, retirement, death, total disability, or other termination of employment. A participant who accumulates less than 1,000 hours of service during a plan year shall not share in the allocation of company contributions (and forfeitures) under Section 5 for such plan year and shall not be given a year of service for purposes of vesting under Section 10, but such participation shall continue until the occurrence of a break in service.

A participant who incurs a break in service or who terminates employment and is reemployed shall again resume participation in the plan as of the date of reemployment.

If the participant is reemployed after a break in service and has no vested rights under the plan, and if the number of consecutive breaks in service equals or exceeds the aggregate number of years of service before the break, such participant shall be treated as a new employee for purposes of participation.

(b) Leaves of Absence: A participant's employment is not considered terminated for purposes of the plan if the participant has been on leave of absence with the consent of the company, provided that he/she returns to the employ of the company within thirty days after the leave or within such longer period as may be prescribed by law. Leaves of absence shall mean leaves granted by the company, in accordance with rules uniformly applied to all participants, for reasons of health or public service or for reasons determined by the company to be in its best interests. For purposes of preventing a break in service, a participant on such leave shall be credited with eight hours of service for each business day of the leave. A participant who does not return to the employ of the company within the prescribed time shall be deemed to have terminated his employment as of the date when his leave began, unless such failure to return was the result of his death, total disability, or retirement. Such participant must further remain in the employ of the company for at least thirty days.

(c) Suspended Participation: A participant who ceases to be an eligible employee but who has not separated from the company shall become a suspended participant. During the period of suspension, no amounts based on his covered compensation from and after the date of suspension shall be credited to the participant's accounts. Amounts previously credited to a participant's accounts shall continue to vest, and the participant shall be entitled to benefits in accordance with the other provisions of the plan throughout the period during which the participant is on suspended status.

SECTION 5.   COMPANY CONTRIBUTIONS

(a) Amount of Contributions: For the current plan year and each subsequent year, company contributions shall be made to the trust in such amounts as may be determined by the company's board of directors. Contributions may not be made in amounts that would permit the limitation described in Section 7 to be exceeded.

(b) Time of Contributions: Contributions for each year must be established by resolution of the company's board of directors, announced to the participants, and paid to the trust not later than the due date for filing the company's federal income tax return for that year (including extensions).

(c) Form of Contributions: Company contributions shall be paid in cash, company stock, or other property as the company's board of directors may from time to time determine. Company stock and other property shall be valued at their then fair market value. No participant shall be required or permitted to make contributions to the plan or trust.

SECTION 6.   INVESTMENT OF PLAN ASSETS

(a) Authorized Investments: Company contributions of cash and other cash received by the trust shall be applied to pay any outstanding obligations of the trust incurred for purchase of company stock and then to purchase additional shares of company stock from current shareholders or newly issued shares from the company. The committee may also direct the trustee to invest funds of the plan in savings accounts, asset loss insurance policies, or insurance policies on the life of any key employee or stockholder (provided that the aggregate insurance premiums for any participant do not exceed 25 percent of the amount allocated to such account), certificates of deposit, short-term securities, other stocks or bonds, and other investments deemed by the committee to be desirable for the trust. Residual funds may be held in cash.

(b) Duties of Committee: Except as otherwise provided in Section 15, all investments shall be made by the trustee only upon the direction of the committee. Except as may be provided in Section 14, all purchases of company stock shall be made at prices that do not exceed the fair market value of such stock at the time of the transaction.

SECTION 7. ACCOUNT ALLOCATIONS

(a) Individual Accounts: The committee shall establish and maintain individual accounts for each plan participant. Individual accounts shall also be maintained for any former participant who still has an interest in the plan. Such individual accounts shall not require a segregation of the trust assets, and no participant, former participant, nor beneficiary shall acquire any right to or interest in any specific asset of the trust as a result of the allocation. One such account shall consist of the allocated shares of company stock purchased and paid for by the trust or contributed in kind by the company, with forfeitures of company stock and with stock dividends on company stock held in the account. Allocations of company stock shall be reflected separately for each class of such stock, and the committee shall maintain adequate records of the cost basis of company stock allocated to each participant's company stock account.

An investments account of each participant shall be credited (debited) as of each anniversary date with each share of the net income (loss) of the trust, with cash dividends on company stock in each company stock account including contributions and forfeitures in other than company stock. It shall be debited for any payments on purchases of company stock and, if applicable, any insurance premium payments.

(b) Allocation of Company Contributions and Forfeitures: Company contributions and forfeitures shall be allocated as of each anniversary date among the accounts of employees who are participants in the plan on the last day of the year or whose participation terminated during the year because of death, total disability, or retirement in the proportion that each such participant's eligible compensation bears to the total eligible compensation of all such participants for that year. Such allocation may not exceed the lesser of $25,000 or 25 percent of eligible compensation for any participant as adjusted by the cost of living.

For purposes of this paragraph, a person whose participation in the plan terminates during a plan year for reasons other than death, total disability, or retirement shall not be considered a participant in the plan on the last day of that plan year.

The net income (loss) of the trust shall be determined annually as of each anniversary date. A portion thereof shall be allocated to each participant's investments account in the ratio on which the balance of his/her investments account on the preceding anniversary date bears to this sum of the balance for the investments accounts of all participants on that date. Account balances shall be reduced by amounts distributed to participants during the plan year. The net income (loss) includes the increase (decrease) in the fair market value of assets of the trust, interest, dividends, other income, and expenses attributable to assets in the investments accounts since the preceding anniversary date.

(c) Allocation Limitations: The total annual additions to a participant's accounts for any fiscal year shall not exceed the lesser of $30,000 [or such greater amount as may be permitted pursuant to regulations issued under Section 415(d) of the Internal Revenue Code] or 25 percent of the participant's total compensation for the year. If the company is contributing to another defined contribution plan, as defined in Section 414(i) of the Internal Revenue Code, for employees of the company, any of whom may be participants in this plan, then any such participant's annual additions in such other plan shall be added to the participant's annual additions from this plan for purposes of this limitation.

If a participant in this plan is also a participant in a defined benefit plan, as defined in Section 414(j) of the Internal Revenue Code, to which contributions are made by the company, then such participant shall be subject to the limitation set forth in Section 415(e) of the Internal Revenue Code. If company stock is purchased from a shareholder of the company and if such shareholder is also a participant in this plan, then the total account balances of such participant's accounts combined with the total balances in the accounts of such participant's spouse, parents, grandparents, children, and grandchildren shall not exceed 20 percent of the total of all account balances under the plan.

If the account balances or the annual additions to a participant's accounts would exceed the limitation described in the preceding paragraphs, then the sum of the annual additions to this plan and any other plan shall be reduced until the applicable limitation is satisfied. The reduction shall be treated as a forfeiture and shall be allocated in accordance with this section to the accounts of participants who are not affected by this limitation. If any amount cannot be so reallocated, then such amount shall be deposited into a suspense account and allocated to the maximum extent possible in succeeding years.

SECTION 8.   VOTING RIGHTS

Company stock held by the trust shall be voted by the trustee in accordance with instructions from the committee with respect to any matter that under state law or corporate charter requires more than a majority vote of shareholders. However, effective January 1, 1980, each participant shall be entitled to direct the voting of shares acquired by the trust and allocated to his/her accounts subsequent to January 1, 1980, with respect to any matter that by state law or corporate charter requires more than a majority vote of shareholders.

SECTION 9. DISCLOSURE AND REPORTING

(a) Summary Plan Description: Within 90 days after the receipt of a favorable determination letter from the Internal Revenue Service relating to the qualification of the plan, and thereafter within 120 days after a participant commences participation (or after a beneficiary first receives benefits under the plan), the committee shall furnish such participant (beneficiary) with a summary plan description as required by Sections 102(a) and 104(b) of ERISA. Such summary plan description shall be updated from time to time as required under ERISA and Department of Labor regulations thereunder.

(b) Summary Annual Report: Within 210 days after each anniversary date, the committee shall furnish each participant (and each beneficiary receiving benefits under the plan) with the summary annual report of the plan required by Section 104(b) of ERISA, in the form required by regulations of the Department of Labor.

(c) Annual Account Statement: As soon as practical after each anniversary date, each participant shall receive a written statement of accounts showing: the balance in each such account as of the preceding anniversary date; the amount of contributions and forfeitures allocated to the accounts for the year; the adjustment to the accounts to reflect the dividends, income, and expenses of the trust for the year; and the new balances in each account, including the number of shares of company stock.

If any error or miscalculation is discovered in an account, the committee shall correct the same if correction is feasible. Statements to participants are for reporting purposes only and no allocation, valuation, or statement shall, of itself, vest any right or title in any part of the plan trust.

(d) Additional Disclosure: The committee shall make available for examination, by any participant or beneficiary, copies of the plan and trust agreement and the latest annual report (Form 5500-C) of the plan filed with the Department of Labor. Upon written request of any participant or beneficiary, the committee shall furnish copies of such documents, at a reasonable charge to cover the cost of such copies, as provided in regulations of the Department of Labor.

SECTION 10. VESTING AND FORFEITURES

(a) Vesting Schedule: If a participant has a break in service or termination of employment for any reason other than as described in Section 11, such participation in the allocation of company contributions and forfeitures will terminate as of the anniversary date preceding the break in service or termination of employment, and the vesting of plan benefits shall be based upon years of service, as determined by the vesting period and in accordance with the following vesting schedule:

Years of Service	Percentage of Vesting
Less than 3 years	0.0%
Three years, but less than 4 years	25.0
Four years, but less than 5 years	32.5
Five years, but less than 6 years	40.0

Six years, but less than 7 years	47.5
Seven years, but less than 8 years	55.0
Eight years, but less than 9 years	62.5
Nine years, but less than 10 years	70.0
Ten years, but less than 11 years	77.5
Eleven years, but less than 12 years	85.0
Twelve years, but less than 13 years	92.5
Thirteen years or more	100.0

(b) **Vesting Upon Reemployment:** If a participant is reemployed following a break in service, such participant's accounts shall be vested according to the vesting period as defined in Section 2.

(c) **Forfeitures:** Any remainder of a terminating participant's accounts that is not vested in accordance with the foregoing provisions shall be treated as a forfeiture. Forfeitures shall be first charged against a participant's investments account with any balance charged against the company stock account. The disposition of such forfeitures shall be as follows:

(1)   If a participant is not reemployed on or before the anniversary date of the plan year next following a break in service, the balance of the accounts shall be allocated as a forfeiture as of such anniversary date. Distribution of a participant's benefits following termination of service may occur prior to the occurrence of a break in service if so directed by the committee.

(2)   If the participant is reemployed on or before the anniversary date of the plan year next following the break in service, the balance of the accounts shall be treated as a separate account subject to distribution.

SECTION 11.   BENEFITS UPON RETIREMENT OR DEATH

Participation terminates as of the anniversary date coinciding with or next following a participant's retirement or death. A participant's plan benefit upon retirement or death shall be the total of the account balances as of the coinciding or next following anniversary date. A participant shall be 100 percent vested upon death or upon attainment of any of the following retirement dates: normal retirement at age sixty-five; deferred retirement beyond age sixty-five upon company request or company approval; disability retirement if the committee determines in a nondiscriminatory manner, on the basis of a doctor's certificate, that a participant has become totally disabled [i.e., the mental or physical inability of the participant to be usefully employed as evidenced by the certificate of a medical examiner satisfactory to the committee certifying such inability and certifying that such condition is likely to be permanent); early retirement after age sixty at the election of the participant, but the vesting schedule of Section 10 may apply if the company does not concur.

SECTION 12. DISTRIBUTIONS OF BENEFITS

(a) Death or Retirement: Upon death or retirement a participant's benefits shall be distributed in a single distribution not later than sixty days after the anniversary date coinciding with or next following death or retirement. The committee may, in its discretion, distribute currently the accumulated benefits and distribute the participant's share of the final year's allocations sixty days after the anniversary date following the death or retirement date. The committee may, at its discretion and after conferring with the participant or beneficiary, direct that the distribution be made in a single distribution at a deferred retirement date or on a life-expectancy installment basis.

(b) Other Terminations: If a participant ceases to participate for reasons other than death or retirement, benefits will be distributed as soon as possible after termination of service. The committee may, at its discretion, direct that the distribution be made in a single distribution at the anniversary date next following the termination of service or within sixty days of each anniversary date; or in a single distribution at death or retirement date (age sixty-five) or within sixty days thereafter; or on a life-expectancy installment basis.

SECTION 13. FORM OF DISTRIBUTIONS

Distributions of plan benefits shall be made in whole shares of company stock except that the value of any fractional shares will be paid in cash. Any balance in a participant's investments account will be applied to acquire for distribution the maximum number of whole shares of company stock at the then fair market value, and any unexpended balance will be distributed in cash. After December 31, 1979, distribution of plan benefits may be made entirely in cash or in the form of company stock.

Distributions shall be made to the participant, if living, and, if not, to the respective estate or beneficiary. A participant may designate a beneficiary upon becoming a participant and may change such designation at any time by filing a written designation with the committee. If the participant is married, a designation of a beneficiary other than the spouse shall be allowed only when a consent in writing by the spouse of the participant is furnished to the committee.

SECTION 14. RIGHT OF FIRST REFUSAL AND PUT OPTION

(a) Right of First Refusal: Unless company stock is publicly traded, all shares of company stock distributed by the trustee may, as determined by the company or the committee, be subject to a right of first refusal. Such right shall provide that prior to any subsequent transfer, the shares must first be offered by written offer to the trust and, if refused, then to the company. If the proposed transfer is at less than fair market value, the price shall be determined by the latest valuation date. If the proposed purchase is by a prospective bona fide purchaser, the offer to the trust and the company shall be at the greater of fair market value, as determined by an independent appraiser (appointed by the committee) as of the latest valuation date, or the price offered by the prospective bona fide purchaser. The trust and the company, respectively, may accept the offer at any time within fourteen days after receipt of such offer.

(b) Put Option: At the time that shares of company stock are distributed to him/her, a participant or a beneficiary shall be granted an option to put the shares to the company. The trust shall have the option to assume the rights and obligations of the company at the time the put option is exercised. The put option shall provide that for a period of up to six months after such shares are distributed to a participant or beneficiary, such party has the right to have the trust and/or the company purchase such shares at their fair market value as determined in (a) above.

SECTION 15.   PLAN ADMINISTRATION

The board of directors shall have the following duties and responsibilities:

(1)   Acting with respect to amending or terminating the plan;
(2)   Acting with respect to the selection, retention, or removal of the trustee;
(3)   Appointing, retaining, and removing members of the committee;
(4)   Periodically reviewing the performance of the trustee, the members of the committee, and any appointed advisors;
(5)   Determining the form and amount of employer contributions.

The company shall administer the plan and is designated as the "plan administrator" under Section 3(16) of ERISA. The company may delegate all or part of its duties to the plan committee. The members of the committee shall be comprised of three persons who shall be appointed by the board of directors and who may be removed by the board of directors at any time with or without cause. The committee is designated as the agent of the plan for the service of legal process and as the named fiduciary of the plan. All decisions required to be made by the committee involving the interpretation and administration of the plan shall be resolved by majority vote either at a meeting or in writing without a meeting.

The committee shall have the following duties and responsibilities:

(1)   Providing for the fair market valuation of company stock as of each annual valuation date (December 31);
(2)   Establishing and maintaining a funding policy for the plan;
(3)   Determining the eligibility of employees for participation in and benefits under the plan;
(4)   Complying with the reporting and disclosure requirements established by ERISA, IRS, and other units of government;
(5)   Making recommendations to the board of directors with respect to amendment or termination of the plan and contributions under the plan;

(6) Maintaining plan accounts and other records;
(7) Authorizing, allocating, and reviewing expenses incurred by the plan;
(8) Communicating with plan participants and the plan trustee;
(9) Investing and controlling the plan assets in a prudent manner.

The committee shall establish rules and regulations and shall take such actions to carry out its duties and responsibilities as may be necessary and proper.

SECTION 16. AMENDMENT AND TERMINATION

(a) Amendment: The company reserves the right to amend the plan at any time, in whole or in part, including retroactive amendments necessary or advisable to qualify the plan and trust under the provisions of Section 401(a) of the Internal Revenue Code. No such amendment shall cause any part of the assets of the plan and trust to be recoverable by the company, or be used for or diverted to purposes other than the exclusive benefit of participants and beneficiaries, or deprive any participant or beneficiary of any benefit already vested, except to the extent that such amendment may be necessary to qualify the plan or modify the duties or liabilities of the trustee.

(b) Termination: Although the company has established the plan with the intention of making contributions indefinitely, the company shall not be under any obligation to continue its contributions or to maintain the plan for any given length of time. The company may in its discretion discontinue such contributions or terminate the plan in whole or in part in accordance with its provisions at any time without any liability for such discontinuance or termination. If so terminated, and the plan is not replaced by a comparable plan qualified under Section 401(a) of the Internal Revenue Code, the accounts of all participants affected by the termination shall become nonforfeitable. The committee and the trust shall continue until the plan benefits of each participant have been distributed.

If the Internal Revenue Service shall fail or refuse to issue a favorable written determination or ruling with respect to the initial qualification of the plan and exemption of the trust from tax under Sections 401(a) and 501(a) of the Internal Revenue Code, all company contributions together with any income received or accrued, less any benefits or expenses paid, shall be distributed in accordance with the preceding paragraph. However, if a contribution is made by the company due to mistake or if a contribution is conditioned on its deductibility and the deduction is disallowed, then such contribution may be returned to the company within one year.

SECTION 17. MERGER, ASSIGNMENT, AND SEVERABILITY

(a) Merger: If the company merges or consolidates with or into another corporation, or if substantially all of the company shall be transferred to a corporation, the plan shall terminate on the effective date of such merger, consolidation, or transfer. If the surviving corporation resulting from such merger or consolidation, or the corporation to which the assets have been transferred, adopts the plan, then the plan shall continue and said corporation shall succeed to all powers and duties of the company. The employment of any employee who is continued in the employ of such successor corporation shall not be deemed to have terminated.

(b) Assignment Prohibited: The benefits provided by this plan may not be assigned or alienated. Neither the company nor the trustee shall recognize any transfer, mortgage, pledge, order, or assignment by any participant or beneficiary of any interest hereunder, and such interest shall not be subject in any manner to transfer by operation of law and shall be exempt from the claims of creditors or other claimants from all orders, decrees, levies, garnishments, or executions against such participant or beneficiary.

(c) Applicable Law and Severability: The plan shall be construed and governed in accordance with ERISA and the Internal Revenue Code and, to the extent not superseded by federal law, in accordance with the laws of the state. If any provision is susceptible to more than one interpretation, such interpretation shall be given as is consistent with the Internal Revenue Code. If any provision of this instrument shall be held by a court of competent jurisdiction to be invalid or unenforceable, then the remaining provisions shall continue to be fully effective.

As evidence of the adoption of this plan, the company has caused its appropriate officers to affix its corporate name and seal hereto on this _____ day of _____
_____ 1977.

THE YOUR CORPORATION

By _____
PRESIDENT

By _____
SECRETARY

(SEAL)

THE YOUR CORPORATION TRUST AGREEMENT

This agreement, between the Your Corporation, hereinafter referred to as the "company," and Any National Bank, hereinafter referred to as the "trustee," is to be effective as of January 1, 1977.

It is the policy of the company to finance and conduct its operations so as to enable its employees to share, through an employee stock ownership plan, equity ownership in the company. The company has adopted the "The Your Corporation Employee Stock Ownership Plan" (the plan) effective as of January 1, 1977. Further, the company has designated the plan and this trust as constituting parts of the plan intended to qualify under Section 401(a) of the Internal Revenue Code.

Therefore, the parties hereto do hereby establish the Your Corporation Employee Stock Ownership Trust and agree that the following shall constitute the trust agreement:

SECTION 1. TRUST ASSETS

Company contributions shall be paid to the trustee, from time to time, in accordance with the plan. All company contributions made and all investments, together with all accumulations, accruals, earnings, and income, shall be held by the trustee in trust as the trust assets. The trust assets shall be received by the trustee and invested pursuant to written instructions to the trustee from the committee. The trustee shall not be responsible for the administration of the plan, the maintenance of any records of participants' accounts under the plan, or the computation of or collection of company contributions, but shall hold, invest, reinvest, manage, administer, and distribute the trust assets as provided herein for the exclusive benefit of participants or their beneficiaries.

Unless otherwise directed by the company or the committee provided for in the plan, the trustee shall hold, invest, and administer the trust assets as a single fund without identification of any part of the trust assets with or allocation of any part of the trust assets to the company or to any participant or group of participants or their beneficiaries.

SECTION 2. INVESTMENT FUND

The investment fund shall consist of all employer contributions and earnings hereon under the employee stock ownership plan. As directed by the committee, the trustee may invest and reinvest the trust assets under the fund, without distinction between principal and income, in company stock in accordance with the terms of the plan and this agreement. The trustee may also, as directed by the committee, place funds in savings accounts or in certificates of deposit issued by any bank or savings and loan association or may invest in stocks and obligations of corporations or of unincorporated associations or trusts or investment companies, or in any kind of investment fund, mutual fund, common trust fund, pooled trust fund, or in insurance policies on any key employees of the company (life insurance premiums for any participant may not exceed 25 percent of the amount allocated to such account), or in any other realty or personalty, interests in oil or other depletable natural resources, and any other similar investment.

The plan assets shall be invested and controlled by the committee, provided that the actual management of trust investments, other than company stock, may be delegated to the trustee or may be delegated to one or more investment managers appointed by the committee. Investments directed by the committee shall not be in conflict with the "prohibited transactions" provisions of the Internal Revenue Code. The trustee shall purchase or sell such shares of company stock pursuant to direction from the committee. The trustee shall have no obligation to seek or request direction from the committee, nor shall the trustee have any power or authority to dispose of any such company stock acquired pursuant to such direction unless directed by the committee. The trustee shall be under a duty to comply with any such direction when given, but shall have no responsibility in connection with any purchase, retention, or sale, other than compliance with such direction.

SECTION 3. POWERS OF TRUSTEE

As directed by the committee, the trustee shall have the power and responsibility to:

(a) Sell, transfer, mortgage, pledge, lease, or grant options with respect to any securities or other property in the trust at public or private sale;

(b) Vote any stock (including company stock), bonds or other securities held in the trust, or otherwise consent to or request any action on the part of the issuer in person or by proxy;

(c) Give general or specific proxies or powers of attorney, with or without powers of substitution, and appoint nominees;

(d) Participate in reorganizations, recapitalizations, consolidations, mergers, and similar transactions with respect to company stock or any other securities;

(e) Deposit company stock or other securities in any voting trust or with a trustee or with depositories designated thereby;

(f) Exercise any options, subscription rights, and conversion privileges;

(g) Sue, defend, compromise, arbitrate, or settle any suit or legal proceeding or any claim due it or on which it is liable;

(h) Contract or otherwise enter into transactions between itself as trustee and the company or shareholders of any of them;

(i) Perform all acts that the trustee shall deem necessary and proper and exercise any and all powers of the trustee under this agreement;

(j) Incur reasonable expenses, to be paid by the company, in carrying out its powers and duties.

As to company stock, as of January 1, 1980, each participant shall be entitled to direct the trustee regarding the voting of shares acquired by the trust and allocated to such accounts subsequent to January 1, 1980, with respect to any matter that by state law or corporate charter requires more than a majority vote of the shareholders.

SECTION 4. RECORDS AND REPORTS

The trustee shall keep accurate and detailed records of all investments, receipts and disbursements, and other transactions as directed by the committee. All accounts, books, and records relating thereto shall be open to inspection by any person designated by the committee or the company at any reasonable time.

Within sixty days after the end of each taxable year of the company or removal or resignation of the trustee or any other date specified by the committee, the trustee shall file a report with the committee. This report shall show all purchases, sales, receipts, disbursements, and other transactions effected by the trustee during the year or period for which the report is filed. It shall contain a description, the cost as shown on the trustee's books, and the market value as of the end of such period of every item held in the trust and the amount and type of every obligation owed by the trust. The trustee may rely without liability upon the valuation of company stock as determined by the committee.

SECTION 5. DISTRIBUTIONS

The trustee shall make distributions from the trust at times and in such amounts of company stock and amounts of cash for the benefit of persons entitled thereto under the plan as the committee directs in writing. After December 31, 1979, distributions of plan benefits may be made in company stock or in cash as the participant or beneficiary may elect. Any undistributed part of a participant's plan benefits shall be retained in the trust until the committee directs its distribution. The trustee shall comply with the provisions of the plan and the regulations of the committee relating to repurchase of such stock by the trust or by the company. If a dispute arises as to who is entitled to or should receive any benefit or payment, the trustee may withhold such benefit or payment until the dispute has been resolved.

If the trustee is notified by the committee that any participant or beneficiary has been adjudicated bankrupt or has purported to anticipate, sell, transfer, assign, or encumber any distribution or payment, voluntarily or involuntarily, the trustee shall, if so directed by the committee, hold or apply such distribution or payment or any part thereof to or for the benefit of such participant or beneficiary in a manner as the committee shall direct. The trustee shall not be obligated to search for or ascertain the whereabouts of any participant or beneficiary and shall mail all required benefits or payments to addresses provided by the committee.

SECTION 6. TRUSTEE LIABILITY

The trustee shall not be liable for any expense or liability hereunder unless due to or arising from fraud, dishonesty, negligence, or misconduct of the trustee. The trustee shall not be liable for the making, retention, or sale of any investment or reinvestment made by the trustee, nor for any loss to or diminution of the trust assets, nor for any action that the trustee takes or refrains from taking that the trustee deems in good faith to be in the best interests of the trust or that the trustee takes or refrains from taking at the direction of the committee or company. These provisions shall conform to ERISA and other applicable law.

All communications required from the company or the committee to the trustee shall be in writing, signed by an officer of the company or a person authorized by the committee to sign on its behalf. The committee shall authorize one or more individuals to sign all communications required between the committee and the trustee. The company and the committee shall keep the trustee advised of the names and specimen signatures of all members of the committee and the individuals authorized to sign on behalf of the committee. All communications required hereunder from the trustee shall be in writing signed by the trustee. All nonconforming actions or procedures shall be void and invalid.

SECTION 7. AMENDMENT AND TERMINATION

The company shall have the right at any time, by written instrument duly executed and delivered to the trustee, to amend this agreement, in whole or in part, or to terminate the trust in accordance with the provisions of the plan. The company shall have the right to amend this agreement retroactively to its effective date in order to meet the requirements of Section 401(a) of the Internal Revenue Code and to terminate this agreement if the Internal Revenue Service fails to determine that the plan and the trust satisfy the requirements of Section 401(a). Upon such failure and termination, all contributions, less expenses and benefits paid, shall be returned to the company if it so directs in writing.

Except as provided in this section, this trust is to be irrevocable and at no time shall any part of the trust assets revert to or be recoverable by the company or be used for or be diverted to purposes other than for the exclusive benefit of participants or their beneficiaries. The committee may, by notice in writing to the trustee, direct that all or part of the trust assets be transferred to a successor trustee under a trust instrument that is for the exclusive benefit of such participants or their beneficiaries and meets the requirements of Section 401(a) of the Internal Revenue Code.

SECTION 8. RESIGNATION OR REMOVAL OF TRUSTEE

The trustee may resign at any time upon thirty days' written notice to the company or be removed at any time by the company upon thirty days' written notice to the trustee. Upon resignation or removal of the trustee, the company shall appoint a successor trustee. The successor trustee shall have the same powers and duties as are conferred upon the trustee hereunder, and the trustee shall assign, transfer, and pay over to such successor trustee all the moneys, securities, and other property then constituting the trust assets, together with such records or copies thereof as may be necessary and proper.

SECTION 9. REPORTING AND SEVERABILITY

As long as this plan is in effect, the company shall file with the Internal Revenue Service and the Department of Labor the information required under the Employee

Retirement Income Security Act of 1974 and the Internal Revenue Code. If the trust and the plan, after initially qualifying under Section 401(a) of the Internal Revenue Code, shall thereafter cease to be qualified by reason of some act or omission on the part of the company, the company agrees to indemnify the trustee and hold the trustee harmless against any liability it may incur for federal or state taxes or penalties.

If any provisions of this agreement shall be held illegal or invalid for any reason, the illegality or invalidity shall not affect the remaining provisions of this agreement. This agreement shall be construed and governed in accordance with ERISA and the Internal Revenue Code and, to the extent not superseded by federal law, in accordance with the laws of the state.

The trustee hereby accepts this trust and agrees to hold the trust assets existing on the date of this agreement and all additions subject to all the terms and conditions of this agreement. In witness whereof, the company and the trustee have caused this agreement to be executed on this _____ day of _____, 1977.

THE YOUR CORPORATION

(SEAL)

By _____
    PRESIDENT

By _____
    SECRETARY

ANY NATIONAL BANK TRUSTEE

By _____

By _____

_____

_____

Further Reading

Bachelder, Joseph E. III, ed. *Employee Stock Ownership Plans*. New York: Practicing Law Institute, 1979.

Bellas, Carl J. *Industrial Democracy And The Worker Owned Firm*. New York: Irvington Publications, 1972.

Bennis, Warren G. *Organizational Development: Its Nature, Origins and Prospects*. Reading, Mass.: Addison-Wesley Co., 1969.

Bernstein, Paul. *Workplace Democratization: Its Internal Dynamics*. Kent, Ohio: Kent State University Press, 1976.

Copeman, George. *Employee Share Ownership and Industrial Stability*. New York: International Publications Service, 1975.

Frieden, Karl. *Workplace Democracy And Productivity*. Washington, D.C.: National Center for Economic Alternatives, 1980.

Friedman, Milton R. *Capitalism And Freedom*. Chicago: University of Chicago Press, 1962.

Galbraith, John K. *American Capitalism: The Concept of Countervailing Power*. Boston: Houghton Mifflin, 1952.

Kelso, Louis O. *The Capitalist Manifesto*. New York: Random House, 1958.

Kelso, Louis O. *Two-Factor Theory: The Economics of Reality*. New York: Vintage Books, 1968.

Marx, Karl. *Capital And The Capitalist Manifesto*. New York: The Modern Library, 1959.

Marx, Karl. *Capital*. New York: Vintage Books, 1976.

Meade, J. E. *Efficiency, Equality And The Ownership Of Property*. London: Allen & Unwin, Inc., 1964.

Menke, John D. *How To Analyze, Design And Install An Employee Stock Ownership Plan*. Greenvale, N.Y.: Panel Publishers, 1976.

Scharf, Charles A. *A Guide To Employee Stock Ownership Plans*. Englewood Cliffs, N.J.: Prentice Hall, 1976.

Speiser, Stuart. *A Piece Of The Action*. New York: Van Nos Reinhold, 1977.

Stern, Robert N. *Employee Ownership In Plant Shutdowns*. Kalamazoo, Mich.: Upjohn Institute, 1979.

Thurow, Lester. *The Zero-Sum Society*. New York: Basic Books, 1980.

Vanek, Jaroslav. *The Participatory Economy: An Evolutionary Hypothesis And A Strategy For Development*. Ithaca, N.Y.: Cornell University Press, 1974.

Williams, Ervin, ed. *Participative Management: Concepts, Theory And Implementation*. Atlanta: Georgia State University, 1976.

Index

About the Author

TIMOTHY C. JOCHIM is Counsel/Consultant for Data Logistics of Akron, Ohio. His articles have appeared in such publications as the *Academy of Management Review* and *Personnel*.